Keeping Score

Keeping Score

The Economics of Big-Time Sports

BY RICHARD G. SHEEHAN

Diamond Communications, Inc.
South Bend, Indiana
1996

Keeping Score
Copyright © 1996 by Richard G. Sheehan

10 9 8 7 6 5 4 3 2 1

Manufactured in the United States of America

Diamond Communications, Inc.
Post Office Box 88
South Bend, Indiana 46624-0088
Editorial: (219) 299-9278
Orders Only:
1-800-480-3717
FAX (219) 299-9296

Library of Congress Cataloging-in-Publication Data

Sheehan, Richard G. (Richard Gerard), 1949–
    Keeping score : the economics of big–time sports / by
Richard G. Sheehan.
        p.   cm.
    Includes bibliographical references (p.).
    ISBN 0-912083-96-4. -- ISBN 1-888698-05-5
    1. Sports--Economic aspects--United States. 2. Professional
sports--Economic aspects--United States.   I. Title.
GV716.S45   1996
338.4'7796'0973--dc20   96-19528
                                                          CIP

Contents

Preface ix

Chapter 1
Keeping Score—A Financial Box Score of Sports Franchises 1

Chapter 2
Baseball—Yes Virginia, There Are Owners Dumber
Than Hockey's 14

Chapter 3
Basketball—Trouble in Paradise? 52

Chapter 4
Football—Socialism in America 77

Chapter 5
Hockey—Crying All the Way to the Bank 106

Chapter 6
Competitive Balance—Does Big Spending or a Big Market
Mean Winning Big? 128

Chapter 7
Revenue Sharing and Competition 155

Chapter 8
Stikes and Lockouts and Salary Caps—A Pox on All Houses .. 180

Chapter 9
Free Agency and Salaries—Are Professional Athletes
Really Underpaid? 200

Chapter 10
Expansion Prospects—Austin and Nashville or Another
Team for New York City? 228

Chapter 11
Colleges—Financial Rankings or Going for the Green 261

Chapter 12
The NCAA, Colleges, and College Athletes—Should
Athletes Be Paid? 286

Chapter 13
Conclusion—The Financial Future of Big-Time Sports 313

To my mother—an avid Boston fan who loves the Red Sox, hates greedy athletes, and would not be willing to pay one nickel in additional taxes to support a municipal stadium.

Preface

Since I was old enough to read, I have first opened the newspaper to the sports section. Only when I knew, for example, whether the Red Sox had won—and the Yankees had lost—and the most recent heroics of Ted Williams, Carl Yastrzemski, or Roger Clemens, only then could I read the rest of the newspaper. Does that behavior reflect a warped sense of priorities? Perhaps. But it is for people with those same priorities that I wrote this book. Nevertheless, this book is a far cry from what I expected when starting this project. Quite frankly, initially I was simply curious about what many may view as an arcane question of finance: what is the rate of return on professional sports franchises versus the return on stocks or bonds? In trying to answer that question, however, I immediately ran into an anomaly. Many owners have repeatedly cried poverty. For example, Art Modell claimed that the Cleveland Browns have lost $22 million in the past two years. (The evidence here suggests that Art Modell may have lost money but the Browns have been quite profitable.) These same owners have then refused to provide any financial information to support their contention of losses. However, despite no cooperation from the owners, much information is available. Having the profit numbers opens up a host of additional questions. For example, are high ticket prices the result of high salaries? Who is hurt and who is helped by a salary cap? Why do strikes in sports appear so difficult to solve? How much would it cost an owner to win one more game? Are professional athletes overpaid? Should college athletes be paid? How should Title IX be enforced given the "profits" in collegiate football? Economics has something to say about all these issues and much more. The general conclusion is that economic factors have altered the face of sports and will continue to influence how all leagues develop. Perhaps surprisingly, the issues raised here—and the ubiquitousness of economic forces—are not new. Walter Camp, George Halas, and Grantland Rice discussed economics and sports more than fifty years ago. The greatest change in that period may be simply the magnitude of the revenues, costs, and salaries.

Preface

Since I was old enough to read, I have first opened the newspaper to the sports section. Only when I knew, for example, whether the Red Sox had won—and the Yankees had lost—and the most recent heroics of Ted Williams, Carl Yastrzemski, or Roger Clemens, only then could I read the rest of the newspaper. Does that behavior reflect a warped sense of priorities? Perhaps. But it is for people with those same priorities that I wrote this book. Nevertheless, this book is a far cry from what I expected when starting this project. Quite frankly, initially I was simply curious about what many may view as an arcane question of finance: what is the rate of return on professional sports franchises versus the return on stocks or bonds? In trying to answer that question, however, I immediately ran into an anomaly. Many owners have repeatedly cried poverty. For example, Art Modell claimed that the Cleveland Browns have lost $22 million in the past two years. (The evidence here suggests that Art Modell may have lost money but the Browns have been quite profitable.) These same owners have then refused to provide any financial information to support their contention of losses. However, despite no cooperation from the owners, much information is available. Having the profit numbers opens up a host of additional questions. For example, are high ticket prices the result of high salaries? Who is hurt and who is helped by a salary cap? Why do strikes in sports appear so difficult to solve? How much would it cost an owner to win one more game? Are professional athletes overpaid? Should college athletes be paid? How should Title IX be enforced given the "profits" in collegiate football? Economics has something to say about all these issues and much more. The general conclusion is that economic factors have altered the face of sports and will continue to influence how all leagues develop. Perhaps surprisingly, the issues raised here—and the ubiquitousness of economic forces—are not new. Walter Camp, George Halas, and Grantland Rice discussed economics and sports more than fifty years ago. The greatest change in that period may be simply the magnitude of the revenues, costs, and salaries.

Chapter 1

Keeping Score — A Financial Box Score of Sports Franchises

"The love of money is the root of all evil."— **I Timothy, 6:10**

"Baseball is a public trust, not merely a money-making industry."
—Ford Frick, baseball commissioner

"If you always tell the truth, you don't have anything to remember."
—Dick Motta, coach, Chicago Bulls

"The trouble with officials is they just don't care who wins."
—Tommy Canterbury, coach, Centenary

Reading the newspaper sports section is becoming increasingly difficult without a background in economics. It sometimes is hard to tell where sports ends and business begins. Multimillion dollar labor contracts, strikes, franchise sales, and expansion talks frequently overshadow who won and how. As an economist, I find it amusing that no branch of human endeavor appears insusceptible to the dismal encroachment of economics. As a sports fan, I find that distressing.

Frequently, the press reminds us that baseball—or football or basketball or hockey—is first and foremost a business. It is, however, a minor league business in comparison with major industries in the U.S. For example, the 28 teams currently comprising Major

League Baseball (MLB) have a combined full time employment of fewer than 5,000 employees. In contrast, General Motors employs over 700,000 while AT&T employs over 300,000. Recent corporate restructurings by GM and IBM each have eliminated over 30,000 jobs, more jobs than in the major sports leagues combined. The combined market value of all 28 MLB franchises is approximately $3.5 billion. In contrast, GE is worth approximately $90 billion—25 times as much as baseball. Warren Buffett, who owns less than 50 percent of the 35th most valuable U.S. firm, Berkshire Hathaway, could buy all the MLB franchises and still have most of his net worth outside of baseball. In fact, he could buy out the NBA and NHL as well.

The point of these comparisons is, bluntly, that major league sports as an industry is strictly minor league. It is a footnote on newspapers' financial pages. To state the obvious: Sports merits its own section in every paper because it is a game. Personally, I would like to see the discussions of strikes, contracts, lockouts, and the like remain exclusively in the business section. I love baseball because it is a game. That it is a business as well is inconsequential to my enjoyment. Nevertheless, this book is written because business affairs keep intruding into sports matters. This book is written for people who believe that the game comes first and financial matters are just accountants' messy details. These are necessary details, however. In this book I attempt to examine some of those messy details and their implications.

WHY LOOK AT THE ECONOMICS OF SPORTS?

Most sports fans would rather not read about multi-million dollar contracts, strikes, labor negotiations, and franchise sales. The economic forces that shape those financial events, however, also have a substantial bearing on the conduct of the game. Do we have an MLB or NBA players strike? How many teams make the playoffs? Which players sign with which teams? Which team plays where? Who wins and who loses? All these questions are substantially affected by underlying economic forces.

One might be tempted to argue that who wins and loses is determined solely by what happens on the playing field. True enough. But what determines who plays for, say, the New York Yankees versus the Kansas City Royals? Consider a few extreme examples. The San Francisco 49ers easily won the 1995 Super Bowl, and sports writers have touted the Steve Young-led 49ers as one of the best teams of all time. The MVP of this triumph, however, was not Steve Young or even Deion Sanders or Jerry Rice, although they won the awards and set the records. It was Carmen Policy, President of the 49ers, who in late 1993 spent over $10 million to sign the talent necessary to beat the Dallas Cowboys and San Diego Chargers and to win the Super Bowl. At the other extreme are the Cincinnati Bengals who have vied for the worst record in the NFL. To someone familiar with the financial numbers, the Bengals' on-the-field misfortune was as predictable as the 49ers' success. The Bengals are at the bottom of the league both in record and in expenditures. To be blunt, the Bengals' ownership has not tried to field a competitive team.

Similar analyses hold true for all leagues. In baseball, the San Diego Padres held a fire-sale of high-priced talent, and they immediately moved from vying for the pennant to struggling to avoid the cellar. The stated reason for their player sale was finances and their inability to make a profit. George Steinbrenner, owner of the New York Yankees, takes in more revenue than any other MLB owner. He has used those funds to spend copiously, although not entirely successfully, to sign the best players possible. The NBA has a salary cap or a limit on the total player payroll allowed for a team. In 1993-1994 only one team was under the salary cap—the Dallas Mavericks. The Mavericks also had the worst record in the NBA. In hockey, Edmonton is a hockey hot-bed but a relatively small-market franchise in comparison to New York or Los Angeles. Edmonton also has drafted and developed talent like Wayne Gretzky and Mark Messier. One was sold to the Los Angeles Kings, the other to the New York Rangers. There should be no arguments now that who plays where—and who wins—is largely shaped by economic forces. Tell me who spent how much and I will tell you approximately how each team will fare on the field.

In sports we keep score in terms of wins and losses. Not all teams are equally successful, and not all teams live up to their potential. The same is true in finance, where we keep score in dollars and cents. Some teams are prosperous and some are not, and some teams fall far short of their financial potential. The financial scoreboard is rarely examined, perhaps in part because sports fans do not find it interesting and in part because the numbers are difficult to obtain. Nevertheless, financial performances have major implications for on-the-field successes. Those implications are the focus of this book.

Can small-market MLB franchises like Kansas City, Milwaukee, and Minneapolis survive? Will MLB be dominated by media-rich teams like the Yankees or the Braves? How can NBA teams like the Seattle Supersonics and Utah Jazz successfully compete with teams like the Los Angeles Lakers and the Boston Celtics? Is the NBA's salary cap responsible for the reversal of team fortunes or are there other factors at work? Can the small-market publicly-owned Green Bay Packers ever hope to contend for the Super Bowl? Can the San Francisco 49ers repeat in the Super Bowl given the 1995-1996 salary cap? Can franchises like the Arizona Cardinals be successful anywhere? Can the Edmonton Oilers contend for the Stanley Cup? Can the Oilers even afford to stay in Edmonton? Can the New York Rangers begin a hockey dynasty? Are the Montreal Canadien's days as the premier NHL franchise over? Are all franchises competently run on the financial end? Is financial competence related to a team's on-the-field performance? Is an owner trying to win a championship or is he more interested in making money, assuming that the two may not always go hand-in-hand? These are some of the fundamental questions shaping the future of team sports, determining who wins and loses, and to some extent, even determining how the game is played and whether the game is played.

I initially focus on which franchises have been financially successful. The information gathered, however, also carries strong implications about which franchises have been well run and which poorly run as well as which have been run primarily with a focus on profits as opposed to a view toward winning. While many owners may not like to hear it, not all owners are equally capable of or equally interested in running a major league sports franchise.

Nor are all owners equally committed to fielding a championship-caliber team. Fans are often criticized for being "fair weather" supporters of a team. In many cases, a team lacking fan support also lacks owner financial support.

The analysis here does not consider only the financial profitability of individual franchises. The average profit in a league, the distribution of profits in a league, and the desires of owners (and to a lesser extent, of players) also have major implications. Those implications are spelled out in detail. For example, in 1994 MLB and the NHL had lengthy and bitter strikes. Both strikes stemmed in part from the owners' contention that they were losing money and had to control players' salaries in order to save the game. A key issue then is the average profit in MLB and in the NHL. My results suggest that the average profit in both leagues has been more than reasonable when compared to the average profit in stocks, for example.

As any good statistician knows, an average can hide a multitude of sins. While league average profits may be substantial, a few franchises may be making most of the money while most franchises are making much less or even losing money. That in fact is the case in both MLB and the NHL. In this respect also, the sports industry is like virtually any other industry; some firms succeed and others fail. In sports, the financial losers have options that may be painful for sports fans. Arguably, both the MLB and the NHL strikes were brought to us courtesy of the financial losers.

While the numbers indicate some teams like the Indianapolis Colts and the Detroit Tigers have had poor financial management, a financial loss does not necessarily indicate that a team is financially mismanaged. The owners differ in their capability of producing an on-the-field winner and in their ability to produce profits. They also differ in their desires to win versus make money. For example, Jerry Jones, owner of the Dallas Cowboys, has spent liberally on both facilities and players to achieve a Super Bowl winner. Ask yourself the question, "how much more do you think he would have been willing to pay—if he had the option—to get the Cowboys in the 1995 Super Bowl?" Do you think John Sawyer, president of the Cincinnati Bengals, would be willing to pay as much?

The financial numbers presented here also have implications for many additional questions. For example, what really are ball player's salaries and are they out of line? Do higher salaries lead to higher ticket prices? What kind of deals do cities have in terms of providing and renting municipal stadiums? Do fans—or should fans—have any voice in team or league affairs? How has the competition between cities for teams changed the nature of sports finance? Are small-market teams at a competitive disadvantage? Is the data really consistent with the notion that big spending equals big winning? What are the implications for the future success of the large-market teams like the New York Yankees relative to small-market teams like the Milwaukee Brewers? Should there be revenue sharing? Should there be further league expansion?

The answers to these questions likely will not please everyone. Arguably, there is something here to offend everyone, especially many owners. The answers, however, are based on careful economic analysis and the most complete information available. No information is withheld and I have no ties to either the players or the owners.

THE FINANCE OF SPORTS

Virtually every recent book on sports has bemoaned the impact of finances. But finance has influenced religion, politics, and every other aspect of life. Why should athletics be different? While most bemoan the impact and go on, I take a different approach here and attack the issue head on. There are parallels between sports and finance that may not be apparent to the average sports fan. I will try to place the financial matters in the language of sports. Think of what follows simply as keeping score. Instead of talking about runs or points or goals, we keep score in dollars. There is one fundamental difference, however, between keeping score in finances and in sports. In team sports, we have a loser for every winner. In finances that need not always be the case—although players and owners appear not always to have taken that point to heart.

While the terminology will be in terms of keeping score, the focus will be on analyzing the financial rules of the game and thus the implications for strategy. Consider a baseball example. The strike zone is approximately from the armpits to the knees and over the plate. Anything else is a ball. The rules are well understood by all—although some who have watched MLB might ask if some umpires need a lesson in anatomy. In theory, life is neat and simple; in practice, it can be more than slightly muddy and maddening. Pitchers attempt to throw all over the strike zone, "nibbling the edges," working inside and out. No matter how hard a pitcher throws, if he sends it down the middle each time he will get hammered. There is a Darwinian aspect to this process. Pitchers that can work the strike zone and that can adapt to the umpire or their own frailties survive. The rest get a real job.

So it is also in finance. The theory is relatively straightforward to someone who has practiced it for years, but the precise application sometimes can be muddy and confusing. Some sports fans now might say I am crazy. Baseball really is simple and finance is confusing, difficult, or impossible. To those who believe that, I suggest the following experiment. Take someone from Russia or China with virtually no knowledge of American sports to a baseball game. Sit in the right field bleachers and try to explain the game. Why is one pitch a ball and the next a strike? Why do baserunners sometimes run on a fly ball and other times stay put? And why after hitting a ball is a batter sometimes called out even before the ball is caught (the infield fly rule)? After doing that, I can tell you that explaining the rules of finance is easy in comparison. And those rules also include a Darwinian survival process.

The ground rules in finance are no less compelling than the ground rules in baseball, although they may sometimes appear as ambiguous as an umpire's strike zone. The umpire's strike zone determines how far inside a pitcher will get a strike called and gives incentives for a pitcher to go inside. Likewise, the rules of finance give incentives to both owners and players. The question here is what are the financial equivalents of "nibbling the edges" of the plate?

The unifying assumption of this book, and of finance in general, is that everyone operates in his own self-interest. For an economist, no further explanation is required. The statement is tautological. For the other 99+ percent of the world, the obviousness of this statement may be in question. What it means is simply that you do what you want to do—subject to constraints—because you want to do it. If you buy a Ford rather than a Chevy, it is a matter of your choice. You prefer the Ford given the available prices, options, etc. If you work in construction rather than in sales, again it is a matter of your choice, given the alternative salaries, the availability of employment, and your talents. Economists define self-interest so broadly that even actions like making charitable donations may fall into that category. You give because it makes you feel better or because you expect an eternal reward.

What then does this unifying assumption of "enlightened" self-interest imply for sports? From the perspective of an owner of a professional sports team, self-interest can be narrowly characterized as an attempt to maximize profits. To be more precise from an economic standpoint, the owner may be concerned with maximizing future profits or, equivalently, the value of the franchise. Economists label the worth of a company the Net Present Value (NPV). I will use this term to refer to what a franchise would potentially be worth to its owner strictly based on economic considerations. You can think of NPV as the potential sale price of a competently run franchise.

More realistically, an owner's self-interest also includes a desire to win. In fact, the typical owner appears quite willing to sacrifice some of the club's potential profits for a winning team or a championship season. Thus, the team owner may not achieve maximum NPV because he is willing to pay to win. A baseball analogy may be useful. Like high profits, a high batting average is desirable, but sometimes it is necessary to sacrifice average to advance a runner—e.g., hit behind the runner, and maybe win a game.

What are the implications of trying to win even at the cost of lowering profits? First, the value or the selling price of the franchise will be greater than the NPV—simply because owners value winning. They are willing to pay for the privilege of owning a winning franchise. (They appear to be much less willing to pay for the privilege of losing.) How much is an owner willing to pay to win—even if it may mean lowering the profitability of the franchise? Historically, some of those numbers have been quite large. The Boston Red Sox under Tom Yawkey (1934 to 1978) did not frequently finish first, either in profits or wins. But Yawkey was quite willing to spend on his players, even when it reduced the team's profits. More recently some owners, including George Steinbrenner of the New York Yankees and Gene Autry of the California Angels, have allegedly attempted to buy a pennant—even though that would lower their team's profits and thus its NPV. For many baseball owners come late September, it's not ERAs or RBIs or even NPVs that matter, but WINs.

To put it another way, owning a franchise has both consumption and investment aspects. You own the club generally because you would like to make money—or at least, you do not want to lose money. The franchise is an "investment." But you also own the club because you enjoy the game; you enjoy the notoriety; you enjoy hob-nobbing with the players; you have civic pride; or you enjoy winning. An economist would say these last aspects reflect your "consumption" of the amenities associated with owning a sports franchise. A non-economist might say that you own the club as a hobby rather than as a business. To the extent that the club is an investment, you are concerned with the bottom line. To the extent that the club is consumption, you are concerned with winning and with enjoying the perks of ownership. Most owners appear to value both consumption and investment.

There is a second implication of wanting profits and wins both. If owners are willing to pay big bucks to win, it should not be surprising that they lose money, and they should not complain about those losses. But that gets us ahead of our story.

KEEPING A FINANCIAL SCORE

In putting financial concerns in terms of sports analogies, the most important consideration is the idea of keeping score. To that end, it is necessary to lay out the ground rules of keeping a financial score. The basic question is how different franchises have fared financially. Which are the rich clubs and which the poor? The next four chapters consider each major league in the U.S.: baseball, basketball, football, and hockey.

I must note at the outset one limitation for anyone who attempts to analyze the finances of major league sports franchises. Virtually no information is released to the public. Most teams are owned either by a limited partnership, by an individual, or as a division of a larger corporation. In virtually all cases—the Boston Celtics, Green Bay Packers, Pittsburgh Pirates, Toronto Maple Leafs, and Vancouver Canucks being the only exceptions—no public accounting of the finances is required. In addition, most clubs refuse to release any financial information, which is their prerogative. Thus, the numbers presented here are generally estimates and are not without error. But they are consistent with other estimates and with all publicly available information, including salary information, ticket prices, attendance, and franchise sale prices.

The lack of information is puzzling. Franchise owners in all sports have been crying poverty in labor talks, in negotiations on leasing municipal stadiums, in considering franchise relocation, and in their requests for dispensation from anti-trust laws. These discussions have all been conducted, however, with a minimal release of information. I find this troublesome. For teams that lease municipal stadiums at below market rates not to provide financial information even to the municipalities from which they rent appears bizarre. And for an organization like Major League Baseball, which has been granted special treatment for anti-trust purposes, to claim that financial information should not be public is a bit hard to fathom. Teams and players have much of the information; only fans are kept in the dark. However, what is in good taste is not the subject here.

The raw numbers presented here are not all that different from those that have been presented elsewhere, for example in *USA Today* and in *Financial World.* If it was a question of reading this book just for the numbers, my recommendation would be to turn to the tables in Chapters 2 to 5 and ignore the rest of the book. But if all you want are the numbers, then you could look at *USA Today* or *Financial World* and use their numbers. The true sports fan, however, is not interested just in the scores; they want to know the how and why behind the scores. That is what I am trying to present here, the story behind the financial game. Who is in sports for the money and not for the game? Who is out there trying to buy a championship? What are the implications of owners' actions for the future of major league sports?

COLLEGIATE SPORTS VERSUS PROFESSIONAL SPORTS

One feature of this book that differentiates it from prior analyses is the extension of the analysis to colleges. To many associated with colleges and universities, this extension may be the most controversial part of this book. If I had a scintilla of tact, as a professor at Notre Dame, I would omit this discussion. However, there are simply too many interesting questions posed by athletic finances for me to leave collegiate financing on the sidelines. Tenure has some advantages, including giving me the freedom to discuss "market values" of collegiate sports programs and the implications of financial factors.

The basic question I ask for collegiate sports is simple. Take the two sports that commonly generate revenue, football and mens basketball; given their costs and revenues, what are their profits and the resulting "market values" or NPVs? The calculations, in principle, are virtually identical to those associated with the pros, although some details differ dramatically. The results indicate that the best of the colleges—including Notre Dame—make as much as virtually all professional teams. However, the overwhelming majority lose money even on football.

There are a number of ways of motivating the discussion of collegiate athletics in nearly the same breadth as professional athletics. The first is, again, with respect to the rules of the game. In most cases, the collegiate and professional rules of the game are identical. The differences (e. g., aluminum bats allowed in collegiate but not professional baseball, a different distance for a three-point shot in basketball, and one foot versus two feet in-bounds for a legal catch in football) do not appreciably alter the character of the games, although they do sometimes alter strategy. Likewise, the financial incentives for colleges and pros are similar.

Now with that last sentence half the college administrators probably dismiss me as not knowing what I am talking about while the other half began to reach for their phones to verbally rend me limb from limb. Let me repeat, the financial incentives for colleges and pros are similar. I make this statement with confidence—even though professional sports is a for-profit endeavor, financial losses and alleged losses notwithstanding, while colleges generally are not-for-profit operations. That difference cannot obscure that colleges and professionals both operate in markets where supply and demand influence all prices, revenues, and costs.

Perhaps the most fundamental difference between college and professional sports is what happens to any excess of revenues over costs. For the pros, the booty is labeled profits and is the property of the owner. For the colleges, any surplus sometimes is returned to the college's general fund and used to subsidize the general educational mission of the institution. Other times it is spent on other athletic programs or facilities.

The point here is not to judge whether the use of any profits is admirable or reprehensible. It simply is to point out that the pressure to turn a profit—or not let costs grow beyond revenues—are similar in the college and pro ranks. Anyone who doubts that has not talked to a college athletic director. In addition, for both colleges and pros, I am comfortable in arguing that the financial rules may have almost as much impact on who wins and who loses as does the team that ultimately takes the field.

Juxtaposing colleges and the pros also provides insight into how financial incentives influence both. For example, one debate at the collegiate level concerns whether college athletes should be paid beyond the value of the education they receive. Viewing collegiate football as akin to the minor leagues, one can argue that free market compensation for college football players would be similar to minor league salaries. With this perspective, we can ask if collegiate football players should be compensated beyond tuition, room, and board. The numbers suggest that many currently are overpaid while others are exploited.

Perhaps the most controversial but compelling reason for examining colleges as well as pros is also the simplest: who is number one? The wealthiest "franchises" among the college ranks are also at or close to the top in terms of NPVs of all sports franchises. Most football fans would probably contend that Michigan, Nebraska, or Notre Dame, for example, could not successfully compete in the NFL. However, their financial successes put them near the top of any financial ranking of "sports franchises." I must emphasize that this does not necessarily mean that they have sold their souls for thirty silver pieces. Certainly, some colleges have attempted to "cash in" financially, have broken any constraints on good sense, have consistently fallen afoul of the NCAA, and have broken any number of laws. When confronted with their transgressions, the administrators at these colleges usually respond that their actions were based upon tremendous pressures to win. They are quite correct, and that pressure to win is both athletic and financial and it holds for both collegiate and professional sports.

Let us proceed to the scores.

Chapter 2

Baseball — Yes Virginia, There Are Owners Dumber than Hockey's

"Baseball is too much of a sport to be a business and too much of a business to be a sport."
—Philip Wrigley, former owner, Chicago Cubs

*"Baseball is a tremendous business for men with big egos. But ego can only take you so far. After that, it has to be a good business proposition."***—Brad Corbett, former owner, Texas Rangers**

"Baseball isn't a business. It's more like a disease."
—Walter O'Malley, owner, Los Angeles Dodgers

"Baseball a business? If it isn't, General Motors is a sport."
—Jim Murray, sports writer

"Under generally accepted accounting procedures, I can turn a $4 million profit into a $2 million dollar loss, and I could get every national accounting firm to agree with me."
—Paul Beeston, president, Toronto Blue Jays

Baseball is a game with a rich statistical history. Analysts like Bill James (*The Baseball Book*, 1992) have studied historical statistics in detail while "rotisserie leagues" of fans with their "own" franchises based on current player statistics flourish. The statistics in turn lead to debates over questions like whether Ken Griffey or Barry Bonds is the best player in baseball or how Frank Thomas or Greg Maddux compare with the greats of yesteryear. The financial numbers, while less well known and less discussed, also lend themselves to some rather heated debates. Some of these debates, like the appropriate solution to the 1994-1995 Major League Baseball (MLB) strike, receive extensive press coverage. Many others, like the implications of revenue sharing, receive virtually no press attention.

THE UGLY FINANCIAL DETAILS—
WHAT GOES INTO DETERMINING THE PROFIT NUMBERS

Though all kinds of fragmentary financial data are available, only Pittsburgh has released complete financial statistics, and then only because they are partially owned by the city of Pittsburgh. Seattle has made public some information, but their numbers raise more questions than they answer. So where do we turn for financial information? Requests to the other 26 clubs elicited no information. Since most MLB teams are either privately owned (or are small divisions of large corporations), they have no legal obligation to release any information to the public. Given the owners' contention that they are losing money, I was under the naive impression that they would be willing to document these losses. In fact, the owners have been singing this refrain about losing money at least since the late 1970s—and arguably, since the formation of the first professional leagues back in the 1870s.

Nevertheless, a tremendous amount of financial information is available.[1] Helping in the search is the fact that some revenues are split equally between clubs and many costs are quite similar across clubs. The details of national television contracts are well documented. Most local media contracts also are public information. General ticket revenues can be readily calculated, and luxury box revenues also are publicly available. Finally, since many stadiums are municipally owned, the terms of those arrangements, including rental payments and the split of any concession and parking revenues, are available under the Freedom of Information Act. Player salaries have been published by *USA Today* and the *New*

---

[1]Andrew Zimbalist, *Baseball and Billions* (New York: Basic Books, 1992), has a particularly insightful analysis of baseball finances, although his approach differs dramatically from mine.

York Times. The salary numbers used here are for the regular 24-player major league roster and do not include *per diem* allowances or pensions, for example. Those are included under "other costs."[2]

The principle unknowns are travel costs, player development costs, game-day expenses associated with the stadium, and administrative costs. Travel costs are assumed to equal $3 million per team. Undoubtedly, there is some variation. This assumption appears generous enough to cover even the highest cost team and includes transportation, hotels, and *per diem* allowances. (Assuming 40 people traveling with the team, including players, coaches and trainers, costs would be $75,000 per person per season or over $450 per person per game.) Game-day expenses including ushers and field maintenance are assumed to run a minimum of $60,000 per home game. A club that owns its own park then would have approximately $5 million in game-day expenses. The Pittsburgh Pirates actual game-day expenses were $4.4 million in 1993. Where the costs are known to be higher, based on contractual stadium arrangements, this number is adjusted upward. Player development costs, including scouting and minor leagues, are assumed to average around $7 million per team; some teams (the Los Angeles Dodgers) are higher while others (the Oakland A's) are lower. The last assumption is about administrative expenses. This category may be the most controversial—and the most ripe for abuse by owners. The numbers here are based on an average of $3 million per team, with New York and Los Angeles adjusted upward for their larger markets. I will defend that number shortly. Other major costs include player fringe benefits such as pensions (approximately $2 million per team plus 10 percent of player salaries).

The only number from the owners that I have not taken at face value is the alleged $7 million per team national television contract for 1994. From 1990 through 1993 each MLB franchise received $13.4 million a year from the national media. When the networks

---

[2] Player costs used here are based on beginning-of-season rosters rather than end-of-season rosters like the "official" MLB numbers. Near the trading deadline, teams out-of-contention frequently trade aging stars or big-salary players to teams vying for the pennant. Most of the salary expense generally is incurred by the team of record at the beginning of the season. Using the end-of-season numbers then can give a distorted picture of team finances. Ideally, it would be preferable to assign some of the salary to each team. However, as part of the trade agreement, one team may agree to pick up more than its pro-rated share of the contract.

declined to renew those contracts, MLB chose to enter the media business and produce the games itself. The owners arbitrarily assigned a value of about $7 million per team for those telecasts. In fact, given the prior media contracts combined with CBS's losses under those contracts, a more reasonable value would have been in the range of $11 or $12 million. To be conservative, I will use a national media value of $8.5 million.

For MLB it is reasonable to determine first what profits were before the most recent labor dispute and then to ascertain how the strike changed MLB finances. That is the approach taken is subsequent sections.

1994 FINANCIAL PERFORMANCE

Assuming that the 1994 baseball season was played to its normal conclusion, what would MLB profits have been? Table 2.1 lists revenues and costs by category for each club, as well as the profits for each club. Arguably, it presents more information about MLB finances than you ever wanted to know. The information included there, however, is vital to a full understanding of how MLB will evolve. What does this table tell us? First and foremost, the profit numbers in the last column indicate that most MLB franchises are doing quite well. True, 10 of 28 lost money; Kansas City, Detroit, Minneapolis, Seattle, and Cincinnati all lost a bundle, in excess of $10 million; but both New York franchises, the Chicago Cubs, Baltimore, and Colorado all had tremendous financial success. These teams all would have made in excess of $17 million had there been a full season. Profits averaged almost $5 million per club, slightly higher in the American League and slightly less in the National. Clearly these numbers present a dramatically different story than what the owners keep repeating, that MLB is losing money. So much for the obvious. Table 2.1 suggests four additional general conclusions.

(1) **Importance of Market Size.** Possibly the most interesting point about the financial data is that small-market teams (that is, franchises located in metropolitan areas with relatively small populations) are not all bleeding red ink. Some are doing very well. Take four similarly sized cities, St. Louis, Baltimore, Minneapolis

and Pittsburgh, all among the smallest cities with MLB franchises. The former two thrive while the latter two struggle. One could argue that Baltimore draws fans from Washington D.C. as well as Baltimore, but D.C. presumably is not a baseball hotbed, given that two teams have fled the city and attendance for those teams was poor. Baltimore would still have profits even if they lost their Washington media money (about $5 million) and their Washington-based gate revenues (about $10 million). One could argue that St. Louis is supported by Anheuser-Busch. But Anheuser-Busch is a public company that pumps suds and not cash into Busch Stadium. To argue that small-market teams like Minneapolis and Pittsburgh cannot compete is to ignore the evidence that Baltimore and St. Louis compete very successfully.

Look at even smaller markets, Milwaukee and Denver, two of the four smallest market teams. Denver leads MLB in attendance while Milwaukee languishes near the bottom. Now the Milwaukee management undoubtedly will argue that it is unfair to compare the Brewers with an expansion franchise. Agreed. But when the Brewers first moved to Milwaukee, did they draw anywhere near the crowds? No. Furthermore, the Colorado Rockies would have been profitable in 1994 even with half the attendance. The Brewers lost money even with national television money, while the Rockies did not need that to be successful; the expansion franchises initially did not receive national television money.

The numbers imply that small market franchises are not automatic money-losers. Some have had substantial financial success, but small market teams do have less margin for error. Franchises in New York, Los Angeles, and Chicago appear to have a guaranteed profit. No such guarantee exists for small market franchises.

(2) **Importance of Alternative Revenue Sources.** Teams that lead the league in financial losses, franchises like Cincinnati, Detroit, Houston, Kansas City, Milwaukee, Minnesota, Pittsburgh, and Seattle, have one common characteristic; far below average gate receipts. Many of these clubs also have complained that they do not receive sufficient fan support. Either their city does not have a history of supporting MLB, or their stadium is too old, or their fans only support a winner. This argument, whether made in

Table 2.1

REVENUES, COSTS, AND PROFITS

(all numbers in millions)	1994 Revenues				1994 Costs		1994 Net Profits	1990-94 Total Profits
	Gate	Media	Stadium	Total	Players	Total		
AL								
Baltimore	36.6	20.3	20.2	81.1	37.5	65.1	16.1	99.9
Boston	27.7	29.0	14.0	74.7	36.3	61.4	13.3	55.4
California	17.9	18.3	10.8	51.0	20.7	45.6	5.5	8.9
Chicago	29.0	17.0	22.5	72.5	38.2	65.8	6.7	60.9
Cleveland	29.0	14.5	20.5	68.0	28.5	55.2	12.8	28.1
Detroit	20.5	22.5	7.3	54.3	40.0	66.8	-12.5	-18.8
Kansas City	20.9	12.0	10.5	47.4	40.5	67.1	-19.6	-48.0
Milwaukee	20.1	12.5	8.1	44.7	23.4	49.5	-4.9	-27.4
Minnesota	20.1	11.5	7.1	42.7	27.6	53.7	-11.0	-13.2
New York	29.4	54.0	12.7	100.1	44.8	76.1	24.0	122.1
Oakland	20.9	21.6	11.5	58.0	33.2	59.3	-1.3	-3.8
Seattle	19.2	13.0	8.0	44.2	27.9	53.5	-9.3	-15.9
Texas	29.8	17.8	18.2	69.8	32.4	59.4	10.4	49.3
Toronto	43.9	21.6	11.7	81.2	41.9	68.9	12.3	52.5
NL								
Atlanta	40.0	26.0	11.4	81.4	40.5	67.4	14.0	10.9
Chicago	30.0	27.0	14.1	75.1	32.2	57.2	17.9	46.1
Cincinnati	24.0	15.2	12.4	55.6	40.0	66.7	-11.1	-16.7
Colorado	36.0	13.5	14.5	68.0	23.0	50.1	18.9	31.6
Florida	27.0	19.5	9.7	60.2	20.2	44.9	15.3	27.8
Houston	21.0	14.5	13.6	53.1	32.0	58.0	-4.9	25.7
Los Angeles	30.5	25.0	15.0	74.5	37.2	67.2	7.3	48.0
Montreal	20.0	14.5	6.7	45.2	18.6	42.2	3.0	29.3
New York	20.5	44.5	13.3	82.3	29.9	59.7	23.1	70.1
Philadelphia	29.5	20.5	10.0	64.0	31.4	58.3	5.7	21.8
Pittsburgh	16.0	17.0	6.0	43.0	20.3	47.1	-4.1	-14.6
St. Louis	26.0	21.0	12.6	63.6	29.0	53.4	10.2	35.5
San Diego	13.5	16.3	7.1	40.9	13.5	37.4	3.5	-3.7
San Francisco	26.0	18.5	16.0	64.5	40.1	67.1	-2.6	43.9
AL Average	26.1	20.4	11.0	63.6	33.8	60.5	3.0	25.0
NL Average	25.7	20.9	11.6	62.2	29.1	55.5	6.9	25.4
Average	25.9	20.7	12.4	62.9	31.5	57.9	5.0	25.2
Maximum	43.9	54.0	25.5	100.1	44.8	77.1	24.0	122.1
Minimum	13.5	11.5	6.0	40.9	13.5	37.4	-19.6	-48.0

MLB or in another professional sport, is amusing at best. The fans do not come—the customers do not buy the product—and whose fault is it? Why, the customers of course! It is like arguing that if GM loses money it is your fault for not buying a new car. To put this argument in context, consider again the Colorado Rockies. Denver had no history of supporting a major league baseball franchise; Colorado played its first season in a large stadium poorly equipped for baseball and, quite frankly, the Rockies were not a very good team, although they were respectable for an expansion team. While the novelty of MLB in Denver undoubtedly boosted ticket sales, with an attendance over 4 million, it strains my credulity to argue that creative marketing did not play a substantial role in the Rockies' profits. Having an entertaining product together with successful marketing does influence profitability.

While the teams suffering large losses uniformly have low gate revenues, the teams at the top of the financial rankings get there by alternate means. Both New York franchises are successful based on their media revenues. They are the only two franchises deriving over 50 percent of their total revenues from the local media. They receive over $40 million each while no other franchise receives as much as $30 million. The three teams with the smallest media revenues, Kansas City, Milwaukee, and Minnesota, average only $12 million, putting them at a substantial revenue disadvantage. The Mets would have made money even if they gave away all their tickets while the Kansas City Royals, with the largest loss in MLB, would have had a sizable profit if they had the Yankees' or the Mets' media revenues. Boston also does very well in local media revenues with its exclusive rights to the populous New England market. All franchises have exclusive rights to some local areas. The Atlanta Braves and the Chicago Cubs also have substantial "local" media revenues because of their tie-ins with TV superstations.[3]

Clubs that succeed based primarily on their gate and stadium

---

[3] Both the Braves and the Cubs profits, in fact, may be understated because the superstations' payments to the clubs may be understated. The motive is simple: the Cubs receive substantial publicity while WGN receives relatively little. If you are engaged in semi-public negotiations with the players' union, being able to hide funds would strengthen your hand.

The superstations also make payments to MLB to compensate other clubs for airing baseball games in another team's exclusive area and potentially lowering their profits. In 1993 those payments were approximately $0.7 million a team.

revenues include Baltimore, Cleveland, Colorado, and Toronto. All have new stadiums, tremendous gate revenues, and extremely favorable stadium arrangements. (Texas is added to that list beginning in 1995.) Whether their success wanes as the novelty of the stadium wears off remains to be seen, although Toronto and Baltimore have seen virtually no drop-off in attendance in the few years their new stadiums have been open (until 1995). In the AL, five teams have new stadiums and those five teams rank one to five in attendance. The New York Yankees are sixth. Detroit, Milwaukee, Pittsburgh, and Seattle recently have made the most noise about needing a new stadium. While these franchises all may be aided by a new stadium or a new lease, it is not clear that a new stadium by itself will restore profitability to any of these franchises. That the economics of a new stadium are open to doubt is corroborated by the franchises themselves: none of these franchises have initiated stadium development on their own, as we should expect them to do if that would restore their profits. All four franchises have feverishly lobbied their state and local governments to build them new homes. Only Detroit has expressed a willingness to be more than a minority contributor to the cost of their new stadium.

The franchise most constrained by its stadium may well be the Boston Red Sox. Fenway Park is one of the most intimate stadiums in the country, but its capacity of under 34,000 seriously limits the Red Sox's gate revenues. In contrast, Detroit, Milwaukee, Pittsburgh, and Seattle are all operating far below capacity and generally are close to the cellar in terms of attendance. While a new stadium may increase gate revenues, there may be a much more effective way to increase attendance. Specifically, the evidence suggests that one factor beyond stadium age or market size is an extremely important determinant of attendance: entertainment. California is last in the AL in gate receipts and San Diego is last in the NL. Both also are last in player payroll. The lesson from California and San Diego: a lack of marquee players plus a lack of victories equals a lack of entertainment and a lack of fans. Building a new stadium may increase attendance, but signing the next Bonds or Griffey may have a greater impact on attendance and may increase attendance at a much lower cost than building a new stadium.

(3) **Magnitude of Players' Salaries.** One result in Table 2.1

may strike a sharp-eyed reader as rather strange. Players' salaries average only 50 percent of total revenues rather than the 58 percent widely reported in the financial press. Why do we have such a difference? The answer is simple: what do you include in revenues and in salaries? The numbers here refer to players' salaries based on the 24-man roster and excludes player pensions but includes all revenues. Depending on the precise definitions employed, the ratio of players' salaries to revenues could be as high as 63 percent or as low as 46 percent. We can debate those numbers just like we can debate the significance of Babe Ruth's 60 home runs in 154 games, Roger Maris's 61 in 162 games, or Matt Williams' 43 in a strike-shorted 115 games. There is no evidence, however, that players' salaries are the driving force behind MLB's financial losses. I will discuss this point in much more detail below.

Players' salaries are the largest component of costs and vary substantially by franchise. The New York Yankees lead both leagues at $44 million, followed by Toronto.[4] At the bottom are San Diego (lowest at $13 million) and Montreal in the NL and California in the AL. Some owners have argued that they cannot compete with the player expenditures of teams like New York, Toronto, and Atlanta. It would appear logical that California and Milwaukee, with payrolls roughly half that of the New York Yankees, should have difficulty competing on-the-field with the Yankees. However, that Montreal with the second lowest player expenditures had the best 1994 record suggests that there is more to winning than simply having the highest payroll. The relationships between market size, player payroll, and wins are examined for all leagues in much more detail in Chapter 6.

(4) **Importance of Idiosyncratic Factors.** All teams face idiosyncratic factors, factors peculiar to their franchise. There is a history of fan support; or there is an unfavorable stadium lease; or it rains too frequently; or players do not like to play there. These factors work for some clubs and against others. Certainly these factors make it easier to make money with an MLB franchise in

---

[4] Looking at the 40-man roster and including pensions, the Detroit Tigers have the highest payroll in baseball. While the individual rankings of the teams change slightly when taking this different view of salaries, the overall implications of the analysis are unaffected.

New York or Los Angeles than with a franchise in Milwaukee or Cincinnati. Owners frequently place all the credit or blame for a franchise's performance on these external factors. Their impact, however, has been wildly overstated. A franchise does sometimes have a run of bad luck. Key players get injured or have subpar years. But the talent and effort of the manager and players also play a role in who wins and loses—both on the field and off.

Idiosyncratic factors are not entirely to blame for a franchise's profits or losses. The owner and team management deserve a lot of credit—or blame. Colorado did not draw over 4 million fans entirely by accident. The Yankees did not receive $47 million in local media revenues just by good fortune. And San Diego did not have the lowest payroll in MLB by chance. The teams that made money made hard decisions that led them to make money. And the teams that lost money generally made decisions—sometimes very bad decisions—that led them to lose money. Those decisions were not all by accident either.

RECONCILING MLB NUMBERS WITH THOSE PRESENTED HERE

Before proceeding, it is important to ask why the 1994 numbers presented in Table 2.1 appear to contradict what the owners are saying: that most of them are losing money. How can I reconcile my numbers and those of MLB? The answer is simple (although accountants might have you believe differently). Three factors are at work. I will consider all three in a simple hypothetical example of a team called the Pirates. All the relevant numbers are laid out in Table 2.2.

Suppose you paid $100 million for this hypothetical MLB franchise. What did you get for your money? Essentially two things: the franchise name and some player contracts. The IRS generally will allow you to declare that you paid $60 million for the name and $40 million for the player contracts. The value of the franchise name "Pirates" basically remains unchanged according to the IRS. However, the player contracts are assumed to lose value as those players age and lose their competitive skills. It does not matter that you have new players developing. Because the contracts lose their value as players' skills decline with age, the IRS will allow you to say that the decline in value is a cost. You can use that cost to lower your taxable income.

Suppose after paying all the bills you had $5 million left over. Most of us would call that profit. But if you amortize that $40 million in player contracts over 5 years, as allowed by the IRS, you can write off 1/5 of that $40 million or $8 million each year and call that a cost. Thus, you have pocketed $5 million but declared a loss of $3 million. This accounting maneuver is perfectly legal and entirely consistent with "generally accepted accounting principles." It is perfect nonsense from the perspective of determining your true profits. With just this one change, in the extreme, you could turn the 1994 average profit into an average loss and have 15 clubs "losing" money.

Now two other factors are important to understand why the owners say that they generally are losing money. Consider administrative costs. I assumed $3 million a year in average administrative costs consistent with actual administrative costs at a wide range of relatively small businesses—and $40 to $100 million in revenues is a relatively small business. MLB's semi-official administrative cost numbers range from $5 to $10 million. Why are they so high? Why are they out of line with other similarly sized businesses? Two possible reasons exist, each with at least some corroborating evidence.

First, these so-called administrative costs may actually include some profits. In the example above, suppose as owner of the Pirates you decide to pay yourself $2 million in salary even though you are a "hands off" owner who lets the general manager call all the shots. Your loss has just increased from $3 million to $5 million because your "costs" have increased by the $2 million of your salary. Again, this transaction is entirely legal. But $2 million that used to be called "profit" now is called "cost." You used to keep the money in your left pocket; now you keep it in your right. The bottom line: this accounting change has only served to further misrepresent the overall financial health of the franchise. Do owners actually do this? While there is no direct evidence in MLB, there is much evidence in football, thanks to a recent lawsuit. The NFL evidence indicates that some owners have given themselves "salaries" as high as $7.5 million for "managing" a franchise with revenues of approximately $50 million!

Yet another way to overstate costs is suggested by Bill Veeck.[5] Talking about the Washington Senator's owner Calvin Griffith, Veeck writes, "You think of that silly operations of theirs, with all the relatives on the payroll performing duties just barely visible to the naked eye, and it is hard to take Calvin seriously." In terms of this example, rather than paying yourself $2 million, hire 10 relatives at $200,000 and keep them safely removed from any responsibilities. Again, administrative costs have increased by $2 million for no good reason.

The last difference between MLB's numbers and mine involves transactions that are not at "arm's length." Suppose that you also

Table 2.2
RECONCILING "OFFICIAL" MLB PROFITS WITH THOSE REPORTED HERE
Hypothetical Example - Pirates
(all numbers in millions)

	Profited Reported Here:		$5
(1)	Franchise Sale Price:	$100	
	Player Contract Values:	40	
	Amortization Cost Allowed	8	
	(for 5 years)		
(2)	Excess Administrative Costs	2	
(3)	Media Rights "Market Value"	10	
	Media Rights Payment	7	
	Media Revenues Excluded from Franchise Income	3	
	Loss Reported by MLB		8

Loss reported by MLB equals $5 million in profits minus $8 million amortization cost, $2 million excess administrative costs, and $3 million in media revenues excluded from franchise income.

[5] *The Hustler's Handbook*, New York, G.P. Putnam's Sons, 1965, p. 144.

own a television station that will broadcast the Pirates' games. Suppose under competitive bidding the local TV rights would fetch $10 million. In fact, however, maybe your TV station pays the Pirates only $7 million. Again, there is nothing necessarily illegal here. It is just a question of whether you keep your money in your TV checking account or your MLB checking account. However, from the perspective of the franchise, you have lowered the reported net revenues by $3 million ($10 million minus $7 million) and raised those of the TV station similarly. This move further increases the paper loss of the Pirates. In sum, you have converted a profit of $5 million into a reported loss of $8 million, all entirely legally.

The owners have a tremendous incentive in their negotiations both with the players' union and with cities to cry poverty. They are engaged in semi-public negotiations that may dramatically alter their profitability. They also have the means to manipulate their books to contend that they are losing money. Table 2.1 indicates that some owners are losing money. That should come as no surprise. In any industry there is a range of profitability. Some make a lot of money, some a little, and some lose. Baseball is no exception. However, there is no evidence that baseball franchises in general would have lost money had they completed the 1994 season—despite the owners' contention. In fact, the evidence overwhelming suggests that baseball has been an extraordinarily profitable venture.

THE PROFIT PICTURE—1990-1994

The last column of Table 2.3 presents total profits over the 1990-1994 period, indicating that some teams have been extraordinarily profitable.[6] Over the past five years the Yankees and the Orioles both earned in excess of $100 million (or would have absent the latest strike). The Mets, the Red Sox, the White Sox, the Rangers and the Blue Jays all racked up over $50 million in profits over this period.

The profit numbers from 1990 to 1993 are consistent with those in 1994. They make it quite clear that owning a franchise in

---

[6] Profit figures from 1990 to 1993 come from *Financial World*, with minor modifications to make them consistent with other available information.

a city like New York, L.A., or Chicago is an effective way to make a substantial profit. The only exception is the California Angels franchise, which has been only marginally profitable. The profit numbers also indicate that small-market franchises generally do not do quite as well as large, but neither do they all bleed red ink. St. Louis and San Diego, for example, are two small-market teams that have taken very different roads to profitability.

MLB franchises have averaged approximately $5 million a year in profits from 1990 through 1994. There are those who contend that the economics of MLB has changed dramatically in the past five years and small market teams can no longer survive under the current financial rules. Bud Selig has stated that the Milwaukee Brewers have made a profit in 20 of the past 25 years, but small market teams cannot cope any longer. The numbers in Table 2.3 indicate that he is incorrect. Some small-market teams have accrued incredible losses. Kansas City has lost almost $50 million while Cincinnati, Detroit, Milwaukee, Pittsburgh, and Seattle have each lost $15 million or more. But Detroit is a relatively large market, and small-market teams like Baltimore and St. Louis are extremely successful. Something else must play a role to explain the differences in profits. In fact, there are two factors.

(1) **Franchises frequently lose money through weak management.** It is not avaricious players or fickle fans that are at fault. A subset of owners simply have not fielded a marketable product. It may not be fashionable to say some owners are incapable of running a successful franchise; however, that is what the numbers suggest. All kinds of businesses fail because managers and owners make some decisions that with 20-20 hindsight are really stupid. Why should baseball be different? Does anyone seriously think all 28 owners have the savvy to run a successful franchise? I do not expect a George Argyos, former owner of the Seattle Mariners, or Bud Selig, owner of the Milwaukee Brewers to agree. It is so much easier to say "I was dealt a bad hand" than to admit that "I played the cards poorly." George Steinbrenner may have said it best: "What happens is that all your life you operated businesses in such a way that you could afford to buy a baseball team, and then you buy the team and ignore all the business practices that enabled you to buy it."

In general, U.S. firms make a profit, although there is a wide range of returns, and firms with big losses generally either go out of business or replace management. Among major U.S. firms, General Motors, Sears, and IBM have recently had major turnover among top executives because of their poor financial performances. Maybe their managers were just unlucky. However, their boards of directors found it necessary to install new management teams because they believed that the poor performances were at least in part due to management failure. MLB is no exception in terms of the range of returns.[7] The Yankees, Orioles, Red Sox, and Mets prosper while the Brewers, Mariners, and Reds struggle. What differs, however, is the lack of market discipline on those franchises losing money. There is only minimal responsibility to report to limited partners; there is a reluctance to admit responsibility for failure; and there are ready scapegoats—players, fans, or the stadium arrangement. The financial numbers suggest management failure at Cincinnati, Detroit, Kansas City, Milwaukee, Pittsburgh, and Seattle.[8] Not surprisingly, the ownership at four of these franchises has changed (Detroit, Seattle, Pittsburgh, and Kansas City). We should expect that firms losing money will change their management or ownership team.

Inefficiency is possible either on the playing field or off, and MLB has enough examples of both. On the field, one would have to look at the success of Atlanta, Philadelphia, Montreal, and Toronto and say that all have operated efficiently. Through 1994 they achieved substantial on-the-field success without breaking the bank financially. Successful clubs also have adopted very different strategies. While the Braves have an excellent minor league system, their success largely has stemmed from attracting players who were free agents. In contrast, Montreal has focused on internal

---

[7] One might argue that the wide range of returns suggests that owning a MLB franchise is more risky than owning stocks. That may be true but it certainly is not obvious. Owning an asset like IBM or the Seattle Mariners is a risky endeavor. It is not obvious which is riskier. The issue is unlikely to be resolved, although evidence from the publicly-traded Boston Celtics suggests that sports actually may be less risky.

[8] Despite Minneapolis's large loss, it is not included on the list since its loss appears to be due to the second reason why a franchise may not make a profit: the owner is more interested in winning than in making money.

player development. Neither strategy is necessarily "correct;" at different times for different clubs, either strategy may produce the best results.

You also can look at the collection of talent in some clubs and their subsequent performance to argue that they were under-achievers. Given their expensive free agent signings and large pay-rolls, the Mets and the Tigers appear to be the biggest underachiev-ers in 1994 —or the most inefficient on the field. On-the-field underachievement (or perceived underachievement) is an easy way to get a manager fired, and a common enough event. It is curious that roughly 5 managers seem to get fired each year, but virtually no GM's or presidents get fired. It is amazing how talented MLB's front offices are and how incompetent managers are!

(2) Some owners are committed to winning even at the expense of profits. An owner presumably would like to make a sub-stantial profit and would also like to win a World Series. The ques-tion then is, how does he trade off between the two goals? The California Angels organization is an interesting case. Gene Autry, the owner, at one time spent lavishly to lure players who were free agents and could sign with any club. He unabashedly attempted to buy a World Series victory and was not particularly worried about the Angels' profits. If they lost $5 or $10 million, that sim-ply was the price he was willing to pay to win the World Series. Despite having the highest payroll in baseball during the mid-1980s, the Angels won only two division championships. Autry has since completely reversed course. Payroll has been cut dramati-cally, and in 1994 was lowest in the AL. He no longer was inter-ested in mounting a serious challenge for the World Series but was content to take what profits the franchise yielded. Stated simply: the Angels in the 1980s were committed to winning even when it meant lower profits; the Angels in the 1990s are committed to profits even when it means losing.

Now I am not stating that any owner likes losing. I am arguing that owners make different financial commitments to winning. Looking at the profit numbers in Table 2.3 and the underlying revenue and cost numbers, we can identify some teams who have greater than average commitments to winning. Atlanta, Minnesota, San Francisco, and Toronto lead the list with high payrolls relative to team revenues and well above average victories. At the other extreme are California, the Chicago Cubs, and San Diego. All appear to place much more weight on profits than on winning. Now some of these owners may object that they do really value winning. That is not the issue. The question is: are they willing to pay to win? If the answer is yes, then their complaints about not making a sufficient profit should fall on deaf ears. If the answer is no, then we should not be sympathetic if their teams have dwindling fan support.

A willingness to spend big bucks for the best talent available is not necessarily bad—or good. It simply means that you should not complain about a $10 million loss when your primary goal is to win a World Series. You can complain about a loss only if your goal is profits, not if your goal is wins or civic pride or ego. My guess is that there are a substantial number of owners—maybe virtually all—who would part with $10 million in a flash for a guaranteed World Series trophy. Of course, that tendency makes MLB profits lower than what owners would like.

1995 FINANCIAL PERFORMANCE

Table 2.3 presents information on 1995 MLB finances, information that suggests a very different financial status at the end of 1995 than at the beginning of 1994. MLB had averaged $5.25 million yearly profit per team for the prior five years. In 1995 the average franchise lost $2.9 million. Through 1994 MLB owners were crying "wolf" about their losses. In 1995 the wolf arrived.

The catalysts for this change? First, national TV money decreased substantially as The Baseball Network (TBN) went down in flames. Second, the strike, lack of settlement, and playing only a partial season soured many fans, with attendance falling about 20 percent. And third, the average player's salary declined, but not nearly enough to offset the revenue losses. Even while the strike was in progress, owners signed hefty contracts with star players. After the agreement to play the 1995 season, big contract signings were relatively rare. Nevertheless, for many franchises the payroll already had been largely established by a few pricey multi-year contracts. As the chapter on salaries will demonstrate, 1995 may have been a watershed year in MLB in terms of changing the entire distribution of player salaries.

In terms of individual franchises, few made a profit. Fans kept coming to new stadiums in Baltimore and Colorado and Cleveland and to a lesser extent Texas, giving all four a profit. Media money kept both New York teams highly profitable. The Chicago Cubs also made money, albeit less than before, and established Cubs fans as among the most loyal in MLB. Pennant races and noteworthy pitching additions in Los Angeles (Hideo Nomo) and Boston (Tim Wakefield) led to increased profits for each.

Nevertheless, the 1995 financial picture generally looked bleak. Media income fell by about $4 million a franchise while gate receipts dropped by almost $5 million. San Francisco's gate fell by $12.3 million, Florida's by $10.6 million, and a number of others were close behind. Teams at the bottom in 1994 gate revenues also suffered in 1995. San Diego dropped from $13.5 to $9.5 million while Pittsburgh fell from $16.8 to $8.8 million. To put these numbers in context, Pittsburgh's total gate would not have paid Cecil Fielder's 1995 salary! Some franchises offset the revenue loss with dramatic payroll cuts. In some cases the owner basically liquidated the team, bringing in whoever would work for the MLB minimum salary to fill the gaps. The two most notable examples were Kansas City and Montreal. Kansas City cut their payroll from $40.5 to $26.6 million while Montreal reduced theirs from an already-low $18.6 million to $12.0 million. Even some of the more profitable and profligate franchises cut back. For example, the Red Sox's payroll decreased from $34.3 to $28.7 million.

What are we to make of the 1995 financial numbers? MLB took a tremendous financial hit in 1995. The last column in Table 2.3 indicates only three franchises improved their finances from 1994 to 1995. Boston and Los Angeles were involved in pennant races while Kansas City dramatically reduced its payroll. All other franchises saw a marked financial deterioration from 1994 to 1995—in some cases close to $20 million. The average change in profits? A decrease of $7.8 million per team! That suggests that

Table 2.3

REVENUES, COSTS, AND PROFITS

(all numbers in millions)	1995 Revenues Gate	Total	1995 Costs Players	Total	1995 Net Profits	1994 Net Profits	Change in Profits 1994 to 1995
AL							
Baltimore	38.5	79.5	40.7	63.6	15.9	16.1	-0.2
Boston	28.7	72.5	28.7	49.6	22.9	13.3	9.7
California	15.9	44.4	29.0	51.2	-6.8	5.5	-12.2
Chicago	21.6	55.9	39.6	62.5	-6.6	6.7	-13.3
Cleveland	33.1	70.0	35.2	58.2	11.8	12.8	-1.1
Detroit	14.5	42.7	35.9	57.9	-15.2	-12.5	-2.7
Kansas City	14.5	34.1	27.6	49.5	-15.4	-19.6	4.2
Milwaukee	12.7	30.6	16.2	39.6	-9.1	-4.9	-4.2
Minnesota	12.3	28.6	24.5	47.3	-18.6	-11.0	-7.6
New York	25.7	91.0	46.7	72.5	18.6	24.0	-5.4
Oakland	14.5	44.6	36.0	58.0	-13.4	-1.3	-12.1
Seattle	17.5	38.5	34.2	56.2	-17.7	-9.3	-8.4
Texas	24.3	57.2	32.4	55.5	1.8	10.4	-8.6
Toronto	36.0	67.4	49.8	71.5	-4.1	12.3	-16.4
NL							
Atlanta	30.7	66.0	45.2	67.0	-1.0	14.0	-15.1
Chicago	25.3	65.0	32.5	53.6	11.4	17.9	-6.4
Cincinnati	14.7	39.5	37.2	59.1	-19.6	-11.1	-8.5
Colorado	36.0	63.9	31.1	54.2	9.7	18.9	-9.2
Florida	16.4	42.6	23.7	45.9	-3.2	15.3	-18.5
Houston	12.1	35.9	31.6	53.7	-17.8	-4.9	-12.9
Los Angeles	26.8	65.0	30.5	56.1	8.9	7.3	1.6
Montreal	11.7	31.4	12.0	33.4	-2.0	3.0	-5.0
New York	13.9	68.9	24.3	50.1	18.8	23.1	-4.3
Philadelphia	19.9	48.3	28.6	51.8	-3.5	5.7	-9.1
Pittsburgh	8.8	30.2	17.0	41.4	-11.2	-4.1	-7.1
St. Louis	17.1	47.8	31.1	51.9	-4.1	10.2	-14.3
San Diego	9.5	31.7	25.9	47.8	-16.1	3.5	-19.6
San Francisco	13.7	42.3	34.9	57.1	-14.9	-2.6	-12.3
AL Average	22.1	54.1	34.0	56.6	-2.6	3.0	-5.6
NL Average	18.3	48.5	29.0	51.6	-3.2	6.9	-10.0
Average	20.2	51.3	31.5	54.1	-2.9	5.0	-7.8
Maximum	38.5	91.0	49.8	72.5	22.9	24.0	9.7
Minimum	8.8	28.6	12.0	33.4	-19.6	-19.6	-19.6

the strike cost owners a minimum of $230 million in 1995. The 1995 data also suggest substantial long-term changes may be coming in MLB finances. Will gate receipts recover? Will owners be able to control costs without collusion? Will national media money—which will average $10.7 million a team beginning in 1996—provide financial stability?

FRANCHISE VALUES

After looking at franchises' profits and losses we can turn to the question of what an MLB franchise is actually worth. What is the Net Present Value (NPV) of a team like the New York Yankees? There is admittedly some uncertainty in the profit numbers. There is, however, even greater uncertainty about what a franchise is worth. To some extent it depends simply on what a potential owner is willing to pay for the assets and the fame associated with owning an MLB franchise. To begin to establish what a franchise is worth, we can ask what someone would or should be willing to pay for the profits of an MLB franchise.

To answer these questions we need an assumption about expected future profits.[9] In fact, I need two sets of assumptions. The first considers profits pre-strike. That is, assume that clubs on average will earn in the future what they have earned before the 1994-1995 labor impasse. Thus, the New York Yankees, who earned $122.1 million from 1990 to 1994, would be expected to continue to average over $24 million per year in profits. Rather than simply assuming that profits remain constant, in the interest of being conservative, I assume that clubs with substantial profits like the Yankees will not be able to maintain these levels. Table 2.4 presents the actual averages as well as the assumed "normal" profits. Except for unusual cases like Cleveland (a new stadium), Atlanta (hiding cable revenues), and California (profits dramatically less than the Dodgers), clubs with profits are assumed to have lower future profits. The numbers in part require arbitrary assumptions

---

[9] We also need an assumption about what interest rates are expected. The appropriate value is what economists call the real interest rate—that is, the interest rate above the expected rate of inflation. Looking at stock returns over the past 50 years in the U.S., it is reasonable to assume a 6 percent average real interest rate on an asset as risky as an MLB franchise.

about matters like future club leases and may change apprecia-bly—either up or down. For example, if New York (either the city or the state) does build a new stadium for the Yankees, you should expect even higher Yankee profits. I also assume no increase in revenue sharing—and thus no decrease in Yankees' profits and cor-responding increase in Brewers' profits (revenue sharing and its im-plications are discussed in Chapter 7).

In contrast, teams currently losing money are assumed to in-crease profits to a minimal positive level of $3 million. The num-bers in Table 2.4 indicate that any competently run club that is concerned with profits should average a minimum profit of $3 million per year. For example, consider Montreal, long thought of as one of the best-run organizations in baseball, as well as a money-losing franchise in a relatively small market with a populace more interested in hockey and less than enthusiastic about baseball. In fact, the Expos have averaged profits of almost $6 million, double what I assume is the minimum profit level. St. Louis also is a small market club and they have averaged over $8 million in profits. If you want to push the figures, you could plausibly argue that every club in baseball should make a minimum of $5 million under rea-sonably competent management and with the 1994 labor pact and media arrangements, assuming their goal was to make money rather than to buy a championship.[10]

Table 2.4 presents pre-strike actual 1990-1994 profits, as-sumed "normal" profits and the calculated pre-strike NPVs in the first three columns. The pre-strike NPVs suggest there are three groups of franchises: the rich, the well-off, and the "other" fran-chises. In the first category are the Yankees and the Orioles. The Yankees had an NPV of over $350 million while the Orioles' was over $250 million. The second category, at around $150 million, includes all the usual suspects: the New York Mets, Boston, the Chicago White Sox, Cleveland and Texas (new stadiums), Toronto, Atlanta, Los Angeles, St. Louis, and Colorado. Bringing

---

[10] Pittsburgh potentially is an exception. However, it is not clear to what extent the consortium owning the Pirates was to blame for their losses since they appeared unable to agree on any-thing— including how to sell the franchise.

Table 2.4

NET PRESENT VALUES

(in millions of dollars)	Average Income Pre-Strike	"Normal" Income Pre-Strike	NPV Pre-Strike	"Normal" Income Post-1995	NPV Post-1995
AL					
Baltimore	20.0	16.0	267	15.0	250
Boston	11.1	10.0	167	13.0	217
California	1.8	4.0	67	3.0	50
Chicago	12.2	9.0	150	7.0	117
Cleveland	5.6	8.0	133	9.0	150
Detroit	-3.8	3.0	50	2.5	42
Kansas City	-9.6	3.0	50	2.5	42
Milwaukee	-5.5	3.0	50	2.5	42
Minnesota	-2.6	3.0	50	2.5	42
New York	24.4	22.0	367	19.0	317
Oakland	-0.8	3.0	50	2.5	42
Seattle	-3.2	3.0	50	2.5	42
Texas	9.9	8.0	133	7.0	117
Toronto	10.5	7.0	117	6.0	100
NL					
Atlanta	2.2	8.0	133	5.0	83
Chicago	9.2	7.0	117	8.5	142
Cincinnati	-3.3	3.0	50	2.5	42
Colorado	15.8	13.0	217	9.0	150
Florida	13.9	6.0	100	3.0	50
Houston	5.1	4.0	67	3.0	50
Los Angeles	9.6	9.0	150	8.5	142
Montreal	5.9	4.0	67	3.0	50
New York	14.0	13.0	217	14.0	233
Philadelphia	4.4	4.0	67	3.5	58
Pittsburgh	-2.9	3.0	50	2.5	42
St. Louis	7.1	5.0	83	4.0	67
San Diego	-0.7	4.0	67	3.0	50
San Francisco	8.8	4.0	67	2.5	42
AL Average	5.0	7.5	125	6.7	112
NL Average	6.4	6.2	104	5.1	86
Overall Average	5.7	6.9	114	5.9	99

up the rear: Detroit, Kansas City, Milwaukee, Minnesota, Oakland, Seattle, Cincinnati, Pittsburgh, and San Francisco with market values of $50 million. The rest are between $67 and $83 million.

The pre-strike NPVs corroborate a point made earlier. One cannot state that large-market teams all are financially successful while small-market teams struggle. The New York teams are at the top and some small-market teams are at the bottom. That is obvious. But the exceptions are important. Detroit and California are large-market, small-profit clubs while St. Louis and Colorado are small-market, large-profit clubs. The general conclusion is that city factors play some role, but an owner's ability to manage the franchise financially is critically important.

The NPVs based on "normal" profits including the 1995 season are presented in the last column of Table 2.4. They indicate NPVs generally are reduced only marginally from their prior levels (compare columns 3 and 5). These reductions are necessarily speculative and make two major assumptions. First, fans are assumed to return and gate receipts to recover to their 1994 levels. And second, owners get a grip on salaries and do not continue bidding up salaries in the absence of increasing revenues. If both things happen, profits will return to MLB and NPVs will be close to their former levels. The small drop under optimistic assumptions reflects the additional risk in most franchises, a risk that these assumptions will prove inaccurate.[11]

MLB now stands at a crossroads. Optimistically, they return to the profits of 1994. Pessimistically, what happens? In a word: "meltdown!" If both assumptions are not met, a number of franchises may not survive through 1997. You can view any franchise with an NPV of less than $50 to 60 million as potentially in trouble.[12] Fifteen teams would be legitimate candidates to fold. Furthermore, if attendance does not pick up, the pool of potential franchise buyers will dry up as well.

FRANCHISE PECULIARITIES

A few points should be noted about some of the financial numbers, primarily with respect to franchises that are losing money.

---

[11] Four franchises have increased NPVs because their 1995 profits suggest there may be less risk or higher profits than calculated based solely on pre-1995 numbers.

[12] Kansas City had a pre-strike loss of almost $20 million and Cincinnati, Detroit, and Minnesota all had losses exceeding $10 million. With an NPV of $60 million, Kansas City would be bankrupt in three years without a capital infusion while Detroit would be out of business in under five years. An NPV less than $60 million may preclude a team from obtaining financing to sign the players required to be competitive.

Detroit. The Tigers lost almost $20 million from 1990 to 1994, despite being a relatively large-market franchise. Attendance was low; stadium revenues were near the bottom of the league; and player salaries were close to the top of the league. All in all, Detroit presented a perfect recipe for low profits and a low market value. The single most likely cause for this state of affairs was managerial neglect and turmoil. The former owner, Tom Monaghan, paid little attention to the team's management and then hired a general manager with no baseball experience. With this approach to management, Detroit's financial mess should be no surprise. The financial evidence suggests that the new owner, Mike Ilitch, has the potential to substantially increase the profitability of this franchise, even without building a new stadium.

Oakland and San Francisco. Oakland and San Francisco share a market and must be considered together. San Francisco should be large enough to support two teams, having a population more than double that of Atlanta. At times, one or the other franchise has prospered but never have the two had concurrent financial success. The data does not allow us to distinguish between competing explanations; less than stellar financial management versus the unfavorable demographics in Oakland, and the notoriously bad weather at San Francisco's Candlestick Park versus greater concern about winning than profits. The Giants free agent signings in particular suggest that their goal is primarily winning rather than profit.

Cincinnati. In Cincinnati, the travails of Marge Schott are well known. To put it mildly, her "controversial nature" (some call it incompetence) is the stuff of legends. Team costs are close to the top of the league, in part padded by administrative expenses associated with her car dealerships. Revenues are close to the bottom, in part because the fans know she runs the club unencumbered by any knowledge of baseball. In her own words, "I wish they'd give me a scorecard with pictures because I still get everybody mixed up." Her limited partners sued her for failing to disclose revenues and for inappropriately charging costs from her car dealership to the team. And her financial controller sued her, in part for allegedly telling him to "cook the books" to lower her taxes. With even marginally competent management, Cincinnati should not be a financial basket case. Schott has been pushing aggressively for a new stadium. The financial evidence does not indicate a new stadium is necessary for the Reds to be financially successful.

Kansas City. The Royals ownership has spent liberally to field a competitive team. In the process, Kansas City led MLB in financial losses. It should be obvious that an MLB franchise in Kansas City cannot spend dollar-for-dollar with the New York Yankees without losing a lot of money. Nevertheless, the Royals kept spending and kept losing. The team is now owned by a trust, charged with finding a buyer committed to keeping the team in Kansas City. If the team remains in Kansas City, fans should expect the new owners to take a dramatically different approach to the team, perhaps unloading all the high-priced talent, simply to keep the Royals afloat.

Pittsburgh. The Pirates have lost a substantial amount of money over the past five years by following the strategy exactly the opposite of the Royals: do not spend money on free agents but try to develop talent internally. While they have had some on-the-field success, they have consistently lost money. Their losses appear to stem from a poor stadium arrangement and an inability to attract fans. Their attendance is better only than San Diego's. The underlying problem with Pittsburgh may be its ownership group, an unwieldy combination of the City of Pittsburgh, private investors, and local corporations. No one in the group appears to have the ability or the funds to provide managerial direction. That makes it difficult to field a quality team—or even to sell the franchise.

Seattle. Seattle, under its former ownership, would be another club near the top of my list of financially poorly run franchises. Seattle has no local or near local competition; from Vancouver to Portland there is no other baseball team. The Mariners should be the Pacific Northwest's team much as the Boston Red Sox are New England's team and the Colorado Rockies are the Mountain region's team. Seattle is bigger than Denver, and the population within driving range of Seattle is a large multiple of Denver's. Three years ago, Denver had as little history of supporting MLB as Seattle. There are also as many ways to spend your entertainment dollar in Denver as there are in Seattle. And the media market in Seattle is substantially larger.

San Diego. Off-the-field financial success differs, and off-the-field financial strategies also may differ. The Yankees, the Braves, and the Giants have all adopted a strategy of going after big-name free agents, a strategy where you have to spend money to make money. Their success has been mixed, with the Yankees scoring big financially while the Giants have been shut out. San Diego has taken exactly the opposite approach. They have dramatically reduced their payroll by unloading virtually all their high-priced talent. Their goal is to reduce expenses and hope that revenues do not decline as rapidly. The Padres, as reviled as they may be by many of their fans, have actually been successful in this strategy. They had the lowest payroll in baseball, and while their gate revenues also are the lowest, they have been profitable. Whether this strategy would be successful in the long run is open to debate. Nevertheless, the Expos, Mets, and Royals have all followed the Padres lead in slashing payroll.

It is interesting to compare the Padres performance with Charlie Finley's behavior with the Oakland A's in the 1970s. His attitude toward the end of his reign is another example of a switch in strategies by an owner, from spending big to not spending at all. The Finley example also makes clear at least one interrelationship between the owners: they are all at least partly dependent on each other for revenues. Finley's attendance in 1977 was beyond woeful. The players used to count the fans in the stands—which was easy because sometimes there were fewer than 500. The other owners were less than thrilled at this state of affairs since gate receipts are split; in the AL through 1994 the home team kept 80 percent of paid attendance and the visitors received 20 percent. No-shows do not count and may be substantial with corporate purchases of season tickets. If you have a three game series with, say, 2,500 attending each game and a $5 average ticket price, the total gate is $75,000. Twenty percent of that is $7,500, which may not even pay for the visiting team's trip. We will come back to revenue sharing and the associated incentive problems in a later chapter that considers revenue sharing in all sports. Baseball has much to learn in that regard both from football and from economic theory.

Chicago White Sox. Among the franchises making considerable profits, the White Sox are a particularly interesting story. The

White Sox had threatened to leave Chicago for St. Petersburg because the old Comiskey Park was unsuitable. The engineering community agreed that Comiskey was structurally sound and could be refurbished for around $10 million. However Jerry Reinsdorf, owner of the White Sox, insisted that without a new park he was leaving. How credible a threat should that have been? Reinsdorf was threatening to leave the third-largest media market for the 21st when he was making $5 to $10 million per year in profits on a franchise he purchased in 1981 for $21 million. The move to the smaller media market would have cost him $2 to $3 million in local television revenues and the smaller population base, after the novelty of the franchise wore off, would have cost him another $2 million plus. For Reinsdorf just to break even St. Petersburg would have had to provide a $4 million plus subsidy per year! While the threat to leave should not have been credible, the state of Illinois blinked and he got public financing for a new stadium. Unfortunately, other major league moguls from Seattle to New York have taken his success to heart and have engaged in full court presses for new municipal stadiums.

New York Mets. The Yankees would appear to be exhibit number one in terms of financial success, although it remains unclear to what extent this is due to the good fortune of location or the financial acumen of Steinbrenner. Following closely behind are Baltimore, Boston, the Chicago White Sox and Cubs, Colorado, Los Angeles, St. Louis, Texas, and Toronto. The New York Mets are conspicuously absent from the list. Despite leading the NL in profits over the last five years, I would rank their performance at best mediocre. Why? They are located in New York City and have an immense reservoir of good will built up. Even my wife is a Mets fan. But from 1990 to 1994 their profits were more than $50 million less than the Yankees. The explanation is simple. They have a surprisingly low attendance. Not only is their attendance less than the Yankees' (although their park is in a much better section of the city), their attendance is less than that of small-market teams like Montreal and St. Louis. The Mets make money because of their lucrative local media contracts. Perhaps the appropriate characterization of the Mets owners: "I'd rather be lucky than good."

New York Yankees. It pains me as a Red Sox fan to say anything positive about George Steinbrenner. However, strictly from a financial perspective, his management of the Yankees appears very successful. While Steinbrenner may have made illegal campaign contributions to Richard Nixon, had questionable dealings with gamblers, bullied players, second-guessed and abused managers, and won fewer pennants than he would have liked, the Yankees' financial affairs appear to be handled with skill. The Yankees handling of local media rights have been exceptional, almost $10 million higher than the Mets. In addition, while one can quarrel with his role as "villain" in his dealings with players and other teams, we expect the Yankees to play the role of the bully. It is a great marketing strategy than Steinbrenner appears to relish.

A General Comparison. The New York Yankees and Kansas City have both followed a strategy of big spending while Pittsburgh and San Diego have both sharply restricted spending. Clearly, MLB owners can and do follow very different financial strategies, even if they have the same goal. The New York Yankees and San Diego have both made money while Kansas City and Pittsburgh have both lost money. Thus, it also should be clear that each of those financial strategies can be successful or unsuccessful.

ACTUAL FRANCHISE PRICES

How do the calculated NPVs compare with the actual sale prices? Table 2.5 presents actual franchise prices when either the *Wall Street Journal* or the *New York Times* reported both a sale and a sale price. Franchise prices in general have increased dramatically, averaging under $10 million in the 1960's and about $100 million in the 1990's. However, there has been a wide range of prices. For example, in 1985 the Pittsburgh Pirates sold for $21.8 million while in 1986 the New York Mets sold for $80.7 million. More recently, the Baltimore Orioles, one of MLB's financial elite, sold for $173 million while the Oakland A's and San Diego Padres, both teams with financial difficulties, sold for about $85 million.

The increase in franchise prices is interesting but not particularly surprising given the profits reported in Table 2.1. Of more interest from a finance perspective is the return. That is, what rate

Table 2.5

SELECTED FRANCHISE PRICES

Date of Transaction	Franchise	Expansion	Purchase Price (in millions)
1961	Los Angeles Angels	Yes	2.1
1962	New York Mets	Yes	1.8
1964	New York Yankees	No	13.2
1968	Kansas City Royals	Yes	5.5
1968	Seattle Pilots	Yes	5.5
1968	Montreal Expos	Yes	12.5
1968	San Diego Padres	Yes	12.5
1970	Milwaukee Brewers	No	10.8
1972	Cleveland Indians	No	11.0
1973	Seattle Mariners	Yes	6.2
1973	Toronto Blue Jays	Yes	7.0
1973	New York Yankees	No	10.0
1974	San Diego Padres	No	12.0
1975	Chicago White Sox	No	9.7
1976	Atlanta Braves	No	12.0
1977	San Francisco Giants	No	12.0
1977	Texas Rangers	No	10.0
1977	Oakland A's	No	12.5
1977	Boston Red Sox	No	20.5
1979	Houston Astros	No	12.0
1979	Baltimore Orioles	No	12.2
1980	Oakland A's	No	12.7
1980	New York Mets	No	21.1
1980	Cleveland Indians	No	15.9
1981	Chicago Cubs	No	20.5
1981	Chicago White Sox	No	21.0
1981	Seattle Mariners	No	13.1
1982	Philadelphia Phillies	No	30.1
1983	Pittsburgh Pirates	No	12.5
1983	Detroit Tigers	No	43.0
1984	Minnesota Twins	No	32.0
1985	Pittsburgh Pirates	No	22.5
1986	New York Mets	No	80.7
1986	Cleveland Indians	No	45.0
1989	Baltimore Orioles	No	70.0
1989	Texas Rangers	No	79.0
1989	Seattle Mariners	No	76.0
1990	San Diego Padres	No	75.0
1992	Seattle Mariners	No	106.0
1992	Detroit Tigers	No	85.0
1992	Houston Astros	No	100.0
1993	San Francisco Giants	No	100.0
1993	Baltimore Orioles	No	173.0
1993	Colorado Rockies	Yes	95.0
1993	Florida Marlins	Yes	95.0
1994	San Diego Padres	No	83.0
1994	Oakland A's	No	85.0
1995	Pittsburgh Pirates	No	85.0

Table 2.6

FRANCHISE VALUES AND RETURNS FOR
TEAMS THAT SOLD MORE THAN ONCE
(When Both Prices Are Available)

Franchise	Year of Purchase	Purchase Price	Implied Annual Return
Seattle Pilots [a]	1969	5.5	
Milwaukee Brewers	1970	10.8	94.6
New York Yankees	1964	13.2	
New York Yankees	1973	10.0	-3.9
Oakland A's	1977	12.5	
Oakland A's	1980	12.7	0.5
Oakland A's	1994	85.0	14.5
Chicago White Sox	1975	9.7	
Chicago White Sox	1981	21.0	13.6
New York Mets	1962	1.8	
New York Mets	1980	21.1	14.7
New York Mets	1986	80.7	25.1
Cleveland Indians	1972	11.0	
Cleveland Indians	1980	15.9	4.7
Cleveland Indians	1986	45.0	18.9
Texas Rangers	1977	10.0	
Texas Rangers	1989	79.0	18.8
San Diego Padres	1969	12.5	
San Diego Padres	1974	12.0	-1.0
San Diego Padres	1990	75.0	12.1
San Diego Padres	1994	83.0	2.6
Houston Colt .45s [a]	1962	1.8	
Houston Astros	1979	12.0	11.6
Houston Astros	1992	100.0	17.7
Detroit Tigers	1983	43.0	
Detroit Tigers	1992	85.0	7.9
Seattle Mariners	1973	6.2	
Seattle Mariners	1981	13.1	9.7
Seattle Mariners	1989	76.0	24.6
Seattle Mariners	1992	106.0	11.7
San Francisco Giants	1977	12.0	
San Francisco Giants	1993	100.0	14.2
Baltimore Orioles	1979	12.2	
Baltimore Orioles	1988	70.0	21.4
Baltimore Orioles	1993	173.0	19.8
Pittsburgh Pirates	1983	12.5	
Pittsburgh Pirates	1985	22.5	34.2
Pittsburgh Pirates	1994	85.0	15.9

[a] The Milwaukee Brewers originally were the Seattle Pilots and the Houston Astros originally were the Houston Colt .45s.

have the owners made on their investment? That question is addressed in Table 2.6 for franchises that have more than one recorded sale price since 1960. For these clubs I calculate the average percentage increase in the value of the franchise between sales. Only twice has an owner sold a franchise for less than was paid, and in many cases the rate of appreciation exceeded 20 percent. The average exceeds 15 percent. Not a bad return for an industry allegedly in financial distress!

Table 2.7 presents the average price appreciation on a yearly basis.[13] To put these numbers in context, compare the averages over the last 5, 10, and 20 years with the percentage appreciation in three stock market indexes over the same periods. Owning an MLB franchise yielded a 15.6 percent annual gain over the last 5 years while the Standard and Poors 500 Index (S&P 500), perhaps the most widely employed stock index, increased only 6.8 percent per year. For every period and every index, owning an MLB franchise like Pittsburgh or Seattle on average would have produced greater appreciation than holding a typical portfolio of stocks. One very important modification must be made to these rates of return, however.

The implied returns in Table 2.7 are based on appreciation of the franchise value only. They do not include operating profits. For example, the Baltimore Orioles were sold in 1988 for $70 million and in 1993 for $173 million. Just the appreciation in market value or capital gain yields an annual return of 19.8 percent, assuming the franchise owner received no profits from 1988 to 1993. In fact, the Orioles have been one of the most profitable franchises in MLB. The numbers in Table 2.1 suggest that Eli Jacobs, the prior owner of the Orioles, received over $65 million in profits from 1988 to 1993, profits that were not reinvested in the club. Thus, the total return equals $103 million (the difference in sale prices or capital gain) plus $65 million (operating income) for a profit of $168 million. The corresponding Orioles' rate of return was approximately 30 percent a year. In contrast, Kansas City's

---

[13] The value for, say, 1990 is the average of the returns for franchises that sold before and after 1990.

Table 2.7

AVERAGE ANNUAL RATE OF FRANCHISE APPRECIATION
(Based on Actual Franchise Sale Prices)

Year	Average Appreciation %
1975	10.9
1976	11.3
1977	11.3
1978	11.0
1979	12.1
1980	12.6
1981	16.9
1982	17.1
1983	20.5
1984	19.3
1985	19.3
1986	17.6
1987	16.5
1988	16.5
1989	16.7
1990	14.2
1991	14.7
1992	14.7
1992	17.9
1994	15.9

Indexes	1989-1995	1985-1995	1975-199
MLB Average	15.6%	16.4%	15.3%
Dow-Jones Industrial Avg.	8.1	12.5	9.3
Standard & Poors 500	6.8	11.0	9.7
Wilshire 5000	7.1	10.7	NA

operating losses more than offset their implicit capital gain giving the Royals a loss of about 5 percent a year.

Clearly the Orioles and the Royals are exceptional cases. What can we say on a more representative note? To calculate the total return, add operating income to the figures in Table 2.7, which states only the capital gain. We could debate what is the appropriate value to use for average profits, but for simplicity I use MLB's 1994 average profits. Taking the owners at their word, the numbers for 1994 should be a conservative estimate of average profits over the last 20 years. That is, the owners complained throughout the abbreviated 1994 season about their poor financial shape. So assume that they were doing at least as well during the prior 20 years as they did in 1994. From Table 2.1 the average operating profits were $5 million per year. On a $117 million franchise, the MLB average, that would imply a return of 4.3 percent on equity. Adding that to the capital gain gives you a total return to owning an MLB franchise of about 20 percent over the last 5, 10, and 20 years. In contrast, the S&P 500 increased by 14 percent over the last 5 years and 15 percent over the last 20. One adjustment should be made to the S&P 500 number. MLB franchises are small businesses and small stocks typically have higher returns, typically with a premium of just under 3 percent over the last 20 years.[14] Thus, MLB's 20 percent return should be compared to a stock return of about 18 percent. The conclusion: on average MLB franchises have made a return that is at least marginally higher than what owners could have made on comparable assets. Furthermore, that return does not include the ego or consumption value of the franchise

There are two warnings to attach to MLB's 20 percent average annual return. First, it likely represents a conservative estimate. If 1994 was a bad year, as the owners claim, and 1990 was a more representative year, then the total return would increase to around 23 percent. And second, this average hides some wide disparities. The Seattle Mariners did not make a lot of money under their former owner. Detroit and Pittsburgh also have struggled to stay afloat. All have had annual returns of 10 percent or less. In contrast, the Yankees have had a return in excess of 30 percent.

Let it be said, profits are not evil and are not the work of the devil. The owners deserve a reasonable return on their investment, and in cases like Baltimore, Colorado, and Florida it is a very substantial investment. Generally, owners through 1994 received a reasonable return. That MLB has made substantial profits, profits in excess of other industries, should come as no surprise. MLB was effectively granted an antitrust exemption by the Supreme Court

---

[14] If you believe that because MLB franchises do not have traded stock, they are relatively illiquid assets, then you might want to include an additional liquidity premium of about 1 percent. The appropriateness of that assumption is open to debate since there appears to be no dearth of interested buyers for franchises.

in 1922. With the monopoly power stemming from this exemption, it would be surprising if MLB did not have profits exceeding those in most other industries. You can view MLB's profits in excess of stock returns, 20 to 23 percent versus stocks' 18 percent, as stemming from MLB's antitrust exemption.

1994-1995 STRIKE—WHO LOST THE MOST?

As an aside, one can ask what was the financial impact of the 1994-1995 MLB strike. Who lost more, the owners or the players? In finance, you do not need a loser for every winner; you can have two winners or, in this case, two losers. It is a question without a solid answer at the moment, but the numbers here give some clues. Roughly 30 percent of the 1994 season was canceled, and 10 percent of the 1995 season. Players lost approximately 30 percent of their 1994 salaries as well as most 1994 performance bonuses plus 10 percent of their 1995 salaries. The total cost to the players: almost $300 million in 1994 and another $100 million in 1995—not counting any long-term decreases in player salaries, possibly reflecting less revenue coming into MLB. The players' loss: $400 million and counting.

For the owners the story is a bit more complex. In 1994 costs declined by approximately $350 million, largely due to the decrease in player salaries. But revenues also declined. Assuming franchises lost about 30 percent of their gate and stadium receipts but two-thirds of their media revenues—the media money is heavily concentrated on the post-season—then owners lost approximately $700 million in revenue, for a net loss of $350 million in 1994. Added to owners' $230 million loss in 1995 this gives them a total loss of $580 million and counting.

Before you conclude that the owners have lost more than the players, remember that the typical baseball player's career is quite short, and the high incomes most associate with MLB players only come after playing a number of years. Thus, relatively speaking, the players may have lost more than the owners. Then why did the players strike? I will return to that in Chapters 7 and 8.

There is one additional strike-related concern. The players have beaten the owners in three complaints of collusion. The players now are considering filing another case against the owners, Collusion IV. What would happen if the owners lose? While the case probably will not be settled for a couple of years, if the ruling is that the owners colluded, the cost to the owners would be staggering. Collusion damages are automatically tripled. Thus, if the players' loss is $300 million for 1994 and $100 million for 1995, the owners collusion payments would be $1.4 billion! Assuming the settlement cost is evenly divided among franchises, each franchise would owe the players $48 million. Given that the 28 MLB franchises are worth a little over $3 billion, the players would effectively own almost one-half of MLB baseball after the final settlement. Including this contingent liability would sharply reduce the value of all franchises.[15]

One other related aside. How much does a franchise benefit from reaching the playoffs or the World Series? The answer is a lot in the short run but probably much less in the long run. For a typical six game playoff series, each franchise would net about $3 million. The Pittsburgh Pirates, for example, netted $2.9 million for their appearance in the 1992 National League Championship Series. The franchises in the World Series would net around another $3 million. Thus, winning the World Series would add roughly $6 million to a club's net revenues. Had Montreal's 1994 regular season success extended into the post-season, the Expos would have had profits of around $9 million. The down-side is that a World Series ticket generally leads to substantially higher player costs when contract renewal time rolls around. Thus, long-run profits may not increase significantly even from a World Series victory. There are two implications. First, Montreal may be the franchise that lost the most with the 1994 strike. The Expos missed a World Series appearance and the profits that go with it, but their player costs increased anyway given their talented team and their low payroll. And second, it is more difficult to repeat as champions because of the higher costs associated with winning.

---

[15] To go one step further, if the typical franchise is purchased 1/3 with cash and 2/3 with debt, MLB would be entirely owned by the players after a collusion ruling against the owners. The sale of the Pittsburgh Pirates apparently was held up by precisely the issue of who would be responsible for any liabilities due to the 1994 strike.

PROFITS VERSUS WINS—WHAT PRICE EGO?

While this chapter has focused on MLB profits, let me reiterate that owners are not motivated exclusively by profits.[16] For some owners, the desire to win may be more important. Indeed, it is difficult to rationalize some of the actions of Steinbrenner, like his managerial musical chair and his offer of $72 million to Barry Bonds and Greg Maddux, without assuming he wants to win baseball games even at substantial cost. Ted Turner, owner of the Atlanta Braves, signed free agents like Greg Maddux, Fred McGriff, and Terry Pendleton, signings that can be easily explained only if his primary goal is to win the World Series.

Does ego play a substantial role? As Bud Selig put it: "All I can say is, if people do it for the ego trip, it's the most horrible ego trip in the world."[17] But when 100 potential buyers contact an owner rumored to be interested in selling, it suggests that a lot of people see a lot of profit or a lot of ego gratification. One also can reasonably ask, given that Selig's Brewers allegedly have been losing money and it is not an ego trip, why is he still involved in baseball?

Can we get any feel for how much owners or potential owners are willing to pay for the ego trip of owning an MLB franchise? How much are owners willing to pay for the privilege of trying to win a World Series? Perhaps the clearest perspective comes from comparing the calculated NPVs with the recent franchise sales. Only recent franchise sales are considered since the current market price for a franchise that sold five or ten years ago would be speculative. Table 2.8 restates the calculated NPVs (generally pre-strike) as well as the adjusted purchase prices for franchises sold since 1992 (also generally pre-strike). The prices of franchises sold one or two years ago are adjusted upward at a rate of 9 percent per year, to take into account 3 percent inflation and a real return of 6 percent. Expansion franchises are excluded since the actual cost of an expansion franchise substantially exceeds the franchise fee because

---

[16] Economists distinguish between maximizing profits in the short-term versus in the long-term. Nevertheless, the evidence indicates owners' actions cannot be explained entirely by either short-term or long-term profit maximization.

[17] (*Forbes*, April 1, 1977).

an organization, minor league arrangements, etc., all must be developed from scratch. That leaves us with eight sales.

In only one case, the Baltimore Orioles, is the purchase price lower than the NPV. This is also the only recently sold franchise that has made a profit. All other franchise sales have been of teams struggling to break even. In most cases the NPV is substantially below the sale price. The relatively frequent sale of teams losing money is not surprising to an economist. It simply represents inefficient owners getting out of a business.

The difference between NPVs and actual prices still requires some explanation. One way to view the difference is as the "psychic return" or the value of the ego trip associated with owning a franchise. Selig's statement notwithstanding, the sale prices versus the NPVs suggest that there are a significant number of individuals willing to pay a large amount of money for the privilege of owning a franchise—independent of profitability. The owners may or may not be attempting to maximize their profits. They are unlikely to be in it simply for the losses.

Table 2.8

NPVs versus PRICES PAID
What Price Ego? or How Much Have Owners "Overpaid" for an MLB Franchise?

Franchise	Purchase Price [a]	NPV [b]	Purchase Price Minus NPV	1994 Franchise Profits	1995 Franchise Profits
Baltimore	189	267	-78	16.1	15.9
Detroit	101	50	51	-12.5	-15.2
Oakland	85	50	35	-1.3	-13.4
Seattle	126	50	76	-9.3	-17.7
Houston	119	67	52	-4.9	-17.8
Pittsburgh	85	42	43	-4.1	-3.5
San Diego	85	50	35	3.6	-16.1
San Francisco	109	67	42	-2.6	-14.9
Average	112	80	32		
Average excluding Baltimore	101	54	48		

[a] Purchase price equals the actual sale price in the year of sale multiplied by 1.09 (for inflation and the real return) for each year since the sale occurred.

[b] NVP is the pre-strike NPV for sales before the strike and post-strike for sales after.

However, as a group they appear to have paid dearly at least in recent years for the right to be one of a select few. To put it differently, it costs to be in the club and if you have to ask how much, you cannot afford it. For those of us who cannot afford it, the answer is about $32 million if you include the Orioles sale, and $48 million if you do not.[18] And you thought ticket prices were expensive?

Of course, neither profits nor egos are the same for all owners. The roughly $40 million ego value is an average. The actual ego value from owning the Yankees may far exceed the ego value of owning the Royals or the Brewers. However, there is insufficient data to be able to calculate the precise ego value of each franchise.

Now if you do not like this explanation for the difference between the calculated NPVs and the actual sale prices, there is one other. I have argued consistently that my profit numbers are conservative. For example, 1994 media revenues could have been $3 million per team higher; promotional revenues could have been dramatically higher; or an owner's other companies could have had dramatically higher profits as a result of his franchise ownership (e.g. Turner Broadcasting Systems or Anheuser-Busch). Let us be a little less conservative for a moment. Suppose that the minimum profit that a well-managed club should earn was $5 million a year (rather than the $3 million used earlier). At a 6 percent real return, this profit would be consistent with a NPV of $83 million, almost exactly the recent selling price of the Padres and Athletics ($85 million). What is the point? You can argue that ego does not influence the price paid for franchises—but only if you are willing to concede that profits should be a minimum of $5 million under the 1994 rules of the game. In this case, total MLB profits in recent years would have averaged approximately $200 million per year. In other words, in order for NPVs to equal market prices, major league baseball profits are being even more grossly understated than suggested here.

The conclusion: either major league baseball has substantial profits or some wealthy individuals are willing to pay a lot to be a member of the MLB-owners club.

---

[18] To be really calculating about this, an owner overpays when buying a franchise but recovers this payment when selling. It would be interesting to examine whether the price of ego has increased over time, but the data isn't precise enough to allow this calculation.

Chapter 3

Basketball — Trouble in Paradise

"I don't like talking about money. All I know is the Good Lord must have wanted me to have it."

—Larry Bird, Boston Celtics

"Statistics are the cancer of basketball."

—Al McGuire, basketball coach, Marquette

"The collective business of selling heros."

—David Stern, NBA commissioner, on the NBA's mission

"A group of owners couldn't even agree on what to have for breakfast."

—Peter Ueberroth, former baseball commissioner

THE BOSTON CELTICS—AN INSIDE VIEW OF NBA FINANCES

The financial ground rules for basketball are identical to those for baseball. Owners want both profits and victories; the NBA has a monopoly on franchises; neither the league nor individual franchises release financial information; and a creative accountant can bend the numbers in more ways than Shaquille O'Neal can bend a backboard. Yet there is one major financial difference: one franchise is publicly owned and traded on the New York Stock Exchange. Shares in the Boston Celtics—actually, the Boston Celtics Limited Partnership—are publicly traded, and as a publicly traded firm, the Boston Celtics are required to file annual financial reports. While the picture is incomplete, these reports present limited official information on the financial health of the NBA.

The Celtics are but one of 27 franchises, and, as we saw in baseball, the finances of different franchises vary widely. In addition, the Boston Celtics Limited Partnership owns the Boston Celtics and, until recently, a television station (WFXT, a Fox affiliate), and a radio station (WEEI, an all-sport channel). The annual report combines information on both the Celtics and these media outlets. Nevertheless, the Celtics annual reports provide much insight into NBA finances.

Table 3.1 presents the latest official revenues, costs, and profits of the Boston Celtics Limited Partnership. Revenues have grown from $70 million in 1991 to over $100 million in 1994 ($84 million including two extraordinary items). While costs also have risen, from $68 million to over $76 million, profits still have increased from under $2 million to over $20 million, despite substantial deterioration in the Celtics' on-the-court record.

These numbers must be carefully interpreted since they also include the media outlets. One could argue that the Celtics' healthy profits are due to these media outlets. In the explanatory notes to Table 3.1 I attempt to separate the media finances. Media revenues and costs are listed directly in the annual report, but the costs listed exclude some important items. First, the TV and radio stations owned the local media rights to Celtics's broadcasts through part of 1994. In 1993 those rights fees cost $8.86 million. These fees are an additional cost to the media and are not included in the top part of Table 3.1 but are included in the explanatory notes. In addition, the broadcast rights fees suddenly jumped by $5.8 million when they were sold to an unrelated station (an increase of over forty percent after increasing less than ten percent in prior years). The increased broadcast fees are consistent with the contention in Chapter 2 that franchises with media outlets may understate broadcast revenues. The media outlets also incurred some general administrative costs. Allocating half the general administrative cost to the media increases media costs by another $5.19 million in 1993 and $8.53 million in 1994. Administration costs also appear "padded" based on the 1994 annual report. In particular, to the extent that the $3.15 million in bonuses and stock options is paid to the owners, it should be labeled profit and

Table 3.1

BOSTON CELTICS FINANCIAL STATEMENTS
Revenues, Costs, and Profits

(all numbers in millions of dollars)	1991	1992	1993	1994
Revenues				
Ticket Sales	16.43	18.52	20.20	20.24
Basketball Playoffs	3.59	3.25	1.50	0
Broadcast Revenues	10.40	12.47	13.40	19.17
Interest Income	0.63	0.44	0.95	2.60
Other Basketball Revenues	2.65	4.03	3.60	5.18
TV & Radio Revenues	37.20	39.66	42.05	38.30
Extraordinary Items	0	0	0	19.33
Total	70.27	77.93	81.69	104.82
Costs				
Reg. Season (e.g. Salaries)	18.34	27.79	24.72	22.47
Deferred Compensation	1.03	0.98	1.42	1.08
Game Expenses	2.60	2.71	2.97	2.76
Basketball Playoffs	1.55	1.51	0.61	0
Franchise Amortization	1.02	1.03	1.27	1.17
Interest Expense	2.48	2.27	3.11	4.39
General & Administrative	9.81	8.91	10.38	17.06
Other Costs	31.96	32.45	31.97	27.39
Total	68.33	76.84	76.44	76.32
Net Income	1.94	1.08	5.23	28.48

Explanatory Notes

	1991	1992	1993	1994
TV & Radio				
Revenues	37.20	39.66	42.05	38.30
Costs	31.96	32.45	31.97	27.29
Share of Admin. Costs	4.90	4.46	5.19	8.53
Celtics Rights Fees	8.35	7.82	8.86	1.83
Net TV & Radio Income	-8.01	-5.07	-3.97	0.55
Celtics - Total				
Stated Net Income	1.94	1.08	5.23	28.48
Franchise Amortization	1.02	1.03	1.27	1.17
Net Interest Cost	1.85	1.83	2.16	1.79
Minus Extraordinary Items	0	0	0	19.33
Net Celtics Income	4.81	3.94	8.66	12.11

not administration cost. Subtracting stated media costs, the broadcast rights fees, and allocated administrative costs from the stated media revenues yields hefty media losses through 1993 and a slight profit in 1994. (The TV and radio stations generally lost money even if allocated no administrative costs.) Thus, the Celtics profits certainly are not overstated by including the media outlets and may be substantially understated.

A further explanatory note indicates another game that can be played with the financial numbers: including franchise amortization as a cost. As noted in Chapter 2 on Major League Baseball economics cannot justify the argument that most team assets depreciate or amortize. The name "Boston Celtics" is not going to be worth 10 percent less next year. The player contracts of Dee Brown, Eric Montross, or Dino Radja, three current Celtics, are not going to be worth 10 percent less next year. Franchise amortization is not a cost and must be added to stated profits to obtain the true profits.

A second item must be added back to yield real profits: net interest cost. In the NBA, most tickets are season tickets and are sold before the season begins. The largest cost is player salaries which are paid either during or after the season. Given the increasing reliance on long-term contracts in the NBA, these costs are not incurred immediately but are stretched far into the future. Glenn Robinson's $67 million, 10-year contract with the Milwaukee Bucks is one well-publicized example. When you receive the revenues before the games and pay the costs after the games, you should earn substantial interest revenue. Thus, saying net interest equals zero and dropping both interest revenues and costs is an extremely conservative approach to the balance sheet.

How an owner finances the purchase of a ball club should have no bearing on what someone would pay for the franchise, although it may affect what the owner nets from the sale and the owner's interest expense. If I borrowed to buy the Celtics or if I paid cash, when it comes time for me to sell, if you are willing to pay $100 million for the franchise, you do not care what my financial structure may be. Your price is $100 million. So interest is not a cost to the franchise and should be ignored when calculating profits.[1] Thus, net interest costs (interest costs minus interest revenues) are added to stated profits to obtain true profits.

There are two extraordinary items on the balance sheet. The first refers to the one-time gain from the sale of the media outlets. It is excluded from revenues and profits. The second is a $5.6 million payment on a life insurance policy on Reggie Lewis. To the extent that it offsets the salary the Celtics owe his estate, it is included in revenues although it should not affect profits.

Adding amortization and net interest costs and excluding extraordinary items, the Celtics' profit equalled $4.8 million in 1991, $3.9 million in 1992, $8.7 million in 1993, and $12.1 million in 1994—not bad for a team whose playing personnel were aging less than gracefully. These numbers, if off-the-mark, understate the Celtics' profitability since they ignore the net costs of the media outlets; they do not add in all possible interest costs; they consider a period when the Celtics had one of the highest payrolls in the league; and they overstate administrative costs. As the payroll drops with departures of Larry Bird, Kevin McHale, and Robert Parrish and as the Celtics move to a new Boston Garden, the Celtics' profits should increase substantially assuming they continue to fill the Garden.

One more feature about the Celtics' publicly traded status make them particularly interesting. We can take the stock price and multiply it by the number of shares of stocks held to determine the total value of those shares. Table 3.2 presents this information. The closing price on December 7, 1995 was $24 per share. With approximately 6.4 million shares outstanding, this suggests that the stock market values the limited partners' share of the Boston Celtics at $153.6 million.

The Boston Celtics stock price also gives us a clue about the riskiness of sports franchises in comparison to other stocks. Since the Celtics were listed on the New York Stock Exchange in 1986, their stock price has fluctuated in a relatively narrow range. That is, their stock price has varied minimally relative to most stocks.

---

[1] Profits here are accounting profits rather than economic profits. Economic profits subtract from revenue all "opportunity costs" including interest costs. Economic profits then are expected to equal approximately zero. The procedure employed here yields the same end result since at the end of the chapter accounting profits are compared to market rates of return.

Table 3.2

BOSTON CELTICS STOCK PRICE RANGE OF CLOSING PRICES AND IMPLIED MARKET VALUES
Approximate Number of Shares: 6.4 million

		Price (per share)	Implied Market Value of Celtics (in millions)	Celtics Record
1990	Low	$14.500	$92.8	52 - 30
	High	19.125	122.4	
1991	Low	14.250	91.2	56 - 26
	High	20.875	133.6	
1992	Low	16.250	104.0	51 - 31
	High	23.875	152.8	
1993	Low	16.375	104.8	48 - 34
	High	21.625	138.4	
1994	Low	17.875	114.4	32 50
	High	24.125	154.4	
1995	Low	19.750	126.4	35 - 47
	High	28.975	184.8	
1995	Dec. 7, close	24.000	153.6	

Given the limited stock price variation, it seems reasonable to conclude that the Boston Celtics are relatively low-risk relative to most stocks. Whether this is true for other franchises is a matter of speculation. However, it suggests that a sports franchise may not be a particularly risky proposition.

LEAGUE NUMBERS—WHO MADE HOW MUCH?
Moving to the league as a whole, Table 3.3 presents information on the revenues, costs, and profits for all NBA franchises.[2]

---

[2] The NBA is the only league where the 1993-1994 numbers are employed. At press time, some figures required for a complete picture of 1994-1995 finances still were unavailable.

Some background on the numbers is in order. Attendance, average ticket prices, and national media contracts are all public information. Local media contracts also typically are known. NBA licensing revenue has been a source of contention with the players' union and estimates have been widely publicized. Playoff net revenues are included with franchises assumed to net between $300,000 and $700,000 per home playoff game depending on their stadium arrangements. (The Knicks playoff income in 1994 was about $9 million.) On team costs, team payrolls have been reported and the pension plan is known. Other major costs include travel (assumed to average $1.5 million per team), insurance (in part, of long-term contracts at an average of $1.5 million per team), and administrative costs (at an average of approximately $3 million per team). Information on luxury boxes and on publicly-owned stadium rentals also is available through Freedom of Information Act requests.

The profit numbers in Table 3.3 suggest that the average NBA franchise is doing quite well, with profits of almost $5.9 million. As in baseball, however, the range of profits is dramatic. Of the $160 million in total league profit, over 70 percent accrues to just five teams: Chicago, Detroit, New York, the Los Angeles Lakers, and Utah. Unlike baseball, however, no team is running up astronomical losses. The Los Angeles Clippers and the Atlanta Hawks have the biggest losses of $4 million and $3 million respectively. Profits tend to be a little higher in the East conference, but that is largely attributable to the influence of the Bulls, Pistons, and Knicks.

There is no simple formula for financial success in the NBA. In baseball, the easiest way to make a big profit is to have a sweet local media contract. In basketball, that helps but is not required. Both Sacramento and Utah are close to the bottom of the rankings in local media revenues. However, both are very profitable. In the NBA, the size of the arena and the ability to fill it consistently are at least as important as local media revenues. For example, the Knicks were the most profitable team in the NBA in 1994 not because of their media revenues—which were high but, unlike the New York Yankees, did not lead the league—but because they sell out a large arena at premium ticket prices.

While most of the numbers in Table 3.3 consider only the 1993-1994 year, the last column presents total team profits during the last five years.[3] The profits in prior years corroborate the financial health of the NBA. On average, NBA franchises have had substantial profits each and every year for at least the last five years. Average profits have declined slightly over the last two years, but there is no real trend; the decrease can be traced to the decline of the Los Angeles Lakers.

The numbers again imply that a few clubs are making tremendous profits: Chicago, Detroit, New York, and the Los Angeles Lakers lead the league. While all these teams have had on-the-court success, in fact, that appears to be only a secondary determinant of their financial success. For example, the Pistons and the Lakers recently have struggled just to make the playoffs yet they remain among the financial elite. The Rockets recently have had more success on-the-court than either the Pistons or the Lakers, winning championships in 1994 and 1995, yet they have not had nearly as high profits. Now there is no reason to feel sorry for the Rockets' owners. They still make a respectable profit and have a very competitive franchise. The explanation of the financial difference between the Pistons and the Rockets: differences in stadium arrangements. The Pistons and the Lakers lead the league in luxury box revenues. They would make money even with a team the caliber of the Los Angeles Clippers.

After the big four in profits come a number of franchises that are doing quite well, averaging profits over $5 million a year. Included in this list are Boston[4], Charlotte, Orlando, Minnesota, Phoenix, Portland, and Utah. What makes these teams profitable varies. The Celtics have the large New England market and made a reasonable profit despite having one of the worst stadium arrangements in the country. Their local media revenues have saved them,

---

[3] Profits from prior years come from *Financial World* with minor modifications to make them consistent with all available information.

[4] The profits of the Celtics are calculated using the same methodology as employed for other franchises. It does suggest lower profits than in the Celtics' financial statements. This is consistent with my choice of conservative financial assumptions throughout and suggests that league profits may be higher than indicated in Table 3.3. However, salary cap arguments presented below suggest that the numbers in Table 3.3 may be more appropriate than those in Table 3.1.

Table 3.3

REVENUES, COSTS, AND PROFITS
(all numbers in millions)

	1994 Revenues				1994 Costs		1994 Net Profits	1990-94 Total Profits
	Gate	Media	Stadium	Total	Players	Total		
East								
Atlanta	11.9	15.7	2.0	36.8	22.5	39.8	-3.0	-10.5
Boston	19.1	22.3	0.5	46.0	21.2	38.2	7.8	34.2
Charlotte	21.8	16.3	0.5	42.2	18.0	34.5	7.7	44.1
Chicago	27.6	16.9	3.0	54.1	19.6	38.6	15.5	71.6
Cleveland	20.2	13.7	5.0	43.0	23.7	42.4	0.6	17.8
Detroit	24.7	17.4	11.0	56.7	15.8	34.7	22.0	123.2
Indiana	10.9	11.0	3.0	30.9	17.2	33.0	-2.1	-19.3
Miami	15.1	11.9	5.0	36.2	17.8	34.0	2.2	17.6
Milwaukee	14.3	10.4	4.0	32.3	15.9	31.3	1.0	6.6
New Jersey	18.3	13.7	0.5	36.9	20.1	37.8	-0.9	2.4
New York	31.9	18.9	14.0	77.5	22.1	44.1	33.4	89.5
Orlando	19.4	14.5	3.0	41.0	20.8	38.5	2.5	27.1
Philadelphia	11.7	14.7	0.5	30.5	15.5	32.1	-1.6	-1.5
Washington	13.8	12.9	5.0	35.3	16.1	32.1	3.2	-2.5
West								
Dallas	12.3	11.4	1.0	28.3	14.3	29.1	-0.8	7.3
Denver	12.7	10.9	5.0	34.2	17.3	33.3	0.9	-4.4
Golden State	16.4	16.0	6.0	42.4	21.2	39.0	3.4	14.9
Houston	15.1	12.9	2.0	40.1	16.8	33.0	7.1	17.6
LA Clippers	13.6	15.4	1.0	33.6	20.2	37.6	-4.0	6.3
LA Lakers	20.7	22.6	13.0	59.9	22.5	44.5	15.4	135.3
Minnesota	17.5	11.9	6.0	39.0	15.5	31.3	7.7	46.8
Phoenix	28.1	16.7	3.0	54.4	21.6	41.8	12.6	52.7
Portland	14.7	18.0	3.0	39.9	23.5	41.4	-1.5	30.4
Sacramento	17.1	9.9	8.0	38.6	15.9	31.7	6.9	22.1
San Antonio	19.8	10.4	3.0	37.6	19.3	36.1	1.5	21.1
Seattle	18.0	13.5	2.0	38.3	16.0	31.7	6.6	13.9
Utah	26.1	11.5	4.0	50.0	17.0	34.0	16.0	42.1
East Average	18.6	14.8	4.1	42.5	19.0	36.5	6.3	28.6
West Average	17.9	13.9	4.4	41.3	18.5	35.7	5.5	31.2
Average	18.3	14.4	4.2	41.9	18.8	36.1	5.9	29.9
Maximum	31.9	22.6	14.0	77.5	23.7	44.5	33.4	135.3
Minimum	10.9	9.9	0.5	28.3	14.3	29.1	-4.0	-19.3

and their move to a new arena will likely launch them into the ranks of the financial elite. From this list it also should be clear that you do not need a big market to compete financially in the NBA. Charlotte, Orlando, Portland, and Utah all are small-market franchises. Charlotte, Orlando, and Utah all have relatively low player expenses—more on that later—and large arenas. Until 1995 Portland had a relatively small arena, but Portland has been a media innovator and has generated large media revenues given its relatively small market. The implication? There are different ways to profits in basketball, and you have to work with what you have. In some cases, that means the stadium; in others it means the media.

In terms of profits, a number of additional franchises have been operating just a notch below the second tier franchises, far from the penthouse but with comfortable profits nonetheless. This list includes Cleveland, Miami, Golden State, Houston, Sacramento, San Antonio, and Seattle. Once again, the list includes a mix of large-market (Golden State) and small-market (Sacramento and San Antonio) teams. None appear in financial difficulty—not even San Antonio, despite their pleas for a new arena.

Finally, Atlanta and Indiana are at the bottom of the league, leading only in financial losses. Indiana has no good excuse. The state is widely known as a basketball hotbed; the arena is large enough to generate substantial income; and by city size Indianapolis is roughly in the middle of the pack. The numbers suggest that Indiana is exhibit A in terms of financial mismanagement in the NBA. Atlanta is a very different case. Like Indiana it has been consistently losing money, despite a reasonably-sized arena. However, Atlanta's loss appears largely due to the magic of accounting. The Hawks' broadcasts over Turner's superstation WTBS appear to be worth much more than currently being paid. Given that WTBS broadcasts 30 games to a nationwide audience, Atlanta should have one of the highest media revenues. If Atlanta was near the top in media revenues they also would show a profit.

Philadelphia and Washington are two more franchises with financial question marks. They are large-market franchises that appear to have lackluster profits at best. Neither has seen recent on-the-court or financial success. While their losses are not as large as Indiana's, their financial performance is less than stellar. New Jersey appears to be another financial underachiever. Metropolitan New York is large enough to support two NBA franchises—it may be large enough to support four or five NBA franchises—but the New Jersey Nets, while generally avoiding losses, hardly qualify as a financial success story.

Dallas and the Los Angeles Clippers do not make the list of financial underachievers. Both have had abysmal on-the-court records, striving to avoid setting new standards for basketball futility. However, both also generally have made profits. While wins do not add a lot in terms of profits, the Mavericks and Clippers have been so far below .500 that even modest on-the-court success could have a significant impact on their finances.

The general moral of Table 3.3: There is more than one way to make a buck in the NBA and there is more than one way to lose one. Some teams with favorable market or arena situations and aggressive and innovative management have done extremely well. Many others, perhaps without quite the same media or stadium advantages also have fared relatively well. At the bottom of the list are a few franchises with either minimal locational, stadium, or hometown advantages or with minimal financial and marketing skills. It is difficult to discriminate between two alternative hypotheses: that a franchise has a bad location or a bad lease versus the alternative that it has bad management. For Indiana, Philadelphia, Washington, and New Jersey, however, given the size of their markets, it appears to be the latter—either that or they have substantially more profits than suggested here.

The numbers in Table 3.3 suggest that the NBA generally is doing very well. While it may not be a money-making machine, neither the owners nor the players appear to be suffering. The owners have averaged about $6 million each in yearly profits. Over the last five years, NBA franchises made a total of over $800 million.

A word of caution is in order when comparing these numbers to any "official" NBA numbers. The owners in the NBA, like their MLB counterparts, have been complaining about difficult financial times. The owners argue that they are suffering despite the NBA's salary cap. In part these complaints likely stem from accounting sleight-of-hand. The NBA's accountants use the same set of tricks as MLB's. Include amortization as a cost—which the records indicate the Boston Celtics do; where possible, understate the revenues from ancillary enterprises including media revenues—possibly done by Atlanta, Boston, and New York; and pay a substantial salary to an owner who performs no substantive duties. These ploys should be ignored and "official" league profits should be heavily discounted.

Another similarity between the NBA and MLB is less clear from the numbers. Some owners are in the league for the money and some for the ego, prestige, or victory. Alternatively, you can argue that some owners view their NBA franchise as a business and others view it as a hobby. If it is a hobby, however, obtaining the talent to win becomes of paramount importance—which can be a matter of some difficulty given the NBA's draft and the relative lack of mobility of NBA players.

While the NBA and MLB have many financial similarities, one important difference is that the NBA has a smaller range of profits, running from a small loss to a large profit. A number of factors are instrumental in narrowing the profit gap between clubs. Two features, neglected elsewhere, deserve mention at this point. First, the NBA has a right-of-first-refusal clause. That is, if another owner makes a salary offer to one of your players, you can match the offer and retain the player. Given that franchises frequently match salary offers, the advantage to an owner of bidding aggressively for talent is substantially reduced. Owners do not have strong incentives to woo someone else's talent because the probability of successfully signing a player is low.[5] And second, basketball appears to have greater domination of the game by limited number of players: a Jordan, O'Neal, or Olajuwon. The big-name players generally do not move. Other owners do not seriously clamor for their services. In addition, because their contribution represents a large component of a team's success, franchises appear very reluctant to let them leave. Can you imagine what would

---

[5] It is open to debate whether owners have conspired to match virtually all salary offers as a way of discouraging recalcitrant owners from aggressively bidding. That is, have owners colluded to eliminate any gain from attempting to bid for player? Suggesting the answer is yes: in some cases, a salary was matched and the player then traded away.

have happened to Chicago's attendance had the Bulls let Jordan sign with another basketball team rather than try baseball?

BEHIND THE NUMBERS—THE ROLE OF THE SALARY CAP AND A POTENTIAL PROBLEM

Table 3.4 presents the relative importance of each revenue source for the league as a whole as well as player salaries as a percent of revenue. Gate revenues on average are the largest source of league income, followed closely by media revenues. There is, however, substantial variation indicating once again that there is no simple rule for financial success in the NBA.

The sharp-eyed reader may be troubled by player salaries averaging only 46 percent of revenues. Why is this noteworthy? The players union and the league agreed that the players should receive 53 percent of 1994 league revenues under the so-called salary cap proposal. Why do these numbers indicate 46 percent rather than 53 percent? The answer is that the 53 percent refers to "Defined Gross Revenues" (DGR) which excludes some categories of revenues that are included here. In fact, the salary cap is an accounting game played by both the owners and the players. The owners excluded some revenues like luxury box rentals from the definition of DGR. That tends to lower the ratio. The owners give the players 53 percent of some revenues. Since the salary cap limits an individual team's ability to sign players, however, each owner has an incentive to try and work around it. How do they do it? Simply offer long-term contracts! Maybe an owner cannot sign a

Table 3.4

FINANCIAL RATIOS

Revenue Sources as a Percentage of Total Revenues
Player Salaries as a Percent of Total Revenues

	Gate	Media	Stadium	Other	Players
East Average	43.4	35.8	8.8	11.9	46.7
West Average	43.2	34.1	10.2	12.5	45.9
Average	43.3	35.0	9.4	12.2	46.3
Maximum	52.7	48.2	21.7	25.2	61.1
Minimum	32.3	23.0	1.2	6.0	27.9

Glenn Robinson or Chris Webber or Anfernee Hardaway to a mutually acceptable contract because he only has pocket change left under the cap. He can increase the amount of money offered and spread it into the future so he can continue to fit under the cap. It is another bit of accounting legerdemain.

This financial game-playing with the salary cap makes it more difficult to ascertain a team's profits. If Milwaukee paid Glenn Robinson, the top 1994 draft pick, $6.7 million per year, with no further changes their $1 million profit would turn into a $5.7 million loss. Can they make money from signing Robinson? The jury is still out on whether they can average $5.7 million more in revenues. To give a rough answer, let us assume that their media revenues will not change appreciably. Media revenues are determined primarily by the market size and not by won-loss record. Let us also assume that the Bucks now will average 6 home playoff games per year. In other words, Robinson will move them from a lottery team to a conference semi-finalist. The home playoff games will generate approximately $1.8 million a year in additional revenue leaving $3.9 million to make up in regular season attendance. If the Bucks net $20 per ticket over 41 home games they must average 4,640 additional fans. There is but one small problem: they average only around 2,000 empty seats!

Now this is not necessarily to say that the contract was a dumb idea. A couple of things could alter the picture dramatically. First, to the extent that the contract is back-loaded or most of the money is at the end of the 10 years, then the Buck's real cost could be much less than $67 million and they would need to sell fewer additional seats. Another mitigating factor is the possibility that Robinson becomes one of the dominating players in the game. Then the Bucks could increase ticket prices because the team is more entertaining—just as the Chicago Bulls substantially increased ticket prices when Michael Jordan reached superstar status.

The numbers in Table 3.3 indicate that the NBA has been extraordinarily profitable. This need not imply that the NBA's financial picture is entirely rosy. The potential problem, however, stems from what many will consider an unusual source—a source many cite as "saving" the NBA from its financial difficulties in the early

Table 3.5

IMPACT OF LONG-TERM CONTRACTS

Hypothetical Example—Pirates

(all numbers in millions)

		1993-1994	1994-1995	1995-1996
Revenues				
	Gate	$15.0	$15.8	$17.3
	Other	19.0	19.0	19.0
Total		34.0	34.8	36.3
Costs				
	Salaries	16.0	16.0	20.5
	Other	16.0	16.0	16.0
Total		32.0	32.0	36.5
Profits		2.0	2.8	-0.2

1980s—the salary cap! The salary cap for the 1993-1994 season was approximately $15.9 million. In fact, only one team, Dallas, was not over the salary cap and many teams were substantially over the cap. To demonstrate the problem, consider the hypothetical Pirates once again. Suppose the Pirates are exactly at the salary cap and want to sign a high first-round draft choice. Suppose the Pirates also had total costs of $32 million with salaries of half that amount and a gate of $15 million and total revenues of $34 million. Finally, suppose that $1 million will be available under the cap to sign this player because of the salary freed up by the player released to make room for the Pirate's star-in-the-making. These numbers are in the first column in Table 3.5.

If the market wage for this player's skills is much higher than the $1 million you have available under the cap, what can you do? Easy, lengthen the terms of the contract! Let us assume that the Pirates initially have no long-term guaranteed contracts. This is a highly unrealistic situation, but it demonstrates what happens when you begin to rely on those contracts. Suppose the Pirates and their draft pick settle on a 10 year $50.5 million contract. The terms: $1 million this year—that is all they are allowed—and $5.5

million for the remaining 9 years. As these contracts go, it is all guaranteed. The Pirates will make the payments even if the player is a bust or develops a bad back. (In addition, there could be a provision to reopen the contract if salaries continue to escalate.) Consider the Pirates' balance sheet next year. Assuming a 5 percent increase in gate receipts because of signing this future star, profits increase by $0.8 million. (Column 2 in Table 3.5.) But what happens further down the road? Looking at year 2, suppose gate revenues rise another 10 percent, a substantial increase. Total revenues have increased to $36.3 but total costs have increased by $4.5 million up to $36.5 million. (Column 3 in Table 3.5.) Initially the Pirates were making a comfortable profit. After two years they are losing money. As long-term guaranteed contracts become a way of life in the NBA, a major problem is potentially developing. The contracts themselves are not the problem. But the long-term guaranteed contracts together with Byzantine accounting may mislead even owners about the financial health of their franchises. In the NBA the problem may not be apparent this quickly or this dramatically. Multi-year contracts have been around for a while, but the length of these contracts has been getting longer and longer—as you should expect in each succeeding round of player signings. A key item for the owners in the 1995 contract renegotiations was restricting the maximum length of contract and thus tightening the salary cap. Nevertheless, the potential is there for these contracts to come back and bite the owners (and players)— especially if the NBA cannot maintain its revenue growth.

In terms of the salary cap, NBA owners are playing two games with the financial books. First, they are playing games with the revenue numbers to make the cap as low as possible. Once they have done that, they are stretching out contracts to get around that same cap. Only an economist would argue that both actions make sense! The owners want to restrict salaries and thus effectively collude to reduce the salary cap. Then, each owner has an incentive to cheat on that agreement to collude, paying more to his players in an effort to obtain a competitive advantage on-the-court.

The bottom line is simple. There are economic pressures at work in basketball and in baseball. In baseball there are no institutions like a salary cap to stand in the way of the market pressures for higher salaries. In basketball, the salary cap stands in the way of higher salaries. In the mid-1980s the cap was a relatively effective constraint. Then accountants recognized that increasing the contract length could circumvent the cap. And that is what we have increasingly seen, the emergence of long-term guaranteed contracts, because they work in the player's self-interest and an individual owner's self-interest as well. The player receives a higher salary and an owner has a more competitive franchise—unless other owners are even more creative in circumventing the salary cap. The 1995 addition of a maximum contract length simply means that creative accountants will search out new ways of circumventing league salary restrictions.

THE 1995 LOCKOUT

For the first time, the NBA was visited by labor strife in 1995. The reasons were similar to those in baseball but with one interesting twist. The 1994-1995 season was played under a no-lockout/ no-strike agreement. At the end of the season, the owners and the union agreed to a settlement. That settlement called for a continuing salary cap, a maximum percentage of revenues that the players can be paid. The owners agreed to raise the percentage of revenues on which the salary cap was based while the union agreed to a cap with more "teeth" placing limits on rookie salaries and imposing a maximum contract length. But a funny thing happened on the way to a settlement: the players refused to ratify the agreement!

In this chapter and the chapter on MLB, I have argued that owners have very different objectives and differing owner objectives (or different financial circumstances) have made labor negotiations much more difficult. In the NBA, it appears that player differences made a contract settlement harder to reach. The superstars, journeymen, and rookies likely have very different perspectives on whether the final contract is a good deal. Rookies did not vote on the contract and they clearly lost from the old contract to the new. Some superstars saw the proposed contract as restricting their ability to bargain for mega-deals while some journeymen were concerned about their income security. After the players ini-

Table 3.6

PRESENT DISCOUNTED VALUES
(in millions of dollars)

Franchise	Average Income	"Normal" Income	Net Present Value
East			
Atlanta	-2.1	5.0	83.3
Boston	6.8	12.0	200.0
Charlotte	8.8	8.0	133.3
Chicago	14.3	15.0	250.0
Cleveland	3.6	6.0	100.0
Detroit	24.6	12.0	200.0
Indiana	-3.9	3.0	50.0
Miami	3.5	3.5	58.3
Milwaukee	1.3	3.0	50.0
New Jersey	0.5	8.0	133.3
New York	17.9	15.0	250.0
Orlando	5.4	5.0	83.3
Philadelphia	-0.3	6.0	100.0
Washington	-0.5	4.0	66.7
West			
Dallas	1.5	3.0	50.0
Denver	-0.9	3.0	50.0
Golden State	3.0	5.0	83.3
Houston	3.5	3.5	58.3
LA Clippers	1.3	5.0	83.3
LA Lakers	27.1	15.0	250.0
Minnesota	9.4	8.0	133.3
Phoenix	10.5	9.0	150.0
Portland	6.1	12.0	200.0
Sacramento	4.4	4.0	66.7
San Antonio	4.2	4.0	66.7
Seattle	2.8	3.0	50.0
Utah	8.4	8.0	133.3
East Average	5.5	6.0	100.0
West Average	6.2	6.3	105.8
Average	5.9	6.2	102.9
Maximum	27.1	15.0	250.0
Minimum	-3.9	3.0	50.0

tially rejected the contract, the union renegotiated some points that appear to improve the lot of non-star players, thus securing a majority of players supporting the modified contract.[6] Differing player perspectives are discussed in more detail in Chapter 9.

WHAT IS THE NET PRESENT VALUE OF AN NBA FRANCHISE?

From profits we turn to the Net Present Values (NPVs) of NBA franchises. As in baseball, NPVs are calculated using "normal" profits and a real interest rate of 6 percent. Table 3.6 presents the actual profits as well as normal future profits assuming the franchise is reasonably well-managed. Conservative assumptions are used to obtain normal profits. Franchises with the highest profits are assumed to make less in the long run. Nevertheless, teams like the Lakers are assumed to maintain their profit advantage. The Lakers would have been one of the most profitable franchises in the league even without Magic Johnson because they are a large-market franchise with good media arrangements and an exceptional stadium arrangement. Recent empty seats in the Forum indicate only that the Lakers are not as profitable now as they were three years ago.

The minimum for a reasonably well-run franchise appears to be about $3 million. Few clubs have averaged below that, even those in very small markets. The Mavericks and Clippers, franchises with the worst recent won-loss records, average about $1.5 million in profits and with even modest on-the-court success should generate profits of at least $3 million per year based on the calculations in Chapter 6.

Whose "normal" profits are greater than their average profits? Atlanta is assumed to make substantially higher profits based on its relationship with Turner Broadcasting. The TV superstation's revenues should make them highly profitable for Turner although he may not acknowledge that fact. Second, Boston, Chicago, Cleveland, and Portland have moved into new arenas that generate substantial additional revenues. The Celtics in particular have had an

---

[6] The role of player agents, while tangential to the story here, also is of interest. Agents were clearly hurt by the contract and they lobbied heavily against it even though it would appear that many of their clients would be better off with a contract than without.

abysmal leasing arrangement in the old Boston Garden and presumably will have a much better deal in the new Garden. Third, New Jersey's normal profits are assumed to equal average actual profits in Boston and Charlotte. A New York City team with reasonable management and marketing should regularly sell out its arena and should be able to negotiate local media revenues at least equal to those of the Los Angeles Clippers. These two moves alone would make the Nets extremely profitable. I have already suggested that Philadelphia and Washington are poorly managed franchises. As large-market teams with a solid core of serious basketball fans in each city, they should have much higher profits, although Washington's Landover location is not ideal. In the West, only Golden State is adjusted upward marginally. As a large-market franchise, it should have profits greater than Sacramento's.

NBA average profits have been $5.9 million while normal profits are conservatively assumed to equal $6.2 million. (Without the new stadiums, normal profits would have been about $5.4 million.) The implied market values range from $250 million to $50 million. In the penthouse are the Chicago Bulls, Los Angeles Lakers, and New York Knicks at $250 million followed by the Boston Celtics, Detroit Pistons, and Portland Trailblazers at $200 million. A number of franchises are in the $100-167 million range including Charlotte, New Jersey (albeit perhaps not under current management), Minnesota, Phoenix, and Utah. Bringing up the rear are Indiana, Milwaukee, Dallas, Denver, Seattle, and Houston. To be at the top you need a large-market franchise and favorable stadium and media arrangements. To be at the bottom you need a small market and poor stadium and media deals. Once again, however, as in baseball, the large-market/small-market distinction does not neatly separate the financial winners and losers in the NBA. For example, Charlotte and Utah are small-market and large-profit franchises while Washington and Dallas are large-market and small-profit franchises. In the latter cases there always are questions about whether the franchise is in a market where NBA basketball is not appreciated, or whether existing management leaves something to be desired. I believe that there is at least a kernel of truth in the latter argument. If Utah, San Antonio, and Sacramento can make

Table 3.7

SELECTED FRANCHISE PRICES

Date of Transaction	Franchise	Expansion Franchise?	Purchase Price (in millions)
1966	Chicago Bulls	yes	$1.25
1967	Seattle Sonics	yes	1.75
1967	San Diego Rockets	yes	1.75
1968	Milwaukee Bucks	yes	2.0
1968	Phoenix Suns	yes	2.0
1970	Chicago Bulls	no	3.3
1970	Buffalo Braves	yes	3.7
1970	Cleveland Cavaliers	yes	3.7
1970	Portland Trail Blazers	yes	3.7
1972	Chicago Bulls	no	5.1
1974	New Orleans Jazz	yes	6.2
1974	Detroit Pistons	no	8.1
1976	Buffalo Braves	no	6.1
1977	Atlanta Hawks	no	7.2
1980	Dallas Mavericks	yes	12.0
1980	Cleveland Cavaliers	no	5.4
1981	San Diego Clippers	no	13.5
1981	Philadelphia 76ers	no	16.0
1982	Denver Nuggets	no	10.0
1982	Houston Rockets	no	11.0
1983	Boston Celtics	no	15.0
1983	Seattle Supersonics	no	21.0
1984	New Orleans Jazz	no	16.0
1984	Milwaukee Bucks	no	19.0
1985	Chicago Bulls	no	16.4
1985	Denver Nuggets	no	17.5
1986	Boston Celtics	no	130.0
1987	Phoenix Suns	no	44.5
1988	Charlotte Hornets	yes	32.5
1988	Miami Heat	yes	32.5
1988	Portland Trail Blazers	no	70.0
1989	Minnesota Timberwolves	yes	32.5
1989	Orlando Magic	yes	32.5
1989	Denver Nuggets	no	54.0
1993	Houston Rockets	no	90.0
1994	Golden State	no	139.0
1994	Minnesota Timberwolves	no	152.0
1995	Toronto Raptors	yes	125.0
1995	Vancouver Grizzlies	yes	125.0

Table 3.8

FRANCHISE VALUES AND RETURNS FOR TEAMS THAT SOLD MULTIPLE TIMES
(When Both Prices Are Available)

Franchise	Year of Purchase	Purchase Price	Implied Capital Gain
Chicago Bulls	1966	1.25	
Chicago Bulls	1970	3.3	27.5%
Chicago Bulls	1972	5.1	24.3
Chicago Bulls	1985	16.4	18.2
Seattle Sonics	1967	1.75	
Seattle Supersonics	1983	21.0	16.8
Milwaukee Bucks	1968	2.0	
Milwaukee Bucks	1985	19.0	14.2
Cleveland Cavaliers	1970	3.7	
Cleveland Cavaliers	1980	5.4	3.9
Buffalo Braves	1970	3.7	
Buffalo Braves	1976	6.1	8.7
San Diego Clippers[a]	1981	13.5	17.2
Phoenix Suns	1968	2.0	
Phoenix Suns	1987	44.5	17.7
Portland Trail Blazers	1970	3.7	
Portland Trail Blazers	1988	70.0	17.7
Denver Nuggets	1982	10.0	
Denver Nuggets	1985	17.5	20.5
Denver Nuggets	1989	54.0	32.5
San Diego Rockets	1967	1.75	
Houston Rockets[a]	1982	11.0	13.0
Houston Rockets	1993	90.0	21.1
Boston Celtics	1983	15.0	
Boston Celtics	1986	130.0	105.4 [b]
Boston Celtics	1995	153.6	1.9 [c]
Minnesota Timberwolves	1989	32.5	
Minnesota Timberwolves[a]	1994	152.0	36.1

Capital Gains	1989-94	1985-94	1975-94
NBA Average	27.5%	25.6%	20.6%
Dow-Jones Industrial Avg.	8.1	12.5	9.3
Standard & Poors 500	6.8	11.0	9.7
Wilshire 5000	7.1	10.7	NA

[a] The Buffalo Braves were moved to San Diego and renamed the Clippers and have been subsequently moved to Los Angeles. The Rockets moved from San Diego to Houston. The Minnesota Timberwolves sale was rejected by the league.

[b] The Celtics' return over the 1983-94 period is 23.3 percent.

[c] Based on December 7, 1995 Boston Celtic stock price.

a profit, it seems hard to believe that with competent management Philadelphia or Washington cannot do the same.

NPVs versus Actual Sale Prices—
What Is an NBA Franchise Worth?

How do the calculated NPVs compare with franchise sale prices? Table 3.7 lists the prices of franchises reported sold either in the *Wall Street Journal* or the *New York Times*. NBA franchise prices have increased tremendously, with increases very similar to those in MLB. Through the 1960s and 1970s franchise prices were less than $10 million. During the 1980s they increased from around $10 million to around $50 million. Sales during the 1990s generally have exceeded $100 million, and the two expansion 1995 teams paid $125 million as well as having to meet stringent financial conditions including selling a minimum of 12,500 season tickets.

We can calculate the capital gains accruing to NBA teams by examining the prices of franchises that sold multiple times. Table 3.8 lists the teams, the reported sale price and the resulting yearly average percent capital gain. No franchise has been reported sold for a loss. The yearly capital gain is in excess of 15 percent during this period. The bottom panel of Table 3.8 also presents the average rate of franchise appreciation or capital gain. The results indicate substantial gains over the last 20 years. Owning an NBA franchise always yielded a gain in excess of the return available from other assets, for example, the Dow Jones stock index. For the last 5 years, the return was 3 to 4 times that of any general stock index! Even during the late 1970s and early 1980s—pre-salary cap— NBA franchises had substantial and increasing returns. With the advent of the salary cap in 1984, these returns increased dramatically, albeit with a delay as owners and potential owners realized significant savings from restrictions on players' salaries. Owners' average capital gain over the last 20 years has exceeded 20 percent per year and over the last 5 years has exceeded 27 percent per year.

To obtain a complete picture of the financial health of the league, however, we must add operating profits to these capital gains. That is, how much did an owner receive in yearly profits plus how much did the value of the franchise appreciate? Assuming 1994 was a representative year—in fact, it appears slightly worse than the recent average—the typical NBA franchise had profits of $5.9 million and an NPV of $108 million for an operating return of 5.5 percent. Adding the operating return to the capital gain yields a yearly average profit of 27 percent for the last 20 years and 33 percent for the last five years. Call the average total return in the NBA roughly 30 percent. Call the NBA extremely profitable.

Finally, let us compare the prices recently paid for franchises with the calculated NPVs. Table 3.9 lists three franchises sold since 1992. In all cases the purchase price substantially exceeded the NPV. As in baseball, the results suggest that owners and potential owners value the perks of ownership. That should be no surprise. Ted Turner (Atlanta Hawks), Jerry Reinsdorf (Chicago Bulls), Gordon Gund (Cleveland Cavaliers), and Paul Allen (Portland Trailblazers) value the consumption or hobby of owning an NBA team. The difference between the purchase price and the calculated NPV is how much owners overpaid for the privilege of being a member of the NBA owners club. The average overpayment is $39 million. The hobby—or ego value—of owning an NBA franchise costs about $39 million.

This $39 million figure carries an asterisk, however. Some NBA franchise owners have businesses that are helped by the franchise. For example, Turner (Atlanta Hawks) and Paramount Communications (New York Knicks) may appear to value the club more than it is worth, but both in sum may be better off if their

Table 3.9

NPVs versus PRICES PAID
What Price Ego? or
How Much Have Owners "Overpaid" for an NBA Franchise?
(in millions)

Franchise	Purchase Price	NPV	Purchase Price Minus NPV	1994 Franchise Profits
Houston	$98	$58	$40	$7.1
Minnesota	152	133	19	7.7
Golden State	139	83	56	3.4
Average	130	91	39	6.1

media outlets are strengthened, perhaps by having access to guaranteed basketball programming. In addition, it is possible that the NPVs are based on too low estimates of profits and the true profits and NPVs are even higher than estimated. However, in basketball as in baseball, both owners and potential owners are willing to pay a high price for the privilege of being associated with an NBA franchise or NBA profits are even greater than previously indicated.

CONCLUSION

What is the NBA's financial bottom line? In many respects, it is very similar to MLB's. On average, franchises make substantial profits; most franchises are profitable and the best are extremely profitable. A few do lose money but much less than their brethren in baseball. In addition, some clubs appear well-run and others appear poorly-run. Finally, some teams appear to have a clear focus on profits while others appear to have a greater interest in winning. This is not to state that all do not value profits, only that not all put the same weight on profits relative to victory. Owners who value victory over profits, however, appear to face greater hurdles in the NBA than in MLB. The hurdle is not the salary cap but the difficulty of obtaining a prime-time player and the limited ability to woo a player from another franchise given the right-of-first-refusal. The only current impact of the salary cap appears to be to disguise the current financial status of the league—perhaps even from the owners themselves.

Chapter 4

Football —
Socialism in America

"Football is the biggest dramatization of American business ever invented." —**Marshall McLuhan, writer**

"I love the game as do the other owners. There isn't an owner in the NFL that is in it for a buck. They're in it because they love the sport."—**Art Modell, owner, Cleveland Browns, on owning a team in the 1980's**

"I had no choice."—**Art Modell, owner, Cleveland Browns, on moving the team to Baltimore**

"It's a very, very serious problem. It's something we have to address with the utmost urgency."—**Art Modell, owner, Cleveland Browns, on franchise movement, just after announcing the Browns move**

"At that rate, he's going to last 150 years."—**H.L. Hunt, businessman, when told his son Lamar would lose $1 million in the first year of the AFL**

The Ugly Details—What Underlies the Profit Numbers

How does NFL finance differ from Major League Baseball (MLB) or NBA finance? In terms of the general principles, there are no differences. All leagues rely on media revenues, ticket sales, other stadium-related revenues including luxury boxes, as well as other income including licensing fees and advertising revenues.

Costs are primarily player-related but also include insurance, game-day expenses, maintenance, travel costs, and general administrative costs. League differences lie in the relative importance of the revenue categories and how those revenues are shared. In both respects, the NFL differs dramatically from other team sports.

The NFL was no more forthcoming with data than any other league. Thus, once again it was necessary to turn to secondary sources. Average ticket prices are available from *Team Marketing Report* while *Sports Business Daily* provided the attendance figures. Combined they yield gate revenues. A franchise's gate revenues must be adjusted, however, since the NFL home team retains only 60 percent of the gate while the visitor gets 40 percent. Media revenues include national television contracts worth $39.3 million per franchise plus local media revenues. The latest local media figures available were for the 1993-1994 season although no appreciable changes have been reported since then. Using the 1993-1994 values is a conservative estimate of 1994-1995 arrangements. In contrast to baseball and basketball, NFL local media revenues are small relative to the national television contracts. For example, the Chicago Bears and the San Francisco 49ers have the largest local media revenues and they receive only about $4 million. Ninety five percent of an NFL franchise's media revenues come from national sources and only 5 percent from local sources.

Other stadium revenues were difficult to ascertain by club. Total luxury box income has been estimated by *Skybox* to be approximately $135 million. The exact distribution of those revenues is unavailable, but it is straightforward to determine how many luxury boxes each club has available and then allocate the money in part based on the number of luxury boxes available. Other stadium revenue comes from sources like concessions and parking. In many cases, a franchise's facilities are privately owned and no information is directly available on this item. For public facilities with available data, responses to Freedom of Information Act requests indicate that franchises net a minimum of $1.5 million in concessions and parking. This value is assumed to be the minimum for private facilities, although most probably are substantially higher. The last two major revenue sources are licensing income and playoff income. In 1994 retailers sold over $3 billion in NFL licensed merchandise yielding each NFL franchise approximately $2.4 million per team in licensing income. Net playoff income is roughly $0.4 million per game, although the exact figure depends on where the game is played.

The major cost item is payroll. It used to be a straightforward exercise to determine a team's payroll. While team numbers are not available to the public, they are available to registered agents. However under the salary cap, the available numbers are much less meaningful, for reasons discussed in Chapter 3 on the NBA's finances. Given the incentives facing a franchise under a salary cap, teams have an incentive to be much more creative in structuring contracts. Thus, the reported numbers have less meaning in 1994 than they had in 1992, pre-cap. Nevertheless, they are the best figures available and are used here and discussed in more detail below. The figures used here are not those employed for salary cap purposes; I will come back to those later. In terms of this year's budget and profit, it matters how much a team paid in bonuses this year. The salary cap spreads those bonuses over the life of the contract. To the extent that bonuses are negotiated and paid this year, those costs are appropriately included in this year's payroll even if under "caponomics" they get counted under some future year's salary cap. For example, Deion Sanders' $35-million, 7-year contract with the Cowboys includes a $13 million signing bonus. While Sanders is paid $13-million in 1995, allegedly he counts only about $2 million against the Cowboys' salary cap.

Another major cost is player pension expense. The calculation underlying the salary cap called for a maximum 1994 payroll of $34.6 million with another $4.4 million allocated for pensions. In fact, league numbers suggest many clubs have subverted the salary cap. Rather than using $4.4 million for pensions, which implies pension costs of 12.3 percent of the salary cap, I use 15 percent of the reported salary number as a better indication of the actual non-salary compensation costs.

Other NFL franchise costs include training camp expenses. Unlike in MLB, NFL training camps cost money rather than make money. The Green Bay Packers report training camp costs of about $1.2 million.[1] I use that as the average for all clubs. Game-day costs include stadium rent as well as costs of hiring ushers, parking attendants, etc. The NFL sets a 60-40 split of the gate between the home and visiting teams to allow the home team to cover the game-day expenses. On that basis, again using Green Bay as a representative case, 20 percent of the home gate receipts would be approximately $400,000 per game. This value is used as a rough guide for game-day expenses. Other costs include travel and hotels. While no NFL numbers are available, information on college football expenses suggest that travel costs likely run about $100,000 per away game and hotel and ground transportation cost a similar amount. Other substantial expenditures include scouting and draft expenses (approximately $1 million), coaches' salaries (varying widely), and insurance (as much as $2 million). Maintenance and depreciation of facilities is another important item and varies substantially depending on what facilities a franchise owns and its stadium arrangements. General administrative costs are assumed to be no more than $2 million. Given an average franchise has approximately $67 million in revenues including over $40 million in TV and licensing revenues simply handed to it, administrative costs over $2 million appear unwarranted. Wellington Mara, owner of the New York Giants, has paid himself as much as $7.5 million in salary and has called that a "cost." Given the Giants' revenues of approximately $30 million beyond national TV and licensing, such a salary is a blatant attempt to artificially depress profits. There is nothing illegal about this; it simply gives a misleading picture of a franchise's profits.

1994 revenues, costs and profits by team are listed in Table 4.1. The general conclusion is that most franchises have made a profit, some a very large profit, and only a few experienced a loss. The Dallas Cowboys lead the NFC with a $24 million profit while the Miami Dolphins lead the AFC with a profit of $13 million. The Washington Redskins had the largest loss at $4.8 million followed by the Seattle Seahawks and Indianapolis Colts at $3.5 million.

---

[1] The Green Bay Packers serve as a convenient reference since they are quasi-publicly owned. While they are not required to release financial information, the *Green Bay Press-Gazette*, a stockholder, regularly publishes summary information.

Table 4.1

REVENUES, COSTS, AND PROFITS
(all numbers in millions)

		1994 Revenues			1994 Costs		1994 Net Profits	1990-94 Total Profits
	Gate	Media	Stadium	Total	Players	Total		
AFC								
Buffalo	19.4	42.0	5.0	68.8	34.6	61.6	7.2	31.0
Cincinnati	14.6	41.6	2.5	61.1	31.9	54.2	7.0	35.2
Cleveland	16.3	42.4	9.0	71.1	34.9	63.4	7.6	36.0
Denver	18.2	42.9	3.0	66.5	31.2	55.7	10.9	41.0
Houston	14.7	41.9	6.5	65.5	38.3	64.3	1.2	27.2
Indianapolis	13.2	41.2	2.5	59.3	39.0	62.8	-3.5	6.4
Kansas City	17.5	41.9	7.5	69.8	37.8	62.5	7.3	44.0
LA/Oakland	14.5	43.0	2.5	62.4	37.7	64.9	-2.4	11.8
Miami	17.1	42.5	16.0	79.0	31.3	66.0	13.0	47.4
New England	16.4	42.0	4.5	65.8	39.8	65.4	0.5	24.2
NY Jets	15.8	42.0	4.0	64.2	35.7	63.9	0.3	15.9
Pittsburgh	15.5	41.9	3.5	64.8	30.9	55.1	9.6	56.6
San Diego	16.5	41.9	5.0	67.3	38.3	64.0	3.3	19.8
Seattle	14.9	42.9	3.0	63.2	40.6	66.7	-3.5	21.2
NFC								
Arizona	15.4	42.0	5.0	64.8	42.5	67.5	-2.7	23.6
Atlant	14.2	41.8	7.0	65.4	36.3	62.0	3.4	11.8
Chicago	16.7	44.9	6.5	71.5	34.2	62.3	9.2	53.7
Dallas	16.7	44.2	30.0	94.8	31.3	70.8	24.0	81.9
Detroit	16.9	41.9	3.0	64.7	38.4	63.3	1.5	14.3
Green Bay	13.9	41.2	4.2	62.7	35.2	63.9	-1.2	6.6
LA/St. Louis	12.8	42.8	5.0	63.0	33.6	57.8	5.2	42.4
Minnesota	15.4	41.9	5.5	65.7	33.9	59.3	6.4	35.8
New Orleans	14.7	41.4	4.0	62.5	38.2	64.4	-1.9	22.2
NY Giants	19.7	43.4	5.0	70.5	34.3	62.8	7.6	27.7
Philadelphia	19.0	42.4	10.0	73.8	34.6	63.0	10.8	52.8
San Francisco	19.5	44.4	9.0	76.8	35.5	68.3	8.5	-1.6
Tampa Bay	13.6	41.5	6.0	63.5	32.1	56.9	6.5	40.4
Washington	16.1	43.9	3.0	65.4	42.6	70.2	-4.8	10.3
AFC Average	16.0	42.2	5.3	66.3	35.9	62.2	4.2	29.8
NFC Average	16.0	42.7	7.4	68.9	35.9	63.8	5.2	30.1
Average	16.0	42.4	6.3	67.6	35.9	63.0	4.7	30.0
Maximum	19.7	44.9	30.0	94.8	42.6	70.8	24.0	81.9
Minimum	12.8	41.2	2.5	59.3	30.9	54.2	-9.5	-1.6

The typical NFL franchise made a profit of $4.7 million in 1994, slightly higher in the NFC and slightly lower in the AFC. Before going into more detail on individual franchise profits, there are three general points to note on revenues and costs.

(1) **Gate Revenues.** In terms of team revenues, differences in gate revenues are much smaller in the NFL than in any other league, running from highs of $19.7 million for the Giants and $19.4 million for the Bills down to the Rams at $12.8 million (in LA) and the Colts at $13.2 million. In contrast, MLB had a range of gate receipts from $47 million to $13 million while the NBA's range was from $32 million to $11 million. The 60-40 split of gate revenues substantially reduces the gate revenue advantage of teams that sell out larger stadiums, like the Bills, or those that can price their tickets at a premium, like the Giants. The teams at the bottom of the gate receipt rankings should come as no surprise: Indianapolis, Tampa Bay, and the Los Angeles Rams (pre-move). While most NFL teams sell out all games, these three virtually never sell out. These clubs inability to sell out has an adverse impact not only upon their revenues but also upon visiting teams' revenues.

(2) **Media Revenues and Shared Revenues.** Media revenues in the NFL are far higher than in any other league. Only baseball's Yankees have comparable media revenues. Almost 95 percent of the NFL's media revenues come from national contracts while the figures for MLB and the NBA are 40 percent and 65 percent respectively. Each NFL team receives almost $40 million from national media while NBA franchises are second and receive roughly $10 million each. The magnitude and the distribution of media revenues goes a long way towards leveling the playing field between franchises like the Dallas Cowboys, New York Giants, and San Francisco 49ers, who on their own might be able to negotiate lucrative television deals, and small-market franchises like the New Orleans Saints, Tampa Bay Buccaneers, and Green Bay Packers that have limited media appeal.

Each franchise basically started the 1994 season with $41.7 million in revenue, $39.3 million from national television contracts and another $2.4 million as its share of NFL licensing revenues. To that add a club's 40 percent share of gate receipts for its away games and the importance of NFL revenue sharing should be obvious.

(3) **Players Salaries and the Salary Cap.** The 1994 NFL salary cap actually set both a maximum and minimum payroll allowed. The maximum a franchise could spend on player payroll in 1994 was $34.6 million, the cap, while the minimum was $27 million. While no club was close to the minimum, 18 of 28 teams exceeded the putative maximum.[2] One potentially surprising result is that the San Francisco 49ers did not exceed the salary cap despite late signings of players like Deion Sanders while the New Orleans Saints, the team that complained most vociferously about the 49ers violating the salary cap by signing Sanders, themselves exceeded the cap. (Even Dallas's 1995 signing of Sanders did not exceed the putative cap.) The important point is that the salary cap, despite being labeled a "hard cap" was not hard to circumvent.

Some also may find it surprising that a number of the most successful teams were also among the lowest in player costs. The Pittsburgh Steelers, Miami Dolphins, and Dallas Cowboys were 3 of the 4 lowest payroll teams in 1994 (Denver was the fourth). The high payroll teams were the Washington Redskins', Arizona Cardinals, Seattle Seahawks, New England Patriots, and Indianapolis Colts. Only the Patriots made the playoffs although the Cardinals were close. Both the Patriots' and Cardinals' payrolls soared in 1994 as both franchises increased their financial commitment to winning. In contrast, the Redskins high payroll appears to be a relic of their prior on-the-field success. The Seahawks and Colts have been less than successful on-the-field. Given high payrolls and at best mediocre results, one might question whether their money has been wisely spent. In sum, the individual team payrolls clearly indicate that a team can play games with respect to a salary cap in terms of shifting money from one year to another, restructuring contracts, and awarding bonuses. To some extent all teams play those games. However, some clearly play better than

---

[2] The most important explanation for how teams effectively exceeded the salary cap is that bonuses are pro-rated over the life of the contract. That is, a $1 million bonus on a 5 year contract would be included under the salary cap at a cost of $0.2 million for each of the next 5 years even though the entire bonus was paid today. The NFL's goal in constructing its salary cap was to make it a "hard cap" or, unlike the NBA's cap, one difficult to evade. In practice, however, if you need more than 25 words to state the cap, creative accountants are going to find loopholes.

others. Given the salary cap, it now seems appropriate to give Player-of-the-Year awards for offense, defense, and finance.

In terms of overall franchise profits, the Dallas Cowboys are in a league of their own. Even though most league revenues are split, their stadium arrangement has no peer in the NFL and the Cowboys retain most of the additional revenues.[3] The implications of Jones' recent deals are detailed later in this chapter. Following the Cowboys are the Dolphins, with the second-best stadium arrangement and the second highest profits—before the recent spate of moves and proposed moves. After that, many franchises fall in the $7-$10 million profit range including Denver, Philadelphia, Pittsburgh, Chicago, San Francisco, Cleveland, Kansas City, Cincinnati, Buffalo, and the New York Giants. Some have been high-cost high-return teams like San Francisco while others, like Cincinnati, have generated profits by keeping expenditures well below the league average and counting on league revenue sharing funds for their profit. In the NFL there is more than one strategy to achieve financial success.

While many of the 28 NFL franchises should be labeled financially successful, some franchises lost money in 1994 including the Indianapolis Colts, Los Angeles (now Oakland) Raiders, Seattle Seahawks, Green Bay Packers, New Orleans Saints, Arizona Cardinals, and Washington Redskins. Of these 7 teams, only two consistently filled their stadium: Green Bay and Washington. The Colts and the Raiders lost money solely because they were in the minority of franchises that could not consistently sell out. Both would have had a profit if they sold out. These two franchises share a number of features. Both have moved in the past because they did not like the financial support in their prior city; they relocated and initially sold out (or were close to it) but subsequently have seen ticket sales fall dramatically. Given the regularity of NFL sellouts, one might question the marketing ability of an owner who has been unable to fill a stadium in either of two cities (Irsay, owner of the Colts) or the wisdom of an owner who would leave a

---

[3] The financial structure of the Cowboys, and of other clubs, includes a large debt burden with substantial interest payments. Thus Jerry Jones, the owner, may not have netted $24 million. Given our focus here, however, the financial structure of the franchise is irrelevant.

stadium that he could fill for one often less than half filled (Davis, owner of the Raiders). Arizona's situation is similar to Indianapolis's through 1993. The Cardinals had dwindling support in St. Louis, moved to Phoenix and were initially greeted enthusiastically. However, over the years attendance fell. While revenues dropped, the Cardinals did not lose money because costs were kept low as well, close to the bottom of the NFL which is where the Cardinals also were found in the standings. In 1994 Arizona hired a new coach, Buddy Ryan, and expenditures increased dramatically. The Cardinals appear to be a team in transition from a low-cost low-performance team. Their loss appears due to that transition. Whether the "new" Cardinals will see profits or wins is open to debate. One certainty about the Cardinals is that Bill Bidwell, the owner, is more peripatetic than most, moving the team from Chicago to St. Louis to Phoenix, and again threatening to leave for greener pastures.

Washington's loss is largely attributable to their high costs. Until recently Washington has been one of the most successful franchises on-the-field and those successes led to some sizeable payroll costs continuing into 1994. Washington also appears limited by their stadium arrangement: no luxury boxes and the smallest stadium in the league.

Seattle and New Orleans have similar financial stories. Both have had troubles at times filling an indoor arena; their ticket prices are among the lowest in the league; they have had only limited on-the-field success at least measured by playoff performance; but they have player costs near the top of the league. Both also have, at best, mediocre stadium arrangements. In sum, both are in less than ideal financial situations.

The final franchise with a loss is Green Bay, which may be the most interesting case of all. Most NFL franchises are owned by individuals, generally very strong-willed individuals. NFL franchise ownership appears to attract the Jerry Jones's, Al Davis's and Wellington Mara's. (Should it be any surprise that George Steinbrenner has been attempting to buy a franchise?) The Green Bay Packers organization, however, is publicly owned by citizens of Green Bay. Based on the Packers financial decisions, they appear to have two goals quite consciously in mind. First, they want to field a competitive team. Green Bay, despite its small size is one of the higher-spending franchises in the NFL. And second, they want to keep ticket prices relatively low and affordable. Their ticket prices are second lowest in the NFL. (Only the New York Jets have a lower average ticket price.) While the Packers are a public corporation, their stockholders receive no dividends. All profits are reinvested in the franchise. Thus, from a practical perspective, the Packers are in a public trust, and increasing ticket prices does not benefit stockholders. The Packers' overall objectives are to be competitive on-the-field, break even financially and charge ticket holders a relatively low price. We should expect the club to approximately break even, in some years recording a slight profit and in others a slight loss. That is their recent history. 1994 happens to show a loss.

The Packers' objectives stand in sharp contract to the Cincinnati Bengals, Los Angeles Rams, or, until 1994, the Arizona Cardinals. In each case, costs were sharply restricted; the teams were basically uncompetitive; but the franchises made a profit based upon revenue sharing income. The Cardinals fired their coach (Joe Bugel) after the 1993 season and the Bengals threatened to fire their coach (Dave Shula) after the 1994 season. The financial numbers strongly suggest that both were made scapegoats by the team owners. Neither had been given a personnel budget that allowed them to field a competitive team.

The Rams' ownership also appears to be in it for the money, a hypothesis strongly supported by their move to St. Louis. The NFL's vote on that move also suggests that all owners are interested in their own profits. While some owners may object, the NFL's vote appears to be entirely self-serving. The teams that initially voted for the move (Rams, Bengals, and Buccaneers) were actively exploring the possibility of moving. All stood to gain from relaxing restrictions against franchise movement. The 21 teams that initially voted against had a substantial self-interest in the Rams not moving. The Rams' move to St. Louis will increase the Rams' revenues and thus league revenues. The increase in league revenues in turn would cause the salary cap to rise thus increasing other franchises' costs. Conservatively, the Rams' revenues will increase by $20 million. The NFL salary cap calls for the players to receive 62 percent of league revenues. Thus, the Rams' move to St. Louis will increase the players' revenue by $12.4 million or $0.4 million per team. The Rams' profits would increase by $19.6 million while other clubs' profits would decrease by $0.4 million. Not surprisingly, other clubs insisted and eventually received a share of the Rams' windfall from moving to St. Louis. A second vote of the league's owners allowed the Rams to move to St. Louis. The key difference with the second vote? The Rams agreed to pay the rest of the franchises $46 million.

THE PROFIT PICTURE—1990-1994

The last column of Table 4.1 presents total profits for the last five years. 1993 NFL profits are calculated as described above while I employ *Financial World's* numbers for 1990 to 1992. The results indicate that with the exception of the San Francisco 49ers, all franchises have been profitable over the last five years. And the 49ers' loss deserves an asterisk. That loss is attributable to a large one-time expenditure at the end of 1993, after the 1993 regular season but before the salary cap was in place. Recognizing that the salary cap was to be implemented in 1994 but that any 1993 payments would not count under the cap, Carmen Policy, President of the 49ers, restructured the contracts of a number of players to increase their 1993 salaries and decrease their 1994 salaries. This process substantially assisted the 49ers in their pursuit of free agents and a January 1995 Super Bowl victory. Thus, the 49ers 1993 loss is better viewed as the down payment on the profits from another Super Bowl. Carmen Policy would have my vote for the NFL's financial Player-of-the-Year.

The only franchises with less than $10 million profit since 1990 are the Green Bay Packers and the Indianapolis Colts. There are no surprises there. As noted above, the Packers are not in it for the profits; they are in it for the game. There is a commitment to take the revenue generated by the team and put it back into the franchise. We should expect the Packers to roughly break even, and we should expect them to win more than their share of games, despite being the smallest-market major league franchise in the U.S.

The Indianapolis Colts, however, are a very different story. They would be my pick for the worst run franchise—at least from a financial standpoint—in the NFL. Whether the goal is to win or to make money does not really matter. The Colts have not been successful at either. Their on-the-field performance has been much worse than average, and their financial performance has been worse than the Packers—and the Packers have not been trying to make a profit. Yet there is evidence that Robert Irsay, owner of the Colts, does at least try for profits. Certainly Irsay did not move the franchise from Baltimore to Indianapolis to improve the team's on-the-field performance. That move can only be explained by a desire to increase profits. When the Colts first moved to Indianapolis, the franchise had tremendous financial success, even when its on-the-field performance was less than stellar. The team initially sold out all its games and had a long waiting list for season tickets. Looking at the gradual decline in the Colts' profits over the last 5 years, one gets the picture of a franchise sliding into financial oblivion. From a finance perspective, it is hard not to argue that the Colts are the worst-run organization in the NFL.

While not currently at the bottom of the financial rankings, Arizona would be another candidate for worst-run organization in the NFL, for the same reasons as the Colts. The difference is that the Cardinals moved to Arizona from St. Louis a few years after the Colts moved from Baltimore to Indianapolis. In other words, the Colts have a head start to losses in a new city. The signs are all there for Bill Bidwell's Cardinals: team support initially high but declining, a history of mediocre or worse teams, profits initially high due to the novelty of a major league franchise but declining dramatically over time.

Other franchises at the bottom of the financial rankings allow much less clear-cut conclusions, the Redskins and Raiders in particular. Both are large-markets franchises with low profits, although the NFL's revenue sharing makes market size relatively unimportant. Both also have owners with a long reputation of wanting to win. Thus, the low profits may simply represent a willingness to spend what it takes to win a Super Bowl. In the Raiders case, however, it also appears that Al Davis, the owner, values profits. If Davis does not value profits—perhaps even more than winning—its hard to explain his move from Oakland to Los Angeles despite enthusiastic support in Oakland; it is hard to explain the continuing turmoil in the Los Angles area about where the Raiders will move next; and it may be even harder to explain his move back to Oakland. Given the turmoil surrounding the Raider's next location and the negative impact that has on attendance and profits, I have to conclude that Davis has not done himself any financial favors and may not be nearly as clever a financial manager as he believes he is. Davis has estimated the move back to Oakland will reduce the franchise's value by $20 million. As detailed below, however, the financial evidence does not support that contention.

For 1990-1994 profits, Dallas again tops the league followed by Pittsburgh, Chicago, and Philadelphia. All have average profits over $10 million a year. Buffalo, Cincinnati, Cleveland, Denver, Kansas City, Miami, Minnesota, Tampa Bay, and the Rams have been almost as successful, averaging profits over $6 million a year. That Cincinnati and Tampa Bay are on this list indicates that on-the-field success is not a requirement for financial success in the NFL.

On average, an NFL franchise had profits of $30.5 million over the last 5 years or about $6 million a year per team. Total NFL profits from 1990 to 1994 were almost $850 million. The league as a whole currently is in very strong financial shape. As in all other leagues, however, the distribution of profits is highly unequal. The Cowboys have almost 1/9 of the league's profits while the 49ers, Colts, and Packers get almost nothing. It is particularly instructive to consider how average profits have changed since 1990, given the dramatic changes in the NFL's financial structure between 1992 and 1994. The introduction of a salary cap could have drastically changed the NFL's finances. Had the salary cap actually restrained player salaries, NFL profits would have increased. In fact, the early results suggest that there has been minimal impact. Before the cap's introduction, the NFL had substantial profits but also had a definite downward trend in those profits. This downward trend may have been due to gradual salary increases with unchanging media revenues. That is, the NFL was in the middle of multi-year television contracts; media revenues were constant while salaries were gradually increasing. Media revenues are the largest component of revenues and player salaries are the largest component of costs. Thus, a small decline in profits from 1990 to 1992 should not be surprising.

There is one other explanation for declining pre-salary cap profits. Looking more closely at the league's decrease in profits, it occurred almost entirely among a few franchises: Buffalo, Cleveland, Indianapolis, Miami, Atlanta, San Francisco, Washington, the Raiders, and the New York Giants. Excluding Atlanta and Indianapolis, these franchises have been among the most competitive in the NFL. Thus the decrease in profits may be explained by a few owners' escalating expenditures in pursuit of a Super Bowl trophy. DeBartolo (the 49ers), Cooke (the Redskins), Mara (the Giants), and Davis (the Raiders) may simply have been increasing their efforts to win.[4] You can look at the decrease in profits from 1990 to 1992 and argue that the league was becoming financially weaker or that some teams were increasing expenditures to become more competitive. While it is not possible to state definitively which explanation is more accurate, that profits did not decline uniformly across franchises suggests that the second explanation is likely at least part of the answer.

What happened in the last two years? 1993 must be viewed as a transitional year. The league had negotiated a contract with the union that called for a salary cap in the subsequent year. Some clubs took the year delay as an invitation for one last spending fling. Teams like the Houston Oilers went out and loaded up to win it all in 1993, buying the best talent available for a run for the 1994 Superbowl—under the theory that money would not buy a championship again. Other franchises like the Cincinnati Bengals delayed player expenditures, calculating that once the cap took effect some high-payroll teams would have to release talented players. These low-cost franchises would save money and then be in

---

[4] Economists might argue these increased expenditures were to increase short-term wins and thus increase long-term profitability. That argument rings hollow. NFL revenue sharing makes it unlikely that a franchise's higher expenditures will generate substantially higher franchise revenues.

better position to compete for talent under the cap. The resulting 1993 spread in team payrolls appears unprecedented in the NFL. The final result: some franchises were successful and some unsuccessful using each approach. Some successes were financial and some on-the-field. For many clubs the profit numbers changed dramatically from 1992 to 1993, once again, as they followed the beat of different drummers.

1994 was the first year under a salary cap. It is too soon to reach any definite conclusions about the implications of the new financial arrangements. (1995 developments are discussed later in this chapter.) Nevertheless, the profit numbers suggest little substantive financial change from the pre-cap years. The average level of profitability is about the same. This result is by construction. The cap calls for players to receive a percent of the revenues that keeps league profits roughly unchanged. The distribution of profits and wins also are roughly comparable, although some franchises have gained and some lost. It also appears reasonable that some owners are still in the game primarily for the money—although they would also like to win—and others still in it primarily for the wins—although they will not give back any profits. Putting Jerry Jones, Art Modell, Al Davis, Wellington Mara, Bill Bidwell, and Robert Irsay in a room and telling them to reach an agreement on what owners should be trying to do with their franchises might make for a very interesting meeting, but I would expect agreement about the same time that I expect Tampa Bay to meet Indianapolis in the Super Bowl. As long as different owners have different objectives and as long as the NFL has substantial revenue sharing, it is likely that the distribution of profits will remain about the same.

Before moving on, one last comment is in order on profits, revenues, and costs over the last 5 years. Much has been written on the AFC's losing streak in the Super Bowl, 10 years and counting. Some sportswriters have argued that the NFC plays a better brand of football. I am not an expert in football strategy so I offer no wisdom on those arguments. However, the financial numbers suggest a different reason for NFC supremacy: the best teams in the NFC simply have spent more than the best in the AFC. When a big-spending team plays a small-spending team, the big spender

Table 4.2

1994 NET PRESENT VALUES
(in millions of dollars)

Franchise	Average Profits	"Normal" Profits	NPV
AFC			
Buffalo	6.2	5.5	92
Cincinnati	7.0	6.5	108
Cleveland	7.2	7.0	117
Denver	8.2	8.0	133
Houston	5.4	5.0	83
Indianapolis	1.3	4.0	67
Kansas City	8.8	8.0	133
LA/Oakland	2.4	4.0	67
Miami	9.5	9.0	150
New England	4.8	4.5	75
NY Jets	3.2	4.0	67
Pittsburgh	11.3	10.0	167
San Diego	4.0	4.0	67
Seattle	4.2	4.0	67
NFC			
Arizona	4.7	4.0	67
Atlanta	2.4	4.0	67
Chicago	10.7	9.5	158
Dallas	16.4	14.0	258
Detroit	2.9	4.0	67
Green Bay	1.3	4.0	67
LA/St. Louis	8.5	7.0	117
Minnesota	7.2	7.0	117
New Orleans	4.4	4.0	67
NY Giants	5.5	5.0	83
Philadelphia	10.6	9.5	158
San Francisco	-0.3	4.0	67
Tampa Bay	8.1	6.0	100
Washington	2.1	4.0	67
AFC Average	6.0	6.0	99
NFC Average	6.0	6.3	104
Average	6.0	6.1	102
Maximum	16.4	15.5	258
Minimum	-0.3	4.0	67

does not always win. If it did, the Colts would have played the Seahawks in the 1994 AFC championship game. However, when a well-run and well-coached big spender meets a well-run and well-coached small spender, as has been the case in many recent Super Bowls, the big spender generally wins. While I do not have data for all Super Bowls, the information over the last few years suggests that the more free-spending team generally is the winning team. Buffalo, Denver, New England, and San Diego all were relatively low-cost teams when they represented the AFC in the Super Bowl. Not since the Miami Dolphins in 1985 or possibly the Cincinnati Bengals in 1988 has the AFC had a big spender in the Super Bowl.

What Is the Net Present Value of an NFL Franchise?

Following the procedure used for MLB and the NBA, we can calculate the Net Present Values (NPVs) of NFL franchises, or what NFL franchises are worth based on their observed profits. Table 4.2 presents the average profit for each franchise as well as the assumed "normal" profit and the resulting NPV. The NPVs are based on a 6 percent assumed real return. As with other leagues, normal profits of the high-profit teams are assumed to be slightly lower than past actual profits. With parity in the NFL we might expect some evening out of won-loss records, with the rich franchises to have profits decreasing toward the league average. However, this trend will be limited by franchises' idiosyncratic features, including stadium arrangements. While MLB and the NBA may see more equalization of profits due to greater revenue sharing, that is unlikely to be the case in the NFL.

A second adjustment made when converting actual profits into normal profits is to assume that all franchises have a minimum normal profit of $4 million. This figure likely is quite conservative. The Buccaneers averaged profits of $8.1 million and the Rams (in LA) averaged profits of $8.5 million, yet neither could consistently sell out their stadium and both had abysmal on-the-field records. These numbers suggest that any owner who focuses exclusively on the bottom line should be able to earn at least $4 million and possibly $8 million in yearly profits. Lower profits indicate either that the owner is trying to buy victory or the franchise is financially mismanaged.

With the latter adjustment, we run the risk of substantially undervaluing a franchise like Green Bay or San Francisco that has been run with a view toward winning rather than a view toward profits. The Packers, for example, could cut all expenditures, reduce payroll to the minimum allowed by the NFL ($27 million in 1994), and rely on funds from revenue sharing to make a profit perhaps as high as $8 million. To the extent that such a strategy is viable, we underestimate the profitability and the NPVs of a number of NFL franchises including San Francisco and Green Bay. I will come back to that point later. For now, I will err on the side of conservatism.

The Raiders', Rams', Cowboys', Oilers', and Browns' numbers all deserve an asterisk given recent franchise moves and proposed moves, new stadiums, and sponsorships. The implications of these changes are presented below. First, let's consider NPVs through 1994 and then consider the impacts of recent developments.

Based on NPVs calculated using profits through 1994, the most valuable NFL franchise is the Dallas Cowboys, valued at $258 million. After that, comes a group of franchises in the $150-167 million range: Miami, Pittsburgh, Chicago, and Philadelphia. At the bottom of the NPV rankings are a wide range of franchises. Some, like San Francisco and Washington, have been among the NFL's elite in terms of on-the-field performance but at a cost of mediocre financial performance and value. Others like Indianapolis, the New York Jets, and Arizona have achieved mediocrity on the field and in finance. Again, the calculations here may seriously understate the value of franchises that are either poorly run or run to win rather than to generate profits. The point of the calculations here, however, is to consider a franchise's NPV based solely upon its prior profitability and not on its victories, the owner's ego, or civic pride.

NPVs versus Actual Sale Prices—What Is an NFL Franchise Worth?

Given the calculated NPVs, what have franchises actually sold for? Table 4.3 lists franchise prices based on sales reported by either the *Wall Street Journal* or the *New York Times*. The results are similar to those reported for MLB and the NBA; franchise prices have increased dramatically. The Dallas Cowboys were an expansion franchise in 1960 costing $0.6 million. By the end of the 1960s franchise prices were around $10 million and increased to around $20 million by the end of the 1970s. During the 1980s and early 1990s the number of reported sales increased substantially and the prices continued to escalate, rising to well over $100 million in the 1990s. Even expansion franchises cost $140 million by 1995. The Tampa Bay Buccaneers, one of the least successful NFL franchises, recently sold for a reported $192 million, with three competing groups bidding in excess of $170 million. As the Rams move to St. Louis, the initial financial arrangement proposed included a new owner for a share of the franchise. News reports of the price and percentage ownership suggested an implied franchise price for the entire team of as much as $200 million. Based on recent franchise sales, it would appear that NFL franchises uniformly have a market price in excess of $175 million at the end of 1994.

While franchise prices are interesting, from a financial perspective the returns implicit in those prices are even more interesting. The top part of Table 4.4 lists all franchises that have sold multiple times and the reported sales prices. The table also presents the implied return—once again, the capital gain—based on those multiple sales. No NFL franchise has been sold for a loss. In fact, every team sold has had an average price increase exceeding 8 percent a year. All franchises experienced substantial capital gains throughout the 1960 to 1995 period. To place these numbers in context, the bottom of Table 4.4 states the average capital gain from owning an NFL franchise versus the capital gain from standard stock indexes. Over the last 20 years, NFL franchises have averaged a 14.5 percent capital gain while the Standard & Poors 500 Index (S&P 500) for stocks averaged 9.7 percent. Over the last 5 years the NFL's capital gain has shrunk but it maintains its advantage over the S&P 500, 12.0 percent versus 6.8 percent. The capital gains in Table 4.6 make it clear that it does not matter what period or what general stock index you consider, NFL owners have averaged a much higher

Table 4.3

SELECTED FRANCHISE PRICES

Date of Transaction	Franchise	Expansion	Purchase Price (in millions)
1960	Dallas Cowboys (NFL)	yes	0.6
1961	Minnesota Vikings (NFL)	yes	1.0
1962	Los Angeles Rams (NFL)	no	7.1
1966	Atlanta Falcons (NFL)	yes	8.5
1966	Miami Dolphins (AFL)	yes	7.5
1967	Philadelphia Eagles (NFL)	no	16.2
1967	New Orleans Saints (NFL)	yes	8.5
1968	Cincinnati Bengals (AFL)	yes	7.5
1974	Washington Redskins	no	15.4
1976	Tampa Bay Buccaneers	yes	16.0
1976	Seattle Seahawks	yes	16.0
1977	San Francisco 49ers	no	18.3
1981	New York Jets	no	20.0
1981	Denver Broncos	no	30.0
1984	Dallas Cowboys	no	60.0
1984	New York Jets	no	40.0
1984	San Diego Chargers	no	42.0
1984	Denver Broncos	no	72.0
1985	Phildelphia Eagles	no	65.0
1985	New Orleans Saints	no	70.2
1988	New England Patriots	no	82.0
1988	Chicago Bears	no	88.0
1989	Seattle Seahawks	no	99.0
1989	Dallas Cowboys	no	150.0
1990	Chicago Bears	no	125.0
1991	Atlanta Falcons	no	118.0
1991	New York Giants	no	147.0
1994	New England Patriots	no	155.0
1994	Miami Dolphins	no	165.0
1994	Philadelphia Eagles	no	185.0
1995	Carolina Panthers	yes	140.0
1995	Jacksonville Jaguars	yes	140.0
1995	Tampa Bay Buccaneers	no	192.0

return from their franchises than they would have received from stocks. Once again, some owners did worse than the NFL average while some did better. However, it appears that even the smallest capital gains in the NFL exceeded those from an average stock.

Table 4.4

FRANCHISE VALUES AND RETURNS FOR TEAMS THAT SOLD MULTIPLE TIMES

Franchise	Year of Purchase	Purchase Price	Implied Return
Dallas Cowboys	1960	$0.6	
Dallas Cowboys	1984	60.0	21.2%
Dallas Cowboys	1989	150.0	20.1
Atlanta Falcons	1966	8.5	
Atlanta Falcons	1991	118.0	11.1
Miami Dolphins	1966	7.5	
Miami Dolphins	1994	165.0	11.7
New Orleans Saints	1967	8.5	
New Orleans Saints	1985	70.2	12.4
Seattle Seahawks	1976	16.0	
Seattle Seahawks	1988	99.0	16.4
Denver Broncos	1981	30.0	
Denver Broncos	1984	72.0	33.9
Philadelphia Eagles	1967	16.2	
Philadelphia Eagles	1985	65.0	8.0
Philadelphia Eagles	1994	185.0	12.3
Chicago Bears	1988	88.0	
Chicago Bears	1990	125.0	19.2
New England Patriots	1988	82.0	
New England Patriots	1994	155.0	11.2
Tampa Bay Buccaneers	1976	16.0	
Tampa Bay Buccaneers	1995	192.0	14.0

Capital Gains	1989-94	1985-94	1975-94
NFL	12.4%	13.2%	14.5%
Dow-Jones Industrial Avg.	8.1	12.5	9.3
Standard & Poors 500	6.8	11.0	9.7
Wilshire 5000	7.1	10.7	NA

The capital gains presented in Table 4.4 are only part of the total returns. That is, NFL owners have seen large capital gains while also receiving substantial operating profit. To obtain the total return to an NFL franchise we add the increase in stock value or capital gain from Table 4.6 to profits from Table 4.3. Over the last 5 years NFL franchises have averaged a capital gain of 12.4 percent a year and profits of $6.1 million a year. The average NPV at the end of 1994 was $102 million. Thus the operating return for the typical NFL franchise was at least 6 percent from 1990 to 1994.[5] Adding the capital gain and the operating return yields the total return to owning an NFL franchise. The result: NFL franchises have averaged an 18.5 percent total return over from 1990 through 1994 compared with a total return of 14.1 percent for the S&P 500. From 1975 through 1994 NFL franchises have averaged over 20 percent total return while the S&P 500 has averaged about 15 percent. NFL franchises, like MLB franchises, are small businesses, and small capitalization stocks have an average return about three percent higher than the S&P 500. Even with this modification, however, owning an NFL franchise appears to be a lucrative endeavor, more profitable than a typical portfolio of stocks.

In fact, this comparison probably understates the NFL's historical advantage over stocks. The calculated total return assumed that $6.1 million is a representative value for profit. In fact, operating profits probably are lower now than they were 5 or 10 years ago. NFL players have had real free agency only in the last few years, and free agency has increased player salaries and decreased owner profits. It should be no surprise that NFL franchises have earned excellent returns or that those returns have fallen somewhat in the last few years. The NFL has had a monopoly in dealing with fans, cities, and players. Monopolists also generally have relatively high profits. The NFL's monopoly power with respect to the players has been weakened with free agency and we should expect this reduction in monopoly power to cut into NFL profits.

PROFITS VERSUS WINS—WHAT PRICE EGO?

The final piece of analysis is to compare prices recently paid for franchises with the calculated NPVs. As in prior chapters, one can ask how much have owners "overpaid" for the privilege of owning an NFL franchise or for membership in the NFL owners club. I consider only franchises purchased since 1991 since prices for prior sales may not accurately reflect their current value. For sales

---

[5] The 6 percent figure uses the average NPV at the end of 1994. If the average franchise value in 1990 was, say, only $85 million, allowing a capital gain from 1990 to 1994, then the operating profit in 1990 would have been over 7 percent.

before 1994, the purchase price is adjusted upward by 9 percent a year to take into account a 6 percent real return as well as inflation. The numbers in Table 4.5 indicate that NFL owners have dramatically overpaid for their franchises. The 6 franchises recently sold have brought an average price of $173 million but have an average NPV of only $105 million for an overpayment of $70 million! If you thought there were a lot of very big egos in the NFL, at least very expensive egos, these numbers suggest you are correct. NFL owners have much more expensive egos on average than MLB ($29 to $42 million) or the NBA ($40 million).

Now there is another way to look at the values in Table 4.5. When calculating the NPVs I noted that some franchise values may be understated. That is, to the extent that some owners have explicitly traded profits for victories, potential profits of some franchises may be understated. Looking at Cincinnati and Tampa Bay, two teams that certainly have not traded profits for wins, one might reasonably conclude that any owner seeking profits should have averaged a minimum of $8 million profit a year. With that minimum level of profits, the minimum NPV increases to $133 million. In this case, owners would have overpaid on average by only $36 million. Nevertheless, ego is still expensive.

Table 4.5

NPVs versus PRICES PAID
What Price Ego? or
How Much Have Owners "Overpaid" for an NFL Franchise?

Franchise	Purchase Price[a]	NPV	Purchase Price Minus NPV	1994 Franchise Profits
Atlanta Falcons	$153	$67	$86	$2.4
New York Giants	190	83	107	7.6
New England Patriots	155	75	88	0.5
Miami Dolphins	165	133	32	15.0
Philadelphia Eagles	185	158	35	10.8
Tampa Bay Buccaneers	192	100	92	6.5
Average	173	103	70	7.1

[a] Purchase price equals the actual sale price in the year of sale multiplied by 1.09 (for inflation and the real interest rate) for each year since the sale occurred.

Taking this logic to its extreme, you can calculate how much some owners have paid to win. For example, the Dolphins have an NPV of $150 million and a recent purchase price of $165 for an overpayment of $15 million. Suppose, however, that the Dolphins' profits could have been higher except for Joe Robbie's (the former owner) pursuit of Super Bowl trophies. In particular, the NPV of $150 million is based on normal profits of $9 million. Suppose that Robbie had been interested solely in profits and by pursuing only profits he could have increased the Dolphin's normal profits to $10 million a year. The Dolphins' NPV would then be $165, just equal to the sale price. The moral: if Robbie was spending an additional $1 million just to win and without concern about profits, then there was no overpayment. In contrast, the Giants would have had to be spending approximately $6 million a year pursuing the Super Bowl for there to be no overpayment. Without this additional spending, the Dolphins and the Giants and the NFL would be even more profitable ventures! Once again we are left with a choice. The NFL has been extremely profitable, even though some owners have been sacrificing profits for victories. Given owners have traded profits for victories, the only remaining questions are how high could profits have been and how much have owners paid for ego? These questions do not have a correct answer for the owners. If they are committed to victory, the example of the 49ers and Packers demonstrates that winning may cost money. Thus owners should not expect the franchise to be extremely profitable! If they are not committed to victory, then they may make a profit, especially with revenue sharing, but they also should expect to be reviled by fans for not fielding a competitive team!

1995 DEVELOPMENTS

1995 may well be a watershed year in NFL history. Two franchises moved before the season began; two expansion franchises bought enough talent to be instantly competitive; Jerry Jones signed endorsement deals that challenged the NFL marketing arm (NFL Properties) and NFL revenue sharing; and two franchises attempted to move after the season. What precipitated all the action? Why did the league that looked most stable at the beginning

Table 4.6
REVISED NET PRESENT VALUES
(in millions of dollars)

Franchise	"Normal" Profits	Revised Profits	Revised NPV
AFC			
Buffalo	5.5	4.5	75
Cincinnati	6.5	5.5	92
Cleveland/Balt.	7.0	19.0	317
Denver	8.0	7.0	117
Houston/Tenn.	5.0	14.0	233
Indianapolis	4.0	3.0	50
Kansas City	8.0	7.0	117
LA/Oakland	4.0	11.0	183
Miami	9.0	8.0	133
New England	4.4	3.5	58
NY Jets	4.0	3.0	50
Pittsburgh	10.0	9.0	150
San Diego	4.0	3.0	50
Seattle	4.0	3.0	50
NFC			
Arizona	4.0	3.0	50
Atlanta	4.0	3.0	50
Chicago	9.5	8.5	142
Dallas	14.0	21.5	358
Detroit	4.0	3.0	50
Green Bay	4.0	3.0	50
LA/St. Louis	7.0	21.0	350
Minnesota	7.0	6.0	100
New Orleans	4.0	3.0	50
NY Giants	5.0	4.0	67
Philadelphia	9.5	8.5	142
San Francisco	4.0	3.0	50
Tampa Bay	6.0	5.0	83
Washington	4.0	3.0	50
AFC Average	6.0	7.2	120
NFC Average	6.3	6.8	114
Average	6.1	7.0	117
Maximum	15.5	21.5	358
Minimum	4.0	3.0	50

of 1995 suddenly go schizophrenic? The answer lies in the changing economics, quite possibly due to the salary cap. The simplest way of stating things may be: the salary cap begat Carmen Policy; Policy begat Jones; Jones begat Modell; and Modell is the embodiment of franchise free agency.

At the end of 1993 Carmen Policy, president of the 49ers renegotiated 1994 player contracts to give the 49ers more room to maneuver under the salary cap, newly-implemented in 1994. Some analysts contend that Policy's moves "bought" the 1995 Super Bowl championship. Policy's moves did make it clear that the NFL's cap had loopholes.

The most important loophole in 1995 allows a franchise to sign a player to a long-term contract with a big signing bonus and an option allowing later years of the contract to be voided. For salary cap purposes, the bonus is spread over the life of the contract. Deion Sanders' 1995 contract is a perfect, albeit extreme, example. He signed a seven-year contract paying a $13 million bonus in 1995; a $178,000 salary in 1995, 1996, and 1997; a $5.25 million salary in 1998; $6.5 million in 1999; and $5 million in 2000 and 2001. Total salary: $35 million for seven years. However, while $13.2 million is paid in 1995, only about $2 million counts toward the salary cap. "Caponomics" spreads the bonus over the seven-year contract. Many franchises have exploited this loophole. Jerry Jones merely happens to be the most aggresive and flamboyant in its use.

The catch with this loophole is that not all franchises can use it—only those teams with up-front cash available. The key to this loophole is the ability to pay big signing bonuses—which means either a large revenue stream or a willingness to borrow against future income. Jones and the Cowboys can simply write a check. Art Modell and the Browns, while a reasonably successful franchise in Cleveland, nevertheless allegedly had to borrow money to pay Andre Rison's 1995 signing bonus.

Which brings us to franchise free agency. The Rams, Raiders, Browns, and Oilers all have been profitable franchises although not among the financial elite. Under the economics of the salary cap and revenue sharing and in their original locales, however, they would likely have been relegated to financial mediocrity and on-the-field mediocrity. Move them to a new stadium with lots of luxury boxes and a great lease and suddenly they are among the elite.

There is one further component to the 1995 changes: the impacts of these changes on other franchises' finances. Consider Jones' deals first. For argument's sake, assume that his recent deals with Pepsi, Nike, and American Express give the Cowboys $50 million. Under the salary cap, the players get about 62 percent of that or $31 million. That represents over a $1-million increase in the salary cap for each franchise. Bottom line: the Cowboys gain $49 million; the players gain $31 million; and all other franchises lose over $1 million each. Jones' actions make great sense for the Cowboys and also pay off for the players but wreak havoc on the other owners. Furthermore, they force the other owners to try and make similar sponsor arrangements further undermining NFL Properties.

What is the total impact of the contract changes and franchise movements? While complete information is not yet available on some of the proposed franchise leases, there is enough information to make preliminary calculations that are presented in Table 4.6. The Cowboys, Rams, Raiders, Browns, and Oilers all generate substantial additional revenue, in sum over $50 million. The players will receive over $30 million of that thus reducing other franchises' profits by over $1 million each. The minimum profit in the NFL would be reduced to about $3 million. The Cowboys retain the ranking as the most profitable franchise in the NFL. However, franchises moved to St. Louis, Baltimore, Tennessee, and Oakland are not far behind. The expansion Carolina Cougars and Jacksonville Jaguars are not listed. However, they also would appear close to the financial elite given their stadium arrangements. Perhaps the most notable change is that the gap between the rich and poor franchises has widened substantially.

Furthermore, without a dramatic change in the NFL's bylaws this is not the end of the changes. The Seahawks, Cardinals, Buccaneers, and Bengals are all making noises about moving. To the extent that a city without a franchise is willing to match the deals offered by Baltimore or St. Louis or Oakland, many cities are in jeopardy of losing their NFL franchise. Revenue sharing together with the salary cap suggests that NFL really stands for a franchise's commitment: "Not-For-Long."

CONCLUSIONS

Before concluding with the NFL, there are two cautionary points to make. The first is on the Green Bay Packers. In my view, the Packers are run the way a sports franchise ought to be run: effectively of the fans, by the fans, and for the fans. In my view, the Green Bay Packers should be America's team rather than the Dallas Cowboys. While it is a small-market team, it has broken even, has relatively low ticket prices, and has fielded competitive teams. That said, I wonder how long the franchise can or will remain in Green Bay? Based on the Tampa Bay price of $192 million, each share of Green Bay Packers stock is worth approximately $44,000. Ultimately, some billionaire is going to figure that the cheapest way to acquire a franchise is to buy Green Bay.

Second, the NFL is in good overall financial health, but it is in a more tenuous position than the numbers may indicate. Financial weakness could be just a TV contract away. National television money is 58 percent of NFL revenues. If a network like Fox loses a bundle on its current football contract, bidding on the next contract might not be as aggressive. Before the last contract negotiation and before Fox entered those negotiations, there was concern that television money would fall because of television losses on prior football contracts. If TV money were to fall even slightly, some franchises could be in real financial difficulty especially if more players receive long-term guaranteed contracts.

Nevertheless, the NFL's bottom line is that it has been exceptionally profitable on average. Like other leagues, NFL franchises have had a range of profits, but the NFL's range is substantially different, running from small profits for Green Bay and San Francisco (when including capital gains) to very large profits for clubs like Dallas, Chicago, and Denver.[6] Over the last 20 years the average total return for all franchises has exceeded 20 percent a year, with the best franchises averaging in excess of 25 percent a year. In addition,

---

[6] I must reiterate a warning that the calculation of profits here deliberately omits the method of financing used to buy a franchise. For example, if the Tampa Bay purchase was financed by borrowing $150 million for 20 years at a 10 percent interest rate, the $17.4 million interest cost is a cost to the owner but is not a cost to the franchise. Nevertheless, the owner will look to the franchise to generate the revenue to cover interest costs, even though the revenue may only come in terms of future capital gains.

it appears that some franchises on the low end of the profit scale are there by choice, choosing to have low profits and high wins rather than higher profits but fewer wins. Again, there are differences between owners in terms of their objectives. The results also indicate that owners differ substantially in their abilities to successfully manage an NFL franchise. However, one fundamental difference between the NFL and MLB is that in the NFL even incompetent owners can break even thanks to NFL revenue sharing.

Chapter 5

Hockey — Crying All the Way to the Bank

"Hockey must be a great game to survive the people who run it."
—Conn Smythe, owner, Toronto Maple Leafs

"As an investment, a hockey team stinks."
—Edward DeBartolo, owner, Pittsburgh Penguins

"I'm an oil man, and I don't drill dry holes twice."—**Jack Vickers, former owner of the Colorado Rockies, on why he sold the team (currently the New Jersey Devils)**

"You can always depend on the owners to do something supremely dumb, sooner or later. It just took them a little longer than usual this time. Congratulations, my dear moguls."
—Clark Booth, sports writer

THE INSIDE VIEW OF NHL FINANCES

Financially, hockey is similar to basketball, sharing seasons and in many cases arenas. While there are important differences, the most notable being the magnitude of the national television contract, one common feature is that both have at least one publicly-traded franchise. In the NHL both the Toronto Maple Leafs and the Vancouver Canucks are publicly owned and must file annual reports. Those reports are a reasonable place to begin to analyze the NHL's financial health. Table 5.1 presents summary information from each club's most recent annual report, 1993-1994 for

106

Toronto and 1992-1993 for Vancouver. Throughout this chapter, all Canadian values have been converted to U.S. dollars.[1]

Both franchises report a profit. Excluding franchise amortization—which makes no sense to call a cost in hockey or in any other sport—Toronto made $5.4 million profit in 1993-1994 while Vancouver made $2.8 million in 1992-1993. However, Vancouver's profit appears due to a one-time expansion fee of $2.8 million (Vancouver's share of the entry fee paid by the expansion franchises). Without the expansion fee, Vancouver apparently would have just broken even. But one further adjustment should be made. All prior numbers are pre-tax while Toronto's and Vancouver's numbers are net of income taxes. Adding income taxes back to calculate the before tax profits gives Toronto an $8.2 million profit and Vancouver a $1.8 million profit, excluding the expansion fee.

The general conclusion from the annual reports: it does not matter how you juggle the numbers, based on Toronto's and Vancouver's annual reports the NHL is on solid if not spectacular financial footing.

These annual reports, however, raise almost as many questions as they answer. Explaining the differences in revenues between Toronto and Vancouver is fairly straightforward. Toronto had higher playoff revenues because they went one round further, and Toronto's media revenues are larger primarily because they are in a larger media market. The only revenue puzzle is why Toronto's "Other Revenues" are slightly less than Vancouver's, despite Toronto's larger market and Vancouver's number referring to a year earlier. Other revenues include NHL licensing revenues, approximately $0.8 million for 1994, as well as income from local marketing and advertising.

The larger puzzles appear under costs in the categories of "Building" and "Other Costs." Vancouver had building costs of $1.67 million while Toronto's were $5.37 million. Why were Toronto's costs $3.7 million higher? Granted, Maple Leaf Gardens is an old building requiring extensive maintenance, but a building

---

[1] The Vancouver numbers have not been further adjusted despite the different year.

Table 5.1

HOCKEY FINANCIAL STATEMENTS

Statement of Income
(in millions of U.S. dollars)

	Toronto 1993-1994	Vancouver 1992-1993
Revenues		
Ticket Sales, Regular Season	$15.47	$16.74
Hockey Playoffs	6.64	2.96
Broadcast Revenues	10.71	4.28
Private Boxes	4.20	0.58
NHL Expansion Fees	0.40	2.78
Other Revenues	5.13	5.90
Total	42.55	33.24
Costs and Expenses		
Hockey Operations (e.g., salaries)	20.34	17.49
Hockey Playoffs	3.73	1.90
Building	5.37	1.67
Other Costs	3.84	7.57
Depreciation	0.72	0.00
Amortization	1.47	0.14
Income Taxes	3.16	1.85
Total	38.60	30.62
Net Income	3.95	2.62
Net Income Plus Amortization	5.42	2.77
Net Income Before Taxes & Excluding Extraordinary Items	8.2	1.8

expense of over $100,000 per home hockey game seems both excessive and out of line with public facilities in the U.S. For example, based on Freedom of Information Act requests to all cities with a public arena used by an NBA or NHL team, the range of rents in the NBA and NHL runs from $3,000 to $10,000 per game with an average of about $7,000. Taking the highest value and assuming 200 nights occupancy per year (much greater than the actual average), you would have $2.0 million rent to cover the facility's costs. To that add, say, $60,000 per game for costs of ushers, security, etc. for 42 home games. The total now is approximately $4.5 million. In sum, Toronto's building costs appear $1 million too high even under very generous assumptions. For Vancouver, the question concerns the category "Other Costs." For a hockey team, how can an item other than building costs or player costs (which includes player salaries and the costs of the minor leagues) be 25 percent of total costs? One logical explanation is that it includes the cost of merchandise, programs, and food sold at concession stands; "other revenues" then include concession stand revenues. If this is the case, though, Vancouver is making only 8.7 percent on its concessions which, given NHL concession pricing, seems unbelievably low.

Nevertheless, taking the annual reports at their word, the most important point about Table 5.1 is that the only official records available indicate that NHL franchises are profitable. Some owners have protested that the NHL is losing money. None have released information to demonstrate those losses. Based on the official record, the only debate is how much money franchises make. The official Toronto and Vancouver numbers suggest profits average about $5 million per franchise.

League Numbers—Who Made How Much?

When we turn to the question of whether other franchises generally are profitable we again face incomplete information. The NHL is the most closed-mouthed of all leagues. For example, the NHL even considers attendance numbers confidential information. The Winnipeg Jets are 36 percent owned by the city and the province, but even city and provincial officials do not see the financial numbers. Nevertheless, attendance numbers are reported in the newspapers; salary numbers are reported in *The Hockey News;* and other information sources generally are the same as for other sports. There are only two major differences from basketball. First, travel costs are somewhat higher since the squads are larger. However, the distances covered are somewhat smaller and the league's cities on average have lower hotel costs. Thus, travel expenses are assumed to average $2.1 million per team. Second, hockey has well-developed minor league and junior league systems subsidized by the NHL. I have been unable to pry loose any direct information on the amount of that subsidy, but Toronto's and Vancouver's annual reports yield some clues. Taking "Hockey Operations" costs and subtracting player salaries allows an educated guess about the maximum expenditure for minor league subsidies. That appears to be about $3.5 million. This number is employed in the cost calculations in Table 5.2. All calculations are based on the assumption of a full season, that is, what profits would have been in the absence of the lockout.

With the exception of substantially lower media revenues, the numbers in Table 5.2 are very similar to those for basketball. On average the NHL appears financially healthy. Franchises averaged $5.5 million profit in 1994-1995. While media revenues averaged only $5 million a team, almost $10 million less than in the NBA, the NHL's gate revenues were slightly higher than the NBA's due to higher ticket prices. Other stadium revenues also were higher in hockey, primarily because more NHL franchises own their stadiums. Game-day costs for basketball and hockey were virtually identical; hockey salaries were substantially less; hockey had minor league subsidy expenses, but basketball had higher player pension costs. The bottom line for the two sports, however, is surprisingly similar. The NBA averaged a profit of $6 million a team while the NHL averaged $6.6 million. The owners' protestations to the contrary, the NHL on average was a very profitable endeavor.

Nevertheless, high average NHL profits, as in other sports, hide dramatic differences in the relative profitability between franchises. For example, total league profits were $172 million in 1994-1995. Of that amount, over $142 million went to just 8 franchises: Boston, Chicago, Detroit, the New York Rangers, Philadelphia, Anaheim, St. Louis, and San Jose. This "elite eight" averaged $17.8 million profit. The other 18 teams totaled $30 million profit or $1.7 million per team. That Boston, Chicago, Detroit, Philadelphia, and the New York Rangers all made substantial profits should come as no surprise. All are old-guard large-market (for hockey) franchises. St. Louis struggled until moving into its new arena. Anaheim's success also should be no surprise

Table 5.2

REVENUES, COSTS, AND PROFITS
(in millions of U.S. dollars)

| | 1995 Revenues | | | | 1995 Costs | | | |
	Gate	Media	Stadium	Total	Players	Total	1995 Net Profits	1990-95 Total Profits
Eastern								
Boston	23.9	11.0	7.4	48.0	12.7	27.2	20.8	80.2
Buffalo	22.9	5.0	3.2	33.5	19.0	33.6	-0.1	-2.0
Florida	20.3	4.0	3.0	30.3	11.7	25.2	5.1	11.0
Hartford	17.1	3.0	3.7	25.3	15.1	29.1	-3.8	-9.0
Montreal	19.6	7.0	7.0	36.1	12.9	27.4	8.7	42.4
New Jersey	24.3	4.8	2.0	36.6	16.5	31.1	5.5	12.6
NY Islanders	20.7	7.0	4.0	33.2	12.7	26.7	6.5	29.1
NY Rangers	28.9	7.2	9.5	52.1	18.0	33.8	18.3	65.3
Ottawa	14.9	3.7	5.0	25.1	9.3	22.4	2.7	14.0
Phildelphia	25.5	7.0	8.0	47.8	14.1	28.8	19.0	43.7
Pittsburgh	26.6	4.9	4.0	41.7	20.1	35.2	6.5	20.1
Quebec/Col.	18.7	5.0	1.5	27.6	13.5	27.2	0.4	5.4
Tampa Bay	16.2	4.0	3.0	24.7	10.5	23.8	0.9	-0.1
Washington	22.3	4.3	6.0	35.6	13.6	27.7	7.9	11.8
Western								
Anaheim	23.3	5.1	10.5	43.4	12.6	27.4	16.0	30.4
Calgary	17.8	4.3	1.6	26.4	14.0	27.8	-1.4	12.8
Chicago	34.1	5.8	14.5	62.7	17.8	39.6	23.1	71.5
Dallas	24.0	3.0	5.0	35.0	14.7	30.0	5.0	-0.1
Detroit	26.4	8.0	13.0	57.9	19.2	36.2	21.7	101.4
Edmonton	11.2	4.0	1.2	17.9	9.2	22.3	-4.4	0.2
Los Angeles	23.4	6.5	6.0	39.9	23.4	43.0	-3.1	28.2
St. Louis	33.7	4.1	11.0	51.5	23.5	40.6	10.9	8.7
San Jose	25.5	3.7	7.0	39.7	11.3	27.3	12.4	21.1
Toronto	22.9	7.0	9.1	43.8	16.5	40.0	3.8	37.8
Vancouver	23.4	4.3	6.0	36.7	17.2	37.4	-0.7	3.4
Winnipeg	11.9	3.0	1.2	18.2	14.1	27.9	-9.7	-21.0
East Average	21.6	5.6	4.8	35.5	14.3	28.5	7.0	23.2
West Average	23.1	4.9	7.2	39.4	16.1	33.3	6.1	24.5
Average	22.3	5.3	5.9	37.3	15.1	30.7	6.6	23.8
Maximum	34.1	11.0	14.5	62.7	23.5	43.0	23.1	101.4
Minimum	11.2	3.0	1.2	17.9	9.2	22.3	-9.7	-21.0
Canada Avg.	17.6	4.8	4.1	29.0	13.3	29.1	-0.1	11.9

since they are owned by Disney and the Disney marketing savvy was liberally applied to push the Mighty Ducks. San Jose is not a franchise that I would have guessed was one of the richest in the league. But then I probably should have surmised that a franchise calculating enough to choose team colors and logo based on extensive marketing research would be one of the most financially successful. San Jose's numbers indicate their success is neither a surprise nor an accident. The Sharks have a big arena—price the tickets at a premium, and sell the place out. In the NHL, that is all you need for financial success.

Buffalo, Hartford, Calgary, Edmonton, Los Angeles, Vancouver, and Winnipeg occupy the other end of the spectrum. Los Angeles's appearance on the list is likely short-term. They have high salaries from long-term contracts, and ownership has been distracted with legal problems unrelated to hockey. That leaves us with Buffalo and Hartford in the U.S. and Calgary, Edmonton, Vancouver, and Winnipeg in Canada, the six smallest markets in the NHL. Buffalo and Hartford have had franchises for a number of years, and neither has ever been tremendously profitable. Even when Buffalo wins it does not make a lot of money, and Hartford has never seen substantial on-ice success. Buffalo and Hartford also are the teams in the two smallest U.S. markets. Does that mean that small market NHL teams cannot make it financially? Perhaps. But before leaping to that conclusion, go back and check out the NBA's Utah Jazz. The Jazz is a thriving NBA franchise in a market even smaller than Buffalo's or Hartford's. Based on the Jazz's performance—substantial profits despite higher salaries and a smaller market—it is far too soon to write off Buffalo and Hartford as viable long-term NHL franchises. However, both franchises clearly need to do something different. One might argue that different management is necessary. Alternately, one might argue that each needs a new arena. Buffalo has a new arena under construction while Hartford has state support for improved facilities. Before leaping on the arena bandwagon, however, it is reasonable to ask whether they fill their current arenas. While half of all NHL franchises consistently sell out, neither Buffalo nor Hartford do. A new arena would help them only if it there would be a lot of new faces in that arena. While new arenas have helped in other cities, there remains the question of whether it is appropriate or justifiable to sink $100-plus million of public funds into a new stadium just to bring the profitability of an NHL franchise up to the league average—and keep that franchise in your city. We will come back to that topic in Chapter 10.

The four Canadian cities on the list of troubled franchises pose a potentially greater problem, especially in light of Quebec's move to Denver and the general Canadian fear that the NHL is deserting Canada. None made a profit in 1995 and none lasted through the second round of the playoffs. All four franchises face serious financial pressures, and those pressures are not going to go away any time soon.

Comparing Calgary and Edmonton is instructive because the comparison suggests that an owner's behavior and the market size both play crucial roles in determining a franchise's profitability. Edmonton's owner, Peter Pocklington, has been one of the most vocal critics of the current financial system. Edmonton has the second lowest payroll in the NHL and has basically dismantled its team since winning the Stanley Cup in 1990. It also has seen attendance and gate revenues fall substantially. There are serious difficulties facing the smaller market teams; however, Calgary faces the same economic pressures as Edmonton and generally has not lost money. Why? It helps to avoid shooting yourself in the foot. The Edmonton hockey fans recognize when "their" team is uncompetitive, and, as Yogi Berra said, "If the people don't come out to the ball park, who's going to stop them?" That Calgary has been profitable despite $5 million more in player salaries and a market 15 percent smaller than Edmonton suggests that the small market Canadian teams can survive, although survival admittedly may be difficult under the current rules. Would a salary cap improve their chances of survival? The potentially surprising answer is no. A salary cap would doom the Calgary, Edmonton, Vancouver, and Winnipeg franchises. More on that in Chapter 8. The key to these franchises' long-term survival: greater NHL revenue sharing. But that brings us back full circle; the NHL is comprised of the "elite eight" and the "other eighteen." Some of the 18 can comfortably survive on their own, but others will not. The owners ultimately will have to come to terms with that among themselves. Revenue sharing will be discussed in more detail in Chapter 7. For now let me note only that revenue sharing and a salary cap are two entirely separate beasts.

Before moving on, there is one other point of interest on the 1995 numbers: player salaries as a percentage of total revenues. NHL players in 1995 received only 40 percent of league revenues, down from 44 percent in 1994. This is less than the NBA average and much less than the Major League Baseball (MLB) or the NFL averages. To bring this percentage up to MLB at 50 percent would require a 13.5 percent across the board salary increase. The NBA is the only league with a percentage close to the NHL, 40 percent versus 46 percent, but the NBA's 46 percent is biased downward by the increasing use of long-term contracts.

The lower percentage of revenues going to player salaries does not prove hockey players are underpaid. Subsidizing minor leagues and the lack of a lucrative national U.S. television contract reduces revenues available to pay NHL players. Hockey's fixed costs, like stadium rentals and travel costs, together with less revenue may simply leave less funds available to pay hockey players. Alternately, NHL players really may be underpaid. NHL players have had less individual freedom to bargain for salaries, have had more limitations on their movement, and have faced greater restrictions on free agency. All these restrictions on markets determining salaries may have caused this lower percentage. My point: there are alternate explanations for this lower percentage. Hockey salaries may be lower because less revenue enters the sport or because players are being exploited.

THE PROFIT PICTURE—1990-1995

Table 5.2 presents total profits for 1990 to 1995 in the last column. Once again, profits from 1990 to 1993 come from *Financial World*. There should be few surprises. The franchises that fared the best in 1994-1995 also generally did well in prior years. Boston, Montreal, the New York Rangers, Philadelphia, Chicago, Detroit, Anaheim, and Toronto combined for a total of $429 million in profits during the last six years out of total league profits of $619 million. These 8 averaged $9.5 million a year in profits while the other non-expansion franchises averaged $1.2 million a year. The only potential surprise, given the performances of some MLB franchises, is that the clubs that have lost money have lost so little money. Of course, that is small solace to the Winnipeg or Hartford owners. To put their losses in context, however, Winnipeg's 6-year $21 million loss approximately equals the Kansas City Royals' loss in 1994 alone.

Consider once again the profitability, indeed the survivability of the small market franchises based on the last five years of profits. Buffalo and Hartford have lost money and appear to have a trend toward greater losses. Winnipeg has lost money every year and the magnitude of those losses is growing. Edmonton and Calgary have slipped from a profit to a loss. Is the demise of the small-market, primarily-Canadian teams inexorable? Based on Table 5.2, the fat lady has not begun to sing, but you might hear her warming up in the wings.

If the jury is still out on the survivability of the small Canadian franchises, it also is out on the success of southern U.S. cities. The first exhibit would be the Calgary Flames, themselves refugees from a hostile Atlanta market. While the performance of small-market Canadian teams lags the league's performance, the performance of the "southern" teams—Florida, Tampa Bay, Washington, Anaheim, Dallas, Los Angeles, and San Jose and arguably St. Louis—also remains in doubt. Washington and St. Louis are the only southern franchises with lengthy histories. Both have less than impressive profits. While there appears to be strong ownership and management in Anaheim, Florida (Wayne Huizenga, owner of Blockbuster Video), and San Jose, and while Dallas and San Jose had success on-ice in the 1994 and 1995 playoffs, there is no track record of great success anywhere in the south. Any owner or potential owner should have serious reservations about putting up $60 million for the dubious honor of bringing the NHL to Phoenix or Houston or Atlanta. In fact, the U.S. cities with the greatest hockey potential may be Minneapolis and Cleveland. More on that later.

One other franchise observes special mention: the New Jersey Devils. There was speculation in the press that the Devils would move to Nashville—in part based on allegations that the franchise lost $28 million over the last several years. While the Devils are not in the NHL's financial elite, there is no evidence to suggest that they have lost money. The state of New Jersey's recent concessions, however, may considerably increase the Devils' profitability.

What Is the Net Present Value of an NHL Franchise?

From the profit numbers once again come the Net Present Values (NPVs), or what is a franchise worth based on the profits it generates. Table 5.3 presents actual average profits, my estimate of "normal" franchise profits, and the resulting NPVs. Once again, my normal profit numbers attempt to be conservative, marginally reducing the income of the most profitable clubs except for Boston and Chicago. Even the increases for the Bruins and the Blackhawks are conservative estimates of the potentially substantial increases in profitability with their moves into new facilities. Buffalo, Montreal, St. Louis, San Jose, and Vancouver also are moving or have moved to new quarters and their increased profits reflect those moves. The other general adjustment sets a minimum "normal" profit of $2 million for franchises like Hartford, Edmonton, and Washington. I am quite comfortable with the minimum numbers used for MLB, the NBA, and the NFL. In each case the league has small market franchises that do considerably better than the minimum. I am less comfortable with the NHL minimum. Calgary has been the closest to a small market success story, but it is not clear whether that success can be maintained. Winnipeg, in particular, is a concern, and as of December 1995 appears committed to playing elsewhere in 1996. It is not obvious that anything short of winning a draft lottery would keep the Winnipeg franchise alive in Winnipeg. Nevertheless, lottery tickets do have some value. In addition, the Jets could liquidate and sell the player contracts and other assets. Just the sale of player contracts would likely fetch over $10 million, and that sets a floor under the value of the franchise. Of course, that is little solace to Jets' investors or fans. The Jets' low normal profit raises a question: is there a way to save the franchise? The answer is yes, if the owners can agree on revenue sharing. That is the subject of Chapter 7. A second question is: should the franchise be saved or moved? That is a much tougher question, at least in part outside the realm of economics. We will return to that in Chapter 14.

What do the NPVs tell us? First, based on their income streams, some franchises like Boston, Chicago, Detroit, and Anaheim should be worth $233 million or more. This value is far higher than any previous estimate of the value of an NHL franchise. It considers the net income stream of the franchise—and the net income streams of the strongest NHL franchises are equivalent to the strongest franchises in any sport. Second, the Mighty Ducks of Anaheim are included among the financial elite of the NHL even before participating in a single playoff game. Certainly a franchise is not built in a year, and including the Ducks in that select few on the basis of two years' profit is a much more speculative call. Any lower value, however would appear unreasonable based on their performance to date. Disney has shown tremendous marketing success in the entertainment industry and their favorable stadium arrangements are not going to change anytime soon. Disney has had a tremendous increase in the value of its NHL investment, in part just by exploiting the Disney name in a different venue. The value of the Ducks should make it clear that the NHL is in the entertainment business first and the hockey business second.

Other franchises that are among the financial elite include Montreal, the New York Rangers, San Jose, and Vancouver, with NPVs between $183 and $200 million. Following them are the New York Islanders, Philadelphia, Colorado (formerly Quebec), St. Louis, and Toronto. All have NPVs in the $100 to $150 million range. All appear on solid if not spectacular financial footing.

Where the NHL differs from other leagues is in the gap between the top and the bottom of the financial ladder. All four leagues have a group of teams at the top with values at $200 million or more. The Detroit Red Wings, Los Angeles Lakers, and Baltimore Orioles, for example, all have roughly comparable market values. No other league, however, has clubs as weak as

Table 5.3

NET PRESENT VALUES (NPVs)
(in millions of U.S. dollars)

Franchise	Average Income	"Normal" Income	Net Present Value
Eastern			
Boston	13.4	17.0	283
Buffalo	-0.3	4.0	67
Florida	5.5	3.5	58
Hartford	-1.5	2.0	33
Montreal	7.1	13.0	217
New Jersey	2.1	6.0	100
NY Islanders	4.9	4.0	67
NY Rangers	10.9	11.0	183
Ottawa	4.7	3.0	50
Phildelphia	7.3	6.0	100
Pittsburgh	3.4	3.0	50
Quebec/Colorado	0.9	9.0	150
Tampa Bay	0.0	2.0	33
Washington	2.0	2.0	33
Western			
Anaheim	15.2	14.0	233
Calgary	2.1	2.0	33
Chicago	11.9	15.0	250
Dallas	0.0	2.5	50
Detroit	16.9	15.0	250
Edmonton	0.0	2.0	33
Los Angeles	4.7	4.0	67
St. Louis	1.5	10.0	167
San Jose	5.3	12.0	200
Toronto	6.3	6.5	108
Vancouver	0.6	11.0	183
Winnipeg	-3.5	1.5	25
East Average	4.3	6.1	102
West Average	5.1	8.2	138
Average	4.7	7.1	118
Maximum	16.9	17.0	283
Minimum	-3.5	1.5	25
Canada Avg.	2.3	6.0	100

Winnipeg, Hartford, Washington, Edmonton, or Tampa Bay. The average NPV in the NBA is $93 million versus $118 million in the NHL, but in the NHL there are 10 franchises with a market value of $60 million or less while the NBA has only 5. You can view $60 million as the cutoff to signal a franchise in trouble. Ten of 26 NHL clubs fit this category. That is not the sign of a league in glowing financial health—although many franchises are extremely healthy.[2]

ACTUAL FRANCHISE PRICES—WHAT IS AN NHL FRANCHISE WORTH?

How do these NPVs compare with franchise sale prices? The NHL is no exception to the rule of dramatically increasing franchise prices. Table 5.4 presents a list of selected franchise sales. A sale is included only if it was mentioned in the *Wall Street Journal* or the *New York Times* and a sale price was indicated. In the NHL there are fewer publicly-reported sales and the list is dominated by the prices of expansion franchises. For example, only one franchise sales price was reported between 1984 and 1990 although several franchises sold during that period. The lads in the NHL are nothing if not tight-lipped.

Even in the NHL, franchises appear to have appreciated substantially in value, at least during the 1980s and 1990s. No owner took a loss on a reported sale. Two sales stand out. First, the Calgary investors who purchased the Atlanta Flames in 1980 appear to have overpaid in comparison with subsequent sales of the Detroit Red Wings and St. Louis Blues. However, an apparent overpayment is common for all leagues when the franchise is to be relocated. Second, the 1994 sale price for the Toronto Maple Leafs may strike some as excessive in comparison to the price for the Hartford Whalers or Quebec Nordiques. These prices actually illustrate only that there are substantial differences in what franchises are worth. In fact, the Hartford owners are more likely to have overpaid than the Toronto owners.

---

[2] One potentially troubling feature of Table 5.3 is that actual profits average $4.7 million versus "normal" profits at $7.1 million, despite my claim to have employed conservative assumptions. The difference is due primarily to a significant number of teams moving into new facilities. Recalculating normal profits with existing facilities leaves actual and normal profits roughly equal.

Table 5.4

SELECTED FRANCHISE PRICES

Date of Transaction	Franchise	Expansion	Purchase Price (in millions)
1967	Oakland Seals	yes	$2.0
1967	Los Angeles Kings	yes	2.0
1967	Minnesota North Stars	yes	2.0
1967	Philadelphia Flyers	yes	2.0
1967	Pittsburgh Penguins	yes	2.0
1967	St. Louis Blues	yes	2.0
1970	Buffalo Sabres	yes	6.0
1970	Vancouver Canucks	yes	6.0
1972	Atlanta Flames	yes	6.0
1972	New York Islanders	yes	6.0
1974	Kansas City Scouts	yes	6.0
1974	Washington Capitals	yes	6.0
1974	California Golden Seals	no	6.0
1974	Vancouver Canucks	no	8.5
1977	St. Louis Blues	no	4.5
1977	Cleveland Barons	no	8.5
1979	Edmonton Oilers	yes	6.0
1979	Hartford Whalers	yes	6.0
1979	Quebec Nordiques	yes	6.0
1979	Winnipeg Jets	yes	6.0
1980	Atlanta Flames	no	20.0
1982	Detroit Red Wings	no	8.0
1982	Colorado Rockies	no	33.0
1983	St. Louis Blues	no	11.5
1984	Hartford Whalers	no	31.0
1988	Quebec Nordiques	no	14.8
1990	Minnesota North Stars	no	31.5
1991	San Jose Sharks	yes	50.0
1991	Pittsburgh Penguins	no	65.0
1992	Ottawa Senators	yes	50.0
1992	Tampa Bay Lightning	yes	50.0
1993	Mighty Ducks of Anaheim	yes	50.0
1994	Florida Panthers	yes	50.0
1994	Hartford Whalers	no	47.5
1994	Toronto Maple Leafs	no	109.0
1995	Quebec Nordiques	no	75.0
1995	Los Angeles Kings	no	113.3
1995	Winnipeg Jets	no	68.0

Table 5.5

FRANCHISE VALUES AND RETURNS FOR TEAMS THAT SOLD MULTIPLE TIMES

Franchise	Year of Purchase	Purchase Price	Implied Capital Gains
St. Louis Blues	1967	$2.0	
St. Louis Blues	1977	4.0	7.2%
St. Louis Blues	1983	11.5	19.2
Vancouver Canucks	1970	6.0	
Vancouver Canucks	1974	8.5	8.7
Oakland Seals	1967	2.0	
California Golden Seals [a]	1974	6.0	17.0
Cleveland Barons	1977	8.5	12.3
Atlanta Flames	1972	6.0	
Atlanta Flames	1980	20.0	16.2
Minnesota North Stars	1967	2.0	
Minnesota North Stars	1990	31.5	9.4 [b]
Pittsburgh Penguins	1967	2.0	15.6
Pittsburgh Penguins	1991	65.0	
Hartford Whalers	1979	6.0	
Hartford Whalers	1984	31.0	38.9
Hartford Whalers	1994	47.5	4.4
Quebec Nordiques	1979	6.0	
Quebec Nordiques	1988	14.8	10.6
Quebec Nordiques	1995	75.0	26.0
Winnipeg Jets	1979	6.0	16.4
Winnipeg Jets	1995	68.0	
Los Angeles Kings	1967	2.0	15.5
Los Angeles Kings	1995	113.3	

Capital Gains	1989-94	1985-94	1975-94
NHL Average	15.1%	13.9%	15.2%
Dow-Jones Industrial Average	8.1	12.5	9.3
Standard & Poors 500	6.8	11.0	9.7
Wilshire 5000	7.1	10.7	NA

[a] The Oakland Seals were renamed the California Seals and then moved to Cleveland and renamed the Barons.

[b] The actual return would appear to be 12.7 percent. However, this value would overstate the true return since the Cleveland Barons and Minnesota North stars merged in 1978. The stated return is based on the combined initial franchise fee of the Oakland Seals and the Minnesota North Stars in 1967.

Franchises with multiple reported sales since 1960 are listed in Table 5.5, and the franchise appreciation or implied capital gain is calculated. With fewer sales we have less information on the implied returns. Nevertheless, as in all other sports, it appears that the average capital gain exceeds 10 percent. Over the last 20 years, the average capital gain for an NHL franchise has been 15.2 percent a year, substantially exceeding the corresponding increase in any general stock price index. For example, the S&P 500 increased 9.7 percent a year over the same period. Thus, the NHL, like the other three leagues, has had an above-average appreciation in asset values.

How much do NHL owners make, considering both the capital gains and the operating returns? Capital gains have averaged 15.2 percent over the last 20 years. Operating income over the last 6 years has averaged $4 million. With an average franchise worth about $118 million we have an operating return of 3.4 percent. The yearly total return: 18.6 percent. In contrast, over the same period the yearly total return for the S&P 500 stocks was 15 percent. Given that small stocks average about a three percent higher return, the relevant average return would be 18 percent. On average, owning an NHL would have been a reasonable investment yielding a slightly above average rate of return.

While few tears need be shed for the financial plight of the owners, there are two mitigating factors. First, the 15.2 percent estimated capital gain contains more than the usual amount of uncertainty since it is based on relatively few franchise sales. The recorded sales have been primarily of weaker franchises where we expect to see relatively small capital gains.[3] Thus, the total percent is more likely to be understated than overstated. That weaker franchises sell more frequently is no surprise. An economist interprets their exit as evidence that the less efficient owner-managers are leaving the hockey industry. Nevertheless, if franchises like the Boston Bruins, Chicago Blackhawks, or Detroit Red Wings sell, we should expect to see a capital gain well in excess of 15.1 percent a year. Second, the 18.6 percent return is an average that includes

---

[3] Of the 16 sales of existing franchises, only two, Toronto and Los Angeles, were sales of financially strong franchises at the time.

a range from Hartford and Winnipeg (below 10 percent) to Boston, Chicago, and Detroit (over 25 percent). Some owners are not making a competitive return while others are doing extremely well—just like in every other league!

PROFITS VERSUS WINS—WHAT PRICE EGO?

For the NHL, like for the other leagues, it is interesting to compare the calculated NPVs with the actual sale prices. The data is presented in Table 5.6. As for other sports, I consider only sales since 1992 and adjust older prices upward by 9 percent a year to take into account both the real interest rate and the rate of inflation. Of the five franchises purchased since 1992, the purchase prices exceed the NPV by an average of $29 million. Once again, I interpret the difference as the amount an owner "overpaid" for the franchise—or how much an owner paid for the ego value of owning an NHL franchise. NHL owners on average have an ego value of $29 million. The amount owners have overpaid for the privilege of owning an NHL franchise is less than that paid for franchises in other leagues. It is not surprising that the ego gratification from owning an NFL franchise ($70 million) or an NBA franchise ($40 million) exceeds that from an NHL franchise.

Table 5.6

NPVs versus PRICES PAID
What Price Ego? or
How Much Have Owners "Overpaid" for an NHL Franchise?

Franchise	Purchase Price[a]	NPV	Purchase Price Minus NPV
Hartford Whalers	$48	$33	$15
Toronto Maple Leafs	109	108	1
Quebec Nordiques	75	33	42
Los Angeles Kings	113	67	46
Winnipeg Jets	68	25	43
Average	83	53	29

[a] Purchase price equals the actual sale price in the year of sale multiplied by 1.09 (for inflation and the real interest rate) for each year since the sale occurred.

Two points should be made on the NHL $29 million number. From a technical perspective one could ask if it makes sense to exclude the Ducks from the calculations. (The Duck's initiation fee was $55 million and the franchise is now worth about $233.) The answer is that the sale price dramatically understated the total start-up costs of a franchise. In addition, it appears that the Disney name also contributed to the profitability of the Ducks. If the Disney name helped convince potential ticket buyers that the Ducks were family entertainment and increased ticket sales, then the franchise value is due partly to the name Disney rather than exclusively to the letters "NHL." While Disney has reaped a large capital gain from the NHL, the NHL may have gained just as much from its association with Disney. If the Disney name nationwide helps to improve the NHL's image, then the Disney-NHL partnership is a win-win situation.

Second, Toronto's NPV and purchase price are virtually identical. This result also should not be surprising and represents a check on the reasonableness of the underlying assumptions. The Maple Leafs are a public corporation and presumably are valued accurately by the market. The similarity of the sale price and the NPV suggests that the NPV likely is a reasonably accurate measure.

THE 1994 NHL STRIKE—ARE HOCKEY OWNERS BONEHEADS OR VISIONARIES?

One aside before concluding: prior to the 1994 season, the owners locked out the players precipitating a strike. It is reasonable to ask what the 1994 hockey strike implies for franchise values and returns and whether the lockout/strike was justified or effective. Consider first where hockey lags furthest behind other sports—national television coverage and the resulting media money. The strike obviously did not help and clearly reduces the value of NHL telecasts. If nothing else, the tension between owners and the union and the potential for future work stoppages will make it more difficult for the NHL to secure a lucrative television deal in the future. Second, almost as important to the NHL is licensing money. In 1993-1994 approximately $1 billion of NHL licensed merchandise was sold, yielding the NHL about $20 million in total revenues or almost $0.8 million per team. While the numbers sound impressive, the NBA's licensing revenue is over 100 percent higher. The strike reduced licensing revenues drastically. While post-strike revenues have picked up, just this cost per team still is close to $0.5 million.

Perhaps the most serious cost of the strike, however, was an apparently non-economic cost: potentially serious damage to the NHL's reputation, which it had been working hard to improve. Fighting had been substantially reduced; Disney had signed on as an owner; and the NHL was coming off perhaps its most successful playoffs ever. The long-term damage to NPVs based in part on damaged reputation is impossible to quantify but hard to ignore. When NHL hockey resumed, attendance for some franchises was down substantially. In sum, the strike cost owners appreciable current and future revenues. Counting fixed costs and lost profits, the total cost to the owners is in the neighborhood of $120 million considering that about approximately 35 percent of the 1994-1995 season was lost. The only franchise with a short-run gain from the strike: Winnipeg! They likely lost less with only a partial season than they would have lost with a full season.

The lockout could have been a worthwhile move if it resulted in appreciable cost savings. However, any savings appear ephemeral at best. For example, one of the key points was whether players should be eligible for free agency at 30 rather than at 31 or 32. Given that relatively few NHL players are over age 30—and even fewer between 30 and 32—the potential savings are trivial. The NHL does have a real financial problem—the financial weakness of as many as 10 teams—even though league profits on average are healthy. If the lockout had been used to solve the NHL's financial problems it could have been a worthwhile move. But revenue sharing remains virtually non-existent and franchises like Edmonton and Hartford will continue to live on the financial edge. The lockout did not lower costs, the lockout did not serve as a vehicle to introduce substantial additional revenue sharing, and it did substantially depress revenues. Was the lockout a smart move? In retrospect, clearly not. All franchises (except Winnipeg) had lower profits or bigger losses in the 1994-1995 season than they would have had with a full season. Some weaker franchises' long-term survival was not enhanced by the strike. Perhaps most troubling to an economist who believes that individuals generally operate in their own self-interest, it is difficult to construct any scenario where the owners' bargaining position was consistent with both rationality and increasing their long-term profits.

CONCLUSION

In sum, what do we find in hockey? The richest clubs are in excellent financial shape. Some of the weak, however, may be heading toward the morgue, perhaps hastened by the strike. This is approximately the point that the NBA found itself in 1984 when they made a number of changes, including introducing a salary cap. The salary cap was one of the most contentious issue of the 1994 hockey strike. Unfortunately, the NHL missed the most important element introduced in the NBA in 1984 with the salary cap—cooperation between the owners and the union. Without cooperation, other institutional changes are pointless.

While the NHL has been profitable overall, there are a number of weak franchises and some franchises would appear to have questionable futures in their current locations. Before the residents of Winnipeg, Edmonton, or Hartford form a lynching party, let me emphasize that I am not recommending that teams leave those cities. I am stating only that with the current financial setup, the economics of the teams in those cities are tenuous at best. Any of those cities could make a substantial financial commitment to the local franchise, for example, in terms of subsidizing the development of a new arena. However, that would be a very high risk endeavor because (1) the population base is relatively small, (2) the current arena does not sell out, and (3) potential owners in cities like Cleveland, Minneapolis, Phoenix, Portland, and Nashville (with available arenas) may have much greater financial resources available to underwrite a hockey team.

Hockey also faces a problem that received greater emphasis in other chapters: a divergence of owner interests. Some have a greater interest in profits and others in wins. The Ducks and the Bruins appear interested primarily in profits while the Penguins and the Maple Leafs may be interested primarily in wins. This conflict underlies the owner-labor strife in all sports. In an owner's words, "We are united by our problems and divided by our solutions." Owners can agree only that players should be paid less and not how to split revenues to ensure the viability of small-market teams. NHL commissioner Gary Bettman and the NHL owners do not appear to be up to the challenge of reconciling conflicting owner interests where some clubs are extremely wealthy and others have only a marginal ability to make ends meet. Their 1994 lockout of the players does not lead me to positive predictions about their ability to handle this fundamentally much more difficult problem. Unfortunately, it is an issue that must be addressed before considering anything other than a stop-gap solution to the player relations problem.

Chapter 6

Competitive Balance — Does Big Spending or a Big Market Mean Winning Big?

"I believe there are certain things that cannot be bought: loyalty, friendship, health, love and an American League pennant."
—Edward Bennett Williams

"I have a lot of money to spend and not a lot of time, and I want a World Series ring." **—Gene Autry, owner, California Angels**

"We hope to bring a small degree of honor to Chicago, and a small degree of cash to ourselves."
—Bill Veeck, owner, Chicago White Sox

"We will scheme, connive, steal and do everything possible to win a pennant—except pay high salaries."
—Bill Veeck, owner, Chicago White Sox

"I gave Allen an unlimited budget and he exceeded it."
—Edward Bennett Williams, owner of the Washington Redskins, on coach George Allen

"The teams that win the most make the most money."
—Vince Lombardi, coach, Green Bay Packers

After considering revenues, costs, and profits in all four leagues, we can now address some general questions. For example, does a large-market guarantee a franchise substantial profits? Does a small-market relegate a team to financial mediocrity? Does big-time spending produce championships? Or do championships produce financial success? This chapter examines the relationships between market size, financial success, and on-the-field success and asks whether there are common themes across sports. A byproduct of this analysis: a ranking of franchise efficiency—which teams win at lowest cost.

All the relationships examined in this chapter are probabilistic rather than deterministic. That is, they hold on average and they hold only with some probability. Suppose you watch a baseball doubleheader. A lead-off hitter might get a total of 10 at-bats. To say that he is a .300 hitter does not mean he is going to get three hits today. He might be in a slump or he might go 2 for 5 each game. That he is a .300 hitter means that over the long haul he will average .300, some weeks higher and some lower. You should expect on average to see him get three hits, but you should not be surprised if he gets one or four. All relationships in this chapter hold in the same probabilistic way.

Do Large-Market Franchises Enjoy Greater Financial Success?

Success has two components: financial and on-the-field. Conventional wisdom states large-market franchises have a substantial financial edge and can use that edge to buy better players and win more games. We could measure the potential edge using 1994 profits, 1995 profits, average profits over the last five years, or "normal" profits. There are many ways the data can be configured—some might say tortured—and I do a lot of that in this chapter. Fortunately, the answers are substantially the same regardless of how you twist the numbers. For simplicity I generally focus on 1994 values (1995 profits for MLB and the NHL are distorted by strikes). In addition, to structure the results simply but dramatically, the format employed generally considers three groups of franchises: the six highest, the six lowest, and those in the middle.

More sophisticated statistical procedures yield the same results and offer no further insights.

Table 6.1 examines whether large-market teams have higher profits. The conclusion: except in football, large-market franchises have larger average profits than medium-market franchises which in turn generally have larger average profits than small-market franchises. That should come as no surprise. In each league except the NFL, teams from New York, Los Angeles, and Chicago consistently top the financial rankings. Conversely, teams

Table 6.1

DOES MARKET SIZE INFLUENCE PROFITS?
1994 Profits by Sport for Different Size Markets

	Baseball	Basketball	Football	Hockey
Average				
Large-Markets	12.7	8.7	5.0	10.6
Medium-Markets	2.9	4.7	5.5	5.4
Small-Markets	-1.0	5.4	2.5	-0.8
Maximum				
Large-Markets	23.6	33.4	10.8	20.6
Medium-Markets	15.4	22.0	24.0	14.8
Small-Markets	18.0	16.0	7.3	6.8
Minimum				
Large-Markets	4.0	-4.0	-2.4	0.5
Medium-Markets	-13.5	-1.5	-4.8	-3.6
Small-Markets	-20.6	-2.1	-3.5	-4.2

from Indianapolis, Buffalo, and Winnipeg, generally the smallest-market teams in the league, are at the bottom of the rankings. That the NFL is an exception also should be no surprise. Each NFL franchise receives almost $40 million from national television contracts, so small-market franchises like Green Bay and New Orleans are not at a discernible revenue disadvantage *vis-a-vis* New York or Los Angeles and franchises potentially are more mobile.

The results suggest that the conventional wisdom is accurate and large-market franchises average higher profits, but this relationship is not exact. Table 6.1 also presents the maximum and minimum profits for each market size. The high and low values suggest two conclusions. First, as the market size decreases, the maximum and minimum profits generally get smaller—consistent with small-market franchises operating at a financial disadvantage. For example, in the NBA the largest profit for a large-market franchise is $33.4 million (the New York Knicks) dropping to $22.0 million for a medium-market franchise (the Detroit Pistons) and to $16.0 million for a small-market franchise (the Utah Jazz). In MLB, the smallest large-market profit was $4.0 million (the California Angels) while the weakest medium-market franchise lost $13.5 million (the Detroit Tigers) and the worst small-market loss was $20.6 million (the Kansas City Royals). Again, the NFL is an exception with no relation between market size and profits. For the other three leagues, average profits decrease as market size decreases; the probability of losing money increases as market size falls; and the maximum profit possible also falls with shrinking market size.

Second, comparing the highs and lows with the averages suggests that size is not perfectly correlated with profits. For example, in MLB the highest profit small-market franchise made $18.0 million (the Baltimore Orioles) while the average large-market franchise made a profit of $12.7 million and the worst large-market profit was just $4.0 million (the California Angels). The conclusion: size does work against franchises in cities like Kansas City, Milwaukee, Minneapolis, and Pittsburgh. A small market makes it easier to lose money. However, some small-market franchises are exceptions to the rule and thrive despite their market size.

Consider two exceptions. The small-market Colorado Rockies had a 1994 profit of $17.9 million and the small-market Baltimore Orioles had a profit of $18.0 million.[1] In contrast to the Rockies and Orioles, the large-market California Angels could manage a

---

[1] Some might argue that Baltimore is not a small-market franchise. Based simply on the population numbers however, for MLB Baltimore is a small-market franchise. Lending support to its small-market appellation is Baltimore's lack of major league basketball or hockey franchises and no recent football franchise. In addition, Baltimore would have been profitable even without Washington D.C. nearby, and the Rockies' numbers suggest they will be highly profitable even when the novelty wears off.

profit of only $4.0 million. The Angels were 21st out of 28 MLB franchises in average attendance while the Rockies were first and the Orioles were fourth. This comparison indicates that an MLB franchise with good marketing and financial management can generate substantial profits even in a small market. With MLB's current system of free agency and revenue sharing, large-market teams like the Angels can be set on autopilot and still generate a modest profit. Medium-market and small-market franchises do not have that luxury. Managerial neglect or turmoil, characterizing the franchises in Detroit, Kansas City, and Pittsburgh, may easily result in sizable losses. In this respect, MLB is just like any other industry and an MLB franchise is just like any other firm. The industry on average makes a profit. An individual firm may have a profit or loss, in part depending on the wisdom and competence of its management. When there is executive turnover or indecision, losses are frequently close behind. In addition, losses often precede executive turmoil and a change in management or ownership. When a firm begins to face financial difficulty, another ownership or management group typically enters—or the firm fades into the sunset. These rules of economics apply to MLB just as surely as they apply to IBM or the corner grocery.

In the NBA the distinction between the large-market and small-market extremes is even more striking. The Utah Jazz, with the smallest NBA market, made a profit of $16.0 million, thanks primarily to its large gate revenues. In contrast, the large-market Los Angeles Clippers did not regularly sell out and lost $4.0 million. None of the six small-market NBA franchises lost this much money. While large-market NBA teams do average higher profits, small-market franchises can make a reasonable profit when well managed, and poorly managed large-market franchises are quite capable of losing money.

The NFL has the weakest connection between market size and profits. Of the large-market franchises, the Raiders (in LA) did the worst, losing $2.4 million. All the small-market franchises did better except the Indianapolis Colts; small-market franchises Buffalo, Kansas City, and Cincinnati earned profits of at least $7.0 million. Except for Green Bay, the Buffalo Bills have the smallest market in the NFL yet they consistently sell out, even in abominable weather conditions. Their profits depend on their ability to sell out. In Los Angeles, the Raiders did not match the attendance numbers even for Green Bay, and the Raiders' loss reflects their inability to sell out. The large-market New York Jets and New England Patriots also have struggled to break even and to sell out. The Patriots' story is particularly bizarre. A former owner moved the Patriots from Boston to the least expensive piece of real estate he could find within 75 miles of Boston, built the cheapest stadium possible, made automotive history with the traffic jams after the Patriots' games, and then wondered why his team received little fan support and lost money! In the NFL, small size does not preclude large profits. The most important factor determining profit in the NFL may be the owner's goal: valuing profits versus victories—although managerial competence is also important. The NFL's revenue sharing process effectively ensures market size does not determine profits.

Only in the NHL does a small market appear to be the kiss of death and a large market appear to guarantee profits. Among the large-market franchises, the Islanders and the Devils have the lowest profits, each close to $1 million. In contrast, among the small-market teams, only Ottawa made more than a trivial profit at $6.8 million. Whether that profit can be maintained once the novelty of the expansion Senators wears off remains open to debate. The evidence from the other small-market teams is not reassuring. Among the non-expansion small-market franchises, only Calgary had a profit, and a tenuous profit at that—less than $1 million, due solely to the Flames' play-off performance. Unlike other leagues, the NHL now has a *de facto* rule: small-market franchises lose money, others do not. No small market NHL franchise is the picture of financial health, like the Baltimore Orioles, Utah Jazz, or Buffalo Bills. The NHL is the only league with a real question about the survivability of the small-market franchises.

For all four leagues, the most profitable small-market franchise does better than the average large-market franchise. The averages are important, and the averages imply that it is easier to make money—or harder to lose money—in a large market. But the exceptions are important. Excluding the NHL, the highs and lows in each league indicate that market size alone does not guarantee financial success or ensure financial ruin. A well-run small-market franchise can be much more profitable than a mediocre or poorly-run large-market franchise. Market size plays a role in influencing financial success, but for most leagues it is but a minor role.

DO LARGE-MARKET FRANCHISES ENJOY GREATER ON-THE-FIELD SUCCESS?

Table 6.1 asked whether size influences profit. The answer was a resounding "yes" for all leagues but the NFL, although the impact is small and holds only on average. Table 6.2 focuses on the other component of success: does market size influence on-the-field success? The answer is an equally resounding "no!" You may find this result counterintuitive. Large market teams have higher profits. Do they buy—or at least attempt to buy—victories and championships? Some large-market owners like Steinbrenner (the New York Yankees) and DeBartolo (the San Francisco 49ers) do

Table 6.2

DOES MARKET SIZE INFLUENCE WINS?
1994 Wins by Sport for Different Size Markets

	Baseball	Basketball	Football 1990-94	Football 1994	Hockey
Average					
Large-Markets	56.8	41.7	45.3	8.9	38.2
Medium-Markets	56.6	38.6	42.9	8.7	39.9
Small-Markets	58.7	45.7	43.0	7.9	29.9
Maximum					
Large-Markets	70	57	69	16	52
Medium-Markets	74	63	64	13	46
Small-Markets	66	55	69	11	43
Minimum					
Large-Markets	47	25	23	4	27
Medium-Markets	47	13	25	2	30
Small-Markets	53	28	25	3	14

try to buy wins. However, the evidence suggests that large-market teams on average are unsuccessful in their attempted purchases. You can go back and cite anecdotal evidence about the success of large-market teams. For example, consider New York City teams in 1994. The Rangers won the Stanley Cup; the Knicks reached the NBA finals; the Yankees led the AL East at the time of the baseball strike; and the Giants just missed the NFL play offs. While citing anecdotal evidence, you should consider the lack of success of the Islanders, the Devils, the Nets, the Mets, and the Jets. On average, New York City teams were just that—about average.

Only in the NFL does there appear to be any evidence of a relationship between size and wins, and even that is very weak.[2] Since the NFL results differ from the other three leagues and the NFL plays substantially fewer games, NFL victories for both 1994 and the last five years are included in the table. In all other leagues, large-market teams average no more wins than other teams. In MLB and in the NBA, small-market teams actually averaged more wins than large-market teams. In terms of on-the-field success, all leagues appear to have taken steps that induce on-the-field parity even in the face of financial disparities. Small-market franchises have not been at a competitive disadvantage over the last year or over the last five years, despite the contentions of some owners, especially in baseball. On average, teams like the Brewers and the Pirates have won more games than the Yankees and the Mets!

Statisticians can torture data with much greater precision than done in Tables 6.1 and 6.2. For example, statisticians can ask questions like, "as the city size increases by 100,000 how much does that add to the bottom line of a franchise, or what is the correlation between market size and wins?" A baseball equivalent would be to ask what the relationship is between team batting average and wins. How many more games should we expect a team to win if its batting average increased from .260 to .270 and everything else remained constant?

---

[2] One modification could be employed for hockey. Since NHL standings are kept by points rather than by wins (two points for a win, one for a tie), it would be reasonable to record points. However, to make the NHL's results comparable to the other leagues', I use wins rather than points. The results using points are virtually identical.

Using regression analysis, relatively high-tech data torturing, how does size influence profits and wins? Regression has the advantage of allowing us to quantify a relationship. That is, regression analysis allows us to calculate on average how much increasing market size will add to franchise profits.[3] Regression indicates that size does not influence victories but does affect profits. The numbers suggest that for each additional person in a metropolitan area, profits of an MLB franchise will rise $0.82, profits of an NBA franchise will increase $0.53, and profits of an NHL franchise will go up $0.40. Profits of an NFL franchise show no appreciable change, a result not surprising given the numbers in Table 6.1. All numbers represent league averages.

What do these numbers imply? For MLB, each additional person in a metropolitan area increases profits of the typical MLB franchise by $0.82. While this value is only an estimate and holds only on average, it is revealing. The $0.82 value suggests, for example, what would happen to franchise profits if you moved a franchise from Pittsburgh to Washington and if you kept all other factors constant, e.g., same stadium lease, same win-loss record, some management, etc. Given Washington's population of 3.9 million and Pittsburgh's population of 2.4 million, we should expect profits to increase by $1.25 million. To put that in context, Pittsburgh's 1994 loss was $4.1 million. Thus, a move to D.C. would still leave the Pirates with a loss. Given the Pirates's loss, the only cities that could financially support the Pirates are New York, Los Angeles, and Chicago. Simply based on city size, there may be nowhere the Pirates could go that would give them a profit if all other factors remained the same. To bring the Pirates back to profitability will require something else: either a change in management, a change in the stadium lease, a change in marketing, etc. Consider an even more extreme example: the Kansas City Royals and their $20.6 million loss. Just based on population, they would

---

[3] The logic underlying regression analysis is simple. Think of a graph with market size on the horizontal axis and profits on the vertical axis. For each team in a league, record where its size and profits place it on this graph. In MLB, for example, you have 28 teams and thus 28 points on this graph. Next, you want to draw a straight line on that graph that approximately characterizes the scatter of points, combinations of size and profits, you have recorded. Regression analysis produces the best possible line.

need a metropolitan population of about 27 million to bail them out of their hole. The moral: in MLB there is a relationship between size and profits but small-market franchises cannot use that as an excuse for poor profit performance. The relationship is not strong enough to save—or doom—any franchise.

Switching to the NBA, Indiana is the only small-market franchise with a 1994 loss. San Diego is the largest city without a franchise, having a population of about 2.5 million. Would a move to San Diego make the Pacers profitable, again if ownership, stadium arrangements, win-loss records, etc. remain constant? The differential in city size alone would increase the Pacers' profits by only $0.6 million ($0.53 per person times about 1.1 million people). They still would be losing money; the greater city size would not make the franchise profitable. In the NBA or in MLB other factors, especially stadium arrangements, have a much greater impact on franchise profits than does market size. Market size has a statistically significant impact on profits. However, the size of the relationship is so small that a move to a larger city by itself is unlikely to pay an appreciable dividend.[4]

The NHL also has a statistically significant relationship between profits and market size. Like in the NBA the impact is relatively small. Each additional person adds approximately $0.40 in profit. What would happen if the Winnipeg Jets were to move to Cleveland or Houston, for example, based on the population differences only? The Jets' 1994 loss would be reduced from $4.1 million to $3.3 million with a move to Cleveland and to $2.9 million with a move to Houston. The larger market would not make the Jets profitable. Something else must change as well. For the NHL, like the other leagues, there is some uncertainty associated with the precise numbers. For example, maybe each additional person adds $.30 or $.50 in profit. The results remain unchanged. For the move from Winnipeg to Houston to lead to profits in Houston, each additional person would have to add $1.40 in profits. Such a result is inconsistent with the data. Thus, the NHL results strongly imply that a franchise relocation to a

---

[4] A move to New York City would be an exception that I will cover in more detail in Chapter 10.

larger city is unlikely to be a big moneymaker unless the ownership changes or stadium arrangements change dramatically. Recent and pending NHL franchise shifts all involve lucrative stadium arrangements.

Market size has a small but statistically significant impact on profits. What about its impact on victories? Regression analysis implies that market size has no impact on wins in any league including the NFL. A team in New York City will win no more games on average than a team in Winnipeg, Buffalo, or Indianapolis, as counterintuitive as that may at first appear. The team in New York City might receive more press coverage when it wins, but on average it wins no more. All leagues have taken steps to ensure parity. The lack of a relationship between wins and market size indicates that those steps have been successful. Gone are the days when a team like Kansas City Athletics served as a major league farm team for the New York Yankees—as they effectively did from the late 1950s through the early 1960s.

The general conclusion on market size and performance: on average bigger means just slightly better as far as profits are concerned; bigger does not guarantee better and smaller does not ensure a loss. Bigger means absolutely nothing as far as wins are concerned. All leagues have parity with respect to market size.

IS THERE A RELATIONSHIP BETWEEN ON-THE-FIELD SUCCESS AND FINANCIAL SUCCESS?

If market size influences profits but not victories, the obvious question is: what relationship exists between profits and wins or between on-the-field success and financial success? To answer this question, it is useful to focus on revenues and costs, separately. The theory is straightforward. You should expect an increase in costs to increase the probability of winning. Owners like Steinbrenner, Turner, DeBartolo, and Jerry Jones appear willing to incur substantial costs to field a championship team. In addition, you should expect a winning team to generate additional revenue. More wins lead to more interest and excitement about the team and thus more revenues, or so the theory goes. Prior statistical evidence also suggests that teams are more likely to raise their ticket prices when they win.

To examine whether there is a relationship between wins and profits, Table 6.3 follows the procedure of Tables 6.1 and 6.2 but ranks teams not by market size but by wins: the top six, the bottom six, and all others. The "winners" have larger profits in all leagues,

Table 6.3

DOES WINNING LEAD TO PROFITS?
1994 Profits by Team Records

	Baseball	Basketball	Football	Hockey
Average				
Winners	6.5	11.0	11.0	6.6
Mediocre	2.6	3.9	3.3	6.3
Losers	4.0	5.3	1.9	3.2
Maximum				
Winners	23.6	33.4	24.0	17.8
Mediocre	22.6	16.0	10.9	20.6
Losers	17.6	22.0	7.0	14.4
Minimum				
Winners	-11.1	0.0	3.3	-2.8
Mediocre	-20.6	-4.0	-3.5	-3.6
Losers	-10.5	-1.6	-4.8	-4.2

although the "losers" do not always have the smallest profits. In MLB winners averaged $6.5 million in profits while other teams averaged just over $3 million. In the NBA and the NFL the differences are even more dramatic. The winners averaged $11.0 million in profits in both leagues and other teams averaged about $4.5 million in the NBA and only $3.0 million in the NFL. In the NHL there is a smaller difference between the winners and the "mediocre" with the winners averaging $6.6 million and the mediocre averaging $6.3 million. But there is a big cost to losing, in particular, a big cost to not making the NHL playoffs, with the losers averaging profits of only $3.2 million.

These results strongly suggest that there is a financial gain from winning. Even if winning costs money, on average there is a profit payoff. However, the relationship between wins and profits is not etched in stone, and there are exceptions to the general rule. For example, in MLB the 1994 Cincinnati Reds were successful on the field but succeeded in losing $11.1 million. The Chicago Cubs maintained their position of lovable losers, having the second-worst record in the NL but making a $17.9 million profit. The worst record belonged to the San Diego Padres, in part by their owner's choice, yet they also made a profit. In the NBA, Detroit has fallen precipitously from its NBA championship level and in 1994 was an on-the-court loser, but not in the financial column where it checked in with a profit of $22.0 million. In contrast, the Atlanta Hawks had one of the best records in the NBA, yet just broke even. In the NFL the San Diego Chargers reached the 1995 Super Bowl and earned a profit of $3.3 million while the Cincinnati Bengals vied for the worst NFL record yet still achieved profits of $7.0 million. Finally, in the NHL, the Buffalo Sabres cracked the ranks of the winners but lost $2.8 million while the Mighty Ducks of Anaheim were mighty profitable but not very victorious. The moral of the story: winners on average have greater profits than other teams. However, winning does not guarantee profits nor does losing ensure financial mediocrity.

The relationship between winning and profits is tenuous because a sports franchise needs two types of management: on-the-field and off-the-field. Success in one need not translate into success in the other. Typically different management teams are responsible for the two areas. Thus teams that lose consistently still may be financially well-managed. Alternately, teams that have hired a skilled coaching staff may have weak financial management. In addition, a team that is mediocre on-the-field may be deliberately mediocre because the owner's goal may be to maximize profits rather than to contend for championships.

More sophisticated statistical tools like regression analysis also can be applied to the relationship between profits and victories. For MLB, regression analysis cannot identify any statistically significant relationship between winning and profit. This result should not be surprising given that even the most successful MLB teams lose almost 40 percent of the time. In addition, some losing teams, like the Mets, make substantial profits while some winning teams, like the Reds, lose money. For the other three leagues, regression analysis does find that another win means more profit. How much more? In the NBA, profits increase by $740,000 with each win; in the NFL, it is $843,000; and in the NHL, the increase is $273,000. Once again, these numbers must be interpreted with care. They indicate the average relationship for all teams in the league and need not hold precisely for any individual team; many factors influence profits and team records are but one. Nevertheless, the numbers are highly suggestive.

When examining the relationship between market size and profits, I concluded that while a relationship exists, its effect is so small that few franchise shifts would be recommended based solely on shifting to a larger market for greater profits. The relationship between profits and wins, however, is a very different story. Consider the NBA. With each win, profits on average increase by $740,000. Suppose Glenn Robinson's addition to the Milwaukee Bucks moves them from 20 to 35 wins, a big improvement but still perhaps not good enough to make the playoffs. This relationship suggests that we should expect the Bucks' profits to increase by about $11 million. If Dallas were to increase their league-low victory total from 13 to 35, their profits could increase by $16 million. In contrast, the Los Angeles Lakers' slide from 63 wins in 1990 to 33 in 1994 could have cost them $22 million in profit. The implication: changing on-the-field success may have a *dramatic* impact on a franchise's profitability.

In the NFL, the estimated increase in profit per game is even larger than in the NBA at $843,000. However, its impact is smaller because there are fewer games played. Again, a couple of examples can illustrate the relationship. In 1994 the New England Patriots made the play-offs and made a small profit as well. Without their improved record, from five wins to ten, the Patriots would have had a loss. The Rams with their move to St. Louis will dramatically increase profits because of the guarantees offered by St. Louis. However, the Rams' profits in L.A. were $5.2 million and could have been $7.7 just by playing .500 ball. From 1993 to 1994 the Buffalo Bills' wins decreased from fourteen to seven. That could have cost the Bills $5.9 million.

An NHL victory is associated with an increase in profits of $273,000. Nevertheless, plausible changes in victories can produce substantial changes in profits. For example, if Ottawa were to increase its wins from a league-low 14 to Tampa Bay's level of 30 we should expect that the Senators' profits would increase by $4.4 million. The Boston Bruins victory total dropped from 51 in 1993 to 42 in 1994. The expected profits lost: $2.5 million. In contrast, the New York Rangers improvement from 34 to 52 wins could have increased their profits by almost $5 million. The small-market Canadian teams are particularly interesting. Calgary made a small profit and won 42 games. Edmonton, Quebec, and Winnipeg won 34 or fewer games. If any had won 40, the numbers suggest that they would have made money rather than losing money. The Winnipeg Jets' record dropped from 40 wins in 1992-1993 to 24 in 1993-1994. Had they maintained their prior performance, they might have made a small profit rather than a $4.4 loss.

Table 6.4

CAN YOU BUY VICTORY?
1994 Records by Team Costs

	Baseball	Basketball	Football	Hockey
Average				
High-Cost	61.1	48.0	9.5	41.8
Medium-Cost	56.3	42.5	8.6	39.1
Low-Cost	54.8	28.8	7.2	33.4
Maximum				
High-Cost	70	57	16	52
Medium-Cost	67	58	13	47
Low-Cost	74	63	15	42
Minimum				
High-Cost	53	33	3	27
Medium-Cost	49	20	2	27
Low-Cost	47	13	3	24

CAN YOU BUY A WIN? OR HOW MUCH DOES A LOSS COST?

If profits in part depend on wins, then the next logical question is, can you buy victory? Table 6.4 begins to answer this question, using a format similar to that employed in prior tables. Clubs are divided into three categories, the six highest costs, the six lowest costs, and all others. For each category in each league, the table presents the average number of wins as well as the maximum and minimum. The conclusion: Yes, you can buy victory! On average, high-cost teams win more games than the medium-cost teams which in turn win more games than low-cost teams. However, this relationship is not exact. There are examples of high-cost teams that have failed miserably, for example the Los Angeles Lakers won only 33 of 82 games in 1993-1994 yet had the highest costs in the NBA. In MLB, the Detroit Tigers are a high-cost team but finished last in the AL East. There also are examples of low-cost teams that led their league. The Montreal Expos had the best record in baseball in 1994 and the Seattle Sonics the best record in the NBA in 1993-1994, yet both rank among the low-cost clubs. There are exceptions to the rule that higher expenses lead to more wins. Later in the chapter we will come back to these rankings in more detail. For now, the point is simply that higher costs on average are associated with more wins.

If increasing costs lead to more wins, then you might surmise that winning also generates more revenues—and that losing costs money. Considerable anecdotal evidence suggests that fans love a winner and avoid a loser like the plague. In the NBA, historically the Los Angeles Lakers have been winners and have drawn tremendous crowds, including the Hollywood elite. Their cross-town rivals, the Clippers have never been successful, fashionable, or had appreciable revenue. In recent years, the Lakers have not been as successful, failing to reach the play-offs in 1994, and some empty seats now are visible where the glitterati once sat. In the NFL, the New Orleans Saints for years languished among the dregs. The Saints played in a virtually empty dome with many present wearing paper bags over their heads (the "Aints"). The team's performance was abysmal and fans were almost nonexistent. However, the stadium was packed when the Saints made the playoffs in

1987. Table 6.5 examines whether the data is consistent with the "fans-love-a-winner" argument. Teams are divided into the six biggest winners, the six biggest losers, and all other franchises. For

Table 6.5

DOES WINNING GENERATE REVENUES?
1994 Total Revenues by Team Records

	Baseball	Basketball	Football	Hockey
Average				
Winners	68.3	48.4	75.6	39.5
Mediocre	63.0	40.8	66.2	33.9
Losers	56.0	37.0	63.6	27.1
Maximum				
Winners	100.7	77.5	94.8	52.6
Mediocre	84.3	59.9	73.8	48.1
Losers	75.1	56.7	65.5	40.7
Minimum				
Winners	45.2	36.8	64.8	27.8
Mediocre	41.6	30.9	59.3	23.5
Losers	40.9	28.3	61.1	17.9

each league and each group the table presents the average, maximum, and minimum franchise revenues. In every case, the winners have the highest revenues and the losers the lowest. While it's unlikely that you needed much statistical evidence to convince you that winners generate more revenues, Table 6.5 documents that relationship nonetheless. Once again, there are conspicuous exceptions to this rule. Some franchises have won and still have not generated large revenues. For example, in 1993-1994 the Atlanta Hawks had one of the best regular season NBA records but revenues substantially below average (although those revenues may be understated due to media arrangements between Turner's Hawks and Turner's WTBS). In the NHL the 1993-1994 New Jersey Devils were second only to the New York Rangers in regular season wins and the Buffalo Sabres were close behind, but both also had revenues well below the league average. Nevertheless, winning generally begets revenues.

Table 6.4 examined the relationship between costs and wins. The conclusion: you could buy victory. Table 6.5 examined the relationship between wins and revenues. The conclusion: wins mean revenues. What happens when we combine these two? Table 6.6 addresses this issue. If I can buy a victory, then you will end up with a loss. So how much will my purchase cost you in lost revenues?

Table 6.6

HOW EXPENSIVE IS IT TO BUY A WIN?
One More Win Would Cost:
(in hundreds of thousands of dollars)

Baseball	Basketball	Football	Hockey
$1,898	$653	$2,801	$922

How Much Revenue Do You Forfeit with a Loss?
One Additional Loss Would Decrease Revenues by:
(all numbers in thousands)

Baseball	Basketball	Football	Hockey
$622	$432	$1,083	$657

To answer that, I employ regression analysis to obtain the most precise estimates possible of the linkage between costs and wins and then between wins and revenues. The first part of Table 6.6 presents estimates of how expensive it is to buy a win. That is, how much would it cost to win one more game? The cost is lowest in the NBA at $653,000 while in the NHL it is $922,000. In MLB to win one more game would cost almost $1.9 million while it costs $2.8 million in the NFL.[5] The relative magnitudes of these numbers should not be a surprise. There is relatively little money

---

[5] The presentation here assumes all relationships are linear. For example, in the NFL one more win costs $2.8 million regardless of whether the franchise would otherwise have won 2 or 14 games. This assumption greatly simplifies the analysis and dropping it does not change any statistical results.

in the NHL in comparison to other sports. Thus, the cost of a win should be relatively low. The low value for the NBA reflects basketball's smaller squad size. The relatively high cost of a win in baseball initially may be a surprise. MLB plays 162 games. Who would pay $1.9 million to win 83 games rather than 82? However, MLB has the lowest winning percentage for its champion. The best team in baseball typically wins only about 60 percent of its games, while the best team in the other three leagues generally wins at least 70 to 75 percent of the time. There is a greater random component in baseball. Thus, to be sure to get that win, you need to spend more money to overcome the innate randomness. In contrast, the NFL's high cost of one more victory is no surprise given the limited number of games played. With fewer games, each win takes on added importance. In baseball, it's uncommon for a team to miss the play-offs by one game and unusual to have a playoff with a regular season tie. In contrast, the NFL uses a detailed list of tiebreakers. Perhaps the most instructive way of interpreting that $2.8 million is to ask how much would Al Davis or Jerry Jones be willing to pay for one more victory? (In 1994 Davis's Raiders missed the play-offs due to a tiebreaker while Jones's Cowboys came up one game short of the Super Bowl.)

The second half of Table 6.6 presents the answer to a related question: how much revenue do you forfeit with a loss? Again based on regression analysis, the results for all leagues suggest that a franchise sacrifices appreciable revenue with each loss. A loss is least expensive in the NBA, with lost revenue of $432,000, and most expensive in the NFL, costing over $1 million. The cost in MLB is $622,000 and in the NHL $657,000. These numbers suggest a measure of how much fans love winners. For example, in baseball, as a team moves from a mediocre 81 wins up to a pennant-contending 95 wins, their revenues on average would increase by over $9 million. These numbers suggest that there is a tremendous financial pressure to win in all leagues.

The magnitudes of the costs and revenues in Table 6.6 appear plausible. The NBA and the NHL trail in terms of total revenues entering league coffers; so we should expect the revenues associated with a victory to be smaller. There is less gain from winning and less cost to losing in the NBA than in the NHL, as expected given the NHL has virtually no revenue sharing—a topic covered in detail in the next chapter. NBA revenue sharing in part insulates clubs from fluctuations in revenue. The NFL has the highest revenue gained from a victory, as expected given the large revenues generated in the NFL and the limited number of games played. You might have guessed that the revenue forfeited with a loss would be even greater than the estimated $1.1 million. The reason this number is not much higher is due to revenue sharing. That is, most NFL money comes from national television contracts and is split evenly. The Cincinnati Bengals and the Tampa Bay Buccaneers receive as much as the San Francisco 49ers or Miami Dolphins. Losing another game does not cost a team any TV money.

Looking at the complete results of Table 6.6, the cost of buying a win varies substantially by sport, from $2.8 million in the NFL to $0.65 million in the NBA. The revenue forfeited with a loss also varies but somewhat less, from the NFL's $1.1 million to

Table 6.7

FINANCIAL STANDINGS—MLB

Cost per Victory
(all numbers in hundreds of thousands)

American League Team	1994 Cost	1995 Cost	National League Team	1994 Cost	1995 Cost
Boston	$538	$577	Montreal	$390	$506
Cleveland	643	582	San Diego	542	683
Milwaukee	666	609	Florida	604	685
California	681	656	Cincinnati	608	695
Kansas City	699	707	Colorado	611	704
Seattle	717	720	Houston	651	707
Texas	728	750	Pittsburgh	688	714
Minnesota	753	845	Los Angeles	695	719
Oakland	767	866	New York	701	726
Baltimore	787	896	Chicago	747	734
New York	799	918	Atlanta	751	744
Chicago	805	919	Philadelphia	804	751
Detroit	870	965	St. Louis	807	837
Toronto	875	1,277	San Francisco	847	852

$0.43 million in the NBA. The general moral: when a George Steinbrenner in MLB spends an extra $1.9 million to buy one more victory, another owner is going to pick up a loss—and is going to drop another $0.62 million in revenues to boot. These numbers are very important in terms of the interrelationships between owners as will be shown in the next chapter.

THE FINANCIAL SCORECARD—WHO WINS AT LOWEST COST?

In this chapter I have focused on *averages.* For example, what relationship exists between average market size and average franchise profits? From the perspective of keeping score, one set of *individual* team numbers is very interesting. A newspaper's sports section typically ranks teams based on their won-loss records. When examining team finances, however, it is more useful to rank teams based on their financial efficiency. In other words, what is their cost per victory rather than their number of victories? Teams that have the lowest cost per victory deserve to be labeled the most efficient. Tables 6.7 through 6.10 rank the teams in each league based on their financial efficiency or cost per win in 1994.[6]

Table 6.7 presents the 1994 and 1995 MLB rankings. The Cleveland Indians led the American League at a cost of $538,000 per victory in 1994 while the Boston Red Sox edged Cleveland for the low cost in 1995 at $577,000 per victory. (The numbers in the tables consider only regular season performances. Including playoff games does not appreciably change the numbers although it does move Cleveland into first places in 1995.) I first looked at these numbers after the 1994 season, and the Indians' first place finish took me completely by surprise. In retrospect, I should not have been surprised. In 1994 Cleveland had the third best record in the AL and had a young team with relatively low salaries and low cost. After the Indians success in 1995, their high ranking should surprise no one. The Red Sox were number two in 1995, based both on their improved record as well as their lower costs— relative to 1994. Milwaukee and California also had low costs per

---

[6] In baseball, an additional adjustment was made, converting the number of wins into their full season equivalent. For example, in the strike-shortened 1994 season the Cleveland Indians won 66 games and lost 47. Their .584 winning percentage would imply 95 wins (actually, 94.6) in a regular 162 game season.

victory in both years, ranking third and fourth in 1995. They got their rankings by following a dramatically different strategy than Cleveland and Boston. Both simply cut costs, not always with regard to the impact on wins.

In the NL, the Montreal Expos led the league in 1994 and 1995, with a cost per victory of $390,000 in 1994 and $506,000 in 1995. Montreal's success also should be no surprise, having led the NL in victories in 1994 and consistently having one of the lowest payrolls in MLB. Montreal has the reputation as one of the best-run franchises in baseball. The numbers in Table 6.7 support that reputation. San Diego and Florida ranked second and third in both years. San Diego's second place finish suggests that cutting payroll may be an efficient move for other franchises, as long as the owner is unconcerned about on-the-field performance. Florida had a high rank largely because they were an expansion franchise with relatively young players and thus a low payroll. (Looking at Colorado's financial numbers indicates that they are no longer an expansion franchise.)

The financial underachievers? No surprises here: Detroit, Toronto, and San Francisco were the worst with large payrolls and mediocre performances. How about other playoff teams? The three 1994 AL division leaders were singularly undistinguished when looking at their cost per victory. The Yankees had the best record in the AL, but with their high costs, they were in the middle of the financial-efficiency pack. The White Sox also were a relatively high-cost team and finished fourth in the AL in terms of cost-per-victory, trailing even the California Angels, the worst team in the AL based on won-loss record. The Texas Rangers led the AL West but finished close to the bottom of the financial rankings. They were a high-cost club with a record substantially below .500. Besides Montreal, the other two 1994 NL division leaders were Cincinnati and Los Angeles. Neither ranked highly here. High costs and a mediocre record put the Dodgers close to the bottom of these rankings. In the NL, only San Francisco was substantially worse than the Dodgers.

Of the 1995 playoff teams, while Boston and Cleveland led the AL, Seattle and New York were also-rans. The Yankees would have had to win 125 games to equal the cost per victory of the Red Sox or the Indians. All the 1995 NL playoff teams were ranked in the middle. Based on regular season performances, there was no substantive difference among them. However, the Atlanta Braves' ranking deserves an additional comment. Adding in their playoff victories, the Braves would have moved into second place behind Montreal. Thus, the Braves low ranking should not be compared with the Yankees. Both have relatively high costs and made the playoffs, but the Braves had a lot more wins while the Yankees had a lot more costs.

Table 6.8 presents the 1994 NBA standings.[7] Atlanta led the Eastern Conference and Seattle led the Western. The Atlanta Hawks tied the New York Knicks for the regular season lead in victories and had slightly below average costs. The Chicago Bulls

Table 6.8

FINANCIAL STANDINGS—NBA
1994 Cost per Victory

Eastern Conference		Western Conference	
Team	Cost	Team	Cost
Atlanta	$698	Seattle	$503
Chicago	702	Houston	569
Indiana	702	Utah	642
Orlando	770	San Antonio	656
New York	774	Phoenix	746
Miami	814	Golden State	780
New Jersey	840	Denver	793
Charlotte	841	Portland	881
Cleveland	902	Sacramento	1,132
Boston	1,194	LA Lakers	1,348
Philadelphia	1,284	LA Clippers	1,393
Washington	1,338	Minnesota	1,565
Milwaukee	1,565	Dallas	2,238
Detroit	1,735		

[7] Some 1995 costs were still unavailable at press time.

Table 6.9

FINANCIAL STANDINGS—NFL
Cost per Victory
(in hundreds of thousands of dollars)

1994		1990-94	
AFC Team	**Cost**	**AFC Team**	**Cost**
Pittsburgh	$4,238	Buffalo	$3,919
San Diego	4,923	Pittsburgh	4,151
Cleveland	4,923	Kansas City	4,190
Miami	6,000	LA Raiders	5,012
New England	6,540	Miami	5,251
Kansas City	6,944	Houston	5,308
LA Raiders	7,211	Denver	5,370
Indianapolis	7,850	NY Jets	5,522
Denver	7,957	San Diego	5,714
Buffalo	8,800	Cleveland	7,563
NY Jets	10,650	Indianapolis	8,638
Seattle	11,117	Seattle	8,638
Cincinnati	18,067	Cincinnati	9,184
Houston	32,150	New England	9,846
NFC Team		**NFC Team**	
San Francisco	4,269	Dallas	4,372
Dallas	5,446	San Francisco	4,610
Minnesota	5,930	NY Giants	5,221
Chicago	6,230	Minnesota	5,239
Detroit	6,360	Chicago	5,285
Green Bay	6,390	Philadelphia	5,388
NY Giants	6,978	Detroit	5,500
Arizona	8,438	Washington	5,772
Atlanta	8,857	GreenBay	6,408
Philadelphia	9,000	New Orleans	7,244
New Orleans	9,200	Atlanta	7,339
Tampa Bay	9,483	Arizona	8,807
LA Rams	14,450	Tampa Bay	9,092
Washington	23,400	LA Rams	10,317

and Indiana Pacers were just a step below Atlanta. Chicago's costs were slightly above average but they had the third best record in the East. Indiana was not quite as successful but had substantially lower cost. The East Conference champion Knicks are in the middle of the financial rankings based on their high costs. Bringing up the rear: the Detroit Pistons. If ever there was an example that you do not have to be successful to make money, Detroit is that case. It cost the Pistons over $1.7 million dollars for each game they won while it cost Atlanta less than $0.7 million. Nevertheless, Detroit made money while Atlanta did not. Milwaukee tied Detroit for the worst conference record, but at least they got there at a lower cost.

In the Western Conference, four teams had better financial records than Atlanta, the leader in the East. They were led by Seattle's cost per victory of $503,000, and Houston, Utah, and San Antonio all bettered Atlanta's $698,000. Seattle's cost per victory was clearly the best in the league, even if they had a disappointing play-off performance. Houston, the eventual NBA champion, was a strong second at $569,000. At the bottom, not surprisingly, was Dallas. The Mavericks, 13 wins gave them a cost per victory exceeding $2.2 million.

It is more appropriate to rank NFL teams based on their records from 1990 to 1994 rather than on their 1994 records alone, although the 1994 rankings are included in Table 6.9 for comparison.[8] Buffalo was the clear leader in the AFC and Dallas in the NFC. That Buffalo was first should be no surprise given their four straight AFC titles. Pittsburgh and Kansas City followed closely behind Buffalo. Both had lower costs per victory than the NFC-leading Dallas. Both Pittsburgh and Kansas City have been successful on the field while maintaining control over costs. In the NFC, Dallas and San Francisco led both lists. Though both had relatively high costs, their cost per victory was relatively low.

At the bottom of the rankings were Indianapolis, Seattle, Arizona, Tampa Bay, Cincinnati, New England, and the Los Angeles

---

[8] All other leagues have much smaller differences between the one-year and five-year rankings, largely because the NFL results are very sensitive to a single additional victory.

Rams. Each victory by one of these teams cost over $8 million during this period. The Rams were the worst at over $10 million per victory based on their limited number of victories and their high costs. In contrast, Cincinnati was at the bottom despite their relatively low costs.

In the NHL, the cost per victory for 1994 and 1995 are presented in Table 6.10.[9] The results differ somewhat by year. For example, in the Eastern Conference, an expansion franchise, Florida, led in 1994 based on low player costs. In 1995 Quebec, a lame-duck surprise, had the lowest cost per victory. Nevertheless, the results generally are consistent from one year to the next. Boston, for example, was consistently near the lowest cost per victory while Hartford and Ottawa were consistently the highest. In the Western Conference, there were even fewer year-to-year changes. Calgary was number one each year while Dallas was close behind.

Table 6.10

FINANCIAL STANDINGS—NHL
Cost per Victory
(in hundreds of thousands of dollars)

Eastern Conference				Western Conference			
Team	Cost	Team	Cost	Team	Cost	Team	Cost
Florida	$511	Quebec	$490	Calgary	$521	Calgary	$592
New Jersey	515	Boston	559	Dallas	581	Detroit	605
Boston	548	Philadelphia	562	San Jose	592	Dallas	663
Montreal	582	Washington	623	Edmonton	606	Edmonton	687
NY Rangers	621	Florida	641	Anaheim	620	San Jose	761
Washington	645	Pittsburgh	676	Vancouver	680	St. Louis	779
Tampa Bay	648	New Jersey	700	St. Louis	703	Winnipeg	838
NY Islanders	648	Montreal	746	Detroit	716	Anaheim	867
Buffalo	653	Tampa Bay	753	Toronto	722	Chicago	874
Pittsburgh	655	Buffalo	771	Chicago	754	Vancouver	912
Quebec	666	Hartford	792	Winnipeg	772	Toronto	937
Philadelphia	732	NY Rangers	842	Los Angeles	1,094	Los Angeles	1,228
Hartford	876	NY Islanders	893				
Ottawa	1,016	Ottawa	1,140				

[9] NHL comparisons actually are made using points rather than victories and then multiplying by two, the point value for a win. This procedure makes the numbers comparable to the costs per victory in other leagues while retaining the NHL's consideration of ties. Using victories instead leaves the results basically unchanged.

Bringing up the rear each year was Los Angeles with few victories, big long-term contracts and high costs. Once again, these rankings do not include playoff performances. Including playoff victories, the New York Rangers would move close to number one in 1994 while Detroit and New Jersey would vie for the best in their conference in 1995.

There are similarities between the NHL and all other leagues. Some teams with low costs and less-than-mediocre records will be near the top of the rankings. Some high-achieving teams will also be near the top. Then some playoff teams will fall closer to the bottom of the rankings based on their exceptional costs. In the NHL, the best example of that would be the Toronto Maple Leafs. You can think of them as the New York Yankees of the NHL.

CONCLUSION

The overall conclusions? First, market size influences profits. Bigger is better. However, the size of the effect is relatively small and holds only on average. Bigger is not much better and bigger is not always better. Market size is only a minor determinant of profits. Second, market size does not influence wins. All leagues have achieved parity between large-market and small-market franchises. While a league could maximize the league's total revenue by allowing large-market franchises to grow stronger, there is no evidence that any league has allowed this to happen. Third, except in MLB, winning means profits. Vince Lombardi on average was correct. The teams that win the most generally make the most money. However, the magnitude of this effect is small. In addition, there are major exceptions. Some teams lose games but not money while others lose money but not games. Fourth, in all leagues you can buy a victory—although it might be expensive. If Gene Autry dies without a World Series ring, it is not because he could not buy a winner, but because he simply was not willing to pay enough. And fifth, more wins generally means more revenues. To state the obvious: fans love a winner.

Chapter 7

Revenue Sharing and Competition

"I found out a long time ago that there is no charity in baseball, and that every club owner must make his own fight for existence."
—Jacob Ruppert, owner of the New York Yankees, on a league profit-sharing plan during the Depression

"It makes a difference whose ox is gored." **—Martin Luther, *Works***

"It is my ball club, my money, and I don't appreciate anyone telling me how to spend my money to run my business. As long as I own this ball club, I will operate my way."
—Charles O. Finley, owner, Oakland A's

"Since the end of the Cold War, Americans have suffered from the lack of a common foe, a pin cushion, a punching bag. With communism dead, we've been shopping for a new demon. Now we have one. It's baseball." **—Clark Booth, sports writer**

Based on analysis of the profitability of each of the four major team sports, Chapters 2 to 5 leave us with four conclusions. First, all four leagues on average have been and remain very profitable. The average return to major league professional franchises has been greater than the average return to stocks. Second, profits are not evenly distributed. In each league, some franchises earn substantial profits while other franchises barely break even or lose money. The New York Yankees, Los Angeles Lakers, Dallas Cowboys and Detroit Red Wings prosper while the Milwaukee Brewers,

Dallas Mavericks, Indianapolis Colts, and Winnipeg Jets struggle. Third, owners have different motives for buying and owning a professional sports franchise. Some are in it primarily for the money while others are in it primarily for wins or ego or civic pride. And fourth, not all major league franchises are competently managed. Some franchises like the Cincinnati Reds, the Indiana Pacers, the Indianapolis Colts, and the Edmonton Oilers have not been well run, assuming that the objective is to make money or to wins games.

The conclusions that each league makes a substantial profit but that the profit is unevenly distributed suggests that some revenue sharing may be appropriate. When a league has an average profit rate over 15 percent but some teams are losing money, there might be a problem in the distribution of league profits, and some mechanism to share league revenues might be appropriate. In fact, each league already has some revenue sharing. For example, all leagues equally divide national television revenues, regardless of a team's number of TV appearances, record, or drawing power. Another example is a league's centralization of the licensing process, and in 1994 each league exceeded $1 billion in sales of licensed merchandise. Licensing revenues are received by the league and are split equally. In football, the Dallas Cowboys' logo sells far more frequently than the Cincinnati Bengals', yet Dallas and Cincinnati each receive 1/30 of the league's revenues. In hockey, the expansion franchises in Anaheim, Florida, and San Jose are three of the five top merchandise sellers, each with colors and emblems carefully chosen to generate as much licensing revenue as possible. Teams like the New York Rangers and Montreal Canadians are also-rans in popularity of team merchandise, but each franchise still receives 1/26 of the NHL licensing revenues. Thus the subsidy implied by revenue sharing can go either from the rich to the poor (Dallas to Cincinnati) or vice-versa (Florida to the New York Rangers).

This chapter considers three questions on revenue sharing. First, how much revenue has been shared in each league? Second, why should any revenue be shared? That is, is there an economic justification underlying revenue sharing and how can the problems associated with revenue sharing be overcome? And third, is there a specific proposal for revenue sharing that begins to address two of the most important problems facing professional sports: (1) How can revenues be split between rich franchises and poor without destroying the incentives for the rich to keep generating prolific revenues? (2) And how can anyone reconcile the split among owners where some focus primarily on the bottom line and others focus primarily on winning? This chapter demonstrates that revenue sharing and two taxes, one on total costs and the other on losing, address both problems. A salary cap effectively addresses neither.

CURRENT REVENUE SHARING ARRANGEMENTS

What revenues currently are shared? For all leagues, the ground rules are strikingly alike. National media money is shared while local media money generally is not; licensing money accrues to the league and is shared while any local advertising money is not; sharing of gate receipts varies by league while luxury box income generally is not shared. NFL gate receipts are split 60-40, with the home team receiving a greater amount justified on the basis of the costs of putting on the game. At the other extreme, the NHL home team retains the entire gate. In the NBA the home team keeps 94 percent of the gate while the league receives the other 6 percent. And in baseball, the American League has a 80-20 split while in the National League the visiting team receives $0.42 per admission.

Based on the average NL price, the visitor would appear to receive approximately 3.8 percent of the gate. But the visitor receives only $0.42 per person actually in attendance and not per ticket sold. Is this difference important? Data is available only for the New York Mets. The Mets reported to the press a 1993 paid attendance figure of 1.9 million, but the "stile attendance" determining the visitors' share of the gate was reported to be only 1.2 million. The evidence suggests that the number of people actually attending Mets games was only 2/3 the announced attendance— unless the Mets understated attendance reported to the other clubs. Does this difference have an appreciable impact? With respect to revenue sharing, the visitors' share of the gate would amount to 3.8 percent absent "no-shows." With 1/3 of the Mets' announced attendance allegedly no-shows, the visitors left the Mets' Shea Stadium with only 2.4 percent of the gate. Since the Mets may not be typical of NL franchises in this regard, I assume that revenue sharing of the gate in the NL is approximately 3.0 percent. Whether it is 2.4 percent, 3.0 percent, or 3.8 percent does not substantially alter our conclusions. (It does lead to questions about whether you can trust any official numbers.)

To see how revenue is shared, it is first useful to summarize what are the average revenues by source for each league. Table 7.1 presents this information as well as the percentage of revenues shared.[1] (1994 data is used to minimize the impact of the MLB

Table 7.1

1994 REVENUE SHARED

	AL	NL	NBA	NFL	NHL	Split
Gate Revenues	$26.1	$25.7	$18.3	$16.0	$19.6	Varies
National Media	8.5	8.5	10.2	39.4	1.0	100%
Local Media	11.9	12.4	4.2	3.0	4.0	0%
Licensing	2.5	2.5	2.0	2.4	0.8	100%
Other Revenues	14.6	13.1	7.2	6.8	8.0	0%
Total Revenues	63.6	62.2	41.9	67.6	33.4	
% of Revenue Split	33.7%	20.2%	31.7%	80.8%	5.4%	
Maximum Revenue	$100.1	$82.3	$77.5	$94.8	$52.6	
Minimum Revenue	42.6	40.9	28.3	59.3	17.9	
Percentage Difference [a]	80.6%	67.2%	93.0%	46.1%	98.4%	

[a] Percent of the average of the maximum and minimum.

and NHL strikes.) In terms of total revenue generated per franchise, the NFL leads all leagues with $67.6 million in average revenue. Of that, $39.4 million per franchise is due to the national media and another $16.0 million per franchise is from gate receipts. Major League Baseball (MLB) is second in revenues. Given the differences in revenue sharing, the table presents the AL and

[1] There are alternate ways of calculating the amount of revenue shared when the split of the gate is unequal. While the percentages reported below would change somewhat based on the method of calculation for all leagues except the NHL, the results and conclusions are unaltered.

NL separately. Gate receipts are the largest component of MLB receipts at about $26.0 million, followed by other revenues (primarily stadium revenues) at $13.8 million and local media at $12.2 million. The NBA lags with total revenue per franchise of $41.9 million. The NBA's two largest income sources are gate revenues at $18.3 million and national media at $10.2 million. Finally, the NHL has total revenue per franchise of only $33.4 million. The NHL relies most heavily on gate revenues, $19.6 million, and other revenues (again, primarily stadium revenues), $8.0 million.

Comparing the leagues, the advantage of the NFL clearly lies in its television contracts. Without them, the NFL would have lower revenue than the NHL. Based on national media revenues, MLB is no longer the national pastime and is not even number two. The NBA now has that honor. However, as noted in Chapter 2, the value of MLB's previous national media arrangement is open to substantial debate—and perhaps should be revised upward. Where baseball is still the most popular is in terms of attendance and gate receipts, where it easily outdistances all other leagues. Perhaps the surprises here are that the NHL has the second highest gate receipts, surpassing the NBA, and that the NFL with so few games still has close to the same gate receipts as other leagues.

The last column in Table 7.1 presents the general split of each category of revenues. These percentages, in conjunction with the different sources of league revenues, makes it clear why some leagues have substantial revenue sharing and others have virtually none. In the NFL, the two largest revenue categories, TV money and gate receipts, are split relatively equally. Thus, the NFL has the greatest degree of revenue sharing. In 1994 over 80 percent of each dollar received by the NFL was shared. In contrast, the NHL has the smallest national media revenues, the smallest licensing revenues, and no split of gate revenues. Thus NHL revenue sharing was the lowest with only 5.4 percent of league revenues shared. MLB and the NBA fall between these two extremes. In the AL, 33.7 percent of all revenues are shared while in the NL only 20.2 percent of revenues are shared. The difference primarily lies in the arrangements for sharing gate revenues. For the NL, the only real revenue sharing is of national media and league licensing revenues.

Sharing of gate receipts is trivial and sharing of local media revenue is limited. The AL shares national media money, league licensing money and adds some sharing of the gate. In the NBA, the percentage sharing of the gate is relatively small, but national media money is shared and is relatively more important for NBA franchises than for MLB franchises.

Another perspective on the distribution of revenues is given by the range of revenues in a league. How do the revenues of the richest and poorest franchises compare? The last three lines in Table 7.1 present the maximum revenue received, the minimum revenue received, and the percentage difference. The results indicate a wide range for all four leagues, smallest in the NFL and widest in the NHL, consistent with the results in the first part of the table. In the NFL, there's a 46 percent difference between the revenues of the Dallas Cowboys ($94.8 million) and the Indianapolis Colts ($59.3 million). While the Colts substantially trail the Cowboys, relative to league average revenues the Colts are not in bad shape, receiving 88 percent of the league's average revenues. Given the importance of TV money to the NFL, this result should not be a surprise. Regardless of how a franchise is run, TV money gives all NFL teams a solid revenue base.

In the NHL, there is a 98 percent difference between the New York Rangers' revenues ($52.6 million) and the Winnipeg Jets' revenues ($17.9 million). In addition, the Jets' revenues are only 53 percent of the NHL's average revenues. If you want another reason for being skeptical about the long-run viability of a Winnipeg franchise, these numbers give you a good one. With no significant revenue sharing in the NHL, teams like Winnipeg and Edmonton are entirely on their own and may not have the revenue base to survive. In the NBA, the maximum percentage difference is almost as high as in the NHL, 93 percent, but Dallas, the lowest revenue franchise, receives 68 percent of the NBA's average revenues. Given Dallas' market size, with a reasonably competitive team, Dallas' revenues should be close to the NBA average.

The AL has a maximum percentage difference of 80 percent between the New York Yankees at $100.1 million and the Minnesota Twins at $42.6 million, and the Twins have 68 percent of

MLB's average revenues. The NL difference is even smaller, only 67 percent between the New York Mets and the San Diego Padres, although the Padres have only 66 percent of average revenues. However, the Padres' low revenues are at least part by choice, after choosing to dismantle a competitive franchise and watch gate revenues fall through the floor as a result. Are the low revenue teams at a disadvantage? Undoubtedly they face a greater financial struggle than the New York City teams. But their on-the-field success need not be in jeopardy, as demonstrated in Chapter 6. Consider one additional example. The minimum-revenue Minnesota Twins won the World Series in 1987 and 1991. The maximum-revenue New York Yankees and Mets last won the World Series in 1978 and 1986 respectively. In sports, location is not a prerequisite for winning.

What may be most noteworthy about the maximum and minimum revenue numbers is the observation that New York City teams lead in all leagues except the NFL, the league with the most revenue sharing. New York City teams have natural revenue advantages over Winnipeg, Buffalo, and Salt Lake City. However, Chapter 6 demonstrated that this revenue advantage has not led to more victories and has led to only marginally greater financial success. New York City teams have both higher revenues and higher costs. Anyone who still believes that market size is the sole or even a primary determinant of financial success should note that Dallas has two entries on the maximum/minimum list: the Cowboys have the highest NFL revenues and the Mavericks the lowest NBA revenues. Market size may play a minor role, but it is a long way from the whole explanation of profits, wins or anything else. Whether a team wins and whether it is well run both contribute more to financial success.

THE ECONOMIC LOGIC UNDERLYING REVENUE SHARING

Should there be revenue sharing? Is there any economic justification underlying revenue sharing? For an economist the answer is simple. In MLB, for example, the Yankees and the Brewers take the field to play a game. They create a win, a loss and entertainment. It is a classic example of a joint product. The fans and the media pay for the entertainment while one of the teams ends up with a win and the other gets a loss. The product obviously is shared, and since the Yankees and Brewers must cooperate to pro-duce it—in terms of agreeing on ground rules—the financial re-wards are appropriately shared. But how are the Yankees and Brewers to split the revenues?

Three issues underlie this apparently simple question. First, you have a set of accounting issues: do you split gross revenues or net and how do you define the revenues to be shared? I will not worry about that set of concerns. Accountants can play what games they will with the numbers but that need not influence ei-ther the actual games or the financial results.

Second, there are equity concerns. What is a "fair" split of the revenues between the Yankees and the Brewers? While that is a major concern to Steinbrenner and Selig, to the rest of us it is just not important unless it has some other impacts on the game. Ef-ficiency arguments made below weigh heavily against an equal split of local revenues. Before considering efficiency, however, there is an equity argument against equally splitting local revenues. In any league we should expect the first franchises to be located in the most profitable cities. New York, Chicago, and Los Angeles have franchises in all leagues (temporarily except the NFL) and sometimes multiple franchises. Detroit, Boston, Philadelphia, and San Francisco also have franchises in all leagues. When you buy an expansion franchise, you should know that it is unlikely to gener-ate the revenue stream of many "old guard" franchises. Thus, it would be disingenuous in MLB for expansion franchises in Colo-rado or Florida to argue that they deserve a share of Yankees' or Dodgers' revenues when the new owners should have known at the outset that they would be among the marginal franchises in the league. I use Colorado and Florida as examples simply because they are the new kids on the block. The same argument holds for Milwaukee, Minnesota, Kansas City, and Seattle. All were expan-sion franchises within the last thirty years and thus have a weak argument for revenue sharing on equity grounds.

Third and most importantly, how can you undertake revenue sharing while not destroying economic incentives? How can you undertake revenue sharing and give owners or potential owners a greater incentive to pursue profits, victories, and the long-run economic health of the league? From an economic perspective, the interesting question about revenue sharing is its efficiency implications. The simplest way of viewing revenue sharing is to think of it as a tax. The general rule in economics is that any tax will distort economic incentives.[2] In this case, we can put the distorting effects of taxes to an advantage. Many things could be taxed, for example, total costs, total revenues, player payrolls (the owners' favorite), or even wins and losses. What is taxed will effect how owners will react to the tax and will impact how owners, players, and fans will fare.

As an example, consider the basics of a tax proposed by owners both in MLB and in the NHL: a tax on total player expenditures, including salaries, bonuses, and fringe benefits. (In fact, this tax was advanced as a fallback position from a salary cap.) The owners' goal was straightforward. Provide incentives to each owner to reduce player payroll. Consider a punitive tax rate of, say, 100 percent on all player costs over the league average when a team's payroll exceeded 110 percent of the league average. Suppose a MLB owner had a payroll of $30 million and the average payroll was $27 million. Suppose he also wanted to spend $5 million more to sign another free agent. By signing that player he would raise his payroll to $35 million or $8 million over the league average. Thus he would also have to pay an $8 million tax to the league. Signing that player would cost not $5 million but $13 million when you include the cost of the tax. Clearly this tax would give owners a tremendous incentive to restrict player payrolls. Furthermore, as all owners struggled to be no more than 110 percent of the league average payroll, the average payroll would decline dramatically. Such a tax would do wonders for owners' profits, but it also would adversely effect a relatively competitive labor market.

In fact, there is no economic justification for such a tax. If owners are truly concerned about escalating costs, they should be concerned about all costs. Why single out player costs? But the

---

[2] The only exception is a so-called lump-sum tax or poll tax that is levied equally on all. A league franchise fee of $0.8 million levied on all clubs to finance league operations would be an example of such a tax. This type of tax, however, does not facilitate revenue sharing.

biggest single flaw in the owners' argument is that their tax proposal focused on taxing all costs and not just on the incremental or additional costs associated with signing a player. There are fixed costs associated with running a franchise. For example, a MLB franchise has a minimum payroll of $2.5 million given the roster size and the minimum salary. Taxing this amount or any fixed cost has no impact on a franchise's operations and is incompatible with revenue sharing. A tax on anything other than incremental costs or revenues is simply bad economics as far as changing incentives is concerned.

A second example of how not to tax has been proposed by some small-market MLB owners. This tax would split all local media money equally among all franchises. Again using MLB as an example, the New York Yankees currently receive $45.5 million a year in local media revenue. Under this form of revenue sharing, the Yankees would receive only 1/28 of this or $1.6 million. They also would receive $10.6 million as their share of other owners' media revenues. However, their media revenues would decline by a total of $33.3 million while Milwaukee's media revenues would rise by $8.2 million and Minnesota's by $9.2 million. In this example MLB is imposing a 96 percent tax rate on local media revenues. (The Yankees keep only 1/28, or 4 percent of their local media revenues.) More problematic is the question of incentives. What would happen the next time the New York Yankees' media contract is up for renegotiations? How much incentive do the Yankees have to bargain aggressively for a higher fee when they keep only 1/28 of the negotiated amount? The moral: equally splitting local revenues would likely have devastating long-run impacts on those revenues. Thus this tax also is bad economics.

ECONOMICALLY JUSTIFIED TAXES TO IMPLEMENT REVENUE SHARING

So how can we set a tax that would be good economics? Let me state the requirements for a good tax system, given the problems facing all leagues. (1) Profits are healthy but are unevenly distributed. Implication: some revenue sharing is necessary, and a tax must fall more heavily on profitable franchises. (2) Owners have different goals; some focus more on wins and others on profits. Implication: two types of taxes are necessary, one on those seeking victory and another on those seeking profits. (3) Taxing revenue will make owners reluctant to take steps to "grow" revenues coming into the league. Implication: avoid taxing revenues; where possible, tax costs instead. (4) Taxes should allow markets to operate without introducing additional distortions. Implication: when player's salaries are determined in a competitive market, there is no need to separately tax this component of costs.

With these suggestions, let us consider a two-part tax, on a franchise's total costs and on its won-loss record. First, consider the "cost" tax and three fundamental questions. Why tax costs rather than revenues? What costs should be taxed? And how high a tax rate is appropriate?

Revenue sharing could be undertaken either by taxing a franchise's revenues or its costs. To date, revenue sharing in all leagues has been done by taxing revenues. As the example above on taxing local media revenues clearly demonstrates, taxing a franchise's revenues ultimately depresses the league's revenues and both owners and players suffer in the long-run. In contrast, taxing costs strengthens owners' existing desires to control costs and to increase profitability. Owners will be better off even if players are not.

What costs should be taxed? Any tax would appear appropriately levied with respect to all costs and not just player salaries, assuming owners are serious about getting a handle on costs and are not simply out to break a union. Player salaries have increased more rapidly than other costs, but player salaries represent only about 50 percent of total costs, and there is no guarantee that another cost component will not accelerate dramatically in the future. While the focus is on all costs, the tax itself should be levied only on incremental costs. For example, if the average cost in a league were $50 million, it would make sense to tax a franchise only on its costs in excess of $50 million, or on its incremental or marginal costs. The goal of the tax is to provide an incentive to keep expenditures below some level.

Now the focus on incremental costs requires some additional explanation, and that explanation is related to how high the tax rate should be and what is the need for revenue sharing in the first place. The tax rate cannot be too high or it will have ugly incentive effects. With a high enough tax rate we could have all franchises fielding a whole new team of rookies each year. But we do not need a tax rate all that high to obtain the desired effect of restricting costs. The main point underlying revenue sharing is that a game creates both a win and a loss and the winner receives more revenues than the loser. Thus, the winner imposes an economic cost on the loser. What is that cost? The answer varies by sport and even by team within sport. In Chapter 6, I calculated on average how much it costs to win one more game and how much revenue a team losses with an additional loss. These two numbers give us the appropriate tax rate. Consider a MLB example with numbers based on the results of Chapter 6. The Yankees sign Wade Boggs to a contract that increases their payroll by $1.9 million. Because of that signing the Yankees on average will win one more game. But the Yankees' win means another franchise's loss and that loss costs $622,000 an average based on the numbers in Chapter 6. Every dollar that Steinbrenner spends costs another owner about $0.33 ($622,000 divided by $1.9 million). Thus 33 percent is the appropriate tax rate on incremental expenditures.

There is some question on what costs should be taxed. The argument made earlier emphasized placing the tax on all costs rather than just on players' salaries.[3] There remains a question of whether this tax should be placed only on costs above some threshold, a so-called "luxury tax" or whether it should be placed on all costs. In MLB, the owners argued for taxing anything over the mean (for player salaries only) while the union argued for a tax only when a teams' salaries exceeded 130 percent of the league average. In this case, the owners appear to have the weight of economic logic on their side. For simplicity assume all clubs spend the same amount and are equally competitive. Then one owner attempted to buy a championship by increasing spending. His

---

[3] There admittedly may be implementation problems when focusing on all costs rather than on player costs only. For example, operating costs in New York probably are substantially higher than in St. Louis or Denver, and some owners have substantial debt service while others have virtually none.

additional expenditures makes his team more competitive and presumably cost other owners money. Those incremental expenditures should be subject to a tax. There is no reason why only expenditures, say, 30 percent above the average impose costs on other franchises.[4]

The magnitudes of the tax by league are presented in Table 7.2. Two numbers are important. First, how much does it cost to win one more game? From Chapter 6, those costs range from $653,000 in the NBA up to $2.8 million in the NFL. The NFL cost is high because of the limited number of games played. MLB's cost also is high because of the relative uncertainty in each game. Second, how much revenue does a franchise lose when the team loses one more game? For example, when the Indianapolis Colts lose a game early in the season, it costs them attendance, increases no-shows, and reduces their revenues at future games by about $1.1 million. The appropriate tax rate is simply the ratio of the revenue sacrificed with one additional loss divided by the cost of winning one more game, or how much one owner's incremental expenditures cost another in lost revenues.

The tax rates in Table 7.2 vary widely by league. MLB has the lowest tax rate of any league, 33 percent. This low rate reflects the high cost of winning one more game, which in turn is due to the greater randomness in baseball. The NFL is the second lowest at 39 percent. The NFL's low tax rate should not be a surprise since it has greater revenue sharing than any other league and revenue sharing reduces the financial gain from winning. For example, the Cincinnati Bengals have not been successful on-the-field but have pared costs and have been successful financially.

The NBA and NHL have substantially higher tax rates than either MLB or the NFL. The only big financial difference between the NBA and the NHL is the magnitudes of their national televi-

---

[4] In fact, the story is substantially more complex than detailed here. All expenditures presumably will increase the probability of winning and thus arguably should be subject to a tax. However, if a franchise's expenditures are below the league average, to the extent that their increased expenditures makes the entire league more competitive, then overall league revenues may increase and all owners may be better off. In fact, the relation between expenditures and impacts on other franchises is undoubtedly highly nonlinear. One might argue for an increasing tax rate as expenditures diverge from the league average. However, a more detailed statistical analysis using nonlinear regression techniques provides no statistical support for such an approach.

Table 7.2

WINNING, LOSING, AND TAX RATES
How Much Does it Cost to Win One More Game?
(in hundreds of thousands of dollars)

MLB	NBA	NFL	NHL
$1898	$653	$2801	$922

How Much Money Does an Owner Lose When Losing One More Game?
(in hundreds of thousands of dollars)

MLB	NBA	NFL	NHL
$622	$432	$1083	$657

What Tax Rates on Incremental Expenditures are Appropriate?
(in percent)

MLB	NBA	NFL	NHL
33%	66%	39%	71%

sion contracts. The NBA has a larger contract and the revenues from that contract are split evenly between clubs. Thus, there is less of a financial loss in the NBA than in the NHL with an in-the-arena loss. However, the cost of one more win in the NBA is slightly lower than in the NHL, presumably reflecting smaller NBA team sizes. The implied tax rates are 66 percent for the NBA and 71 percent for the NHL. In each league, when one owner increases his costs, he forces another owner to sacrifice substantial revenues.

The tax rates calculated in Table 7.2 are based on the average cost of a loss. In fact, this actual cost varies from franchise to franchise and from the beginning to the end of the season. For example, another win generally is worth more in New York or Boston or Los Angeles than it is in Milwaukee or Minnesota or Seattle because of the size of the markets. In MLB, one more win in Seattle might bring another 5,000 fans over the course of the season, while one more win in New York might bring another 20,000 fans. In addition, network television ratings are higher if the Yankees play the Dodgers in the World Series than if the Reds play the

Twins. Those higher TV ratings in the long run translate into more revenue for all teams. While this effect potentially is large, there is no point in discussing it further because it is an argument for systematic league imbalance in terms of wins and losses that would favor larger markets. There is no evidence that large-market franchises have any on-the-field advantage. Economic efficiency may suggest that large-market franchises should win more. This is not consistent with economic equity, which appears to be foremost in owners' minds.

Perhaps the most important feature of this type of tax is that it begins to address one of the major problems underlying much economic strife in sports: the problem of differing owner desires. Some owners primarily want profits and some victories. How does this tax address that? Owners that want victories and champion-ships will still choose to spend more. DeBartolo and Steinbrenner and Turner can spend all they want. As they spend more and—perhaps—win more they also impose costs on other owners that place a higher value on profits. Presumably the money from the tax on costs will be used to reimburse those owners who choose not to increase spending and who end up losing more frequently. Owners that want championships can still attempt to buy them if they wish, but only to the extent that they compensate other own-ers for the costs of losing.

Now this "cost" tax by itself is not the entire solution. Of course, all owners want both wins and profits, but the relative importance placed on each may differ dramatically. The tax above is on those that want to win and are spending freely to do it. They have to pay a penalty for the costs they are imposing on those that want profits. Those who want to win can still spend as freely as they want, but they must internalize the costs they impose on other owners. But owners who primarily want profits also impose costs on other owners. Why? They have little incentive to field a competitive team unless profits are at stake. The NFL may be the most dramatic example because of its revenue sharing. The Cin-cinnati Bengals have been quite profitable because they have not spent money on player salaries—and thus have not been competi-tive on-the-field. Playing in Cincinnati's Riverfront Stadium in

December is no picnic. The empty stands will not make it a lucrative visit, even if the competition is light as well.

League revenues will be higher in the long-run when the games and the races are tight, although any one team might be able to reduce short-term expenditures and lose games but gain profits. What can be done to reduce this incentive? One suggestion: tax less-successful franchises.[5] Give owners who focus only on profits a greater incentive to win. In some cases, franchises have effectively stopped trying to field a competitive team. The Bengals, Buccaneers, and Rams in the NFL and the Angels, Cubs, and Padres in MLB have recently fit this mold. Taxing their losses would likely stimulate more interest in winning and may increase league profitability.

The first tax takes the Steinbrenner's and Turner's and taxes them for their free-spending ways. The second takes the Bill Bidwell's (owner of the Arizona Cardinals) and Tom Werner's (former owner of the Padres) and says field a competitive team or pay a price. The former says of the win-at-all-cost owners pay attention to those concerned with profits. The second says of the only-profits-count owners that you must also be concerned with the on-the-field competition. Thus both sets of owners must move closer to a common middle ground that explicitly gives weight to both controlling costs and fielding a competitive team. Both types of owners may continue with their original focus, but the economic incentives push them toward a compromise. Furthermore, a compromise between the owners is a prerequisite for an agreement with the players.

REVENUE SHARING—A BASEBALL EXAMPLE WITH ECONOMICALLY JUSTIFIED TAXES

How would such a set of taxes work in practice? Using baseball as an example, the "cost" tax would be 33 percent on any expenditure in excess, say, of the MLB average of $57 million (using 1994 values). The "loss" tax is necessarily arbitrary because there is no hard evidence on what owners lose when games and races are

---

[5] Gary Becker made a similar proposal in *Business Week* (October 10, 1994).

uncompetitive. To make it concrete and yet to keep this second tax smaller than the first, consider a loss tax only when a team loses more than 55 percent of its games. Let the tax equal how far below .450 a team falls times the average league revenues. For example, in 1994 the San Diego Padres' won only .402 percent of its games, and average league revenues were $62.9 million. Thus the Padres would pay a tax of .048 times $62.9 million or about $3 million. When the Padres do not field a competitive team they impose a cost on all the other teams in the league and this tax forces the Padres to consider that impact.[6]

Table 7.3 presents how these two taxes would have impacted MLB profits in 1994 assuming that both taxes are based on teams' current performance. A sum of $35.2 million is raised by the cost tax and another $8.0 million by the loss tax for a total of $43.2 million. A total of 15 teams pay the cost tax for having above average costs. However, five pay less than $0.5 million. Six teams pay the loss tax, including one expansion franchise. You could argue that expansion franchises should be excluded from the loss tax for their first few years or the loss tax should be based on records over a multi-year period or the cost tax should be adjusted for different cost-of-living indexes in different markets. These types of considerations are potentially useful complications but represent minor tinkering with the general idea.

In terms of paying taxes, not surprisingly, the Yankees are the largest taxpayer at almost $6 million. No one else pays more than $4 million. Toronto, Atlanta, Los Angeles, and San Francisco pay over $3 million with the cost tax, with Detroit and Cincinnati close behind. Only two teams pay an appreciable sum under the loss tax, San Diego at $3 million and California at $2.6 million.

---

[6] A couple of technical points should be mentioned on this tax. First, it uses league average revenues rather than costs. The reason for the switch from cost to revenue: the purpose of this tax is to encourage less-than-competitive clubs to increase their spending and to field a competitive team. Since the tax has the goal of increasing some clubs' spending and costs, it makes more sense to tax revenues rather than costs. Using average costs instead would leave the results unaltered. Second, this tax shifts from incremental revenues to total revenues despite my contention above that taxes generally should be placed on incremental values. With this tax, it is the tax rate which is determined incrementally and thus the tax can be levied on the level. In addition, while the tax is levied on a level, the rate of the tax typically will be relatively low. With the proposed tax, for 1994 the Padres pay the highest rate of 4.8 percent since they had the worst record.

Through the 1994 season, both teams had traded, sold, or refused to sign most of their expensive ball players. They were uncompetitive on the field and were one of the worst attractions as a visiting team. (The Twins joined that group in 1995.)

The two taxes together generate $43.2 million in tax revenue. What is to be done with this revenue? Given that all leagues face a problem not of insufficient profits but of an unequal distribution of profits, it would seem reasonable to take the revenue raised and return it to franchises with revenue below the league average. What mechanism you employ should not seriously weaken poorer franchise's incentives to generate their own revenues. Consider a mechanism that returns taxes proportionately to all franchises with revenues less than the league average. In 1994 13 franchises had revenues less than the league average. The total shortfall was $185 million. With $43.2 million in tax revenues, those shortfalls can be made up at the rate of $0.31 per dollar ($43.2 divided by $185). San Diego and Minnesota, with the revenues of about $40 million, or almost $18 million below the league average, gain approximately $5 million. Kansas City, Milwaukee, Seattle, Montreal, and Pittsburgh receive in excess of $3 million each. These franchises have experienced real financial difficulties. This system of taxes and revenue sharing would help them all. It would not guarantee them profits, however.

Table 7.3 also calculates the net change in profits from the two taxes as well as any money returned through revenue sharing. The last column presents the franchise's 1994 profits given taxes and revenue sharing. The New York Yankees lose the most under this tax arrangement although they still have profits of $18.0 million. Toronto, Atlanta, Los Angeles, San Francisco also are losers with this arrangement, although all except San Francisco still have comfortable profits. The biggest gainers under this arrangement are Milwaukee, Minneapolis, Montreal, and Pittsburgh. While San Diego and California receive large subsidies, they also pay large taxes for their poor on-the-field performance. Detroit, Kansas City, and Cincinnati also receive substantial subsidies, but those subsidies are largely offset by high taxes based on their high costs.

The nature of these taxes is to subsidize teams that are well-run

Table 7.3

REVENUE SHARING—MLB
Tax on Higher Player Costs and on Weaker Team Performances

	Cost Tax	Loss Tax	Revenue Sharing	Net Change in Profits	New Profit Levels
		(in hundreds of thousands)			(in millions)
AL					
Baltimore	$2,344	$0	$0	-$2,344	$13.7
Boston	1,150	0	0	-1,150	12.1
California	0	2,598	2,899	301	5.7
Chicago	2,599	0	0	-2,599	4.1
Cleveland	0	0	0	0	12.8
Detroit	2,922	0	2,095	-827	-13.3
Kansas City	3,004	0	3,777	722	-18.9
Milwaukee	0	0	4,435	4,435	-0.4
Minneapolis	0	0	4,922	4,922	-6.0
New York	5,984	0	0	-5,984	18.0
Oakland	454	166	1,193	574	-0.7
Seattle	0	786	4,557	3,770	-5.5
Texas	493	0	0	-493	9.9
Toronto	3,612	0	0	-3,612	8.7
NL					
Atlanta	3,103	0	0	-3,103	10.9
Chicago	0	1,030	0	-1,030	16.9
Cincinnati	2,889	0	1,778	-1,111	-12.2
Colorado	0	0	0	0	18.9
Florida	0	410	657	247	15.5
Houston	18	0	2,388	2,370	-2.5
Los Angeles	3,061	0	0	-3,061	4.2
Montreal	0	0	4,313	4,313	7.4
New York	411	0	0	-411	22.7
Philadelphia	130	0	0	-130	5.5
Pittsburgh	0	0	4,849	4,849	0.7
St. Louis	0	0	0	0	10.2
San Diego	0	3,037	5,361	2,324	5.9
San Francisco	3,024	0	0	-3,024	-5.6
Sum	$35,197	$8,027	$43,224	$0	$138.6

and yet still have difficulty making ends meet. According to base-ball insiders, the two franchises that have come closest to meeting this criteria are Montreal and Pittsburgh. Both teams, just by avoiding losing records and keeping costs under control, receive over $4 million in tax subsidies. This tax system, with low tax rates and a carefully selected base, cannot bail out a club like Detroit, Kansas City, or Cincinnati that is awash in red ink. It can do two things, however. It can and does reward those clubs that are "doing things right" or fielding a competitive team at a relatively low cost. It also provides an even greater incentive for owners to be finan-cially prudent and exercise appropriate oversight over fielding competitive teams. In a word, this set of taxes cannot give all own-ers the same set of incentives. However, it does bridge the current chasm between those in the league primarily as a business and those in it primarily as a hobby.

You can argue that this system is not perfect and I would be the first to agree. I doubt there is a perfect tax system. With this proposal, you could raise at least three complaints. First, Detroit receives a $2.1 million subsidy even though Detroit is a large mar-ket franchise and should have above-average revenue. That prob-lem cannot be easily remedied, although it would appear that Detroit's $13 million loss even with revenue sharing should pro-vide a tremendous incentive to improve front office management. Second, San Diego receives a subsidy for below-average revenues even though their lower revenues are partly their own fault. The tax system could be changed to eliminate that subsidy. For ex-ample, double the tax on losing. Then San Diego would be pay-ing taxes of $0.7 million or a $6.1 million tax for a losing record minus a $5.4 million subsidy for low revenues. Increasing the loss tax sufficiently would penalize any team following San Diego's strategy of unloading their stars. However, such a tax rate also potentially is punitive and could put a losing franchise in a hole they cannot climb out of. And third, you could complain that there are still a lot of teams losing money. My reply: there sure are and there should be. Revenue sharing by itself will not and should not save any franchise. Each owner is primarily responsible for his own financial well-being and should not look to other owners, to players, or to fans to bail him out. If he cannot make it, he should sell out. No owner should expect anyone to subsidize his hobby or his incompetence.

REVENUE SHARING—AN NHL EXAMPLE

Before concluding on revenue sharing it is appropriate to examine the NHL in more detail, since it has the least current revenue sharing and the greatest percentage disparity between rich and poor franchises. The financial costs and incentives in hockey are somewhat different than those in baseball. Thus the tax rates must also differ. Nevertheless, the same general philosophy underlies the proposal: how to make all owners value both profits and victories. Table 7.4 considers two taxes, a cost tax and a loss tax, similar to the MLB example. Based on the costs on owner imposes on another by winning, presented in Table 7.2, the appropriate tax on costs in the NHL is approximately 70 percent, the highest of any league. Once again, this tax is imposed only on costs in excess of the league average. Los Angeles, Detroit, Toronto, and the New York Rangers are the highest-cost franchises and they pay the most under this tax, all in excess of $4.8 million (1994 values are used to avoid problems with the 1995 NHL lockout). Even Buffalo pays $2.2 million. While 13 of 26 NHL teams would pay this tax, only 8 would pay more than $1 million. Again, the distribution of costs in the NHL is extremely unequal!

The loss tax also must be changed since the NHL focuses on points rather than wins (two points for a win, one for a tie). A season winning percentage of .45 corresponds to approximately 76 points. It also roughly corresponds to the cutoff for making the playoffs. Taking 76 points as the starting value, let each point below cost a franchise a tax of 0.1 percent of average league revenues. Ottawa, with an NHL-worst 37 points would be taxed at a rate of 3.9 percent (39 points below the 76 point cutoff times 0.1 per point). The cost to Ottawa for failing to field a competitive team: $1.3 million. Revenue sharing is set up the same as in the MLB example. Funds are allocated in proportion to a club's revenues.

The two taxes raise a total of almost $40 million. There are 13 clubs with below-average revenue, and the total amount that their revenues fall short of the league average is $103 million. Thus

Table 7.4

REVENUE SHARING—NHL

**Revenue Sharing of Gate Receipts and Tax on
Higher Player Costs and on Weaker Team Performances**

	Cost Tax	Loss Tax	Revenue Sharing	Impact of Sharing Gate	Net Change in Profits	New Profit Levels
			(in hundreds of thousands)	(in millions)	(in millions)	(in millions)
Eastern						
Boston	$0	$0	$0	-$0.7	-$0.7	$19.9
Buffalo	2,226	0	1,982	0.7	0.5	-2.3
Florida	0	0	2,405	0.7	3.1	8.9
Hartford	0	434	3,829	1.6	5.0	0.8
Montreal	38	0	0	-0.2	-0.2	11.3
New Jersey	0	0	2,136	1.8	3.9	4.5
NY Islanders	0	0	1,982	1.9	3.9	4.9
NY Rangers	4,896	0	0	-2.5	-7.4	10.4
Ottawa	0	1,301	2,983	1.8	3.5	10.3
Philadelphia	1,004	0	0	-0.4	-1.4	8.4
Pittsburgh	3,713	0	0	-2.4	-6.2	-2.3
Quebec	0	0	3,598	1.6	5.2	4.0
Tampa Bay	0	167	3,791	1.4	5.1	5.6
Washington	413	0	0	-0.4	-0.9	5.4
Western						
Anaheim	0	167	0	-1.3	-1.5	12.9
Calgary	0	0	2,752	0.8	3.6	4.5
Chicago	3,454	0	0	-4.1	-7.5	7.8
Dallas	227	0	0	-1.3	-1.5	5.1
Detroit	5,596	0	0	-2.3	-7.9	6.9
Edmonton	0	400	5,753	3.4	8.7	7.7
Los Angeles	5,789	334	0	-2.0	-8.2	-3.6
St. Louis	2,936	0	1,905	-0.8	-1.9	-5.5
San Jose	0	0	0	-2.2	-2.2	9.0
Toronto	5,323	0	0	0.6	-4.7	0.7
Vancouver	721	0	712	1.2	1.1	3.8
Winnipeg	0	634	5,946	3.2	8.5	4.4
Sum	$36,339	$3,435	$39,774	$0	$0	$143.5

franchises with below-average revenue will receive about $0.40 on the dollar of their shortfall from league revenue sharing.

To this point, the NHL and MLB examples are comparable. These adjustments by themselves, however, may not be sufficient to allow franchises like Winnipeg to survive. Let us add one more revenue sharing wrinkle: the NFL's 60-40 split of the gate (again, this would be paid admission and would not include luxury box revenues). Table 7.4 demonstrates how these taxes, revenue sharing, and splitting the gate would alter each franchise's profits as well as stating the new level of profits for each club. The richer franchises remain richer. However, franchises like Winnipeg no longer lose money. Only 4 franchises would now lose money: St. Louis, Los Angeles, Buffalo, and Pittsburgh. St. Louis is an aberration and has profits using 1995 values based on their new arena. The ownership of the Los Angeles Kings has been embroiled in non-hockey legal issues and probably deserves to be losing money. What about the small-market Canadian franchises? All would be doing quite well, with Winnipeg and Calgary each having a profit of about $4 million. The Canadian franchise in the weakest financial shape with revenue sharing would be Toronto. They are a high-cost club and pay a substantial tax based on those costs. Toronto ownership has been criticized even by other general managers for their profligate spending for mediocre talent. The revised profit numbers suggest those criticisms are well deserved.

REVENUE SHARING IN THE NFL

Virtually all NFL franchises have been quite profitable. One can make the argument that the NFL's success is rooted in their revenue sharing, even as different owners appear to have very different objectives. With the NFL's current revenue sharing arrangements, there is little reason or justification for additional revenue sharing. There is, however, a strong case against allowing owners like Jerry Jones to cut their own deals with whomever they choose. Ultimately, Jones' deals with Nike and Pepsi, for example, reduce the value of the league's deals with Reebok and Coke. When the league's deals through its marketing arm, NFL Properties, come up for renewal they will be negotiated downward and total league revenue may fall.

Notre Dame's television contract with NBC illustrates the underlying principle. The College Football Association (CFA) negotiated a television deal with ABC in the late 1980's that ABC interpreted as giving it the TV rights to all CFA home games, including Notre Dame's. When Notre Dame, which had not signed the CFA-ABC contract, decided to sign with NBC instead for $35 million, ABC insisted that its payment to the CFA be reduced by about $35 million.

Jerry Jones quite likely can make more money marketing the Cowboys on his own than he will receive from the Cowboy's share of NFL Properties income. Jones may well have the panache to run NFL Properties substantially better than it currently is being run. Jones, however, is totally off-base when he says that the average franchise is better off doing its own marketing than going through NFL Properties. With 30 franchises each doing its own marketing, the competition for deals with the prime sponsors like Nike likely will drive the value of those deals down for most teams. Teams like the Cowboys and 49ers may be better off but most teams will lose, and many smaller-market teams could lose dramatically. Is the average NFL owner better off with a marketing monopoly and shared profits or with 30 marketing competitors? With apologies to Ben Franklin, NFL owners had better hang together or else competitive markets will hang them all separately.

CONCLUSIONS

What is the bottom line on revenue sharing? Revenue sharing can be simply an out-and-out attempt by small-market franchises to expropriate the wealth of richer teams. In baseball, owners like Bud Selig, Carl Pohlad of the Twins, and Marge Schott may simply be trying to pick George Steinbrenner's pockets for his New York City media money. If that is the case, for most of us it may be interesting theater but it is not interesting from either a finance or a sports perspective.

Revenue sharing does have a strong economic justification based upon the cooperation required between teams to generate league revenues. Since the game is a joint effort, economic theory can be employed to suggest how revenues can be split to provide positive rather than negative incentives. Maintaining the appropriate incentives suggests that whatever tax is employed, the tax rate should fall far short of the prohibitive rates that owners suggested in both baseball and hockey during the 1994 strikes. Tax rates on incremental costs in the 30 percent range in MLB and around 70 percent in the NHL can be justified on economic grounds based on the cost that winners impose on losers in terms of lost revenues. Even a tax rate of 10 percent on **all** costs or on player payroll is devoid of economic justification. That type of tax would have negative efficiency effects and generally appears designed only to artificially reduce player salaries below what a competitive market would set.

The system of taxes and revenue sharing presented here addresses a fundamental problem of sports: that owners are in it both as a business and as a hobby and the weights that different owners place on these two goals sometimes differ dramatically. Taxing both excess costs and excess losses should move owners to roughly the same page in the playbook and should reduce losses at competently managed small-market franchises. This system of taxes also has the potential to reduce tensions between players and owners. Owners would have an incentive to more carefully monitor all costs, including player payroll, because of the cost tax. But owners also would have an incentive to make sure they field a competitive team because of the loss tax. This system of taxes will not suddenly increase owners' profit rates to 30 percent—which is where some owners apparently believe they should be—but as long as the games go on, why should the rest of us care?

Chapter 8

Strikes and Lockouts and Salary Caps — A Pox on All Houses

"Only free men can negotiate. Prisoners cannot enter into contracts." **—Nelson Mandela**

"I once loved this game, but after being traded four times, I realize it's nothing but a business. I treat my horses better than the owners treat us." **—Dick Allen, former baseball player**

"This strike was never for the Hank Aarons, Carl Yaztremskis, or Willie Mayses. It was for the four-year players who pass up college, spend three to five years to make the majors, and have a career ruined by a dead arm or leg."
—Howard Cosell, on the 1972 baseball player's strike

"Money is not the issue. The real issue is the owners' attempt to punish the players for having the audacity not to crawl."
—Marvin Miller, executive director of the baseball players' association, on the 1972 players strike

"Grantland Rice, the great sports writer, once said, 'It's not whether you win or lose; it's how you play the game.' Well, Grantland Rice can go to hell as far as I'm concerned."
—Gene Autry, owner of the California Angels, on criticism of his signing of players to expensive long term contracts

Let me begin this chapter with a contention that should irritate all involved in the negotiations in any sport that has recently been or is still on strike. Neither the owners' position nor the players' position is logically defensible from an economic perspective. Enough fans and sportswriters have made that point already. I will analyze each position, taking each to its highly illogical conclusion.

Owners in all sports have steadfastly argued that they need a salary cap and some restrictions on free agency. They contend that without some restrictions, unbridled competition between them will drive some, presumably the small-market teams, to financial ruin. By salary cap the owners typically mean the maximum team payroll allowed. Typically, salary caps are associated with salary floors, that is, a minimum salary sum that a team must pay. Free agency simply means that a player can sell his services to the highest bidder; that is, he is a free agent in terms of being able to negotiate the best deal possible with any owner willing to negotiate with him. Until the 1970s, players in all leagues were bound by a "reserve clause" to the club with which they initially signed.[1] When a player initially signed a pro contract, that contract contained language that bound the signing player to a team for life unless the team chose to sell the contract. Even though the contract might call for a player to receive a salary for only one year, the club reserved the rights to the player for all subsequent years. A player was not free to negotiate with other teams even after the original contract expired. Currently, all sports have free agency, albeit limited in some form. The NBA and NFL have salary caps, the NBA since 1984 and the NFL since 1992. One of the most contentious issues of the 1994 strike in MLB and the lockouts in the NHL and the NBA was the issue of a cap.

ECONOMIC BACKGROUND

Before worrying about salary caps and free agency, let me review the salient points of Chapters 2 to 5. First, the owners have

---

[1] It was not uncommon in baseball for parents to sign a contract for a minor that precluded him from choosing who he played for or from having any voice in determining his salary even at age 35 or 40. One of the issues in the 1994 NHL strike was the age at which a player would become a free agent and be able to negotiate his contract without constraints. The NHL owners position: when an 18 year old signed with a club, he would be bound to that club until age 32.

been crying poverty for years, but actually major league sports, overall, are extremely profitable. The average return to owners of major league franchises in each league equals or exceeds average stock market returns. And second, while all leagues have high average returns, all leagues also have teams that are genuinely losing money, in some cases, lots of money. However, when teams are losing money, in most cases the evidence strongly suggests that it is not small market size or unfavorable stadium facilities that are responsible, although both may play a role. Rather, it appears that the primary culprit is the owner's financial negligence or the owner's pursuit of victories rather than profits.

The problem is not that owners are losing money on average: they're not and they haven't. They do have two problems. First, they are not making as much profit as they would like, largely because they want to win games and championships without paying competitive prices for their talent. On this problem, I am not sympathetic. The owners might like a 100 percent return rather than a 18 to 25 percent return. If this is the owners' most serious problem, my advice to them would be rather ungenerous: don't expect much sympathy from anyone and try not to destroy the games while trying to raise the returns even higher.

The second problem is that some owners are in it for the money and some are in it for the glory, ego, or wins. On this issue, I am more sympathetic. Steinbrenner, Ted Turner, and Edward DeBartolo have been more than willing to trade profits—lots of profits—for wins. Others like Bud Selig, Tom Werner (former owner, San Diego Padres), and Peter Pocklington (owner, Edmonton Oilers) are much less willing or able to trade profits for wins or are not quite so enthusiastically seeking championships. Compounding the problem: some owners are extraordinarily wealthy and have the financial ability and willingness to bankroll a team, if not attempt to buy a championship; some owners are blessed with a franchise that generates enough revenue to satisfy King Midas and are also willing to use those funds to field the best team money can buy; and still other owners are only wealthy enough to own a team, but not wealthy enough to compete financially in pouring great sums of money into a franchise in the pursuit of victories. A few owners like Bill Bidwell of the Arizona Cardinals depend on their clubs for their livelihood.

The second problem need not be a large-market versus small-market issue. It is more likely to be a rich-owner versus poor-owner issue or an owner who wants to win at all costs versus an owner who wants to maximize profits rather than wins. If the fundamental problem in pro sports is one of different perspectives, say winning versus making money, then there is no easy solution. A salary cap or limits on free agency need bear no relationship to a solution. Why are they so favored by owners? Quite simply, because they are something that the owners can agree on irrespective of their goals, profitability or wealth. These "solutions" do not address any real economic problem; they do address the common owner desire to increase profits.

What else can be said about the owners' position? Most notably, it is logically inconsistent. The owners have steadfastly fought real restrictions on franchise movements—at least whenever those restrictions would have reduced franchise profitability. They have endeavored to maintain and to promote competition among cities for franchises, a topic discussed in more detail in Chapter 10. The owners have also played one television network against another to obtain the most lucrative TV deals possible. To state the owners position most bluntly: the market system should work to determine where franchises are located; the market system should work to determine television broadcast fees; the market system should work to determine ticket prices; but the market system should not be allowed to work in setting player contracts. In that market there should be some checks on the ability of players to be paid what the market—and other owners—ay they are worth. Do the owners see the irony in this contrast?

TAXING PAYROLL

How about a tax on player salaries instead of restricting player mobility? If the justification is simply to reduce player salaries, we have a salary cap in disguise. However, one might argue for a tax for a different reason, as was done in the prior chapter, albeit with a focus on total costs rather than on player payroll only. Winning and losing are both part of the game. Teams like the Montreal Canadians need teams like the Winnipeg Jets, simply to have someone to beat. But the winning team may cost the losing team money. Consistent losing makes it harder to fill a stadium, except perhaps with Cubs and Mets fans. Thus, if an owner attempts to buy a championship, the result may be to cost other teams money (economists label this an externality).

The numbers presented in Chapter 6 indicate that it costs an MLB franchise almost $2 million to win one more game while losing a game means losing revenues of $0.6 million. These two numbers give us a tax rate of 33 percent for MLB. There is no economic rationale for a prohibitive penalty on an owner with a payroll a few million over the league average. A prohibitive penalty is simply a coercive and collusive step to restrain owners from paying market wages and should be ruled illegal. It should also be unnecessary. There is a logic for a tax based on costs imposed on other owners. In MLB a 30 to 35 percent tax on costs over the league average should be more than sufficient to do what a cap or tax should be designed to do: compensate for costs one owner imposes on other owners and provide appropriate incentives for the Steinbrenners to carefully consider all their expenditures. Could an owner attempt to buy a championship? Certainly, but if he does, he will also be paying a tax to the other owners. So why do we need a salary cap? The owners' self-restraint will provide that.

Now you may be doubled over with laughter at the thought— owners' self-restraint. They do have some, perhaps just not very much; the tax would give them more, and only a little more would appear necessary. Consider the example of baseball. There has been no salary cap and no reserve clause restrictions on players with more than six years major league experience. In theory, an owner should have been able to buy a championship relatively easily—albeit perhaps expensively. Had Steinbrenner wanted, he could have signed all the top talent that came on the market, Bonds, Maddux, et al. Would it have been expensive? Absolutely. Would it have produced a World Series Championship? Quite probably. Was Steinbrenner willing to do it? No. Now he certainly was willing to pay, as indicated by a *New York Times* headline

"Bonds and Maddux Offered $72 Million." But neither Bonds nor Maddux signed with the Yankees. I take this as an indication of Steinbrenner's self-restraint, albeit defined much more loosely than many would define it. Steinbrenner wanted to sign Bonds and Maddux but not at the prices that they wanted to play for the Yankees. Maybe it would have taken $100 million or $150 million. That Steinbrenner did not raise the ante that high indicates he has at least a shred of self-restraint.[2] If Steinbrenner had wanted to spend $200 million a year in salaries, he likely could buy a team that would be virtually unbeatable. It might not fill Yankee Stadium because there would be no suspense in the games. He and his partners would likely lose a bundle in the process. But it could be done. Why hasn't he done it? One answer is that he has some self-restraint. A better answer, for an economist at least, is that while he values winning, he also values profits, and he is not willing to pay that much for a championship.

Now there is one last point on the owner's position that needs to be mentioned, if only briefly. The owners have argued that some constraints need to be placed on free agency and on player mobility in the interests of maintaining competitive balance. If players can sign with whomever they wish, so the argument goes, rich teams will sign the best talent, competition will decrease, and ultimately league revenues will go down. There are only two problems with this argument. First, there is no recent evidence to support it. Pick a five- or ten-year period before and after free agency in any sport. More teams won championships under free agency than without free agency. The owner's argument is contradicted by the data! And second, restricting free agency restricts players from selling their services to the highest bidder; it does not restrict owners from selling player contracts to the highest bidder. MLB has a long history of weaker or poorer franchises selling their stars to the stronger and richer franchises. The Red Sox sale of Babe Ruth to the Yankees comes to mind. In hockey, Pocklington, owner of the Edmonton Oilers, has resoundingly opposed free agency and players selling their services to the high bidder.

---

[2] It also may indicate that at least some players, like some owners, may be motivated by factors other than money, since Bonds appears to have signed with San Francisco for less.

Pocklington also has consistently sold his star players, including Wayne Gretzky, to financially stronger franchises. Putting it most baldly, restricting free agency only restricts the players from selling themselves; it does not restrict owners from selling them. It should not be surprising that owners like that policy. However, it has no economic justification.[3]

The bottom line on the owners' position is simple. The owners can only be viewed as a gaggle of greedy hypocrites as long as they simultaneously play one city against another or one TV station against another to wring the best contract possible, and yet say that players should be denied the unfettered ability to pit owner against owner to wrest the best possible contract. Limits can work both ways. How would the owners feel if Congress restricted a franchise's ability to negotiate with more than one city about its location or its stadium arrangements? We should not be surprised that the owners would take such inconsistent positions. Each position by itself will serve to increase the owners' profits. The owners, however, should not expect anyone to take them seriously until they present logically and internally consistent arguments.

Next up, the players' position.

A Salary Cap—Who Gains and Who Loses?

It would be convenient if the players' position was the model of logical consistency, truth, and justice. Unfortunately, life is not quite that simple. The players' position also has problems. I have argued that a salary cap is unnecessary if revenue sharing is addressed head-on. However, if the owners still wanted to have a salary cap, perhaps as a fail-safe mechanism if revenue sharing did not work as planned, the players should offer no objection—in theory. The key is not the existence of a cap. The key is whether

---

[3] Now someone might say that MLB is a good example of where limits exist on the ability of an owner to sell off a team. There was one example where a sale was disallowed based on the best interests of baseball. (Does anyone seriously believe that the next commissioner would attempt to stop such an action by an owner?) Charlie Finley was temporarily blocked from selling players to the Red Sox and Yankees. Finley ultimately got his wish and unloaded his high-priced talent. MLB's most recent fire sales occurred in San Diego and Montreal. The Padres unloaded all their high-priced talent except Tony Gwynn, and the Expos have not signed their stars when they became eligible for higher salaries. These examples clearly indicate that there is no effective constraint on an owner's ability to sell a player's contract—except for a player specifying in his contract that he has the right to approve any potential trade.

the cap will be binding and whether it will lower player salaries. As caps have been presented, that is exactly their purpose.

The players' union in hockey was allegedly entirely unwilling even to discuss a salary cap. The owners in hockey proposed a 60 percent salary cap. When that was rejected, the Associated Press reported that, according to Harry Sinden, president and general manager of the Boston Bruins, the owners suggested the union pick a number for a cap, just to get the discussion going. Well, 100 percent seems like a logical starting point. After all, the players now effectively do have a salary cap, although it is not labeled a cap. The current cap is 100 percent of revenues—assuming that an owner is not so hungry for victory that he will pay literally any price for the best talent, including a price above the franchise's total revenue. To date, no owner in any sport has come close to this ratio. Thus, it would appear realistic to assume that 100 percent is a reasonable upper limit. The catch here is that the 100 percent limit is not binding. That is, it has not restricted and does not restrict player choice or owner choice. It has no effective impact on either the owners or the players. This type of cap simply is not worth arguing about, let alone striking about.

Presumably the cap could be lowered substantially from 100 percent and still not represent a binding constraint simply because of the franchise's other expenses. So assume the salary cap is 75 percent. No team in any sport has had salaries exceeding 75 percent of the league average of total revenues, although in MLB the Yankees have come close. Given game-day expenses and administrative and travel expenses, it is unlikely that any owner would be willing and able to pay over 75 percent of revenues in salaries. Simply stated, the 75 percent cap is just that, a cap, not a minimum that clubs must reach but a maximum that clubs may (or may not) reach but cannot exceed.

In addition, the cap should be set at a level such that all teams are not at the cap, as is approximately the case in both basketball and football. If all teams are at the cap, then the cap simply is a binding constraint to lower salaries and by itself has no impact, as we will see in a moment, on equalizing profits between rich and poor franchises. To the extent that it lowers overall costs, it will increase a league's total profits. But again this increase in profits is accomplished only by short-circuiting the free market. That may be the owners' desire, but such a cap if imposed unilaterally should be rejected by the courts as a restraint of trade.

That some cap exists is not debatable. The only potential questions are (1) whether there should be some league-mandated upper bound, (2) how high that bound should be, and (3) whether there should also be a minimum.

Should there be a league-mandated upper bound? I really don't care, and you shouldn't either, nor should the unions. The unions might as well pack that argument in and let the owners win that point. There are enough other arguments the owners deserve to lose. The unions should agree to a salary cap of, say, 75 percent and let the games go on. There is virtually no cost of doing that—assuming that you have the other appropriate incentives like revenue sharing and prohibitions against collusion. The cap should be set high enough, however, so it generally does not interfere with the workings of the marketplace; although you might design it to provide another safety valve for small-market clubs (or for owners who are unwilling to pay to win). The funny thing about the salary cap, though, is that it may financially benefit the large-market clubs much more than the small-market clubs.

A salary cap can be structured in any number of ways, and its impact on team finances depends critically on the cap's structure. While the differences might appear trivial, they have major differences in their implications, so bear with me on the details. The bottom line in advance: under a salary cap which owners are the financial winners and which the losers is less than obvious. George Steinbrenner and the Yankees could be the biggest financial winners with a salary cap in baseball! In the NBA, the biggest winner might be the Knicks; in the NFL, the 49ers; and in the NHL, the Rangers.

Plan A: Salary caps typically allow a franchise to have a team payroll no greater than a fixed percentage of the average league revenues. For example, in 1994 the NFL used 64 percent of "defined gross revenues" (declining slightly in subsequent years). While discussion focuses on the cap, there also is a salary floor or minimum payroll for each team. In 1994 the maximum for the NFL was $34.6 while the minimum was $27 million. Let us ignore the salary floor for this first cap proposal.

What are the implications of this type of cap? Rich franchises profit tremendously; the players lose; and poorer clubs become marginally more competitive. Consider extending this type of cap to baseball using the Yankees and Brewers as an example. Franchise revenues in 1994 would have averaged about $62.9 million without a strike. With a cap of 50 percent, the MLB 1994 average, each club could pay a maximum of $31.5 million in salaries. The Yankees' payroll would have had to shrink from $44.8 million, a drop of $13.3 million (I ignore any gradual phase-in since that does not affect the overall results). Most of this cut in payroll would go straight to the bottom line: attendance will likely fall only marginally and the Yankees' profits would increase dramatically. Of course, Steinbrenner would not be able to use those profits for player salaries, but he could use them to improve the facilities, the scouting, and the front office, all of which might improve the Yankees' chances of winning.[4] Alternately, Steinbrenner could simply pocket the savings. The Brewers, with a payroll of $23.4 million, would not have to do anything under this payroll cap. Their costs would remain unchanged. If teams like the Yankees spent less, the Brewers would likely be slightly more competitive, but their revenues likely would increase by less than $1 million.[5]

The effect of this plan across all clubs would be that players would lose salaries equal to the sum of what individual teams are currently paying over the cap. In 1994, 15 MLB teams exceeded the hypothetical cap by a total of $95 million. Reducing payrolls

---

[4] This discussion assumes that owners like Steinbrenner would not attempt to subvert the cap—which probably is not a good assumption. However, strategies to avoid the cap simply add another level of problems to the analysis.

[5] The exact calculation is rather complex, but a simple example can demonstrate the basic point. Suppose only the Yankees must decrease their payroll and suppose only the worst teams in the American League gain. If the Yankees' payroll decreases by $13.3 million, we expect them to win approximately 7 fewer games. If the weakest 7 AL teams each pick up one of those victories, then based on the numbers in Chapter 6 each of the weakest franchises would gain one more victory and would see an increase in revenues of about $400,000.

by that amount yields an average pay cut of 10 percent for MLB players. While the typical fan might not be particularly sympathetic toward baseball players with an average salary in excess of $1 million, there is no evidence that such a pay cut would reduce ticket prices by one cent, a point I will come back to in the next chapter. All the money saved likely would go back to the owners in terms of increased profits. As noted previously, while the owners deserve a reasonable return on their investment, they already are doing quite well with average returns of 18 to 25 percent per year. If MLB had imposed this type of cap in 1994, the average level of profits would have increased from $4.9 million to $8.3 million and the rate of return would have gone from 20 percent up to 23 percent.

Financially, in this cap plan and in most cap plans, the rich clubs gain and the players lose. The small-market clubs' costs are not reduced, and while small-market clubs' revenues may increase marginally, the rich clubs' revenues may have offsetting decreases. Owners who value profits more than wins are unlikely to change their behavior significantly with a salary cap. Small-market clubs may choose to compete more aggressively for talent, but for arguments' sake assume that they do not. (The distribution of talent is a much more complex subject than I suspect even the owners realize, as will be demonstrated later.) On the field, clubs like the Yankees will not fare quite as well while small-market clubs gain. Does the league as a whole gain? Only if talent becomes spread more evenly, races become tighter, and thus attendance rises and total revenues increase. The owners have emphasized this argument. Unfortunately, as demonstrated in Chapter 6, the likely increase in revenues will be microscopic.

Plan B: Now consider a salary cap where the cap refers to the league average salary and all teams must pay that amount (rather than having the option of paying below the cap). In basketball and football, in theory, there is a salary range for franchises. However, in the NBA the range runs roughly from the cap to 40 percent above the cap. In the NFL the allowed 1994 range was from $34.6 million to $27 million. In practice, however, virtually all teams are at or within the length of the football of the maximum. Thus, from a practical perspective the cap is not just a maximum; it also effectively serves as a minimum.[6]

With this type of cap, sticking with the baseball example, the Yankees again would have to cut their payroll but the Brewers must increase theirs. The players would end up with the same overall salaries, though there would be a change in where many were playing. The Yankees would have to cut some high-priced talent while the Brewers would have to sign some. Again, the Yankees gain financially. The Brewers, however, are likely to lose rather than gain financially. Why? Again taking 50 percent of average league revenues as the salary cap, all MLB franchises must now spend $31.5 million on salaries. The Brewers current payroll is $23.4 million. Thus, the salary cap will require them to increase their payroll by $8.1 million. Will their revenues increase by that amount? Quite frankly, the odds are better that Bob Uecker returns to MLB next year and hits over .300.

For the Brewers not to lose more money under this salary cap they will have to increase their revenues by at least $8.1 million. Can they do this? National broadcast revenues are set by contract. Thus, the additional revenues must come from local sources. Let us assume that the Brewers could increase local media revenues by 25 percent. That is probably too high because local media payments are linked more closely to market size than to number of wins, but let's be generous. That would generate about $1.4 million and would mean that gate and stadium revenues must increase by $6.7 million for the Brewers to break even. If the Brewers net $10 per seat (which they don't), can they realistically expect to sell 670,000 additional tickets because of a salary cap that is both a maximum and a minimum? They have two chances: fat and slim. The Brewers' attendance must increase from 1.8 million to 2.47 million, and the Brewers did not draw this many fans even when they were in playoff contention. Furthermore, the Brewers would have to draw this many additional fans just to break even, assuming an extraordinary increase in revenues! The conclusion: the idea

---

[6] Teams play accounting games with the cap, as noted in Chapter 3 on the NBA. Those games are becoming more prevalent even in the NFL with a so-called "hard cap." The Dallas Cowboys and San Francisco 49ers have been particularly creative in skirting the cap.

that the Brewers and other teams currently losing money would be helped by a salary cap requires Herculean assumptions. Realistically, the answer to their financial problems is not a salary cap but revenue sharing. And there is no logical argument to link revenue sharing with a salary cap.

So what does this type of cap imply? Large-market teams again win financially—assuming that their revenues do not decline as rapidly as their costs—while small-market teams probably lose big. Owners like Steinbrenner and Turner will be affected non-financially since they will not be able to attempt to buy a pennant. This type of salary cap need not substantially constrain players—as long as the cap is not set lower than what the free market would set.

This example of a salary cap raises an additional concern. It is not clear that owners have even begun to consider the impacts of a salary cap on the game itself. For example, with a MLB salary cap of, say, $31.5 million, how do you buy the strongest team possible? If "good pitching dominates good hitting," then I'll buy the best pitchers possible. The other players will be the best I can get for whatever money I have left. Thus, pitchers' salaries will increase relative to hitters', and the game itself will change to emphasize pitching—especially if I can tinker with the design of my park to help my pitching. I am no expert on baseball strategy, but I do know that dramatic changes in the economic incentives like imposing a salary cap can have implications on the very nature of the game that are not widely understood but that may dwarf the implications of changes like the designated hitter rule.

Plan C: This plan is the same as Plan B, but with no presumption that all teams will raise their payrolls to the salary cap. It also appears to be the theory underlying the plan that team owners have in mind. Two numbers then become important: the highest payroll allowed and the lowest. Don't worry for the moment about the games accountants can play with the salary numbers. MLB owners have suggested a cap of 50 percent. If we add a minimum of 40 percent of the league's average total revenue, then clubs would need a minimum payroll of $25.2 million. As in Plan A, the cap calls for 15 clubs to reduce player salaries by $95 million. The 7 clubs below the minimum would have to increase their payrolls by a total of $36.7 million. The players' overall loss would now be $58.3 million ($95 minus $36.7) or a 6.6 percent salary cut.

Now if you wanted to be more realistic about it, you could pick a cap higher than 50 percent and ask what the cost would be. So take an easy case having a certain symmetry with the owners' proposal. Suppose that the maximum is set at 60 percent of average revenues while the minimum is set at 40 percent. What would happen? Any team with a payroll in excess of $37.7 million would be required to reduce their payroll. In 1994, 8 teams would have had to lower their payrolls by a total of $24.4 million. This would almost exactly offset the salary increases required of the teams below the minimum. The bottom line: the players would have a minimal net change; the rich teams would be forced to spend less and poor teams would be forced to spend more. Presumably, the players break even while competitive balance increases.

In sum, what are the implications of Plan C? With either a 50 percent or a 60 percent maximum, financially speaking, the rich get richer and the poor get poorer, although the poorer franchises are not hit quite as hard as in Plan B. Beyond that, there are a lot of questions. Two stand out. First, precisely what are the maximum and minimum rates? To the extent that the maximum is more of a constraint than the minimum, then the players lose. That should be no surprise since it appears to be why salary caps are so popular among owners. Their goal: make the maximum binding on most clubs and include a minimum to make sure that no owner violates some sense of good taste.

Second, what happens to the distribution of players? This distribution shapes who wins and loses, how competitive the league is and potentially at what rate league revenues grow. The assumption is that a more equal distribution of talent will make for more competitive games and championship races, and thus will increase the revenues available both to owners and to players. Whether that actually will happen depends on (1) how the distribution of players changes, (2) how tight games and league races become, and (3) whether more fans actually take more interest. The evidence in Chapter 6 suggests that league revenues will not increase dramatically.

In fact, to the extent that teams like the Yankees become less competitive and the Brewers become more competitive, league revenues could fall. National television ratings are substantially higher when the Yankees or Dodgers play than when the Brewers or Reds play. Putting the Brewers rather than the Yankees in the World Series costs MLB money because TV money ultimately will be smaller. In addition, teams like the Yankees likely will lose more gate revenues than teams like the Brewers will gain simply because they are in a bigger market.

It is important to note that financial gains are not the only important thing at stake with a cap. Steinbrenner, for example, will probably gain financially under a salary cap. That need not make him better off. Steinbrenner had the option in 1994 of not paying $44.8 million in salaries, either by not offering some players a contract or by selling the contracts of some of his players. That he voluntarily chose to pay $44.8 million in salaries and that a salary cap will force him to do something he would not do voluntarily suggests that he is not better off with a salary cap, looking at both financial and nonfinancial concerns. Once again, we return to the point that owners value both profits and victories, and some appear quite willing to sacrifice profits for victories.

This section presented three alternative perspectives to a salary cap. There are a lot of other twists: a cap for rookies, constraints on free agency, binding salary arbitration, etc. Table 8.1 briefly lists some of these issues and the underlying economic concerns. Including these factors does not change the general points raised here, but they do raise a host of additional issues. For example, is it appropriate for a union to bargain for rookie salary caps when none of the bargaining members would be subject to those caps and the rookies have no say in the process? Is revenue sharing an appropriate topic for collective bargaining discussions? And what constraints should be placed on salary arbitration?

THE SALARY CAP—OVERALL IMPLICATIONS

So why the big push for a salary cap? The only ready argument that makes economic sense is that the owners collectively would like to pay players less and they would like restricted competition

Table 8.1

ISSUES SEPARATING OWNERS AND PLAYERS

(1)
Free Agency
Player's Position: No limits on eligibility.
Owner's Position: Highly restricted to limit salary costs.
Economic Analysis: Should the market set salaries or should player salaries be artificially restricted by arbitrary regulations?

(2)
Salary Arbitration
Player's Position: Favored when there are limits on free agency.
Owner's Position: Opposed, since it may increase players' salaries and introduce uncertainty about salary costs.
Economic Analysis: A second-best solution. If the market cannot be used to set salaries, an arbitrator who determines what salaries would be set in the market is preferred to fixing salaries at arbitrary levels.

(3)
Draft
Player's Position: A necessary evil to maintain parity.
Owner's Position: A necessary evil to maintain parity.
Economic Analysis: Efficiently allocates players to maintain parity, but at a potentially sizable financial cost to players entering the league. Need not produce parity if owners can sell player contracts.

(4)
Rookie Salary Limits
Player's Position: Circumvents NBA's problem of hyper-escalation in rookie salaries.
Owner's Position: Favored since it helps to control costs.
Economic Analysis: Salary limit bargained between two sides that have no stake in the costs imposed on rookies. Necessary only if there is a salary cap.

(5)
Salary Caps
Player's Position: If it's spelled C-A-P, it's B-A-D.
Owner's Position: Required to restrict spending on players and to maintain parity.
Economic Analysis: Both unnecessary and irrelevant for reasons detailed in chapter.

(6)
Payroll Tax
Player's Position: Concern that it represents a salary cap in disguise.
Owner's Position: An alternative vehicle to hold down spending on salaries.
Economic Analysis: Justified only if aim is to force an owner to recognize costs imposed on other clubs.

(7)
Revenue Sharing
Player's Position: Not generally considered.
Owner's Position: Some favor and others oppose. Only limited implementation outside the NFL.
Economic Analysis: Only mechanism needed to achieve financial parity. Must be implemented carefully or league revenues may atrophy.

for players. John Harrington, president of the Boston Red Sox, has publicly admitted as much. With a salary cap that effectively restricts many owners, league profits would go up as player salaries were held down. But if the salary cap is set below what salaries the free market would determine, why should anyone but the owners be in favor?

The owners have advanced two additional arguments in support of a salary cap. The first is that a salary cap would give owners more control over the largest component of costs. That argument is totally without merit. Without a salary cap an owner has virtually complete control over player costs. Binding arbitration may increase the cost of a player above what an owner wants to pay, but the owner may trade the player before it is time to pay his salary. Adding a salary cap actually takes some discretion away from an individual owner, depending on the exact nature of the cap. An owner might have to spend less—or more—than desired and thus loses some control. As far as imposing control is concerned, any owner can follow the lead of the San Diego Padres in 1992 and sell off the high-priced help.

The second additional argument for a salary cap is that it would facilitate the "future economic growth of the game" according to an ad by MLB owners in *USA Today* (11/9/94). If the owners knew what costs would be, they could invest in the game and increase the total revenues coming into the sport. There is an element of truth to this point, but the way in which owners have presented the argument suggests that it is simply window dressing. Why? Three quick reasons. First, owners now know their costs. The only uncertainty concerns the results of arbitration and arbitration was a compromise to restrain salaries of younger players. Second, if owners really were concerned about overall control, why do they focus on one component of costs, players' salaries? Why not focus on total costs or on total revenues? And third, to say that owners would have a greater incentive to "grow" the game suggests that there are unexploited profit opportunities. Does this mean that owners currently receiving a 20 to 25 percent return will not undertake some potentially profitable actions that they would undertake if their returns were 23 to 28 percent instead? Pardon my skepticism.

The bottom line is that there is no solid economic argument for a salary cap and there are lots of solid economic arguments against one. Most important: the salary cap distorts economic incentives. In addition, while people in the NBA may not like to hear this, there is no evidence that a salary cap actually works!

Basketball, with a salary cap since 1984, is widely cited as an example of a successful cap. There should be no debate that basketball was struggling when the cap was introduced in 1984 and has staged a remarkable recovery. However, relatively little of that fiscal success was due to the salary cap. The 1984 agreement also brought increased revenue sharing, a real sense of partnership between the players association and the league (e.g. on drug testing), and the injection of substantial marketing savvy. These factors played a much greater role than the salary cap in reviving the NBA's financial fortunes.

What is the evidence? The strongest evidence is in terms of incentives. Many NBA franchises in the early 1980s were suffering losses. The partnership between the players and the owners, perhaps forged in a spirit of desperation, led both to ask how league revenues could be increased so that the franchises would survive and the players would keep their lucrative employment. The salary cap simply provided the mechanism to restrict player salaries when those salaries were going to be restricted anyway, potentially as franchises folded.

Recently there has been no concern about NBA franchises failing and the salary cap has become a binding constraint on virtually all teams. That is, most teams would opt to pay players more if the salary cap did not stand in the way. While much legalese has attempted to close the loopholes and make sure teams abide by the letter if not the spirit of the cap, there are ways around it. For the 1993-1994 season only the Dallas Mavericks were below the cap. (The Mavericks, perhaps not coincidentally, also had the worst record in the NBA.) The most obvious example: multi-year guaranteed contracts for rookies. Glenn Robinson has tremendous basketball potential and may well be one of the game's dominating players over the next ten years. But consider his 10-year, $67 million contract with the Milwaukee Bucks. Based on other salaries in the league, Robinson probably should have been paid in the range of $3 to $4 million for 1994-1995. Given the 1994 salary cap of $15.9 million per team, Robinson's pro-rated salary would represent 42 percent of payroll. The Buck's did not have the room under the cap to sign him for even $2 million. So they just extended the length of the contract to get around the constraint imposed by the cap. The Bucks are not alone in this subterfuge. Anfernee Hardaway, Larry Johnson, and Chris Webber also have well-publicized, long-term contracts that may well be justified based on their playing skills but are strangely structured to avoid running afoul of the salary cap.[7]

View a salary cap like a government regulation. Initially a problem arises and a regulation, perhaps imperfect, is put in place to deal with that problem. Over the years, those who are regulated find loopholes around the regulation. The problem itself may go away, but regulations rarely do. Is this the fate of the salary cap? In addition, the discussion of NBA finances in Chapter 3 argued that the salary cap currently distorts the perceived financial health of the league.

I cannot argue that basketball would have been better off without a salary cap for the last ten years. I can argue that the cap has outlived its usefulness and the NBA should consider additional revenue sharing instead. That the NBA is now thriving and was struggling when its salary cap was introduced is not open to debate. That the salary cap together with innovative marketing and a spirit of cooperation between players and owners explains the improved finances of the NBA also is not open to debate. What is definitely open to debate, however, is whether the salary cap was or is the most effective vehicle for achieving financial success in the NBA or in any other league.

CONCLUSION

Let us briefly review the major points in the last two chapters. First, revenue sharing between clubs is economically justified because they produce a joint product: wins, losses, and entertain-

---

[7] Deion Sanders and Drew Bledsoe have long-term contracts in part to skirt the NFL's salary cap.

ment. Second, there is no economic justification for a salary cap or a reserve clause; both unnecessarily short-circuit the free market. Third, owners can agree on a salary cap, even while they disagree about whether they are in the game for profits or victory, but players oppose any cap. And fourth, an owner who wins imposes costs on one who loses, and this relationship between owners provides a sound economic justification for a tax on excessive owner spending. This tax is appropriately levied only on incremental expenditures, however. Similarly, an owner who does not field a competitive team imposes costs on those who do since attendance rises when games are close, and this relationship provides justification for a tax on losses.

So is a labor stoppage, either strike or lockout, justified? Chapters 2 through 5 documented that each league on average has substantial profits and a rate of return equal to or greater than available elsewhere. That finding should surprise no one since each league is a monopoly. The players and owners can haggle all they want about how they should split those monopoly profits. As they haggle, they should keep in mind three facts. First, markets do work. Salary caps subvert the market and are inappropriate and ultimately ineffective; revenue sharing and taxes on incremental costs and losing teams can augment the market and should resolve at least some conflicts. Second, each league has a monopoly for that sport but is part of a much larger industry—the entertainment industry—where it faces intense competition. Shutting down for a season or part of a season places the league at a major competitive disadvantage in this broader industry. And third, in sports you have a loser for every winner; in economics you can have two winners—or two losers.

Chapter 9

Free Agency and Salaries — Are Professional Athletes Really Underpaid?

"I didn't know what a free agent meant until I saw my first paycheck." —**Peter Gent, formerly of the Dallas Cowboys**

"It isn't the high price of stars that is expensive. It's the high price of mediocrity." —**Bill Veeck**

"No court in the world can make a Gene Autry or a George Steinbrenner pay a player $3 million. The courts cocked the gun. The owners pulled the trigger."
—**Ruly Carpenter, president, Philadelphia Phillies, on free agency**

"Isn't it amazing that we're worth so much on the trading block and worth so little when we talk salary with the general manager."
—**Jim Kern, pitcher, Cleveland Indians**

What are professional athletes really paid? How has their compensation changed over time? And how does their compensation compare with a more typical worker's compensation? Underlying these questions, for many fans, are two complaints. One common sentiment among fans is that professional athletes are overpaid. To put it concretely, my mother has a visceral dislike—she won't use the word "hate"—of Roger Clemens because his salary is so high and he appears unappreciative of his fame and fortune. She wants the Red Sox to win except when Clemens pitches. Another complaint is

200

that high player salaries have caused ticket prices to become prohibitively expensive. With 1995 NFL, NBA, and NHL average ticket prices over $30, attending a major league game is expensive family entertainment. Are either of these complaints justified?

STATISTICAL BACKGROUND

To determine if professional athletes are overpaid we first need to determine how well paid they really are. While it may seem obvious that professional athletes' salaries are extremely high, simple statistics give a misleading picture of the average pro's finances—although most would argue that they are well compensated by any measure.

Major league baseball is the initial focus because there are more MLB salary statistics available. The economic pressures that produce the distribution of baseball salaries are similar to those in basketball, football, and hockey. Thus the findings should be similar in all sports.

Despite Benjamin Disraeli's contention that there are "Lies, damn lies, and statistics," it is useful to consider some statistical background at the outset. There are alternative ways to define "average" and in sports, some important differences are hidden in the details. Two measures of average are particularly important: the mean and the median. Consider a simple example to demonstrate the difference. Suppose a baseball team had the distribution of salaries given in Table 9.1. There are two "stars" with salaries of $5 million each, seven "quality" players with salaries of $1 million each, 10 "role players" with salaries of $300,000 each, and five "rookies" with salaries of $100,000 each. What is the "average" salary? The total payroll is $21 million, divided by 24 players yields a mean average of $875,000. But over 70 percent of the team is making a dramatically lower salary. An alternative approach is to arrange the salaries in descending order and ask what salary lies in the middle of this order. This salary is the median average salary and in this example is $300,000. Precisely how you define the average makes a substantial difference in this case. Generally, "average" refers to the mean.

Why make a big issue out of this point? Whether the average

Table 9.1

BASEBALL SALARIES
Hypothetical Example
What is Meant by "Average?"

Player Status	Number	Salary
"Star"	2	$5,000,000
"Quality"	7	1,000,000
"Role"	10	300,000
"Rookie"	5	100,000
Total	24	21,000,000

Mean Average Salary = $875,000 = $21.0 million
    divided by 24 players
Median Average Salary = $300,000 = 12th and 13th
    largest salaries

is $875,000 or $300,000, it is still a lot more than most of us make. The example demonstrates, as counter-intuitive as it may sound, that the typical player does not make the mean average salary. This example is not an aberration either. In pro sports, the typical player generally makes much less than the mean. In addition, keep in mind that the mean average is not of all players but is only of the best of the best, and generally the players make those salaries for a very few years.

MLB SALARIES

Table 9.2 presents MLB average salaries from 1970 through 1995, when available presenting both the mean and the median. The numbers generally exclude bonuses, but baseball bonuses are only a small fraction of total salaries. Three points about these salary numbers bear some comment. First, the obvious: baseball salaries have increased astronomically over the last 25 years. While the mean salary in 1970 was a healthy $29,300, the mean salary in 1994 was a lottery-winning $1.1 million. Inflation was not nearly high enough to explain the salary growth. A salary of $29,300 in

1970 is equivalent to $112,600 in 1994 dollars. So MLB players have grown much wealthier. But you didn't need an economist to tell you that.

Table 9.2

AVERAGE SALARIES IN BASEBALL

(all salaries in thousands)

Year	Mean	Median	Minimum	Percentage Increases	
				Years	Mean Increase
1970	$29.3	N/A	$12	1970-75	8.8%
1975	44.7	N/A	16	1976-81	29.7%
1980	143.8	N/A	30	1981-86	17.5%
1985	371.2	N/A	60	1986-89	6.6%
1990	587.5	N/A	100	1990	20.2%
1991	823.3	$362	100	1991	42.5%
1992	985.2	350	109	1992	19.7%
1993	1,088.0	496	109	1993	10.4%
1994	1,182.0	500	109	1994	8.6%
1995	1,095.7	290	109	1995	-7.3%

N/A indicates not available.

Second, salaries escalated dramatically since free agency. An owner might decry the impacts on profits and the changes that money has made in the way the game is played. Economists, however, would contend that salaries were artificially depressed prior to free agency. Until the early 1970s, an owner could sell "his" players without their consent or pay them whatever he deemed appropriate, limited only by a maximum 20 percent pay cut. The player's only choice: play for him or quit baseball. From 1970 to 1975, the last five years before free agency, MLB players averaged an 8.8 percent yearly salary increase while inflation averaged 6.5 percent. Thus their real salaries, after inflation, rose 2.3 percent a year. In the five years following the advent of free agency, salaries increases averaged 29.7 percent a year. Inflation averaged 9.8 percent leaving players with a real gain of almost 20 percent a year. The salary increases accompanying free agency strongly suggest that the players were catching up to where they would have been all along if their salaries had been set by a free market.

Once this surge was over, salary growth slowed substantially—assisted by owner collusion in bidding on free agents. From 1986 to 1989 players' salaries increased by 6.6 percent and inflation averaged 4.2 percent leaving players a net gain after inflation of 2.4 percent—almost exactly the real increase prior to free agency. Free agency led to much higher salary **levels**. But free agency has not lead to higher salary **increases** once player salaries have reached free market levels.

From 1990 to 1992 salaries escalated again, almost as rapidly as they did in the first year of free agency (42.5 percent in 1991 versus 47.7 percent in 1977, the first year of free agent wages). The cause: a new television contract that dramatically increased the revenue entering MLB. While the escalation in television revenues led to higher franchise market values, it also led some owners to bid more aggressively for free agents. An owner whose primary goal was to win a World Series was given almost $10 million in additional television money to go out and buy the team to win it. Other owners had to ante up on salaries or fall behind in the standings. Salaries immediately jumped dramatically and then continued to increase as (1) arbitration awards were indexed to free agent signings and (2) player contracts negotiated before the TV deal came up for renewal. Nevertheless, salary growth slowed substantially through 1994 and then salaries declined in 1995. These developments should have been expected given MLB's decrease in national media money and 1995 drop in attendance. Given the limited new revenues in MLB, there should be no further dramatic increases in average salaries—unless some new large revenue source comes along. In sum, skyrocketing salaries have been created by skyrocketing revenues; as revenue growth slows, salary growth should slow. The 1995 salary numbers are down substantially, reflecting the decrease in MLB revenue.

The third important implication of Table 9.2 is that the distribution of salaries among players has become much more unequal. For example, the ratio of the mean salary to the minimum salary was approximately 2.5 to 1 in 1970 and had increased marginally to 2.8 to 1 by 1975, just before the dawn of free agency. Then the ratio of the mean to the minimum jumped to 4.8 to 1 by 1980 and has continued to rise since, increasing to 5.9 to 1 in 1990 and to 10.8 to 1 in 1994. This change is largely driven by economic factors and has important implications for the likely evolution of MLB.

Before considering those implications, we must take a harder look at the distribution of MLB salaries. Salary averages can hide a multitude of sins so consider the entire 1994 MLB distribution of salaries, plotted in Chart 9.1 (1995 appears to usher in a new era that will be discussed shortly). The chart indicates that approximately 250 of the 700 MLB players made between $109,000 to $200,000 and just over 100 more made $200,000 to $400,000. The chart also makes clear that few players were paid like Bobby Bonilla ($6.3 million), Joe Carter ($5.5 million) and Rafael Palmeiro ($5.4 million). The more typical ball player earned less than $600,000. MLB's minimum salary of $109,000 is still a lot of money, but it also is a long way from Bobby Bonilla's standard of living. Exclusively from a salary perspective, younger or less talented players have more in common with the typical fan than with a Bobby Bonilla.

Parenthetically, you might ask why Bobby Bonilla was the highest paid MLB player in 1994 if you think all baseball decisions

Chart 9.1

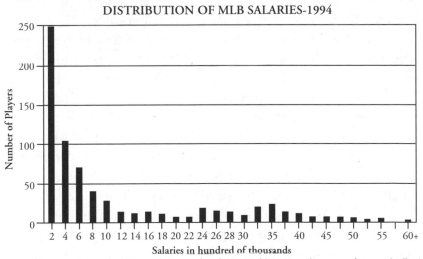

DISTRIBUTION OF MLB SALARIES-1994

Number of Players

Salaries in hundred of thousands

(2 corresponds to under $200,000, 4 corresponds to $200,00 to $400,000, ... 60 corresponds to over 6 million)

Chart 9.2

DISTRIBUTION OF BASEBALL-PLAYING ABILITIES

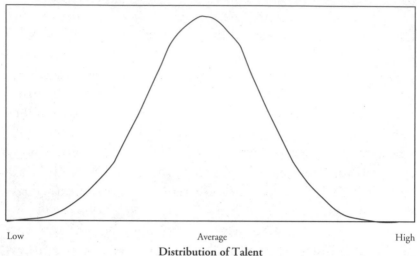

Low   Average   High

Distribution of Talent

are rational. Frank Thomas and Jeff Bagwell, 1994 MVP winners, were not among the top 100 highest paid players in 1994. Since then Thomas and Bagwell have negotiated contracts that puts them near the top of the salary rankings. Nevertheless, just like for the rest of us, achievement is but one determinant of salary. In MLB, luck, how a contract is structured and whether a player has been eligible for free agency all play important roles.

Another way of looking at the distribution of salaries is to compare it with the distribution of talent. Abilities across a wide range of skills follow what economists label a "normal" distribution that looks like a bell-shaped curve and is plotted in Chart 9.2. Let this bell curve represent the distribution of baseball playing skills. Who plays in the majors? The best 700 players in a population of 250 million (for simplicity consider only the U.S. population) or approximately the best 0.0003 percent of the population. Alternately, 1 in 357,000 people is a MLB player. Only the extreme right hand tail of that distribution makes it to the major leagues. Even the worst of the pros—a Bob Uecker who has made a career out of how bad a ball player he was—actually is one of the most talented baseball athletes in the world. This point is fairly obvious, however; why belabor it? Compare Chart 9.1 with the right tail of Chart 9.2. Using some imagination, the two distributions are approximately the same shape. The moral: in MLB the distribution of salaries mirrors the distribution of abilities, focusing exclusively on the extreme right tail of the talent distribution.

Chart 9.3 presents the 1995 MLB salary distribution, contrasting it with the 1993 distribution.[1] While the mean average salaries are almost identical, the distribution of these salaries differs dramatically. 1995 salaries are substantially higher for the best paid players but most of the rest make less in 1995 than in 1993. The salaries for the very best appear to have sharply escalated while those a step below have fallen appreciably. The total amount paid in salaries is about the same, but much more now goes to the top few players. In addition, there are a lot more players receiving the major league minimum salary. The increasing number of those at the minimum in part may reflect an increase in injuries. More players were on injured reserve resulting in more minor leaguers being called up to the majors. However, part of the increase in

Chart 9.3

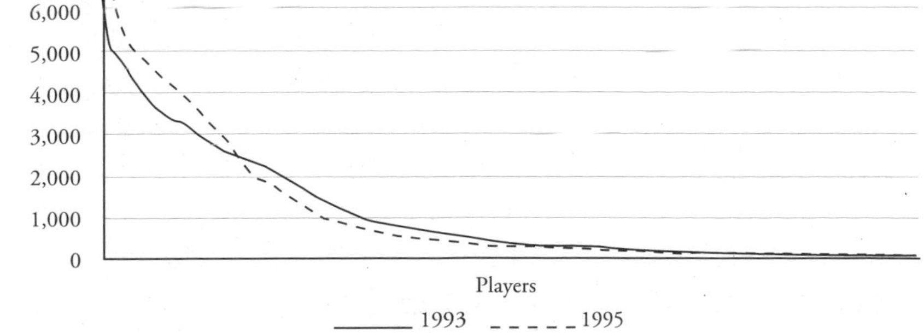

DISTRIBUTION OF MLB SALARIES
(all salaries in hundred of thousands)

Players

———— 1993   _ _ _ _ _ 1995

[1] Comparing 1994 and 1995 yields conclusions similar to those reported below. 1993 is employed rather than 1994 because the 1993 and 1995 average salaries are virtually identical whereas the 1994 average is slightly higher. Thus, comparisons using 1994 and 1995 salaries could mix a changing average with other changes in the distribution.

lower salaries appears to reflect a trend toward using less costly players in utility roles. That is, rather than sign an aging veteran for bench depth, some franchises appear more willing to go with rookies and take their chances.

The changes from 1993 to 1995 may be the beginning of a fundamental restructuring of MLB salaries. Not all contracts were renegotiated between 1993 and 1995. As those contracts expire and are renegotiated, the trend to greater salary dispersion will likely increase. Stars will be paid more. The rest will have to settle for less. A question to ponder: as the economic interests of different groups of players begins to diverge, how long will the MLB Players' Association be able to speak with one voice for the players?

Yet another way to look at the distribution of salaries is to divide players into so-called deciles, that is, the highest paid 10 percent, the second highest paid 10 percent, etc., and then ask what the average salary of each decile is or, what is the average salary of the highest paid 10 percent?). Chart 9.4 presents these averages for the last four years and corroborates an earlier point. The best paid MLB players do extremely well and have done increasingly well relative to their lower paid brethren. From 1991 to 1995 the average salary of the top decile has increased from under $3 million to over $5 million. In contrast, the average of the sixth decile increased from $0.5 million to $0.6 million in 1994 before declining to $0.35 million in 1995. The average of the lowest decile has remained basically unchanged at approximately $0.1 million. A large fraction of players earn high but not outlandish salaries.

Chart 9.4 also gives a different perspective on why player costs have escalated over the last five years. The players whose salaries have increased the most were already the best paid. That is, average salaries in deciles 1 through 7, the lowest paid 70 percent, hardly rose from 1991 through 1994 and then fell in 1995. Most of the additional payroll costs from 1991 to 1994 were due to salary increases of the highest paid 30 percent of baseball players. MLB payrolls increased by approximately $250 million from 1991 to 1994. Of this amount, the costs of the top 30 percent increased by $210 million. The salaries of the stars and potential stars were the driving force behind MLB's player cost increases.[2] 1995 payrolls would have fallen precipitously except for the salary increases of players in the top 15 percent, many of whom had contracts predating the most recent labor dispute.

What is causing this widening gap between the salaries of stars and role players? The answer: the competitive market is at work. The Bonds's, Clemens's, and Thomas's are receiving dramatic salary increases because they contribute substantially to their team's success. Bill James in a yearly series of books documents how stars and superstars contribute—beyond an average player—to the success of their teams. He attempts to determine how many more games a team would win with Wade Boggs at third base rather than Archi Cianfrocco or Dean Palmer or Sean Berry. A Wade Boggs could be the difference for the Yankees between first-place and also-ran status. A Bobby Bonilla may lead a team from mediocrity to a pennant. As Walter O'Malley, owner of the Dodgers stated, "God save us from owners who are just one pitcher away." Given some owners' penchants for winning, that may be all the

Chart 9.4

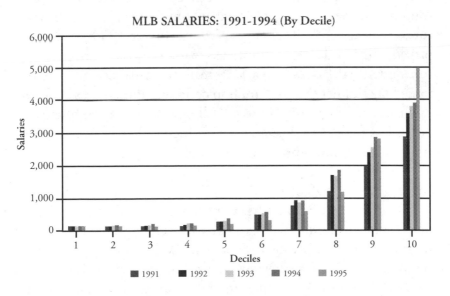

MLB SALARIES: 1991-1994 (By Decile)

1991   1992   1993   1994   1995

---

[2] Many of the players in the bottom 70 percent are not eligible for free agency or arbitration, and their salaries often are far below what they would be in a free market. In many cases the players in the bottom 70 percent will not play in the majors long enough to qualify for free agent status.

justification needed to sign a superstar for what appears to be a ridiculously high price. But there is another reason as well. Fans want to see them play. I enjoy seeing the Red Sox play, but the games I really want to see are those when Roger Clemens pitches. Clemens puts bodies in the stands; Clemens contributes substantially to the Red Sox bottom line, even if people go to Fenway just to boo him. I'll watch the Red Sox when Aaron Sele or Erik Hanson is pitching, but with a touch less enthusiasm. An economist would say the demand for Red Sox tickets increases when Clemens pitches.

The effect is the same in every sport. Watching the Celtics with Larry Bird was a special event, even when Bird was hobbled with a bad back. Watching the Celtics with Dino Radja or Rick Fox is not the same. They are talented players but they lack Bird's magic. Ask the question: how much would you be willing to pay to watch Michael Jordan play basketball? Would you pay as much to watch if Toni Kukoc takes Jordan's place? What if it's Simpkins or Buechler or Caffey instead?

Expected on-the-field and in-the-stands improvements lead owners to bid up prices for stars or apparent stars. Meanwhile, the solid but unspectacular players for whom there are more substitutes see relatively little change in salary. In late 1994, while the players struck and owners threatened to impose a salary cap, Houston signed Jeff Bagwell to a $6.9 million contract and Seattle signed Jay Buhner to a $4.1 million contract. If there was a salary cap, every dollar more paid to a Jeff Bagwell or a Jay Buhner is a dollar less for a Dave Magadan or a Vince Coleman. Again, it's simple economics; supply and demand!

SALARIES AND THE SALARY CAP

Let us briefly return to the salary cap and examine its implications for the distribution of player salaries. Three points stand out. All should be fairly obvious. First, some well-known players will get the axe, not because their skills have eroded below major league levels but simply because they are more expensive. Quarterback Phil Simms' 1994 release by the New York Giants is exhibit A. Paul Tagliabue, Commissioner of the NFL, denied Simms was cut due to the cap. Tagliabue can issue any statement he wants about why Simms was released. The real answer to why Simms was cut: the Giants were $4 million over the cap and releasing Simms cut that gap in half. In MLB, given the choice between a rookie costing $109,000 or an "old-timer" like Kevin McReynolds at $2.9 million or Andre Dawson at $4.3 million, teams will increasingly opt for youth when those big contracts are not guaranteed. In 1995 dozens of MLB veterans were offered the choice of leaving baseball or working for a fraction of their prior salary. Big contracts at some point become a liability and increase a player's chances of being released. This economic pressure existed even without a cap, but a cap intensifies that pressure.

Second, introducing a cap into an existing system of contracts and prior agreements will be disruptive both to clubs and players. For a player to negotiate a contract without a cap and then suddenly find the rules changed in the middle of the contract certainly is going to seem unfair to him. A salary cap makes guaranteed contracts much more important for players. Just ask Phil Simms. Football players are quickly going to recognize that $300,000 guaranteed may be a better deal than $500,000 with no guarantee. Furthermore, teams will recognize it as well. An NFL general manager with a 1995 salary cap of $37 million can make his limited payroll dollars go substantially further if he guarantees the money.[3]

Even with gradual phase-in of a salary cap, some team's ability to be competitive may be jeopardized. For example, introducing a salary cap of, say, $35 million in MLB (approximately the owners' proposal) would mean that Atlanta, Toronto, and the Yankees would have to slash their payrolls by over $10 million. How competitive do you think the Yankees would be if they had reduce their payroll by $10 million? To put that in concrete terms, based on 1995 salaries the Yankees would have had to release Don Mattingly, Wade Boggs, and Paul O'Neill, for example, to get under the cap. The Braves would have had to cut Greg Maddux and Tom Glavine. Those names were not picked accidentally.

---

[3] Two recommendations to general managers: guaranteed contracts can free up substantial funds under the salary cap to more aggressively pursue free agent talent. Combining them with substantial incentive clauses for making the playoffs or the Super Bowl would appear to increase the competitiveness even of a team like the Tampa Bay Buccaneers.

Teams like the Yankees and Braves would have to release stars to get under the cap. The role players are not paid enough to make the big dent required in the payroll.

A salary cap will fundamentally change the salary negotiation process itself, as demonstrated by the NBA's experience with a salary cap since 1984. NBA players now insist on multi-year guaranteed contracts, but with multi-year contracts come incentive problems. The evidence primarily from MLB suggests that players on multi-year contracts spend more time injured and have poorer performances than predicted by their pre-contract performance.[4]

Third, consider the entire distribution of salaries. Superstars will continue to command extraordinary salaries. Michael Jordon, Troy Aikman, Wayne Gretzky, and Barry Bonds will receive a market determined salary under almost any salary structure. In addition, the major league minimums are unlikely to be reduced. So when owners insist on a salary cap, who will get nailed? The majority of players in the middle, anyone without the marquee power of a Bonds or Clemens or the salary of a rookie. This is why sports strikes and lockouts appear so intractable: because a salary cap cuts the "silent majority" of players. Consider MLB's proposed 50 percent salary cap one more time. In Chapter 8 I argued that this cap would require a 12 percent cut in the average salary. Where will this come from? The bottom 30 percent earn at or just above the minimum. It cannot come from them. The top 20 percent are the marquee players with substantial individual bargaining power. It will not come from them. The only ones left are the 50 percent in the middle. To have an overall salary cut of 12 percent, the salaries of this middle must be cut by over 30 percent. Clearly, players will object vociferously to this type of proposal.

Over a longer term, a salary cap means the stars will exit the league earlier. A Carlton Fisk, Pete Rose, or Nolan Ryan will not play in the twilight of his career unless he is willing to take a dramatic pay cut. We might never see another pitcher win 300 games,

---

[4] There need be no conscious shirking. However, guaranteed pay may remove a slight subconscious edge from an athlete's performance and that slight edge may be the difference between winning and losing. Alternately, higher-than-warranted salaries may reflect the "winner's curse." That is, a team signing a free agent typically is the high bidder and to the extent that there is a dispersion of bids, the highest bid may overestimate the player's true contribution.

not because the game has changed or the use of pitchers has changed, but because the financial incentives underlying MLB have changed.[5] Cal Ripkin's streak of consecutive games may end not due to an injury or a manager giving him a day off. It may end because he is not offered a contract renewal. As a fan, the possibilities implied by the changing financial structure of the game I find both sad and troubling.

THE ENTIRE DISTRIBUTION OF SALARIES—INCLUDING THE MINOR LEAGUES

One final point on baseball salaries. Major league baseball, with approximately 800 players is but the tip of the proverbial iceberg. Approximately 4,400 additional players are in the minor leagues. Minor leaguers never see free agency or big bucks. They get paid by the month an average of less than $2,000 and work on average about four months. The average yearly minor league salary is approximately $8,700, excluding players on the 40 man major league roster.

Approximately 600 players enter baseball in any single season. Of those, about 100 will see time in the majors but relatively few will last the six years needed to reach the status of unrestricted free agents. Financial success is only for the lucky and talented few. Minor leaguers may never become free agents. Once a baseball player signs even a one year contract, he could play for 20 years in the minors and never be free to play for who he wanted or to bargain for his salary.

Considering all professional baseball players, majors and minors alike, the mean average salary is approximately $170,000. The general conclusion on baseball salaries is that the pool of players has three groups. One group is the extremely talented few that make exceptional money. The second group is made up of other major leaguers—"role" players and rookies—who do well even though their salaries never make the news. The third group is the

---

[5] The incentives have changed for both owners and players. The owners may want to release fading stars sooner and the players themselves may not want the headaches of continuing to try to perform at their usual levels. Roger Clemens, for example, may well be on track to win 300 games. One question is: does he want to stay in the majors 10 more years to do it, given his already sizable earnings?

majority, players just good enough to make the minors. Those who toil in the obscurity of the minors better play for the love of the game rather than for the love of money because they face long odds against collecting a big paycheck.

SALARIES IN GENERAL—1974 TO 1994

How do baseball salaries compare with salaries in other sports? The top part of Table 9.3 presents the mean salaries since 1974, just before the dawn of free agency. For reference, the table also presents salaries for other types of employment. The second half of the table considers rates of change. All numbers are adjusted for inflation and are in 1994 dollars. Clearly, salaries in all major leagues have increased tremendously. From 1981 to 1994, the mean salary in MLB increased from $303,400 to $1,182,000; the mean in the NBA from $295,200 to $1,380,000; in the NFL from $147,600 to $737,000; and in the NHL from $177,100 to $525,000. In contrast, over the same period the salaries of other workers have stagnated. For example, the mean salary for manufacturing workers has fallen from $27,100 to $26,300. Adjusting for inflation, there has been no general change in salaries over the last 20 years. Some have increased marginally while other have decreased marginally. This stands in sharp contrast to sports salaries. In 1974, the mean MLB salary was 5.5 times the average manufacturing salary. By 1984, that ratio had increased to 16.9 and by 1994 the mean MLB salary was 44.9 times the average manufacturing salary!

In terms of salaries in sports, baseball, and basketball have led while football and hockey have lagged. The average salaries in baseball and basketball have risen roughly in tandem. Some may find this surprising because the structure of the wage negotiation process has differed substantially between the two sports. Basketball salaries have increased since 1984 under a salary cap while baseball salaries have increased without a cap. This need not imply that a cap does not lower salaries. It may indicate only that basketball owners and players have found mechanisms around the cap. Looking at the revenues entering the sport versus the number of players in the sport, the parallel increases in NBA and MLB salaries is not at all surprising. NBA revenues average about 2/3 of MLB's revenues. NBA team size is about 2/3 of MLB's. League revenues per player are approximately equal; thus average salaries are approximately equal.[6]

Football and hockey are different stories. The average NFL salary has averaged a little over half the MLB average. The revenues generated by the NFL and MLB are roughly the same.

Table 9.3

SALARIES IN AND OUT OF SPORTS
Levels
(in thousands of 1994 dollars)

		1974	1981	1984	1991	1994
Baseball	Majors	$123.3	$303.4	$472.1	$931.6	$1,182.0
	Minors		8.9	8.8	8.7	8.7
Basketball			295.2	464.7	903.1	1,500.0
Football			147.6	258.2	510.1	776.0
Hockey			177.1	213.8	278.1	558.0
Doctors			151.0	155.5	186.8	183.0
Production Workers (all)		24.3	21.8	21.9	20.2	19.9
Construction Workers		33.3	34.1	34.2	30.4	29.9
Mining Workers		27.1	37.4	37.6	35.9	34.5
Manufacturing Workers		22.4	27.1	27.9	25.9	26.3

Rates of Increase

		1964-74	1974-81	1981-91	1991-94
Baseball	Majors	3.6%	13.7%	11.9%	8.3%
	Minors			-0.1	0.0
Basketball				11.8	18.4
Football				13.2	15.0
Hockey				4.6	26.1
Doctors				2.4	-2.0
Production Workers (all)		-0.8	-0.5	0.6	-1.5
Construction Workers		-1.1	-0.6	0.0	0.3
Mining Workers		-0.4	-1.3	0.0	0.3
Manufacturing Workers		-1.4	1.9	-0.5	0.5

[6] Baseball also has greater player development costs, but basketball has higher facility costs.

Football teams have approximately twice as many players suggesting that salaries should be approximately half MLB's level. But MLB has much more extensive player development expenses (e.g. minor leagues), suggesting that NFL salaries should be somewhat greater than half MLB's. Recent NFL salary growth has been greater, but this likely does not indicate any long-term trend. It only reflects the fact that real free agency was slow coming to the NFL. The approximate relationship between MLB and NFL salaries may be surprising given that football has a 16 game regular season versus baseball's 162 games. The relationship, however, is just one more indication that salaries are determined by revenues entering the sport. The greater the revenues, the higher the salaries.

Given the NHL's overlap of seasons and of arenas with the NBA, one might expect hockey salaries to move in tandem with basketball salaries. In fact, they have not. The difference is partly due to hockey's more regional appeal and the resulting lack of a lucrative national television contract. NHL's revenues are approximately 80 percent of the NBA's. NBA team size is approximately 60 percent of the NHL's team size. These two percentages together suggest that NHL players should average a salary approximately half their NBA counterparts (NHL player development costs and minor leagues might reduce this somewhat). The NHL average salary was 60 percent of the NBA's in 1981 but had dropped to under 40 percent in 1994. Low NHL revenues can explain low NHL salaries but cannot explain why this percentage has fallen. That drop appears to be due to restrictions on free agency. If players are restricted in their ability to negotiate for salaries, it should not be surprising to find lower salaries.

Considering all four leagues, the most important determinant of salaries appears to be the league revenues, with players' ability to engage in unfettered salary negotiations a close second. Salaries have escalated when television revenues have increased; salaries have stagnated when television revenues have stagnated. Salaries are largely determined by revenues, and there is a *de facto* salary cap in all leagues based on the revenue into the league.

Before concluding on average salaries, it is important to note once again that the mean salary may not represent the typical

Chart 9.5

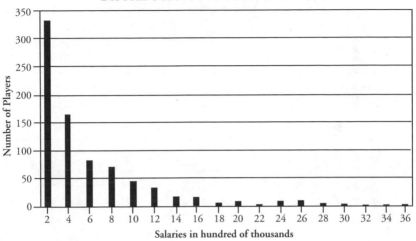

DISTRIBUTION OF NFL SALARIES-1994

player's salary, and there may be information in both the mean and the overall salary distribution. Thus, Charts 9.5 to 9.7 present the salary distributions for the NFL, NHL, and NBA. The shape of the distributions for both the NFL and the NHL is remarkably similar to that for MLB. The conclusion for the NFL and the NHL, like for MLB, is that the mean does not describe the typical NHL player's salary. The best of the NFL and NHL do extremely well, although the highest paid in football and hockey substantially lag the best in baseball. The rest of the NFL and NHL players survive quite comfortably but with salaries under $600,000. Hockey minor leaguers, however, are another story with the top minor league, the IHL, paying a maximum of $62,000.

Chart 9.7, presenting the distribution of NBA salaries, indicates a more equal distribution of salaries. The majority of players earn over $1 million but none make more than $4.2 million. The more egalitarian distribution in the NBA may be due to the salary cap; it may be due to the players being more willing to "share the wealth;" or it may be a statistical artifact, due solely to the accounting games being played to be consistent with the salary cap. While all leagues play games with the financial numbers, NBA salaries are

Chart 9.6

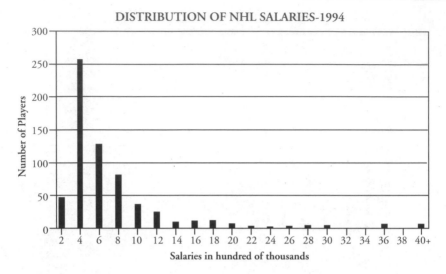

DISTRIBUTION OF NHL SALARIES-1994

Number of Players

Salaries in hundred of thousands

probably the least informative given the games played with salaries due to the salary cap.

One final point on salaries. If you want to compare salaries, it is important to carefully select the reference group. Viewing professional athletes primarily as entertainers, one could ask what do the top entertainers earn. The answer, based on *Forbes'* annual survey of top entertainers' salaries, is that a big salary advantage lies with the entertainers. No athlete generates the revenues or earns the salary of an Oprah Winfrey or Bill Cosby. If you view professional athletes as highly skilled professional workers, then you might ask what do the top doctors or lawyers earn. The answer is that the advantage lies with the doctors and lawyers. Lawyers like F. Lee Bailey can earn much more than the best athletes. Only if you consider professional athletes regular "working stiffs" is there a big salary advantage to the athletes.

Ticket Prices and Salaries—Higher Salaries Do Not Cause Higher Ticket Prices

The conventional wisdom is high player salaries cause high ticket prices since the money has to come from somewhere and the fan ultimately pays the price. Owners encourage this line of thought. For example, MLB owners promised lower ticket prices if replacement players were used during the 1995 season. Unfortunately, there is virtually no truth to this line of thought.

Owners are in the sports business to make money and to win games. They might sacrifice profits to win games. But most are far from altruistic with respect to the fans, and they are not going to sacrifice profits by charging lower ticket prices just to give fans a good deal.[7] The basic assumption underlying an owner's behavior: charge the highest price he thinks people will pay. Considering just the gate receipts, what price will maximize ticket revenues? If an owner can consistently fill a 15,000 seat arena at an average ticket price of $30, why charge $25? Furthermore, if he charges $30 rather than $35, it indicates that he believes that attendance will fall substantially if he raises prices. For example, at $30 a ticket he receives $450,000 per game. If he raised the price to $35, he would need to sell only 12,900 tickets to make the same revenue. If he expected to continue to sell out, he should increase the price by $5 and pocket $75,000 additional per game.[8] When he sets the price, it does not matter whether the team payroll is $30,000 per game or $300,000 per game. The owner will ask what is the profit-maximizing ticket price and then charge that price.

Suppose player salaries rise, will the owner raise ticket prices? The answer is no! The $30 price maximized ticket revenues. If he raised ticket prices the owner would lose money because player salaries rose and because ticket revenues declined. An owner faces two distinct markets, a market for tickets and a market for players. An owner is going to work to set the best deal possible in each market and there need be no relationship between the two markets. Higher ticket prices need not influence player salaries and higher player salaries need not influence ticket prices. However, higher ticket prices may lead to higher player salaries if players are free to

---

[7] As noted in Chapter 4 on football, the Green Bay Packers are one noteworthy exception - because they are effectively owned by the fans.

[8] There are a number of issues including nonlinear relationships and the price elasticity of ticket demand that are ignored for simplicity. Adding them would complicate the analysis but not change the basic result.

Chart 9.7

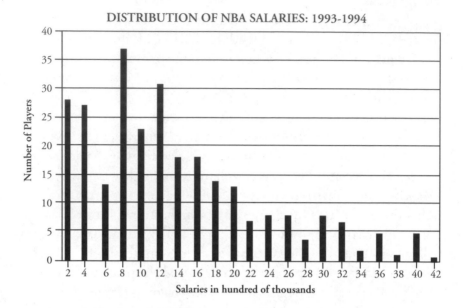

DISTRIBUTION OF NBA SALARIES: 1993-1994

Number of Players

Salaries in hundred of thousands

negotiate and if they recognize that owners are receiving greater ticket revenues, and thus are in a weaker bargaining position in terms of holding the line of salaries. The evidence for all leagues, most dramatically for MLB, indicates that player salaries increase after league revenues increase. There is no evidence that increases in player salaries occur before league revenues increase.

In contrast, fans and owners do not negotiate over ticket prices. Ticket prices rise only when an owner believes it is in his best interest to raise them. Higher ticket prices will be associated with higher player salaries only if those higher salaries also imply a more entertaining team. Consider the Milwaukee Bucks signing Glenn Robinson to a 10-year $67 million contract. That contract probably will be associated with increased Bucks' ticket prices. Nonetheless, the contract itself is unlikely to have caused higher ticket prices. The Bucks will be more entertaining with Robinson. Economists would say Robinson's addition to the Bucks will increases the demand for tickets, and the price rises as a result. Thus, it is increased ticket demand or the additional entertainment value of the Bucks that drives up ticket prices. Higher ticket prices may be timed to occur when player salaries increase, but that timing does not imply that higher salaries cause higher ticket prices.

SALARIES AND PLAYER CHOICES

Chapters 2 to 5 on the profitability of sports franchises spent a lot of time discussing different owner's possible goals—and criticizing some owners. I argued that some owners want to win even at great costs while others primarily are in the game for the money. I also argued that this conflict is an extremely detrimental force in sports—as esoteric a contention as that may be—since it underlies owner-union squabbles in all sports. However, there also exist differences among players that may similarly shape the games—and some players also deserve criticism. The split among NBA players over the proposed 1995 contract is likely the first of many financial rifts among players.

The questions for players are similar to those for owners. To what extent are they in the game to win versus being interested exclusively in the money? And how do the financial interests of stars, bench-warmers and rookies differ? Clearly, players want to be paid the millions generally implied by a free market and do not want constraints on their ability to bargain for higher salaries. Yet at some point, players face a tradeoff between more money and winning, even without a salary cap. Under a cap, both football and basketball players have allowed their contracts to be restructured to allow the franchise to sign additional players that would increase their chances of winning. Magic Johnson is said to have taken a salary cut to allow the Lakers to sign another player and improve their chances of winning another championship. Deion Sanders signed with the San Francisco 49ers in 1994 despite a higher salary offer from the New Orleans Saints. His motive? The 49ers had a better chance of winning the Super Bowl. Sanders valued a potential Super Bowl victory more than the Saints' money. Of course, the possibility also existed that winning the Super Bowl would lead to additional endorsement income and potentially higher future salary offers.

Even without a salary cap, teams have a limit on what they can or will spend. That limit is determined largely by team revenues and an owner's desire to win. For argument's sake, consider a baseball team with an existing payroll of $28 million and an effective salary limit—unknown to players and their agents—of $30 million. A player likely has a rough idea about how high a team payroll this owner will tolerate. If he can negotiate a $5 million salary and if he values winning, this may not be the team for him. If this team signs him for $5 million, it likely will cut $3 million in salaries elsewhere. A reasonable player should assume that those cuts will adversely affect the team's prospects for winning. If he values winning, he might be willing to sign elsewhere for less money. Some owners want a championship trophy and have paid a lot to try and get one. Presumably, many players want a championship ring and with free agency may accept a lower salary to try and get one.

What are the implications of players' choices, including wanting to go with a winner? First, stronger clubs may be able to maintain their advantage. If the money is the same, a player may choose the San Francisco 49ers over the Tampa Bay Buccaneers or the Montreal Canadians over the Ottawa Senators. Second, large-market franchises might have an advantage either if they have a higher effective salary cap (what an owner is willing to spend) or if they have a higher probability of winning or if endorsement money is more readily available. Would an athlete prefer to play in New York or in Milwaukee based exclusively on income opportunities? As noted in Chapter 6, however, there is at best only weak evidence that large-market clubs have been able to successfully exploit this advantage. Third, non-salary considerations may influence where athletes want to play, meaning wins as well as personalities are potentially more important than money. An owner's player relations may play a greater role than market size. For example, George Steinbrenner's well-publicized criticisms of players like Dave Winfield could offset the advantages of playing in New York, or Buddy Ryan's coaching style could offset the disadvantage of playing in small-market Phoenix. When money is not the only important factor either for owners or for players, perhaps it should not be surprising to find only weak relationships between wins and financial variables.

Fourth and perhaps most important, the current turmoil between owners and players has largely been over issues of economic control, whether its an individual player's freedom to negotiate his salary or the league's ability to set a salary cap. Without free agency or salary arbitration, players have virtually no control. For example, a new player in the league can sign with the team that drafts him or can opt not to play and hold out. When a player like Glenn Robinson holds out before signing, he endures almost universal approbation from fans and sportswriters. Fans, generally interested only in winning, want Glenn Robinson in training camp from day one. Most fans have limited interest in or tolerance for the machinations in contract negotiations between player and owner. In most cases, however, the owner holds all the cards. Glenn Robinson can negotiate only with the team that drafted him.. If that team offers him only slightly more than he could earn playing in Europe and much less than the competitive market for his skills, his choice is to play for a below-market salary or hold out. Holding out is the athlete's only mechanism for gaining some control. The cost of a lengthy hold-out for a player, however, is likely much greater than the cost to the team. Given an athlete's short career, sitting out a season may cost 20 percent or more of career income. Only when a player becomes eligible for free agency does he have any real control. At that point he can ask how much does he value winning, relations with his current team, and money.

Major league players have formed unions largely to obtain some economic control, and we should expect a union to do its best for current players. During player strikes and lockouts, however, the striking players have stressed that, while they were losing a substantial fraction of their lifetime income, they were making the sacrifice for future generations of players just as prior players had sacrificed for them. They should carefully consider both the future distribution of salaries and the implications for the games. Are they bargaining so that the top 10 percent can make multimillion dollar salaries while the rest labor at the minimum? If that is the case, then it is not clear that fans or future players will be particularly receptive to their arguments.

Chapter 7 addressed the issue of revenue sharing for owners, noting that the game is a joint product. It also is a joint product for the players. In MLB, a Greg Maddox might start 40 games per year; 10,000 additional fans might come each time he pitches; club revenues might increase $12 per fan for a total increase of $4.8 million. Should he receive most of that money, the owner receive the rest, and the rest of the lineup receive nothing? Based on market power and the existing rules of free agency, the answer is yes. But if winning is a joint product, if fans show up because Maddox wins, and if winning is really a team thing, then the economic answer is that all the players should be included in the split of that $4.8 million. The point is simple. Nothing should preclude owners from sharing revenues, just as they share the game's output of wins and losses, but revenue sharing should be the owners' decision. Likewise, nothing should preclude players from sharing their revenues, just as they share a team's success, but that should be the players' decision. In addition, fans might be substantially more sympathetic with the players if the major leaguers agreed to revenue sharing, possibly by taxing themselves to subsidize minor league players. For example, a 4 percent tax would generate sufficient revenues to double the average minor league salary.

A union has a responsibility that includes an analysis of how to split the salary pool, recognizing that fans come to see the stars but the stars need the cast for the production. Any union that ignores this point does so only at its own peril and at a peril to the game. Salaries of the Griffeys, Aikmans, Gretzkys, and Shaqs will increase in the short term. Salaries of mid-level players may fall. MLB's salary shift from 1993 to 1995 dramatically illustrates this point. The top salaries jumped but mid-level salaries plummeted. The long run implications of a more unequal salary distribution for fan support and for players entering the game suggest potential problems 10 or 20 years down the road.

The recent initial refusal of the NBA players to ratify a union-agreed contract indicates that players are becoming more aware of their potentially divergent interests. The contract initially endorsed by the union called for a tax on salaries of superstars as well as a more binding salary cap. The tax on superstars' salaries led players like Michael Jordon, Patrick Ewing, and Scottie Pippen to object while the more binding salary cap led many journeymen players to object. After the owners and the union renegotiated and concessions were made on the salary cap, the union did ratify the contract, albeit not without a sometimes acrimonious discussion and vote. The minority position among the players was to work without a contract implying, so some argued, virtually complete free agency. Some players likely would have profited substantially from no contract, including Jordon, Ewing, and Pippen. The majority likely would not. Hence this position was rejected.[9]

A more dramatic type of revenue sharing would involve restructuring player contracts. Rather than players receiving only a salary, players might be willing to reduce their salary demands in return for partial ownership of the franchise. Such a proposal has the potential to dramatically reduce the conflicts between players and owners because the players themselves would be owners. In addition, many current and former players including Magic Johnson, Dan Marino, and Walter Payton have expressed interest in owning franchises. The primary drawback is that the owners would no longer be members of an exclusive club, and in most leagues it would take a rule change to open up this club.

A CAVEAT TO POTENTIAL PROFESSIONALS

Given professional athletes' salaries, one message should be conveyed to any aspiring athlete. The salaries of professional athletes tempt many to think about pursuing a career, say, in the NBA. Virtually without exception, based on the money, the best advice is to look elsewhere. The average salary of people with professional basketball aspirations versus those who have aspirations to be a doctor, for example, likely give a big advantage to the would-be doctors. According to the *National Federation Handbook Annual,* there are approximately 16,500 high school basketball teams with 521,000 players. For arguments' sake, let us focus only on the best senior at the top half of all schools and assume that those 8,250 are the only ones that have realistic dreams or hopes of playing pro ball. (The movie *Hoop Dreams* suggests that the appropriate number may be much higher. It may be more realistic to assume that everyone who tries out for a team has the goal of being

---

[9] Agents' role in this disagreement should not be ignored. David Stern, Commissioner of the NBA argued that agents led the revolt against the agreement. Agents' role in the disagreement can be debated. What cannot be debated is the revised salary cap's negative impact on agents' incomes. Thus, to the extent that agents are interested in their own financial well-being, they would oppose the new cap, even if some of their clients would gain from the agreement.

the next Michael Jordan.) After four years of college, approximately 40 of those 8,250 will play in the NBA. Ignore the CBA and the European leagues because kids do not dream of playing pro basketball in Fort Wayne, Yakima, Barcelona, or Milan. Now those 40 new NBA players will receive an average salary of about $1.25 million. A few will get substantially more but most will get much less. With 40 people making $1.25 million each, the class will be paid a total of $50 million, but there were 8,250 or more striving to make the cut. Divide that $50 million 8,250 ways and you end up with a mean average basketball salary of $6,060. Even those few with an apparently plausible hope of playing pro basketball on average will have a basketball salary less than the minimum wage. Even a very talented basketball player likely will have greater financial success as a carpenter, computer programmer, or newspaper reporter because of the much greater demand for carpenters, computer programmers, and newspaper reporters.

The numbers for football are similar. In the 1992-1993 school year, there were approximately 900,000 high school football players. Of those players, perhaps 150,000 were seniors and maybe one in ten has hopes of playing professional ball. That leaves 15,000. Of this number, less than 200 will make it to the pros. The starting salaries for those first few draft picks may be quite high, but the salary cap is approximately $2 million per team for rookies. For 28 teams that is a total of $56 million. The 200-odd players that make the pros average $280,000. First round draft picks will get dramatically more, others will get much less, and then there are the other 14,800 who get zilch. The mean average income for the entire class is approximately $3,784, again below minimum wage. We can go one step further. Those that do make it to the pros on average play only 3.1 years. Even in a short career one of the top players can make enough to live comfortably for the rest of his life. However, the vast majority of athletes in any sport are marginal pro players, albeit still among the best athletes in the world. Their salary is likely to be around $200,000. Not bad for a 22 or 25 year old. But what happens at age 27 or 30 or 35? After taxes he will not have saved enough to live on, and from high school to college to the pros he well may have accumulated enough physical damage to severely restrict the type of work he can do.

In sum, the best professional athletes make a very comfortable living for a relatively short playing career. Then, their income earning capabilities are severely reduced. The merely very good professional, considering only income, may be better off financially not ever playing pro ball. The great majority of exceptional and dominating high school athletes only make it to the minor leagues (or to college in the case of basketball or football). It is only the best of the best of the pros, the Michael Jordans or Troy Aikmans or Ken Griffeys, that make gigantic salaries. Looking at the headline salaries or even the mean average salaries disguises the actual income of the vast majority of athletes in any sport.

CONCLUSION

Are professional athletes underpaid? The answer is major leaguers are paid very well, but minor league salaries probably do not generate a lot of enthusiasm among talented athletes. The best of the best in any sport make headline-grabbing amounts; the rest of the best are down in the agate type. The answer to whether they are overpaid or underpaid depends on how much revenue they add to a franchise's bottom line. If Roger Clemens brings in an additional $10 million for the Red Sox, or Wayne Gretzky generates an additional $15 million for the LA Kings, or Shaquille O'Neill produces an additional $20 million for the Orlando Magic, can you justify paying them only $1 million? A utility infielder, a second string lineman, a seven foot NBA bench warmer, and a career minor-leaguer generate far less revenues and get paid far less. The dozens of technical studies that have considered the issue have uniformly concluded that professional athletes are not overpaid.[10] They also have concluded that restrictions on free agency and underpayment go hand-in-hand. Owners invariably have exploited athletes when given the opportunity. In contrast, athletes have never had the opportunity to exploit owners. Sorry Mom, Roger Clemens deserves the money!

---

[10] Four of the most widely cited studies are Roger Noll, ed., *Government and the Sports Business* (Washington, D.C.: The Brookings Institution, 1974); Gerald Scully, "Pay and Performance in Major League Baseball," *American Economic Review* (December 1974) ; Gerald Scully, *The Business of Baseball* (Chicago: University of Chicago Press, 1989); and Andrew Zimbalist, *Baseball and Billions* (New York: Basic Books, 1992).

Chapter 10

Expansion Prospects — Austin and Nashville or Another Team for New York City?

"War is hell, but expansion is worse."
—Bill Fitch, coach, Cleveland Cavaliers

"If pro football expands one more time, I'm quitting smoking and making a comeback."
—Hugh McElhenny, former running back, San Francisco 49ers

"It's just not the same game today. There are so many teams that there are only two or three good players on most of them."
—Maurice Richard, former forward, Montreal Canadians

The question of expansion and the associated issue of franchise relocation goes hand in hand with the discussion of salary caps and limits on free agency. The former restricts the number of franchises and allows owners to play one city against another. The latter restricts players' abilities to play one owner against another. Both are excellent examples of how owners have structured markets to their advantage.

Owners, whether in baseball or in team tennis, face inexorable economic incentives and have responded predictably to those incentives. First, they want to restrict player mobility and have attempted to stack labor negotiation rules against the players. Those policies have limited salaries and franchise costs. Second, owners want to restrict entry into their fraternity. The more teams, the more TV money must be split; the more teams, the greater competition for players and the smaller the probability of signing the next Michael Jordan, Wayne Gretzky, Babe Ruth, or Joe Montana; the more teams, the fewer attractive cities without a franchise waiting with open arms and open wallets to bail an owner out of whatever financial difficulties he may encounter in his present locale. Limiting franchise entry generally increases revenues for existing franchises.

All major leagues have severely limited the number of franchises. Jeffrey Newman has recounted one example.

> At a convention of the Society for American Baseball Research in 1993, architecture critic and ballpark consultant John Pastier showed a slide of 'the most important ballpark built in the last ten years.' As we braced ourselves for yet another recitation of the virtues of Camden Yards, Pastier flashed before us the hideous image of the Suncoast Dome in St. Petersburg. As long as this ballpark exists and stands empty, he told us, any team in the nation can extort virtually anything it wants out of its municipality: new stadium construction, more favorable lease terms, luxury boxes, etc.[1]

With expansion a continuing topic in baseball, speculation abounds about which cities may be chosen. Tampa-St. Petersburg recently had a lawsuit against MLB for previously denying them a franchise; Phoenix investors have claimed they have been promised a team if they obtain a commitment to build a stadium; Congress has rattled the cage of baseball owners about Washington, D.C.'s lack of a team. After expansion franchises were awarded to Miami and Denver, beginning play in 1993, suitors were upset in cities from Buffalo to Phoenix. Then Tampa and Phoenix were

[1] Private correspondence.

awarded franchises and groups in Indianapolis and Washington, D.C. were upset.

All four leagues also have recently expanded or are scheduled to expand. The NHL has pursued the most aggressive expansion over the last five years, adding teams in Anaheim, Miami, Ottawa, San Jose, and Tampa Bay. Two expansion franchises entered both the NBA and the NFL in 1995, and the NFL debates further expansion in Los Angeles. Expansion franchises generate revenues for existing teams since the franchise entry fee is split among the existing franchises. For example, the NBA's fee of $125 million each for the Toronto and Vancouver franchises generated $250 million for the league or $9.3 million for each existing franchise. That's a strong motive for league expansion.

FRANCHISE LOCATION IN GENERAL

The most important point about franchise location should also be the most obvious: the best markets have already been taken. An owner or potential owner who wants to make money will not seek a franchise in South Bend, Duluth, or Lubbock if Indianapolis or Washington, D.C. is available. The New York's, Los Angeles's, and Chicago's have franchises. Table 10.1 lists the population and number of major league franchises in the largest metropolitan areas in the U.S., Canada, and Mexico as of May 1995.[2] Even a cursory examination of the list suggests that owners of major league franchises are not stupid. The largest cities have the greatest number of teams. All the largest cities have a major league franchises in all sports, except Washington, D.C. in baseball. As the city size decreases, the probability of having a major league franchise also decreases. Charlotte, Orlando, and Salt Lake City are the smallest cities in the U.S. with a major league franchise.[3]

Based on Table 10.1, one could guess that a MLB expansion franchise in Buffalo, Columbus, or San Antonio, for example, might be profitable at the outset. The novelty and excitement of

---

[2] This date is deliberately set before recent franchise moves in the NFL. The musical franchises or franchise free-agency has not yet played itself out, and the NFL's absence from LA appears temporary based on both the underlying economics and NFL league announcements.

[3] Throughout this chapter, for reference purposes the Green Bay Packers are assigned to the Milwaukee metropolitan area.

Table 10.1

POPULATION AND SPORTS TEAMS BY
METROPOLITAN STATISTICAL AREAS
1990 Census Population Data

Rank (U.S.)	City	Population (in thousands)	Number of Major League Teams [a]			
			Baseball	Basketball	Football	Hockey
1	New York	19,342	2	2	2	3
2	Los Angeles	14,532	2	2	2[b]	2
3	Chicago	8,240	2	1	1	1
4	San Francisco	6,253	2	1	1[b]	1
5	Philadelphia	5,899	1	1	1	1
6	Boston	5,455	1	1	1	1
7	Detroit	5,187	1	1	1	1
8	Dallas	4,037	1	1	1	1
9	Washington	3,924	0	1	1	1
10	Houston	3,731	1	1	1	0
11	Miami	3,193	1	1	1	0
12	Seattle	2,970	1	1	1	0
13	Atlanta	2,960	1	1	1	0
14	Cleveland	2,760	1	1	1[b]	0
15	Minneapolis	2,539	1	1	1	0
16	San Diego	2,498	1	0	1	0
17	St. Louis	2,492	1	0	0[b]	1
18	Pittsburgh	2,395	1	0	1	1
19	Baltimore	2,382	1	0	0[b]	0
20	Phoenix	2,238	0[b]	1	1	0
21	Tampa	2,068	0[b]	0	1	1
22	Denver	1,980	1	1	1	0[b]
23	Cincinnati	1,818	1	0	1	0
24	Portland	1,793	0	1	0	0
25	Milwaukee	1,607	1	1	1	0
26	Kansas City	1,582	1	0	1	0
27	Sacramento	1,481	0	1	0	0
28	Norfolk	1,443	0	0	0	0
29	Indianapolis	1,380	0	1	1	0
30	Columbus	1,345	0	0	0	0
31	San Antonio	1,325	0	1	0	0
32	New Orleans	1,285	0	0	1	0
33	Orlando	1,225	0	1	0	0
34	Buffalo	1,189	0	0	1	1
35	Charlotte	1,162	0	1	0[b]	0
36	Hartford	1,158	0	0	0	1
37	Providence	1,134	0	0	0	0
38	Salt Lake City	1,072	0	1	0	0
39	Rochester	1,062	0	0	0	0

Table 10.1 continued

Rank (U.S.)	City	Population (in thousands)	Number of Major League Teams [a] Baseball	Basketball	Football	Hockey
40	Greensboro	1,050	0	0	0	0
41	Memphis	1,007	0	0	0	0
42	Nashville	985	0	0	0 [b]	0
43	Oklahoma City	959	0	0	0	0
44	Dayton	951	0	0	0	0
45	Louisville	949	0	0	0	0
46	Grand Rapids	938	0	0	0	0
47	Jacksonville	907	0	0	0 [b]	0
48	Richmond	866	0	0	0	0
49	West Palm Beach	864	0	0	0	0
50	Albany	861	0	0	0	0
51	Raleigh	856	0	0	0	0
52	Las Vegas	853	0	0	0	0
53	Austin	846	0	0	0	0
54	Birmingham	840	0	0	0	0
55	Honolulu	836	0	0	0	0
56	Greenville	831	0	0	0	0
57	Fresno	756	0	0	0	0
58	Syracuse	742	0	0	0	0
59	Tulsa	708	0	0	0	0
60	Tucson	667	0	0	0	0
61	Omaha	640	0	0	0	0
62	Scranton	638	0	0	0	0
63	El Paso	592	0	0	0	0
64	Albuquerque	589	0	0	0	0
	Toronto	3,751	1	0 [b]	0	1
	Montreal	3,068	1	0	0	1
	Vancouver	1,547	0	0 [b]	0	1
	Ottawa	863	0	0	0	1
	Edmonton	823	0	0	0	1
	Calgary	723	0	0	0	1
	Winnipeg	647	0	0	0	1 [b]
	Quebec	622	0	0	0	1 [b]
	Mexico City	20,899	0	0	0	0
	Guadalajara	3,370	0	0	0	0
	Monterrey	2,939	0	0	0	0
	Caracas, Ven.	3,217	0	0	0	0
	San Juan, P.R.	2,900	0	0	0	0
	Havana, Cuba	2,077	0	0	0	0

[a] The table excludes franchises that had not played a game before August, 1995.

[b] In MLB, Phoenix and Tampa will be added in 1996. In the NBA, expansion franchises were added in Toronto and Vancouver in 1995. In the NFL, Los Angeles's team moved to St. Lou and Oakland and expansion franchises were added in Carolina and Jacksonville in 1995. In th NHL, in 1995 Quebec's team moved to Denver and Winnipeg's team is committed to move

MLB will fill a lot of seats and sell a lot of popcorn. But what will happen after ten years when the novelty has worn off and the franchise has to compete for a limited entertainment dollar? Fewer people seek entertainment in Buffalo, Columbus, or San Antonio than in New York or Los Angeles.

The implication: expect an expansion franchise to have a market value less than that of the New York Yankees or the Los Angeles Dodgers, and expect an expansion franchise's market value to be close to the bottom of the league. Why? Basic economics. Thirty years ago you could have started a MLB franchise in Kansas City or Indianapolis. Owners who presumably did not want to lose $10 million a year chose Kansas City. While they may have had intense loyalty to Kansas City, if they thought they would lose $10 million in Kansas City and make money in Indianapolis, we probably would now have the Indianapolis Royals. Kansas City's population is about 200,000 more than Indianapolis'. If a fraction of them attend a couple of games a year, a Kansas City franchise might be profitable while an Indianapolis franchise might not.

We should expect the oldest franchises generally to be the most profitable, assuming no population shifts. Consider the oldest sport, baseball. Which owners have complained the loudest about the need to share revenues? If news reports are accurate, the clubs suffering the most and crying the loudest include Cincinnati, Kansas City, Milwaukee, Minnesota, Montreal, Pittsburgh, San Diego, and Seattle. Five were created through league expansion since 1968; one has relocated; and only Cincinnati and Pittsburgh have a long history in their current locale. Except Montreal, all are in small markets by MLB standards. Thus, a club in financial distress is probably in a smaller-than-average market and is probably a recent expansion franchise.

Go one step further and consider all MLB expansion franchises granted since 1968, excluding Colorado and Florida since their financial grade is incomplete. The franchises: Kansas City, Milwaukee, Montreal, San Diego, Seattle, and Toronto. Only Montreal and Toronto are in above average sized markets, largely because MLB was slow to expand to Canada. In addition, each of these franchises except Toronto has had well-publicized financial difficulties, although the numbers in Chapter 2 indicate that both Montreal and San Diego, in fact, have been profitable.[4]

We should expect an expansion franchise to be located in a relatively small city, to be less profitable, and to have a below-average market value. Potential owners of expansion franchises should know this before buying in. As the league prospers, an expansion franchise may share in that success, but when the league struggles the expansion franchise will likely have the hardest time staying afloat. Chapter 7 made a strong case for revenue sharing, based on the relationships between owners. Revenue sharing makes sense for a league in terms of allocating funds coming into the league and possibly for helping weaker franchises through difficult financial times. However, while a league may have justification for revenue sharing, there is no justification for the owner of an expansion franchise to seek revenue sharing. When buying an expansion franchise in Milwaukee, due diligence should tell a potential owner that revenues will be limited compared with those of the New York Yankees. To return in five, 10 or 20 years and demand additional revenue sharing may appear logical from the perspective of a close-to-insolvent owner. However, it violates one tenet of a market economy: *caveat emptor.*

Before moving on to the main agenda—what additional cities could support a franchise—it is worthwhile to reiterate a point previously emphasized. A franchise's financial success depends on at least five factors beyond population. First, it depends on stadium arrangements. The most profitable teams like the Dallas Cowboys generally have favorable stadium deals. Second, profits depend on an owner's goals. Some owners emphasize winning while others emphasize profits. Third, managerial competence is critical, especially for small-market franchises. Not all franchises have been well run. Fourth, winning helps. There is ample evidence that winning teams produce greater revenues, and few cases

---

[4] Toronto's profitability undoubtedly is due in part to their stadium arrangement, with a retractable roof and an adjoining hotel. While the Blue Jays have been extremely profitable, the city and the province have taken a financial bath on the stadium. Attributing those losses to the Blue Jays would drastically reduce Toronto's profits. While the stadium now has been sold to the club, the price was well below the cost. Thus, the Blue Jays will not absorb any of the losses, and the city and province have had to write off the majority of their stadium investment.

where losing contributes to the cachet of a team—although the Mets in the 1960s and the Cubs in almost any year may be counter examples. And fifth, idiosyncratic city or locational factors may influence success. For example, the willingness of people to drive from Nebraska, Utah, and Arizona to see a baseball game in Denver has contributed to the success of the Rockies. Likewise, Canadians' passion for hockey allows a major league franchise in Calgary while similarly-sized U.S. cities like Las Vegas, Richmond, and West Palm Beach could not support an NHL franchise.

EXPANSION PROSPECTS—MLB

To marshal the facts on potential expansion differently, Table 10.2 presents information on cities that have MLB franchises or that have some realistic hope of a franchise. For cities with a MLB franchise, the table lists the population, mean household income for the metropolitan area, and the franchise market values. Market values equal Net Present Values (NPVs) plus franchise "ego value" throughout this chapter. In MLB, the market value is NPV plus approximately $40 million. The apparent prerequisites for an expansion franchise would appear simple: a city should have a population exceeding 900,000 and should not be within a reasonable drive from another MLB franchise. For cities meeting these criteria, the table lists the population, mean household income, and the distance to the nearest MLB franchise.

A cursory inspection of the table corroborates what has been reported in the sports press. For MLB expansion, Tampa and Phoenix were the front-runners and were reasonably granted expansion franchises. Except for Washington, D.C., they were the largest U.S. metropolitan areas without a MLB franchise. Washington, D.C. has a much larger population but its proximity to Baltimore's Camden Yards leads many owners to discount the ability of D.C. to support a franchise. That two franchises have already left the capital does not enhance D.C.'s contention that it can support a MLB franchise. However, a dispassionate look at the numbers suggests that Washington may be a stronger candidate for long-term success than either Tampa or Phoenix. Not only is the population appreciably larger, on average it also is substantially wealthier. Since entertainment expenditures increase with increasing income, Washington would appear to be a strong market in the long-term.

Tampa-St. Pete has made attractive offers to entice existing franchises to relocate. Assuming an expansion franchise would receive the same deal, Tampa-St. Pete was the odds-on favorite for an expansion franchise based on the short-term profitability of the team. Based on profits over the next five years, a MLB franchise in Tampa could easily be the financial equal of the Colorado Rockies, a financially successful small-market franchise. However, twenty years down the road the picture likely will look very different. After the tax breaks expire and the stadium ages, would you prefer a franchise in a small media market with a low-income population (Tampa) or in a much larger media market with a much wealthier population (Washington)? Twenty years from now, Washington will have a MLB franchise; Tampa may not.

The information in Table 10.2 suggests rough estimates for the market values of potential expansion clubs. The Washington Senators would appear to have a minimum market value of $100 million based on population and income. In fact, the value could easily exceed $160 million depending on stadium arrangements. In contrast, Phoenix and Tampa would have base market values of about $80 million. Smaller size and lower income hurt. Both could be worth another $50-$65 million more (for a total of $130-$145 million) based on stadium arrangements. However, even good financial arrangements will not save a team with a poor stadium, and whether the Suncoast Dome is a good environment for baseball is open to serious debate.

At a minimum one additional city appears capable of supporting an expansion franchise and perhaps as many as eight. If Milwaukee and Kansas City can support a MLB franchise—and the financial numbers in Chapter 2 leave some doubt about that—then Portland also would qualify. It has a larger population and virtually the same average income. Indianapolis, San Antonio, and New Orleans also may be viable candidates. They already support major league franchises in other sports, and they have larger populations than Kansas City had when it received an expansion franchise.

Table 10.2

BASEBALL EXPANSION PROSPECTS

Rank (U.S.)	City	Population (in thousands)	Mean Household Income	Distance to Nearest MLB Team (in millions)	Estimated Market Values (in millions)	Number of Teams
1	New York	19,342	58,812	0	357	2
					257	
2	Los Angeles	14,532	52,786	0	190	2
					90	
3	Chicago	8,240	51,772	0	192	2
					157	
4	San Francisco	6,253	59,014	0	82	2
					82	
5	Philadelphia	5,899	51,388	0	98	1
6	Boston	5,455	57,899	0	257	1
7	Detroit	5,187	48,733	0	82	1
8	Dallas	4,037	48,195	0	157	1
9	Washington	3,924	64,378	30	x	0
10	Houston	3,731	48,195	0	90	1
11	Miami	3,193	44,378	0	90	1
12	Seattle	2,970	49,125	0	82	1
13	Atlanta	2,960	50,788	0	123	1
14	Cleveland	2,760	44,072	0	190	1
15	Minneapolis	2,539	51,095	0	82	1
16	San Diego	2,498	49,293	0	107	1
17	St. Louis	2,492	51,095	0	107	1
18	Pittsburgh	2,395	40,729	0	82	1
19	Baltimore	2,382	50,266	0	290	1
20	Phoenix	2,238	44,472	300	?	1
21	Tampa	2,068	39,361	205	?	1
22	Denver	1,980	48,336	0	190	1
23	Cincinnati	1,818	44,727	0	82	1
24	Portland	1,793	44,369	145	x	0
25	Milwaukee	1,607	44,831	0	82	1
26	Kansas City	1,582	44,868	0	82	1
27	Sacramento	1,481	45,822	75	x	0
28	Norfolk	1,443	40,708	170	x	0
29	Indianapolis	1,380	45,147	165	x	0
30	Columbus	1,345	43,728	130	x	0
31	San Antonio	1,325	37,510	190	x	0
32	New Orleans	1,285	37,340	320	x	0
33	Orlando	1,225	44,098	205	x	0
34	Buffalo	1,189	40,507	60	x	0
35	Charlotte	1,162	43,568	370	x	0
38	Salt Lake City	1,072	41,331	370	x	0
41	Memphis	1,007	40,226	240	x	0
42	Nashville	985	43,550	215	x	0
43	Oklahoma City	959	39,726	190	x	0
45	Louisville	949	40,253	115	x	0
46	Jacksonville	907	41,840	320	x	0

Table 10.2 continued

Rank (U.S.)	City	Population (in thousands)	Mean Household Income	Distance to Nearest MLB Team (in millions)	Estimated Market Values (in millions)	Number of Teams
	Toronto	3,751	N/A	0	140	1
	Montreal	3,068	N/A	0	90	1
	Vancouver	1,547	N/A	125	x	0
	Mexico City	20,899	N/A	800	x	0
	Guadalajara	3,370	N/A	850	x	0
	Monterrey	2,939	N/A	420	x	0

Market Values of 'x' indicate no team.
N/A indicates not available.

Other cities with a more uncertain claim include Sacramento (possibly too close to Oakland and San Francisco), Norfolk (probably not viable if D.C. had a franchise), and Columbus (problematic because its market would be hemmed in by Pittsburgh, Cincinnati, and Cleveland).

Where controversy enters would be my selection of the two most economically viable long-term locations for an expansion franchise, even better than Washington, D.C. Mexico City is my second choice. Its population is nine times larger than Phoenix's or Tampa's and it is growing rapidly. Current per-capita Mexican income is about one-sixth of U.S. levels, but economists generally predict that its income will increase substantially. Total Mexico City income exceeds that of all but the largest 10 U.S. cities. While the distribution of income also is important, the evidence suggests that the baseball-attending population of Mexico City would be more than sufficient to support a MLB franchise. In addition, adding an expansion franchise in Mexico City would make the nascent Mexican television market much more receptive to MLB. The prescription for Mexican success: a big stadium, cheap tickets, as much Mexican talent as possible, and a national television deal. MLB in Mexico City would be a substantial gamble but with a return possibly exceeding that of the Colorado Rockies.

What is the best location for an expansion franchise? New York City! Its population is almost as large as Mexico City's and the average income is much higher. A NYC franchise has virtually no risk. Skeptics might argue that NYC cannot support three MLB franchises but the numbers strongly argue otherwise. A mid-size MLB market, Atlanta for example, has a population of about three million. Chicago's population of 8.2 million comfortably supports two franchises. New York City's population is 10.1 million higher than Chicago's. Furthermore, New York City had three very profitable franchises before the Dodgers and Giants left.

Looking at the local media contracts of the Yankees and the Mets, another franchise in New York City would introduce more competition and drive down the values of their media contracts and their franchises. George Steinbrenner and Nelson Doubleday (owner of the Mets) would object, but why should anyone else care? More competition in NYC would reduce the revenue advantage of the NYC teams and might reduce the tensions between small-market and large-market franchises. In addition, another MLB franchise in New York might mean that a NYC team would appear in the World Series more frequently.

My recommendation: locate the team in Brooklyn. Call it the Bums after the Brooklyn Dodgers' nickname "Dem Bums." Model the stadium after the Dodgers' old Ebbetts Field, and market the team based on a return to tradition. Then pray for Steinbrenner in a fit of pique or stupidity to move the Yankees to New Jersey.

Two additional points are important on MLB expansion. First, no one should be surprised when the owner of an expansion franchise claims he is losing money after a few years. Owners overpay for a franchise. The numbers in Chapter 2 show that the ego value of a MLB franchise or the average overpayment is $40 million. What is the implication? Suppose a franchise costs $100 million and franchise appreciation is expected to be about 15 percent, the MLB average. To make the stock market return of approximately 18 percent, the owner will need an operating profit of 3 percent or $3 million per year. However, the typical purchaser will borrow a large amount of the purchase price. If the owner paid $50 million in cash and borrowed the other $50 million at a 10 percent interest rate, he must net $5 million a year to cover the interest expense. While the owner needs $5 million in cash to cover his interest expense, he receives only $3 million after operating expenses. The franchise is not losing money, but the owner does have a cash flow problem that largely stems from how the deal was structured. The 18 percent average return primarily is due to franchise appreciation not realized until the club is sold, but the interest payments on the borrowed money come due yearly. To survive, an owner must have "deep pockets" to meet the yearly paper losses.

Second, while the franchise owner may lose money in the short-term, the local business community may benefit handsomely from an expansion franchise. A major league franchise gets a city mentioned on the national news every time the team plays. Even if a MLB expansion franchise in Indianapolis or Portland set new records for on-the-field baseball futility, Indianapolis or Portland would get mentioned on the evening news 162 days a year. From the perspective of Indianapolis or Portland businesses, that advertising could be worth more than a franchise owner's loss. It could also explain why so many cities and much of their business communities lobby so intensely for major league franchises. Community leaders may be true fans and simply want to attend a ball game. Alternately, they may think MLB is good advertising for their city or the additional money spent will create revenue and jobs. Unfortunately, the evidence suggests that sports franchises do not create appreciable revenues or jobs. Business and civic groups have commissioned myriad studies that purport to show the advantages of having a sports franchise. Unfortunately, most of these studies begin with the assumption that there will be revenue and job gains and then attempt to document the size of the gains. They begin by assuming the answer. The hard studies that examine whether there is a gain from having a sports franchise find little net gain.[5]

There will be winners from obtaining a MLB franchise. For example, the city gains prestige and publicity. Some firms near the stadium have increased business. They will lobby hard for a franchise. But there also are losers. Who will receive less of the entertainment dollar or who will pay more in taxes? A franchise may

---

[5] Robert Baade and Richard Dye in "Sports Stadiums and Area Development: A Critical Review," *Economic Development Quarterly*, August 1988, pages 265-75, thoroughly review the contention that a sports franchise leads to economic development. They find at best only weak support for that argument. No scholarly economic study has found any substantial local development gains from having a sports franchise.

not receive direct support, but there may be extensive indirect costs ranging from site preparation expenses to additional police expenses. To the extent that those expenses are not offset by additional taxes, then the taxpayer loses. In addition, when building a stadium a city all too frequently takes a large piece of prime real estate, builds a stadium in the middle, and then paves the rest for parking. The stadium occupies about five acres while the parking lots may take fifty. Taking 55 acres of prime commercial real estate and paving fifty generally is not the optimum use of that land. This setup also isolates the stadium from the rest of the community and reduces the potential positive impacts of a franchise.[6]

EXPANSION PROSPECTS—THE NBA

Table 10.3 presents the same information for basketball as Table 10.2 presented for baseball. For baseball, the expansion prospects are straightforward; for basketball, the crystal ball is murkier. Some small-market franchises have done well, for example the Charlotte Hornets and the Utah Jazz, while some big-city franchises have struggled, including the New Jersey Nets, the Golden State Warriors, and the Philadelphia 76ers.

Some might argue that basketball also appears more sensitive to regional preferences. That is, North Carolina is basketball country while Nebraska is football country. Until looking closely at the regional numbers for all sports, that was my view. However, the importance of regional differences appears grossly overstated. Looking at profit and attendance numbers, Indiana is not basketball country—Hoosier Hysteria to the contrary. After the fact, one can look at the numbers and make up any number of stories about differences in tastes. I don't buy them. If you could have predicted that Portland, with a small population and high market value, was basketball country before it received an NBA franchise, then I might believe your story. But if it is obvious that Portland or Charlotte are basketball hotbeds, why were franchises established in

---

[6] Many successful stadiums have been integrated into the city like Wrigley or Camden Yards or even Busch Stadium in St. Louis. However, integrating the stadium into the community may cost the team owner some profits with lost parking or concession revenues. George Steinbrenner and Marge Schott both now seek sufficient land to build an entertainment complex around their baseball franchise.

Buffalo, Cincinnati, Kansas City, Milwaukee, St. Louis, San Diego, and Seattle before Portland or Charlotte?

The list of cities without an NBA team that might support an expansion franchise includes many cities that have had a franchise leave greener pasture, including Buffalo, Cincinnati, Kansas City, St. Louis, and San Diego. Nevertheless, the best bets for basketball expansion may be St. Louis, San Diego, Buffalo, and Pittsburgh. All have stadiums available. While placing a market value on a potential franchise in any of these cities is fraught with uncertainty, it would appear that with reasonable stadium arrangements these franchises could have market values of $150 million. Baltimore's size suggests it could support a franchise, but its proximity to the Washington Bullets' arena in Landover, Maryland makes a Baltimore franchise problematic. In addition, the Bullets moved from Baltimore to Landover. New Orleans is frequently mentioned as a candidate for an NBA franchise and has attempted to purchase the Minnesota Timberwolves. However, New Orleans already has lost one NBA franchise (to Salt Lake City) and the only existing feasible arena is the Superdome, a poor venue for basketball.

The importance of stadium arrangements has been mentioned for both basketball and hockey. Key components include the ambience and the closeness of the action. No NBA franchise has had long-term success in a multi-purpose football-basketball facility. The quality of the basketball teams that played in the facilities may have had some role, but the facilities appear partially responsible. Fans generally are not enthusiastic about spending $30 a ticket to watch a basketball game when they sit so far away they cannot distinguish Shaquille O'Neal from Mugsy Bogues. Without a new facility, New Orleans does not look like a viable site for an NBA franchise. Tampa suffers using the same logic. A favorable lease could make a franchise profitable in the short-term, but its long-term success is questionable.

The table suggests that Cincinnati, Kansas City, Columbus, and Norfolk and possibly Jacksonville, Louisville, Memphis, Nashville, and Oklahoma City under the proper circumstances could support an NBA franchise. Whether those circumstances—suitable stadium arrangements and community support—exist is

Table 10.3

BASKETBALL EXPANSION PROSPECTS

Rank (U.S.)	City	Population (in thousands)	Mean Household Income	Distance to Nearest NBA Team (in miless)	Estimated Market Values (in millions)	Number of Teams
1	New York	19,342	58,812	0	289	2
					176	
2	Los Angeles	14,532	52,786	0	289	2
					126	
3	Chicago	8,240	51,772	0	289	1
4	San Francisco	6,253	59,014	0	122	1
5	Philadelphia	5,899	51,388	0	139	1
6	Boston	5,455	57,899	0	172	1
7	Detroit	5,187	48,733	0	239	1
8	Dallas	4,037	48,195	0	89	1
9	Washington	3,924	64,378	0	105	1
10	Houston	3,731	48,195	0	97	1
11	Miami	3,193	44,378	0	97	1
12	Seattle	2,970	49,125	0	89	1
13	Atlanta	2,960	50,788	0	122	1
14	Cleveland	2,760	44,072	0	139	1
15	Minneapolis	2,539	51,095	0	172	1
16	San Diego	2,498	49,293	115	x	0
17	St. Louis	2,492	51,095	235	x	0
18	Pittsburgh	2,395	40,729	185	x	0
19	Baltimore	2,382	50,266	30	x	0
20	Phoenix	2,238	44,472	0	189	1
21	Tampa	2,068	39,361	80	x	0
22	Denver	1,980	48,336	0	89	1
23	Cincinnati	1,818	44,727	100	x	0
24	Portland	1,793	44,369	0	239	1
25	Milwaukee	1,607	44,831	0	89	1
26	Kansas City	1,582	44,868	410	x	0

another question. Of these cities, Nashville appears the most promising given their new arena.

The list of potential expansion cities includes a number that have had prior franchises leave town before finding success elsewhere - including Buffalo, Cincinnati, Kansas City, St. Louis, and San Diego. Does losing one franchise suggest that a city will not support another? The Clippers were the last NBA franchise to move, traveling from San Diego to Los Angeles in 1984. Most NBA franchises were financially challenged in the early 1980s. Despite the Clippers move, they continue to struggle. This suggests that their problems were not due to their San Diego location.

Table 10.3 continued

Rank (U.S.)	City	Population (in thousands)	Mean Household Income	Distance to Nearest NBA Team (in miless)	Estimated Market Values (in millions)	Number of Teams
27	Sacramento	1,481	45,822	0	105	1
28	Norfolk	1,443	40,708	140	x	0
29	Indianapolis	1,380	45,147	0	89	1
30	Columbus	1,345	43,728	170	x	0
31	San Antonio	1,325	37,510	0	105	1
32	New Orleans	1,285	37,340	320	x	0
33	Orlando	1,225	44,098	0	122	1
34	Buffalo	1,189	40,507	190	x	0
35	Charlotte	1,162	43,568	0	172	1
38	Salt Lake City	1,072	41,331	0	172	1
41	Memphis	1,007	40,226	335	x	0
42	Nashville	985	43,550	215	x	0
43	Oklahoma City	959	39,726	190	x	0
45	Louisville	949	40,253	115	x	0
46	Jacksonville	907	41,840	125	x	0
	Toronto	3,751	N/A	210	?	1
	Montreal	3,068	N/A	255	x	0
	Vancouver	1,547	N/A	125	?	1
	Mexico City	20,899	N/A	750	x	0

Market Values of 'x' indicate no team.

N/A indicates not available.

The same argument applies to many other "jilted" cities. Losing a team may reflect more on the owner's managerial competence or greed than on a city's lack of support, however impolitic a suggestion that may be. The owners of most franchises are generally talented in their fields. Their fields, however, generally are not professional sports, and their ability to translate their talents into financial success in sports is not always apparent. Because it only takes $100 million and an extra serving of ego to own a major league franchise, owners in major league sports may be more likely to fail—especially if they treat the franchise as a hobby rather than a business. This argument is not likely to appeal to owners. An owner facing difficulties in a city can say that his performance has been unsatisfactory or that the city does not appreciate his team. The owner's standard answer is the latter. That may be the case. Maybe 2.5 million people in San Diego did not appreciate a quality product in the Clippers, or maybe the owner of the Clippers did not market and field a quality product.

In terms of possible international expansion, while Mexico

City could support a MLB franchise, it probably would not currently support an NBA franchise. Mexican baseball players are abundant; Mexican basketball players are virtually nonexistent. European expansion would appear more feasible in the short-term given the proliferation of European leagues and the enthusiastic reception of U.S. teams in Europe. The logistics and finances of an NBA franchise in Europe, however, are at best speculative.

NBA teams began play in Toronto and Vancouver in 1995. Will basketball translate well into Canada? The answer is unclear. The expansion fee for each was $125 million. The numbers in Table 10.3 suggest that the Toronto and Vancouver franchises are worth roughly $100 to $125 million with average stadium arrangements. Both franchises also were required to pre-sell a minimum of 12,000 season tickets suggesting that stadium arrangements could be substantially better than average. However, both franchises reached this number with difficulty and could see a dramatic drop-off when the novelty of an NBA franchise wears off - and Vancouver's 18 losses in a row suggest the novelty may not last long. Without exceptional managerial talent or exceptional luck, both franchises are candidates for long-term financial losses.

EXPANSION PROSPECTS—THE NFL

Jacksonville and Carolina joined the NFL in 1995. Further expansion is virtually a foregone conclusion. Table 10.4 presents football expansion information. The two obvious candidates for expansion were St. Louis and Baltimore before St. Louis snared the Rams and Baltimore snatched the Browns. Both had a club leave for greener pastures, but for a smaller market. The Cardinals moved from the 17th largest market to the 20th and the Colts moved from the 19th to the 29th. Neither the Cardinals' nor the Colts' move appears to have increased their long-term profitability. In contrast, recent moves of the Raiders from the 2nd largest market to the 4th, the Rams from the 2nd to the 17th, the Browns from the 14th to the 19th, and the Oilers from the 10th to the 42nd, all appear to have yielded dramatic profit increases. Clearly they also demonstrate a trend to move from larger cities to smaller. It also is clear that L.A. is the premier site for expansion.

Table 10.4

FOOTBALL EXPANSION PROSPECTS

Rank (U.S.)	City	Population (in thousands)	Mean Household Income	Distance to Nearest NFL Team (in miles)	Estimated Market Values (in millions)	Number of Teams
1	New York	19,342	58,812	0	137	2
					120	
2	Los Angeles	14,532	52,786	50	187 [a]	0
					137 [a]	
3	Chicago	8,240	51,772	0	212	1
4	San Francisco	6,253	59,014	0	120	2
					253 [b]	
5	Philadelphia	5,899	51,388	0	212	1
6	Boston	5,455	57,899	0	118	1
7	Detroit	5,187	48,733	0	120	1
8	Dallas	4,037	48,195	0	428	1
9	Washington	3,924	64,378	0	120 [a]	1
10	Houston	3,731	48,195	190	303 [b]	0
11	Miami	3,193	44,378	0	203	1
12	Seattle	2,970	49,125	0	120	1
13	Atlanta	2,960	50,788	0	120	1
14	Cleveland	2,760	44,072	120	187 [a]	0
15	Minneapolis	2,539	51,095	0	170	1
16	San Diego	2,498	49,293	0	120	1
17	St. Louis	2,492	51,095	0	420	1
18	Pittsburgh	2,395	40,729	0	220	1
19	Baltimore	2,382	50,266	0	387	1
20	Phoenix	2,238	44,472	0	120	1
21	Tampa	2,068	39,361	0	153	1
22	Denver	1,980	48,336	0	187	1
23	Cincinnati	1,818	44,727	0	162	1
24	Portland	1,793	44,369	145	x	0
25	Milwaukee	1,607	44,831	0	120	1
26	Kansas City	1,582	44,868	0	187	1

NFL expansion franchises cost $140 million in 1994, very much in line with the market values listed in Table 10.4. Football franchise values are not as sensitive to city size as values in other leagues. The lack of correlation between city size and franchise values in the NFL likely reflects two fundamental financial differences. First, the NFL relies much more heavily on shared revenues. As noted in Chapter 7, most NFL revenue is shared, with national media money accounting for almost 60 percent of NFL revenues. With the NFL's reliance on national media money, a franchise could be profitable almost anywhere. Birmingham, Alabama (the 54th largest market), Tulsa, Oklahoma (59th), or Omaha, Ne-

Table 10.4 continued

Rank (U.S.)	City	Population (in thousands)	Mean Household Income	Distance to Nearest NFL Team (in miles)	Estimated Market Values (in millions)	Number of Teams
27	Sacramento	1,481	45,822	75	x	0
28	Norfolk	1,443	40,708	140	x	0
29	Indianapolis	1,380	45,147	0	120	1
30	Columbus	1,345	43,728	130	x	0
31	San Antonio	1,325	37,510	190	x	0
32	New Orleans	1,285	37,340	0	120	1
33	Orlando	1,225	44,098	180	x	0
34	Buffalo	1,189	40,507	0	145	1
35	Charlotte	1,162	43,568	330	NA	1
38	Salt Lake City	1,072	41,331	370	x	0
41	Memphis	1,007	40,226	335	x	0
42	Nashville	985	43,550	0	303	1
43	Oklahoma City	959	39,726	190	x	0
45	Louisville	949	40,253	115	x	0
46	Jacksonville	907	41,840	170	NA	1
	Toronto	3,751	N/A[c]	210	x	0
	Montreal	3,068	N/A	255	x	0
	Vancouver	1,547	N/A	125	x	0
	Mexico City	20,899	N/A	800	x	0

Market Values of 'x' indicate no team. NA indicates not available yet.

[a] Market values for the Raiders, Rams, Browns, and Oilers are for their old homes. The market value for the Redskins does not include the impact of their proposed new stadium.

[b] Market values for the Raiders, Rams, Browns and Oilers are for their new homes.

[c] Household income not available for cities outside of the U.S.

braska (61st) could be profitable. Even cities not in Table 10.1 like Austin, Texas; Jackson, Mississippi; or Salem, Oregon could be viable given the experience of the Green Bay Packers.

Second, the structure of the seasons is much different. Baseball has 81 home games while football has only eight excluding the playoffs. In baseball a successful club could average 40,000 attending while an unsuccessful one might only average 15,000. At $10 a ticket, the 1994 MLB average, the difference exceeds $20 million. In football, with fewer home dates, the differences in gate receipts is much smaller, even without revenue sharing. This has heightened the importance of stadium arrangements. Thus, a smaller city that is willing to bid aggressively for an NFL franchise now has a reasonable prospect for obtaining one.

EXPANSION PROSPECTS—THE NHL

Table 10.5 presents hockey expansion information. One can-

Table 10.5

HOCKEY EXPANSION PROSPECTS

Rank (U.S.)	City	Population (in thousands)	Mean Household Income	Distance to Nearest NFL Team (in miles)	Estimated Market Values (in millions)	Number of Teams
1	New York	19,342	58,812	0	213 130 97	3
2	Los Angeles	14,532	52,786	0	263 97	2
3	Chicago	8,240	51,772	0	280	1
4	San Francisco	6,253	59,014	0	230	1
5	Philadelphia	5,899	51,388	0	130	1
6	Boston	5,455	57,899	0	313	1
7	Detroit	5,187	48,733	0	280	1
8	Dallas	4,037	48,195	0	80	1
9	Washington	3,924	64,378	0	63	1
10	Houston	3,731	48,195	230	x	0
11	Miami	3,193	44,378	0	88	1
12	Seattle	2,970	49,125	760	x	0
13	Atlanta	2,960	50,788	420	x	0
14	Cleveland	2,760	44,072	115	x	0
15	Minneapolis	2,539	51,095	350	x	0
16	San Diego	2,498	49,293	115	x	0
17	St. Louis	2,492	51,095	0	197	1
18	Pittsburgh	2,395	40,729	0	80	1
19	Baltimore	2,382	50,266	30	x	0
20	Phoenix	2,238	44,472	350	x	0
21	Tampa	2,068	39,361	0	63	1
22	Denver	1,980	48,336	0	180	1
23	Cincinnati	1,818	44,727	225	x	0
24	Portland	1,793	44,369	535	x	0
25	Milwaukee	1,607	44,831	80	x	0
26	Kansas City	1,582	44,868	410	x	0

not discuss hockey expansion without paying more attention to differences in tastes. Few residents of Atlanta, Houston, or Seattle are likely to have played hockey as youths and may be less familiar with the game. Thus, these cities may be relatively inhospitable sites for hockey expansion although they are the largest cities currently without a franchise. Small-market NHL franchises almost uniformly are in a financial struggle. In addition, southern franchises like Dallas, Tampa, and Washington also struggle. Transplanting hockey to southern cities may require more than a normal amount of managerial talent. While Atlanta may attract an expan-

Table 10.5 continued

Rank (U.S.)	City	Population (in thousands)	Mean Household Income	Distance to Nearest NFL Team (in miles)	Estimated Market Values (in millions)	Number of Teams
27	Sacramento	1,481	45,822	75	x	0
28	Norfolk	1,443	40,708	140	x	0
29	Indianapolis	1,380	45,147	165	x	0
30	Columbus	1,345	43,728	170	x	0
31	San Antonio	1,325	37,510	255	x	0
32	New Orleans	1,285	37,340	340	x	0
33	Orlando	1,225	44,098	180	x	0
34	Buffalo	1,189	40,507	0	97	1
35	Charlotte	1,162	43,568	330	x	0
36	Hartford	1,158	N/A	0	63	1
38	Salt Lake City	1,072	41,331	565	x	0
	Toronto	3,751	N/A	0	138	1
	Montreal	3,068	N/A	0	247	1
	Vancouver	1,547	N/A	0	73	1
	Ottawa	863	N/A	0	91	1
	Edmonton	823	N/A	0	63	1
	Calgary	723	N/A	0	63	1
	Winnipeg	647	N/A	0	55	1

Market Values of 'x' indicate no team.

N/A indicates not available.

sion franchise, keep in mind that the Flames left Atlanta with its 3 million population for Calgary and its population of 0.7 million. While the Flames have not made tremendous profits in Calgary, they have done better in Calgary than they did in Atlanta.

The NHL experience suggests one additional point on expansion. The Mighty Ducks' valuation suggests one factor may be much more important than location in deciding a franchise's success: who is included in the ownership group. Strong management and marketing may not overcome a poor location but will substantially increase the probability of success in a reasonable location. When a league can bring in the entertainment marketing skills of a Disney, owner of the Ducks, the probability of success for the franchise increases substantially. When a franchise is partially owned by a municipality, like the Winnipeg Jets, it likely will struggle. Nevertheless, in the absence of another ownership group like Disney, it is not clear that any further NHL expansion is appropriate.

EXPANSION—THE DOWNSIDE

Franchise expansion is not without costs including diluting the revenues of existing franchises. First, national media money must be split more ways. For example, in the NFL, with 28 teams each team receives about $40 million in national television money; adding two franchises reduces each team's share to $37.3 million, assuming no increase in TV revenues. Second, the talent pool is diluted in the same ratio. A team's chance at the next Joe Montana, Troy Aikman or Barry Sanders falls by 3.5 percent. The Dallas Cowboys would be but one of 30 teams vying for the best talent rather than one of 28. That could have serious repercussions at the turnstiles, more so in MLB or the NBA than in the NFL. And third, a team will to have to play the expansion franchise, and expansion franchises at first generally are dogs.

Finally, expansion may shift the balance of power. Expansion adds franchises in smaller cities and changes the mix of large-market versus small-market teams. Large-market franchises comprise less of the league. Thus, with expansion we should expect to see additional support for revenue sharing. The small-market franchises in baseball, for example, may increasingly push for a piece of Steinbrenner's local media pie. We should also expect to see large-market franchises increasingly likely to oppose expansion, recognizing that it may injure their long-term financial prospects. In MLB, the Yankees, Mets, Dodgers and Red Sox may be increasingly likely to oppose further expansion lest the large market teams get outvoted on other issues, e.g. related to labor negotiations. Large-market clubs will be more likely to ask whether adding franchises will make the sport more popular and less likely to value the one-time bonanza provided by expansion clubs' initiation fees.

FRANCHISE RELOCATION

All leagues except possibly hockey appear to have cities that could financially support an expansion franchise. Then why have all leagues except hockey been so slow to add franchises?[7] For example, when Kansas City received a MLB franchise its population was approximately 1.3 million. Today there are nine cities that large without major league baseball and one city three times that size without a franchise. One can make many arguments like there

---

[7] One can argue that hockey has expanded much more aggressively than other leagues in an effort to increase its popularity throughout the U.S.

are insufficient players with major league talent. They all ring hollow. The NHL has expanded the most. No one can watch a tape of NHL action in 1964 versus 1994 and credibly argue that the level of play has deteriorated.[8] The real reason that few expansion franchises have been awarded is economic.

The owners in any league are as much of a cartel as OPEC - and perhaps more successful than OPEC over the last twenty years. *Webster's Dictionary* defines a cartel as "a combination of independent industrial or commercial enterprises designed to limit competition or fix prices." While the leagues may contend that they need to cooperate in terms of determining the rules of the game and setting schedules, their cooperation goes far beyond these matters. The league bargains for a national media contract and prohibits competition among teams for national media money. The league sets rules for bargaining with players that also limit competition among teams. And the league places restrictions on franchise mobility giving teams an effective monopoly when dealing with the municipality where they are located. These actions suggest all major leagues act as cartels. The focus here is on just one of their restrictions: constraining franchise mobility and granting teams local monopoly power in dealing with their hometown government.

The local monopoly argument is a powerful reason in favor of limiting the number of franchises and restricting expansion. The reason is the St. Petersburg Principle. As an owner, it is nice to be wanted. Your current locale may be where you call home, and there's no place like home. But some of those other places might be willing to pay you a handsome premium to leave. To put things less tactfully, it helps to be talking to St. Pete when you are negotiating a better deal with Chicago over a new Comiskey Park and the terms of the new lease. It helps to have St. Pete on the line when you want Candlestick Park refurbished. And it helps to have St. Pete on hold when the Kingdome needs a new roof.

---

[8] Considering population growth relative to league expansion, it appears that relatively fewer players make the majors now than twenty or thirty years ago. In the NHL in 1964 virtually all players were drawn from a small Canadian pool. Now the NHL includes many more U.S. citizens as well as Swedes, Finns, and Russians. The NBA now draws talent from around the globe including Croatia, Russia, Nigeria, and Australia. MLB only recently has seen players from Japan and Korea but has had a large contingent of players from Latin America and the Caribbean.

For all leagues, many more cities can support viable franchises—at least in the short-term—than there are franchises available. This limit on franchises could be due to large-market owners not wanting to share the wealth. An owner in New York or Chicago does not want to share revenues with a potential owner in Austin or Nashville. However, small-market clubs may actually gain more from the excess demand for teams. Excess demand for teams means that cities are going to compete for teams. Chicago and Tampa-St. Pete competed for the White Sox; Los Angeles and St. Louis competed for the Rams; and when an expansion franchise is contemplated, ownership groups across North America compete for prize. The notion of teams competing for a city is extremely rare, occurring only when there are competing leagues. For example, when the American Football League (AFL) began play in 1960 the Chiefs located in Dallas to compete against the Cowboys, and when the World Hockey League (WHL) started in 1972 the Whalers located in Boston to compete against the Bruins.[9]

Typically there will be more competition for small-market franchises. Moving a team from New York, Los Angeles, or Chicago rarely makes financial sense—despite Georgia Frontiere's move of the Rams from L.A. to St. Louis or Jerry Reinsdorf's threatened move of the White Sox from Chicago to Tampa Bay. Owners especially in MLB want as large a market as possible for the additional media and gate revenues. The franchises most likely to move are those in small-market cities and that have poor stadium arrangements. In MLB, Pittsburgh, Kansas City, and Cincinnati may be the most likely. In the NBA, Indiana is the prime candidate. The story is a little different in the NFL. Since all franchises make money, a city like St. Louis must aggressively pursue a franchise, effectively promising even greater profits. However, as St. Louis has demonstrated, any city willing to pay enough can attract a franchise. In addition, since a team plays only eight regular

[9] One could view the Raiders' move to Los Angeles as competing with the Rams and the Clippers' similar move as competing with the Lakers. However, the Los Angeles market is large enough that there has been very little financial competition. The one case where there may really have been competition is between the Oakland A's and the San Francisco Giants. Jesse W. Markham and Paul V. Teplitz, *(Baseball Economics and Public Policy.* Lexington, MA: Lexington Books, 1981), present evidence that the A's move to the San Francisco area put the Giants and the A's in competition for a limited baseball entertainment dollar. It would appear that this competition was unintentional and that MLB expected both teams to be financially successful.

season games per year, a large population base is not as important for healthy ticket sales. The NHL could see the greatest shifts with Winnipeg the most likely candidate to move.

No one interested in profits generally should move a team from New York, Los Angeles, or Chicago to Portland, Columbus, or Orlando, but moving from one small market to another may make much sense for two reasons. First, the franchise initially will be a novelty and will sell tickets because it is "the" event. The Arizona Cardinals and Indianapolis Colts are perfect examples of this phenomenon. After a few years, the novelty wears off and ticket demand returns to a more normal level. Nevertheless, short-term gate receipts and short-term profits increase substantially. The Cardinals are the prime example of the Nomadic Football League, moving from Chicago to St. Louis to Phoenix and now eyeing Los Angeles. Each time Bidwell has moved the Cardinals, their profits have jumped only to slide back down once the new locale was familiar with the team.

Second, the potentially larger gain comes from the competition between cities. For example, what was St. Pete willing to do to obtain a MLB franchise? Prior negotiations as reported in the sports press suggest a lot. Suppose you owned a weak franchise; say, you were struggling in Seattle. St. Pete offered an attractive lease, a substantial guarantee on season tickets, and more goodwill than you thought possible in Seattle. The difference between your profits in St. Pete versus Seattle could exceed $10 million. What do you do? Going back to Seattle and asking for a better deal is a popular owner pastime. From an owner's perspective, he is fostering competition between cities and allowing competitive market forces to work. The interaction between an owner and two cities in this tango of who is going to pay how much to whom is a classic example of a branch of economics ironically called game theory.

It is worthwhile to describe exactly how game theory applies. Assume an owner attempts to maximize profits, although he may also have other goals including winning. Cities also are engaged in a maximization process, although that process is much more complex for at least two reasons. First, there is no single decision maker. The mayor, city council, business community and others all may be involved. Second, the goals of some of these decision makers including the mayor may be much more complex. Low taxes, increasing employment, building a city's prestige, and reelection all may be components of a mayor's objective. The game begins when an owner enters negotiations with two cities. One city seeks not to lose a team; the other seeks to gain a team. Since a team means prestige and potentially increased employment, each mayor is willing to offer concessions either in terms of lower taxes or, perhaps more politically palatable, a better deal on a municipally-owned stadium. Where does the "game" enter? If I am the mayor seeking to attract your team from another city, I likely will offer you an attractive package on taxes and stadium arrangements. In turn, you will likely return to your current city and outline my offer. Does that city sweeten its arrangements for your franchise? If that city stands pat, to use a poker analogy, they have called your bluff. You can move your franchise—the city lost its bet—or keep it where it is. Either way, the game is over and the winning and losing cities are decided. More likely, however, your current city may sweeten the arrangements if only marginally. You then relay this sweetened offer to me to see if I will make a counteroffer. This cycle can be repeated almost infinitely, and through this process the owner extracts the maximum advantage (what economists label "rent") from the high bidder.

There is one additional twist to this game. As the franchise owner, you do face constraints. While most leagues have some limited legal ability to restrict your franchise's movement, the other league owners also have some moral suasion, especially if they view you as a potential renegade. As an owner you belong to a very exclusive fraternity. Having the rest of the fraternity members angry with you, perhaps for overly aggressive negotiations, is not a position most individuals want to be in—especially given the high costs of joining the fraternity, although the Raiders owner, Al Davis, may be an exception. However, if the profits from the negotiations are large enough, it may overcome the approbation of your fraternity members.

THE DOWNSIDE OF COMPETITION BETWEEN CITIES FOR FRANCHISES

From an economic efficiency perspective, it is appropriate that the cities that want franchises the most and are willing to pay the most should have franchises. If Washington is willing to pay $10 million per year for the Pirates and Pittsburgh is not, economists would argue that it is efficient for the Pirates to move to D.C. In addition, at least some businesses in cities with a major league franchise benefit substantially. For example, hotels and restaurants near the stadium profit. Thus, it is not unreasonable for an owner to bargain with the city to capture some of those ancillary benefits. Nevertheless, there is a downside to this rosy picture of the competitive market serving to allocate teams efficiently to the cities that want them the most. Consider three problems.

First, the benefits of having a major league sports franchise have been systematically overstated. Typically, it is only a relatively narrow set of interest groups that gain when a sports franchise comes to town. Nevertheless, these hotels, restaurants, and developers will lobby intensely to attract a franchise. The losers are much more likely to be diverse, to suffer only a small loss, and not to lobby on the issue. This is a standard problem in public finance. The San Francisco Giants are a concrete example. They covet a new stadium in the Bay area. The issue has been taken to the voters repeatedly and has failed repeatedly but has stubbornly refused to die. While most voters are unwilling to pay the additional taxes required for a new stadium, some deep-pocket interests have strong financial incentives to keep the issue alive. Had the issue not required a referendum, it is likely that those special interests would have succeeded in obtaining authorization to build a new stadium.

Second, aggravating the first problem, public authorities value both low taxes and prestige, and prestige is tied in part to major league sports. If most taxpayers value only low taxes and if a referendum is not required to authorize a new stadium, then those public authorities will overpay for prestige. For example, when Toronto offered the Blue Jays a below-market lease on the Skydome, the city had to make up that money somewhere. When St. Louis or Baltimore or Oakland or Nashville offered sweetheart deals to NFL franchises, the cities must find additional revenues somewhere. Someone's taxes are increased. Furthermore, there is no guarantee that the people who benefit from the new facilities are the ones paying those higher taxes.

And third, owners have systematically limited the number of

franchises. Thus, we see free competition among cities but not among teams.[10] Consider another example. Steinbrenner has threatened to move the Yankees to New Jersey. New York City and state officials have suggested spending $250 million for improvements to Yankee Stadium to keep the Yankees. George Steinbrenner and his limited partners may gain tremendously if these changes are made. Some neighborhood businesses also may gain. But will the typical New Yorker, who ultimately will foot the bill, be better off? The answer is unclear, and the question is unlikely even to be seriously discussed. The political power lies with the organized few rather than the diffuse many—even if the many have more to lose. If New York City could attract another team, its bargaining power would be very different. But MLB grants exclusive territory to a franchise, and another team cannot come to the New York City area without Steinbrenner's approval.

One additional implication of this bargaining between cities for existing teams frequently is ignored. To the extent that a Steinbrenner cuts a deal with a city, he and the city become partners. The implication: when a decision is made that influences the franchise, be it on expansion or negotiating a labor agreement, it influences not just Steinbrenner but also his limited partners— including the residents of New York City. Steinbrenner may not have a written obligation to report to all his limited partners. However, to the extent that there are verbal commitments or implicit agreements when negotiating with a city, those commitments are binding and may have strong implications for other decisions. For example, some sports analysts have argued that fans should have no say in labor-management impasses in sports. Those sports analysts are wrong. When an owner does not field a team, e.g., due to a strike, the owner and the players may be the ones most hurt. But the taxpayers of New York or Chicago or Seattle are the owners' silent partners. When the game is not played, the taxpayers lose. The taxpayers have an implicit contract with the owners to put on a game and to pay the resulting taxes. When owners cannot resolve

---

[10] The argument can be made that anyone can start a new league, and in that sense there is competition. That argument is the same as saying that the automotive market is competitive since anyone can start the next Ford or General Motors. The argument is technically correct but economically uninformative.

their labor problems and cannot field a team in a municipal stadium or in a publicly-subsidized stadium—which includes virtually every major league stadium in North America—then a strike does not involve just the owners and the players. Taxpayers are silent partners and should have a voice.

FINANCIALLY, SHOULD ANY TEAMS RELOCATE?

In MLB, Kansas City, Pittsburgh, and Seattle appear to be the franchises most likely to relocate. Are there any locations that would dramatically increase the market value of the Royals, Pirates, or Mariners? Consider moving the Pirates from Pittsburgh to Washington, D.C. The numbers in Chapter 6 suggest that the franchise's profits would increase by $1.25 million with the same stadium arrangements (the population difference of 1.6 million times $0.80 per person). A favorable stadium package could add $10 million in profit while the novelty of MLB might add another $5 million in franchise profits through short-term increased ticket sales in D.C. However, the long-term difference in profits between the two cities would likely be virtually inconsequential assuming similar stadium arrangements.

A comparison between Seattle and Washington weighs more heavily against D.C. On the surface, the move from Seattle to D.C. would appear to increase the Mariners' market value like the Pirates. The Mariners have two additional considerations, however. First, without additional stadium work they may continue to struggle in Seattle. The stadium was built cheaply and it shows. While the stadium is a major negative, there is a potentially even larger offsetting positive. There is no nearby city with MLB. If you live in the Pacific Northwest, Seattle should be your team. The Mariners should be the Colorado Rockies of the Pacific Northwest. Fans from Vancouver to Portland should be coming to Seattle to see the Mariners, and the Mariners have the potential to be one of the most profitable franchises in MLB. Their population base includes Washington, Oregon, and Vancouver, over nine million people. They should sell out every night. The Boston Red Sox are tremendously profitable not because of Boston but because they are marketed to the entire New England region. Likewise,

Seattle should be marketed to the entire Pacific Northwest. Moving the Mariners would not appear to be financially intelligent.

In baseball, the only franchise shifts that would appear profitable without a tremendous stadium arrangement would involve a move to New York City. Moving a team like the Kansas City Royals to New York might be the one thing the Royals could do to restore profitability. There would be a certain poetic justice in having Kansas City's team move to New York and compete against the Yankees after the Yankees effectively used Kansas City as a farm team during the early 1960s. However, such a move undoubtedly would be opposed by many baseball owners.

A list of the NBA teams most frequently mentioned as ready to move begins with Minneapolis. An ownership group in New Orleans attempted to buy the Timberwolves for over $150 million. However, the league office blocked the sale. The NBA argued that Minneapolis had a reasonable stadium arrangement and had played to capacity crowds despite mediocre teams. Unless the stadium arrangement was phenomenal, a move to New Orleans may be a losing proposition. There is a smaller population; local broadcasting revenues would likely be lower; and the Superdome is not a good venue for basketball. San Antonio also has made noises about moving if they do not get a new arena. While their current arena is not a good basketball venue, the franchise has been financially successful and would not appear likely to relocate.

Denver, Indiana, and Milwaukee are the weakest franchises and thus would appear more realistic candidates for relocation. But a primary determinant of location—beyond stadium arrangements and market size—is a team's ownership status. For example, to the extent that Melvin and Herbert Simon, owners of the Indiana Pacers, remain committed to Indianapolis, the Pacers will remain there, their losses notwithstanding. However, when the ownership changes hands, the probability of a franchise shift increases dramatically. NBA franchise relocation is better predicted by ownership changes or a deep-pocketed potential owner entering the game or stadium availability than by what might be thought of as strictly economic factors. On that basis, Denver with ongoing discussions about a new stadium may be unlikely to lose its franchise. St. Louis, Nashville, and Buffalo with new stadiums may be more attractive if the stadium arrangements are sufficiently sweet.

When speaking of sweet stadium deals, the NFL's Rams' arrangements with St. Louis come to mind. The Rams have been given a new practice facility, will pay below-market rent for a new 70,000 seat stadium, and have virtually been guaranteed a profit of at least $15 million annually. The stadium arrangements move the Rams into the financial elite. Until 1995, the NFL generally saw less discussion of possible franchise shifts, excluding the movements of the peripatetic Al Davis, owner of the Raiders. Greater revenue sharing removed much of the incentive to relocate a franchise, equalized market values, and produced smaller gains from any move. In addition, the obvious candidate for a team, Baltimore, witnessed the Colts' departure in 1984 and the Colts remain the weakest franchise.

"Caponomics" changed this placid picture. With a salary cap and substantial revenue sharing, franchises now aggressively search for revenue that they do not have to share. Stadium income like luxury box revenues and Personal Seat Licenses (PSLs) are the current favorites. Now any city that can put together a financial package emphasizing revenue the team will not have to share will be seriously listened to. St. Louis's successful overtures to the Rams were just the opening move. St. Louis gave every city in the country—and virtually every owner—a lesson in how to attract a franchise. Franchises from Seattle to Cincinnati to Washington look at what St. Louis offered the Rams and ask is there anyone out there willing to make us a similar offer? The Raiders, Browns and Oilers all have already taken the bait. Art Modell's move of the Browns, in particular, makes it clear that "everyone has a price." With Los Angeles currently without a team, other franchises appear to be positioning themselves for a move to L.A. Early favorites: Arizona—with a track record of willingness to move; Cincinnati, with a financial history of putting profits above winning; and Seattle, owned by a Los Angeles resident unhappy with his Seattle lease. Likewise, Cleveland is an attractive site with its rabid football fans and a strong financial commitment to improve the stadium.

Finally, in hockey, there is one obvious city to move out of but no obvious place to move to. Winnipeg is the weakest franchise and may be too small a market to support an NHL franchise. However, there is no city where the Jets could move without long-term financial risk. In addition, there are strong non-economic ties to Winnipeg reinforced by the city's partial ownership of the franchise. Atlanta, Houston, and Seattle are the largest cities without an NHL franchise but none is a hockey hotbed. Minneapolis and Cleveland are next in size and both have arenas available. However, both also have had teams depart due to lack of support. Prior failures may have been due to the prior owner rather than due to city factors, and a new franchise might receive substantial support. Again, the key is the stadium's financial arrangement. In Winnipeg's case, however, there has been little incentive for the general partners to leave as long as the city and province have had to reimburse them for any loss and they did not need to share any financial records with the city and province. Phoenix will be home to the former Winnipeg Jets beginning with the 1996-97 season, and with the right arena arrangements, the team may be successful there.[12]

Hartford and Edmonton and perhaps Florida are other franchises potentially contemplating moves. While Florida has been relatively successful, it also has an inferior facility and an owner whose enthusiasm for ownership may have dimmed.[11] The New Jersey Devils also were widely believed to be leaving for Nashville until New Jersey renegotiated the Devils' lease. Nashville has a standing offer to any team of a new arena and a "guaranteed" profit of $10 million. But its small size and southern locale rightly give owners second thoughts about moving there as a long-term solution to any financial problem.

---

[11] Wayne Huizenga was viewed as the type of owner the NHL wanted to attract. However, Huizenga's sale of his firm, Blockbuster Entertainment, appears to have reduced his gains from owning a hockey franchise.

[12] The Jets aren't alone in pursuing a new home outside of Canada—Quebec has already moved to Colorado, and Edmonton is likely to move within the next year or two.

Chapter 11

Colleges — Financial Rankings or Going for the Green

"I had a friend with a lifetime contract. After two bad years the university president called him into his office and pronounced him dead."

**—Bob Devaney, football coach at Nebraska,
on lifetime contracts**

"A coach simply must resign himself to the fact that he is no longer involved with the educational process, but with entertainment."

—Ralph "Shug" Jordan, football coach, Auburn

"Basketball was fun in high school, but you find as you get into the big time college ball that it gets to be a business and less pleasure."

—Darryl Brown, basketball coach, Fordham

"A college racing stable makes as much sense as college football. The jockey could carry the college colors; the students could cheer; the alumni could bet; and the horse wouldn't have to pass a history test."

—Robert Hutchins, president, University of Chicago

"Everything that has happened in college football since 1939 has confirmed the wisdom of our course."

**—Robert Hutchins, on the University of Chicago's
decision to eliminate football**

"Football is the only activity on any campus that brings all the alumni back to the university."

—Carmen Cozza, football coach at Yale

"Athletics control this university, and they always will."

—Allison Jones, Alabama fan, on Alabama being placed on probation by the NCAA

The profitability of big-time college sports programs has yet to be thoroughly examined in a public forum. The NCAA and the College Football Association (CFA) both undertake surveys of the financial health of their members. Neither release information by school, however. Other studies that have examined the financial arrangements underlying collegiate athletics, for example Murray Sperber's provocative book *College Sports Inc.*, typically have focused on financial abuses and mismanagement, of which there allegedly are a lot. Nevertheless, by focusing on a few schools that have had serious financial problems, one runs the risk of misrepresenting the overall financial health of collegiate athletics.

I focus on schools with Division IA football programs and consider the football and men's basketball programs only. The rational for this focus is simple: these programs are virtually the only ones that generate appreciable revenue. The revenue generated by Michigan's football program dwarfs that generated by all other Michigan athletic programs except men's basketball. The net revenue generated by Florida's football program exceeds the gross revenue generated by collegiate soccer. For a few schools, hockey or baseball or women's basketball yield some net revenue.[1] However, the net revenue generated by these programs is inconsequential in comparison to the revenues from big-time collegiate football or men's basketball.

Many colleges are no more enthusiastic about revealing financial information than are professional teams. However, state colleges generally are required under Freedom of Information Acts to

---

[1] When including all costs, there likely are less than a dozen schools making money on hockey and less than half that making money on baseball or women's basketball. With increasing attendence and interest in women's basketball, however, more schools may be profitable in the future.

make public information on college sports finances. Thus, for schools from Michigan to Florida to Southern Mississippi to Oregon, a substantial amount of information is available.[2] Interpreting the information, however, is frequently problematic because accounting conventions vary widely. Nevertheless, most schools responded by providing either their response to a CFA survey or the NCAA financial audit information, thus simplifying comparisons. Most of the data refers to 1994.

Information from schools that did not respond (including private schools) was calculated based on game attendance and ticket prices, NCAA tourney money, number of times on television, and costs of similar football and basketball programs. For example, while program costs for football vary substantially between conferences, within a conference there are similarities. The reported football costs for ACC schools varied from $3.1 to $6.4 million with the more successful programs generally spending more money. In contrast, Mid-American Conference (MAC) schools generally spent around $1.6 million on their football program.

Before reporting the numbers, a word of caution is in order on their interpretation. Every college has its own set of accounting conventions some of which make no economic sense and serve to give a misleading picture of athletic finances. For example, Notre Dame's athletic budget excludes most of its television revenue from its football contract with NBC; Michigan's athletic revenue (like most schools) excludes licensing income; and Oregon with the highest reported football costs ($8.6 million) includes items generally excluded from football budgets. Thus, some adjustments must be made to the reported numbers to obtain comparable statistics for all schools.

Private schools are assumed to have little gift income directly attributable to collegiate athletics. Prior studies have shown at best a tenuous association between winning football games and alumni contributions. However, excluding gifts from the net revenues of private universities undoubtedly reduces the profit numbers of

---

[2] Only three schools flatly refused to provide any information, Indiana, Pittsburgh, and Temple. Their actions are troublesome. How can a state supported institution tell taxpayers that it will not provide information on whether public funds are being used to subsidize college football?

those schools. Notre Dame is a perfect example. While Notre Dame's football record is unrelated to the amount of contributions it receives in any year, its prior football success certainly has contributed to its current reputation and contributions. Notre Dame without football would be just one of many competitive private mid-west schools like Dayton or Xavier, without its current national constituency and national list of benefactors. The decision to exclude most gifts at private universities was necessary given the inability to separate donations to the athletic program versus those to the university's general fund. Giving an athletic dorm (no longer allowed under NCAA rules) or donating funds for a scholarship dedicated to the left offensive tackle generally show up in the athletic department's budget. Donations to the general fund generally do not. For example, if football tickets are difficult to obtain, alumni may be required to donate a minimum of $50 to be placed in a lottery for the available tickets. If alumni are contributing just for the right to buy tickets, that revenue properly is attributed to the athletic department, but under standard accounting practices it goes directly to the university's general fund. The numbers reported below frequently are not exact because much information is not reported. Nevertheless, they are the best estimates available of what typically are closely guarded secrets.

A final word about the numbers. My goal here is to calculate the net revenues in football and men's basketball. I do not examine the total financial health of a sports program. A school like Wisconsin with a small football surplus and a large sports program will be deep in the red for its total athletic budget. In contrast, a school like Tennessee with a large football surplus, at least one other sport that generates revenue (women's basketball), and a relatively small overall sports program could have a large surplus in its total athletic budget. The point here is not to analyze the impact of programs that are euphemistically labeled "non-revenue." No one asks if a college's philosophy department or library generate a profit. Similarly no one realistically asks if the fencing program or cross-country program generates a profit. However, many have asked whether the football and men's basketball programs generate a profit, and that is the question addressed here. The answer to that question underlies many further questions including the general role of athletics on campus, the appropriate level of support for women's athletic programs, and whether athletes should be paid.

WHO PROFITS AND WHO DOES NOT?

Table 11.1 lists by conference and by school the net revenues (or profits) for all schools with Division IA football plus the basketball powers of the Big East. Virtually no other school qualifies as a financial power in terms of collegiate athletics. DePaul, Marquette, and Massachusetts are the closest but do not even receive honorable mention among collegiate athletic financial powers. The general conclusions from Table 11.1: (1) some schools generate tremendous net revenues; (2) there are dramatic differences both between and within conferences; and (3) some schools are losing a bundle on allegedly moneymaking sports like collegiate football. These conclusions remind you of those for the pros.

First, consider differences within conferences. The ACC has a range of net revenue from Clemson at $10.2 million to Duke at $2.4 and Wake Forest at $2.5 million. The Duke and Wake Forest numbers could be understated because the private school numbers exclude gifts. However, Clemson still would have a substantial advantage. Differences in other conferences are even more dramatic. Syracuse leads the Big East financially with net revenues of $8.2 million followed by West Virginia and Pittsburgh at $6.5 million each. Miami, while not a laggard, has not had financial success to match its on-the-field success. At the other end of the spectrum is Temple with a loss estimated at $0.8 million. Temple's basketball program appears to generate a small surplus that is more than offset by the deficits incurred by its football program. Those deficits may be why Temple refused to provide any financial information. The Big Eight has even greater intra-conference differences. Nebraska ($13.6 million) and Oklahoma ($10.7 million) lead while Kansas State ($1.7 million), Oklahoma State ($2.2 million) and Missouri ($2.3 million) lag.

Table 11.1 strongly suggests a relationship between on-the-field success and financial success. Programs that win more also generally make more money. However, Miami's net revenue sug-

Table 11.1

NET REVENUES
By Conference and By College (in Millions)

	Net Revenue		Net Revenue		Net Revenue
ACC		**Big West**		**Southwest**	
Clemson	10.2	Arkansas State	-0.2	Baylor	1.5
Duke	2.4	Louisiana Tech	0.2	Houston	0.1
Florida State	7.0	Nevada	0.4	Rice	0.9
Georgia Tech	3.3	Nevada-Las Vegas	-1.1	Southern Methodist	1.4
Maryland	4.7	New Mexico State	-0.7	Texas	4.2
North Carolina	8.0	Northern Illinois	-0.6	Texas A&M	5.9
North Carolina State	6.6	Pacific	-1.0	Texas Christian	0.9
Virginia	5.2	San Jose State	-0.9	Texas Tech	3.3
Wake Forest	2.5	SW Louisiana	0.8		
		Utah State	-0.2	**Western Athletic**	
Big East				Brigham Young	10.9
Boston College	3.2	**Mid-American**		Colorado State	1.9
Miami	4.4	Akron	-0.9	Fresno State	3.1
Pittsburgh	6.4	Ball State	-1.2	Hawaii	2.6
Rutgers	1.4	Bowling Green	-1.3	New Mexico	2.1
Syracuse	8.2	Central Michigan	-1.1	San Diego State	1.7
Temple	-0.4	Eastern Michigan	-1.1	Texas-El Paso	1.5
Virginia Tech	0.5	Kent State	-1.7	Utah	0.8
West Virginia	6.5	Miami (Ohio)	-0.8	Wyoming	0.1
Connecticut	1.3	Ohio	-1.6		
Georgetown	2.5	Toledo	-0.6	**Independents**	
Providence	1.6	Western Michigan	-1.5	Cincinnati	0.6
St. John's	2.6			East Carolina	0.3
Seton Hall	1.5	**Pacific Ten**		Louisville	3.0
Villanova	1.7	Arizona	6.4	Memphis	5.1
		Arizona State	3.7	Notre Dame	15.3
Big Eight		California	3.2	Southern Mississippi	0.6
Colorado	6.3	Oregon	0.4	Tulane	1.4
Iowa State	4.8	Oregon State	3.3	Tulsa	0.1
Kansas	3.4	Southern California	7.7		
Kansas State	1.7	Stanford	6.4		
Missouri	2.3	UCLA	11.5		
Nebraska	13.6	Washington	13.5		
Oklahoma	10.7	Washington State	1.3		
Oklahoma State	2.2				
		Southwestern			
Big Ten		Alabama	13.6		
Illinois	5.2	Arkansas	4.5		
Indiana	7.0	Auburn	11.2		
Iowa	7.5	Florida	15.9		
Michigan	17.6	Georgia	12.2		
Michigan State	9.5	Kentucky	5.7		
Minnesota	4.9	Louisiana State	6.6		
Northwestern	2.4	Mississippi	3.5		
Ohio state	12.6	Mississippi State	2.5		
Penn State	12.0	South Carolina	2.1		
Purdue	4.5	Tennessee	11.2		
Wisconsin	1.2	Vanderbilt	3.5		

gests that the relationship between victory and profit is not perfect. (In fact, Miami's football program's net profit in 1995 depends on one factor: participation in a top-tier bowl. Without such participation, Miami's football program loses money.) Most conferences have the same situation, a financial division between the rich and the poor, and that division generally mirrors the division between the programs that are successful versus unsuccessful on the field. Of course, the question remains, does football success generate profits or do profits permit football success? While the numbers in Table 11.1 cannot address this issue, further analysis of the gross revenue numbers suggest that there is an element of truth in both.

Dramatic differences in net revenues also exist across conferences. The SEC and Big Ten both average $7.7 million in net revenue. In the SEC the "Big Five" of Alabama, Auburn, Florida, Georgia, and Tennessee have net revenues over $11 million each—and each also has had recent problems with the NCAA. The SEC's "Seven Dwarfs" have profits of no more than $6.6 million. The seven are dwarfs both in terms of football success and profits. The Big Ten faces a similar situation. The league average includes the "Big Three" of Michigan, Ohio State, and Penn State, each with profits of $12 million or more, and the "Littler Eight" with profits ranging from Michigan State's $9.5 million to Wisconsin's $1.2 million. Given the apparent correlation between football success and financial success, Wisconsin's trip to the Rose Bowl in 1994 is even more surprising. To the extent that winning breeds financial success, however, one might expect that Wisconsin's financial picture will improve.

The Big Eight, the PAC Ten, and the ACC have roughly comparable average net revenues of about $5.5 million each. Of these conferences, the ACC has the most equal intra-conference distribution of revenues and the PAC Ten has the least. The Washington Huskies and UCLA Bruins dominate the PAC Ten while Oregon and Washington State struggle to break even.

The SWC used to be one of the major conferences in the country, especially in football. Recently it has fallen on hard times and will cease to exist after 1995. Another indication of how far the conference has fallen is its financial status. The SWC has average net revenue of only $2.3 million, less than the football members of the Big East ($3.8 million) and less than the WAC ($2.8 million). The SWC team with the highest net revenue, Texas A&M, still falls short of the average team in the Big Ten and the SEC. Simply stated, SWC teams are no longer competitive. Given Arkansas's football success in the SWC before its switch to the SEC and its initial lack of success in the SEC, no one should be surprised that the SWC is not competitive. When Arkansas was in the SWC it was one of the conference's financial powers. In the SEC it is a financial also-ran. Most member schools in the SWC will merge into an expanded Big Eight. The financial numbers suggest that Nebraska, Oklahoma, and Colorado initially will not be challenged even by Texas and Texas A&M.

The WAC average net revenue of $2.8 million is potentially misleading. BYU's net revenue is $10.9 million while the rest of the conference averages $1.8 million. Some sports analysts have speculated that BYU will switch to the PAC Ten conference. The financial numbers suggest that BYU has more in common with the PAC Ten than with the WAC.

Among the independents, only Notre Dame is a financial heavyweight. Memphis is a reasonable second, roughly the equal of Texas A&M. The rest of the independents have sports programs that are, at best, on financial thin ice.

Schools in the final two conferences, the Big West and the Mid-American, generally lose money both in football and in basketball. For example, in the MAC the average cost of a football program is around $1.6 million while revenues average only $0.7 million. No conference member appears to make money on its football program. A similar situation prevails in the Big West. Costs run slightly higher with more travel, but revenues also are slightly higher. The only schools close to making money are Louisiana Tech, Nevada, and SW Louisiana. Even UNLV loses money—both in football and basketball!

IS BIG-TIME COLLEGIATE FOOTBALL THE TICKET TO FINANCIAL SUCCESS?

A casual inspection of Table 11.1 indicates that most big-time collegiate sports programs appear to make money and that programs having more on-the-field success also have greater financial success. To some, the obvious implication is that dear old State U. should just increase the football budget, compete for national championships, and then watch the money flow in. The numbers here are entirely inconsistent with that view. First, given NCAA restrictions, many obvious ways to increase expenditures are not legal. Athletes cannot be paid beyond tuition, room and board; there are limits on the number of coaches; athletic dorms soon will be prohibited; and recruiting regulations and limitations are virtually beyond belief. Simply stated, most universities cannot simply increase football expenditures from $2 million to $6 million. Second, even if a school did substantially increase its financial commitment to football, it is not clear that its on-the-field performance or financial performance would improve at least in the short-term. Schools that have attempted to substantially upgrade their athletic programs have not had concomitant financial success. Miami's on-the-field record has been excellent but their financial status appears to have improved only marginally. Louisville has attempted to follow Miami's lead, even hiring the same coach. However, they have been unable to duplicate Miami's on-the-field success, and even if they did they probably would not have substantially increased their net revenues.

Other schools that have attempted to upgrade their program generally have moved from Division IAA to Division IA. No school has made that jump and also made significant profits. While schools like Louisiana Tech may have the goal of big profits, the reality is far different. Schools like Marshall, currently playing Division IAA, are said to be considering the switch to Division IA. The precipitating factors are money and scholarships. Division IA teams have been reducing the number of games played against IAA teams. Since qualifying for a bowl and the resulting payday requires a minimum of 6 victories against IA opposition, Division IA teams are less interested in playing IAA teams. When a IAA team does play a IA team, typically it is at the IA team's home field and the IAA visitor is guaranteed a substantial fee. That fee averages about $250,000, somewhat more if the visitor will be the victim of a thrashing at Nebraska and perhaps less if the visitor entertains hopes of winning at Arkansas. Fewer IAA games at IA schools means fewer big paydays and more financial pressure on IAA schools.

Complicating the issue is the debate among IAA schools over the maximum number of scholarships. One proposal under consideration would reduce the maximum from the current 63 down to 50. Many schools and conferences currently award less than the maximum. Thus, reducing the maximum would have no impact on them and might make them more competitive with the Division IAA powers. Schools like Marshall that offer the maximum number of scholarships would be at a greater disadvantage when they do succeed in scheduling a Division IA school.

Does it make sense for a team like Marshall to make the jump to IA? Not based on finances. If Marshall moves to IA it will be easier to schedule games against other IA teams. However, IA allows 85 scholarships versus IAA's 63. The cost differential for 22 additional scholarships plus additional recruiting and travel costs and additional salaries will use most of that additional revenue. In addition, any team likely to make the switch from IAA to IA probably is a IAA power and likely participates in the IAA playoffs— which typically means more games and more money. After moving to IA, a team like Marshall will be closer to a doormat than a power and may well see attendance and revenues drop precipitously. In sum, the financial incentives to join Division IA football appear illusory at best.

One can reasonably question whether it is even appropriate to ask if football contributes to the financial success of a university. No one asks if the philosophy department or the library is losing money, although it frequently is asked of the football program or the athletic program in general. For the former there is no question or debate about how they fit into the overall educational mission of the university. For the latter there is a significant debate. For football and men's basketball programs—the revenue-generating programs—one can argue that the revenue generated can be used to further the overall educational mission of the college. For football and basketball programs that lose money, one must seriously reconsider their contribution to the overall university mission.

THE TOP 25

Based on Table 11.1, which collegiate sports programs have had the greatest financial success? Table 11.2 ranks the collegiate Financial Top 25 plus others receiving consideration. Subjective factors enter into any Top 25 ranking and Table 11.2 is no exception. Accounting differences across universities make comparisons sometimes imperfect. However, the Table does provide substantial insight into overall strengths and weaknesses. For example, the differences between Nebraska, Alabama, and Washington are small and accounting differences could easily reverse the order. However, there is a significant difference between Michigan and Ohio State or between Ohio State and Iowa for example. In addition, private schools may be penalized by excluding most donations to the general fund. For example, if you believe that just ten percent of the contributions to Notre Dame's general fund were the result of its football program, then Notre Dame would be number one. In any event, the numbers in Table 11.2 are just like a poll. You may not believe them or like them. However, they are the best numbers available based on reasonable assumptions about costs and revenues.

There should be few surprises on the list. That Michigan is number one should be no surprise. They consistently sell out the largest collegiate football stadium; they are a member of arguably the most financially successful conference; they are second in sales of licensed merchandise; and they have a highly lucrative basketball program. Florida's number two rank took me by surprise. The item that pushed them from a second ten ranking all the way to number two was contributions to their athletic program. Without them and without state aid, they would have been ranked 15th, right behind Clemson. Third is Notre Dame. No surprise here. Money from televised football games plus the most licensing income plus consistent appearances in a big-payout bowls and no need to share those revenues adds up to a high ranking. The only surprise may be that Notre Dame is not number one.

Nebraska, Alabama, and Washington are in a virtual tie for the fourth, fifth and sixth spots. All have large stadiums consistently filled with rabid fans who contribute heavily to their school's athletic coffers. Just behind them comes Ohio State, Georgia, Penn

State, UCLA, Tennessee, and Auburn. The same factors—large stadiums, loyal fans, and successful programs—influence their success, albeit in somewhat different proportions. Ohio State and Tennessee are helped most by their stadiums. Georgia and Auburn rely more on contributions, while basketball and licensing play a greater role for UCLA.

By the time you get to the bottom of the Top 25, the level of financial success of the programs has changed dramatically. While the athletic programs at Indiana, North Carolina State, LSU, and West Virginia are not paupers, they also are on a very different level than Penn State or UCLA. In addition, the difference between the bottom of the Top 25 and the best of the rest appears to be relatively small. For example, the difference between West Virginia and Miami may simply reflect differences in the assumptions concerning donations.

When looking at the Top 25, sports writers frequently ask which conference is strongest. Based on financial criterion, the SEC and Big Ten dominate. The SEC has five of the top twelve teams while the Big Ten has the top spot and six ranked teams. No other conference has more than two ranked teams, and the SWC has no team ranked.

Net Present Values

For professional teams, I calculated profits and then asked what was the Net Present Value (NPV) or what was a franchise worth based on the income stream that it generated. The same methodology can be employed to ask what is the NPV of the income stream generated by, say, Michigan's football and basketball programs. That is done here with one modification. In general, costs for the football and basketball programs did not include administrative overhead and maintenance of facilities. In other words, since a university would employ an athletic director even if it did not have a football program, his salary and staff were not included in the costs associated with football and basketball. When calculating the NPV of a university's football and men's basketball programs, however, it would appear appropriate to include all costs including administrative overhead and maintenance

Table 11.2

TOP 25

Net Revenues and Net Present Values (in millions)

Rank	School	Net Revenues	NPV
1	Michigan	17.6	252
2	Florida	15.9	223
3	Notre Dame	15.3	213
4	Nebraska	13.6	185
5	Alabama	13.6	185
6	Washington	13.5	184
7	Ohio State	12.6	169
8	Georgia	12.2	162
9	Penn State	12.0	158
10	UCLA	11.5	150
11	Tennessee	11.2	145
12	Auburn	11.2	145
13	Brigham Young	10.9	140
14	Oklahoma	10.7	137
15	Clemson	10.2	128
16	Michigan state	9.5	117
17	Syracuse	8.2	95
18	North Carolina	8.0	92
19	Southern California	7.7	87
20	Iowa	7.5	84
21	Florida State	7.0	75
22	Indiana	7.0	75
23	North Carolina State	6.6	68
24	Louisiana State	6.6	68
25	West Virginia	6.5	67

Pittsburgh [6.4], Stanford [6.4], Arizona [6.4], Colorado [6.3], Texas A&M [5.9], Kentucky [5.7], Virginia [5.2], Illinois [5.2], Memphis [5.1], Minnesota [4.9], Iowa State [4.8], Maryland [4.7], Arkansas [4.5], Purdue [4.5], Miami (Florida) [4.4]. Net Revenues in brackets.

of facilities. While these numbers vary somewhat across schools with the Michigans and Nebraskas having higher costs, in the absence of information I assume that the fixed costs associated with each program are $2.5 million. This is subtracted from net revenue, and NPV is calculated as in Chapters 2 through 5 using a 6 percent interest rate. The NPVs for the Top 25 programs are presented in the last column of Table 11.2.

The results for colleges are remarkably similar to those for each pro league. A few collegiate sports programs have extremely high NPVs, values comparable with the best of the pro sports franchises in any league. If the University of Michigan's football team played the Detroit Lions, you might need dental records to identify the Michigan players after the game. However, Michigan, Florida, and Notre Dame have NPVs far exceeding the NPV of the Lions. Programs like Nebraska, Ohio State, and Tennessee also have very healthy NPVs. However, by the time you get to the bottom of the Top 25, the numbers are not particularly impressive. West Virginia's football and basketball programs appear financially solid, but its NPV is virtually identical to that of the Washington Bullets, and the Bullets are a financially mediocre NBA franchise.

I argued in Chapter 5 that an NPV of $50 million was the minimum value for a financially healthy professional sports franchise. Using the same criterion for a college, only 31 of 103 colleges playing Division IA football would qualify as financially healthy. Even programs like Illinois, Texas, Miami (Florida), Kansas, and Wisconsin do not meet this standard. While that criterion may be a harsh measure by which to judge collegiate sports, it does suggest that most colleges have football and basketball programs that are not quite the revenue sources that they may think.

ALTERNATE VIEWS

As with professional franchises, there are a number of ways that the financial numbers can be juggled, and there are a number of alternate ways we could examine the financial information on collegiate football and basketball programs. However, the results are remarkably robust with respect to these alternate views.

Table 11.2 considered the financial performance of the strongest collegiate sports programs. What about the health of all Division IA teams? Chart 11.1 attempts to give a simple graphical perspective on the financial health of all collegiate football and men's basketball programs. This chart presents two ways of looking at profits. First, consider ranking the net revenues of all colleges in Table 11.1 and then plotting those revenues from high to low. Second, consider ranking the net revenues of all colleges after excluding donations and any state support.[3] Both these rankings are presented in Chart 11.1. The solid line presents the net revenues from football and men's basketball programs. It confirms the point made earlier: most so-called revenue producing sports programs do appear to produce revenue. The best produce over $14 million, the more typical yield $2 to $4 million, while a few lose money. However, subtract donations and state support and the profitability picture changes. The dashed line suggests that the profitability of many programs is in part the result of voluntary contributions to the program rather than income earned by the program. Finally, consider again that administrative costs and facilities costs generally are excluded from the official statistics, and again assume that those costs are $2.5 million. Then a program must have reported net revenue of $2.5 million to break even. Excluding gifts and state support, however, there are relatively few programs that meet this criterion and a number of programs that fail this criterion very badly.

Chart 11.1 suggests that collegiate sports finances look very similar to professional sports finances. A few do extremely well; many do acceptably; some simply do not make it. The only question at the collegiate level is how many universities fall into the third category.

Table 11.3 addresses exactly that question: of the 103 schools that have Division IA football, how many do not make a profit? This table presents a number of ways of approaching the answer. Simply examining the reported costs and revenues—and ignoring administrative and facilities costs—gives the numbers in column one. Eighty five schools make money and only 18 lose money.

---

[3] Donations and state support that could be identified were separated. Undoubtedly, not all of these sources were identified.

However, we should consider the number that have a suitable cushion for any unforeseen contingencies or cost increases. For the pros, I argued that an NPV of $50 million or more indicates sound financial health. For colleges, I use a more conservative criterion since they generally operate on a smaller scale and in theory they are not-for-profit enterprises. Given the potential for year-to-year fluctuations and the uncertainty in the financial numbers, it appears that a surplus of $1 million would be the minimum indicator of financial health. On that grounds, only 71 Division IA universities have football and men's basketball programs that are financially healthy.

Chart 11.1

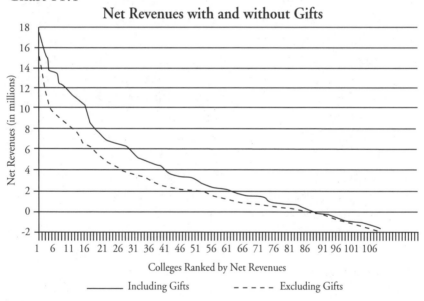

Net Revenues with and without Gifts

Colleges Ranked by Net Revenues

———— Including Gifts   – – – – – Excluding Gifts

The second adjustment would be to subtract administrative overhead and maintenance costs from official net revenues. Again assuming these costs are approximately $2.5 million, only 54 Division IA schools now earn a profit while 49 lose money. Again, requiring a net revenues of $1 million to indicate financial health, the number of universities with financially healthy football and men's basketball programs shrinks to 41.

The final adjustment would be to exclude gifts and state contributions to athletic department budgets. How much do these programs earn versus how much are given to them? Subtracting contributions leaves only 41 programs making money and only 31 making more than $1 million. Thus, the strictest standard suggests only thirty percent of Division IA colleges have football and men's basketball programs that can be classified as financially healthy.

Regardless of which set of assumptions you believe are most appropriate—I personally favor the last—the overall conclusions remain the same. A few make a lot of money. Many survive, although arguably with some difficulty. And some lose money. From any perspective, the best programs—the Michigans, Floridas, and Notre Dames—do very well. However, their success should not fool any school into thinking that its program also can be turned into a dramatic money maker. That would appear to be the easy path to NCAA probation. Whether colleges generally make money is open to debate.

Finally, the total profits of all schools with Division IA football programs sums to about $420 million including gifts and excluding administrative costs. Subtracting administrative costs drops

Table 11.3

HOW MANY SCHOOLS MAKE MONEY?
Division IA Football Schools Only

	Ignoring Administrative Expenses	Including Administrative Expenses	Including Administrative Expenses & Excluding Gifts
Number Making Money	85	54	41
Number Losing Money	18	49	62
Number Making More than $1 Million	71	41	31

the profit total to $280 million while further subtracting donations reduces profits to less than $10 million. Do big-time collegiate sports make money? The "industry" just breaks even!

FOOTBALL AND BASKETBALL INDIVIDUALLY

To this point the discussion of collegiate athletic finances has focused on football and men's basketball programs together. What can be said about these programs examined separately? Table 11.4 presents the Top 25 football programs based on net revenue. Administrative costs are excluded. When there was ambiguity about where donations to the athletic program belonged, for traditional football powers—most schools on the list—they were attributed entirely to the football program. The rankings for football look

Table 11.4

TOP 25

Net Revenue—Football

Rank	School	Net Revenues
1	Florida	15.2
2	Michigan	14.4
3	Notre Dame	14.3
4	Washington	13.5
5	Alabama	12.9
6	Nebraska	11.8
7	Georgia	11.5
8	Auburn	11.0
9	Penn State	10.1
10	Ohio State	9.8
11	Oklahoma	9.5
12	Tennessee	9.1
13	Clemson	8.0
14	UCLA	8.0
15	Brigham Young	7.9
16	Michigan State	7.0
17	Southern California	6.5
18	West Virginia	6.0
19	Texas A&M	5.9
20	Colorado	5.7
21	Stanford	5.3
22	Louisiana State	5.1
23	Syracuse	4.8
24	Florida State	4.8
25	Iowa State	4.2

Iowa [4.1], Arizona [4.0], Arkansas [4.0], Pittsburgh [3.9], Texas [3.8], Miami (Florida) [3.7], North Carolina [3.6], North Carolina State [3.5], Mississippi [3.2], Vanderbilt [3.1], Texas Tech [3.0], Virginia [2.8], Hawaii [2.7], Kentucky [2.7], Arizona State [2.6].

very similar to the overall rankings. Florida moves up to the top spot, but the top three stay the same. Except for some minor juggling at the bottom of the rankings, the order is basically unchanged. The only noteworthy difference: Texas A&M now moves into the rankings, albeit close to the bottom.

Counting "others receiving votes" at the bottom of Table 11.4, the list includes all football programs that made in excess of $2.5 million. Thus, the single criterion to get mentioned on the football financial rankings is that you cover both your variable and your fixed costs.[4] Once again, the numbers suggest that big-time college football is not the revenue generator that many have alleged—except at the top schools like Michigan, Florida, and Notre Dame.

Chart 11.2 presents another way of looking at the football numbers. Net revenues for all schools are ranked from high to low and then graphed. The evidence, like that in Chart 11.1, indicates that the best do very well but profits drop dramatically from the top group to the second best and then to the rest. Taking $2.5 million as the cut-off for real profitability, the numbers indicate that the

Chart 11.2

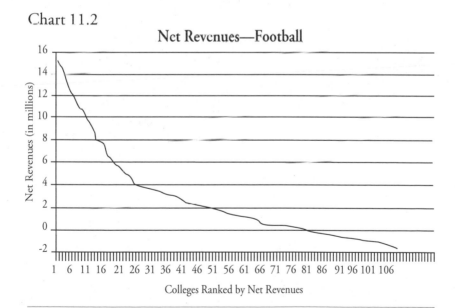

Net Revenues—Football

Net Revenues (in millions)

Colleges Ranked by Net Revenues

---

[4] A very few programs like Oregon have included fixed administrative costs in the numbers they report to the CFA and NCAA. Others like Nebraska and Michigan, given their facilities, likely have maintenance expenditures that, together with administrative overhead, bring their fixed costs well over $2.5 million.

majority of football programs lose money, sometimes lots of money.

Turning to basketball, Table 11.5 presents the Top 25 ranking for men's basketball. This ranking differs substantially from the overall ranking in Table 11.2. In addition, the net revenues are much smaller and the differences between the best and the rest are dramatically smaller as well. At the top are traditional basketball powers. Indiana, North Carolina, and UCLA's presence at the top of the financial rankings should surprise no one. They have three of the most storied basketball programs in the country. Iowa's ranking may be a surprise, but the Big Ten is an excellent basketball conference with substantial television revenues, and Iowa has a large facility generating substantial gate revenue. The Big Ten has eight schools in the Top 25. The ACC and the Big East have five each while the PAC Ten has two. If on-the-field success and financial success are correlated—as they appear to be—then we should expect the Big Ten, and to a lesser extent the ACC and the Big East, to dominate the basketball rankings.

No basketball program has had sustained on-the-court success without some financial success with a single exception: UNLV. When UNLV won big, it made some money but not nearly enough to move into the financial elite. When UNLV has not won big, it has lost money. Chart 11.3 presents all the basketball numbers ranked from high to low. Profits are not as high as in football, but there is a smaller probability of losing money.

Many schools have recently joined Division I in basketball, moving up from Division II, the NAIA, or even Division III. The underlying logic is simple: their goal is the pot of gold at the end of the NCAA tourney. However, despite substantial revenue sharing, the results here suggest that there should be a lot of disappointed gold diggers. The major programs do make substantial sums. However, many schools struggle just to break even. Even among the football powers, 22 schools lost money on basketball in 1994. While schools like Coppin State, Arkansas-Little Rock, and Cleveland State were not surveyed as part of this study, the numbers here suggest some rather harsh economic facts of life. Counting coaches' salaries, grants-in-aid, travel, and maintenance of facilities, a basketball program will cost a **minimum** of $0.5 million. To

Table 11.5

TOP 25

Net Revenue—Basketball

Rank	School	Net Revenues
1	Indiana	4.5
2	North Carolina	4.4
3	UCLA	3.5
4	Iowa	3.5
5	Syracuse	3.4
6	Michigan	3.2
7	Minnesota	3.1
8	North Carolina State	3.1
9	Brigham Young	3.0
10	Kentucky	3.0
11	Louisville	2.8
12	Illinois	2.8
13	Ohio State	2.8
14	Purdue	2.8
15	St. John's	2.6
16	Memphis	2.6
17	Boston College	2.5
18	Duke	2.5
19	Georgetown	2.5
20	Maryland	2.5
21	Michigan State	2.5
22	Pittsburgh	2.5
23	Virginia	2.5
24	New Mexico	2.4
25	Arizona	2.3

Wake Forest [2.3], Florida State [2.2], Clemson [2.2], Tennessee [2.1], Georgia Tech [2.0], Northwestern [1.9], Penn State [1.9], Nebraska [1.8], Villanova [1.7], Kansas [1.7], Providence [1.6], Seton Hall [1.5], Louisiana State [1.5], Oregon State [1.3], Connecticut [1.3].

be even marginally competitive will cost about $1.0 while the top schools will spend $1.5 million or more. Schools like James Madison, Dayton, Prairie View, and San Francisco are going to be hard pressed to generate $0.5 million in revenue from basketball. For some schools, the only financially viable alternative is to hit the

Chart 11.3

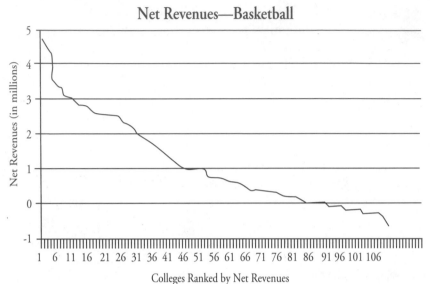

Net Revenues—Basketball

Colleges Ranked by Net Revenues

road for as many away games as possible and collect the financial guarantees associated with those games. Of course, if you play 18 away games for the financial guarantees, one might reasonably ask whether the players are student-athletes or are low-paid mercenaries for State U. That is the subject of the next chapter.

In contrast, the absolute minimum cost for a football program appears to be around $1.6 million and that only buys you a program like Ball State or Arkansas State. Even some Division 1AA programs spend more than that. To be relatively competitive, that is, any school with hopes of cracking the Top 25 (on-the-field and not financially), you must spend a minimum of $3.0 million and then take your chances. Many schools that have spent substantially more—including South Carolina, Kentucky, Oregon State, Duke, Oklahoma State, and Purdue—with little to show.

TITLE IX IMPLICATIONS

A heated issue in collegiate sports concerns the implications of Title IX, the federal mandate that women be granted equal opportunities or equal access at colleges. The most common application of Title IX has been in the sports arena, although there are serious questions about whether that was Congress's original intent. The strong interpretation of Title IX advanced by many pushing women's sports has been that if females make up fifty percent of the student body, then fifty percent of the athletes and the athletic scholarships should go to women. The counter-argument has been that football should be excluded from the equation since it generates net revenue rather than costing a university money like most sports, including women's sports. That is, the Congressional intent of Title IX was to exclude football.

Consider a simple example. Suppose a school offers eleven sports each for men and women excluding football, and suppose that on average it gives fifteen scholarships per sport. Adding football's 85 (maximum) scholarships gives 415 scholarship athletes.[5] Of these, 165 or approximately forty percent are female. Many schools through similar arithmetic have set a goal to allocate forty percent of the athletic scholarships to females. For example, the Big Ten has set that as a conference goal. Implicitly, this calculation excludes football from the Title IX consideration, presumably because football generates net revenue.

What are the implications for football versus female athletes? If football does not generate a profit and must be subsidized by the university, then the argument for excluding it from Title IX discussions is entirely inappropriate. Florida, Michigan, and Notre Dame can legitimately argue that forty percent of their student-athletes should be female based on Title IX considerations and based on the net revenues generated by their football programs. Akron, Brown, Temple, and UNLV cannot.

Brown University recently was party to a lawsuit where the University contended that forty percent was appropriate, but female athletes sued arguing that it was insufficient. Brown lost the suit. Brown's football program does not make money. Thus, from an economic perspective it would appear that the court ruling was correct. Football should be included in the calculations of percentages of scholarship athletes when football does not make money.

Allowing different standards for schools that make money versus those that lose money would further exacerbate the difference

---

[5] This example ignores the common practice of splitting scholarships, a practice that would substantially complicate the example but would not alter the general conclusion.

between the haves and the have-nots. That problem, however, was not addressed by Congress. Given how Title IX is being interpreted, there is no easy solution that would appear fair to all parties concerned. Of course, a substantially deeper question is why Title IX is being applied singularly to sports and has not been applied in a wider university framework.

The overall moral here: the case for additional women's scholarships may be much stronger than even proponents have argued. Furthermore, the argument should not be viewed as taking scholarships from males to give to females. Rather, it is a question of the extent that a university subsidizes its female athletic programs versus the extent that it subsidizes its male athletic programs. When a football program loses over $1.5 million, it would appear likely that athletic programs for women are underfunded.

CONCLUSIONS

Asking whether college football makes money is akin to asking have you stopped beating your wife. If you answer that football loses money, many on campus will ask why football should be subsidized. If you answer that football makes money, some on campus will ask whether that is appropriate at a not-for-profit institution and whether football players are being exploited.

The overall implications for the financial status of football and basketball programs are simple. The Michigans, Notre Dames, and Floridas do very well and compare favorably with most professional franchises. The next tier of 25 to 30 schools does relatively well but the remaining Division 1A programs either barely cover or do not cover all costs. Football programs may make more money but they also can lose more money. Basketball programs are less costly and appear less likely to lose money. Virtually all football and men's basketball programs other than Division IA lose money. That is not necessarily a problem, any more than it is a problem that the philosophy department or the library loses money. However, if the football program loses money, one must examine the rationale for that program's existence and for its appropriation of funds in exactly the same manner as one would appropriate funds to the philosophy department or the library.

That is, how does the football program fit into the overall educational mission of the university? This is not a question typically asked of collegiate football programs. It is a question that should be seriously addressed at schools from Temple to Wisconsin to Houston to Washington State.

The chapters evaluating the NPV's of professional teams concluded by calculating the "ego value" associated with owning a sports franchise. No comparable calculations are possible for colleges.[6] However, this does not imply that substantial ego is not involved. Nonfinancial considerations like school pride undoubtedly have led alumni and boosters to contribute funds and to steer recruits to old State U. And it just as likely has led some administrators to fund football better than the philosophy department or the library. The "bragging rights" associated with a winning football team appear to exceed the "bragging rights" associated with a top-notch philosopphy department.

---

[6] Those calculations were based on comparing NPV's with actual sale prices. College sports teams are not sold. Thus, no comparison is possible.

Chapter 12

The NCAA, Colleges, and College Athletes — Should Athletes Be Paid?

"We've stopped recruiting young men who want to come here to be students first and athletes second."
—Sonny Randle, football coach at Virginia

"Some year I'm going to write our book, and it's going to say 'I wish I have never recruited this player. He's eaten $5,000 worth of groceries and has cost us $10,000 overall, and he's scored one point. He's a dog."
—Abe Lemons, basketball coach at Texas, on press guides

"It's like recruiting for college, only the money's on the table instead of under it."
—Bruce Coslet, New York Jets coach, on free agency

"As long as I pay for your room, board, tuition, and fees, you're not like other students. I gave you a free ride. The moment I don't pay for a thing you'll be like the others."
—Barry Switzer, football coach at Oklahoma, on charges he dominated his players' lives

"An athlete who does not graduate is grossly underpaid as an entertainer. One who graduates is overpaid."
—Joe Paterno, football coach at Penn State

Chapter 11 addressed the profitability of big-time collegiate sports and concluded that the best programs do extremely well, the next level survives comfortably, and the rest struggle—and frequently fail—just to break even. How has this distribution of profits arisen and what are its implications? Each professional sports league has a monopoly in that sport although each league competes for the overall entertainment dollar. In contrast, collegiate football is not as well organized or as tightly structured as the NFL, for example. The National Collegiate Athletic Association (NCAA), the primary collegiate sports governing body, is a strong central organization with significant power over individual teams/colleges—as colleges currently or recently on probation like Alabama, Auburn, and Washington can attest. However, some of the controls that in the pros are centralized in the league (NFL) office, are in the colleges centralized in individual conference offices. For example, conferences like the Big Ten and the SEC have negotiated television rights for all conference schools. Other controls that the pros have centralized in the league office have in the colleges been centralized either in the NCAA or in the College Football Association (CFA), an association of the largest football schools. For example, rules on the conduct of the game including player substitutions and scoring options after a touchdown have been determined by the NCAA. In addition, individual colleges and universities have ceded less power to organizations like the NCAA than individual professional franchises have ceded to the NFL. For example, schools make their own licensing and scheduling arrangements and generally do not have revenue sharing agreements.[1]

THE ROLE OF THE NCAA—CARTEL OR CHARITABLE ORGANIZATION?

One can look at the NCAA and argue that it fulfills basically the same functions as the NFL league office in terms of central administration and setting the ground rules. However, negotiations for television rights are centralized in the NFL league office while collegiate television rights are retained by the individual schools. Thus one can argue that the NFL is a monopoly while

---

[1] There are two major revenue sharing exceptions. First, the NCAA basketball tourney revenues in part are split among all schools that have Division 1A basketball programs. And second, conferences have revenue sharing arrangements, typically of television money and bowl money.

college football is not. Then the NCAA would appear to be a collegiate effort to form a cartel and operate like a monopoly. In contrast, the NCAA's literature suggests that its first objective is to protect the student-athlete, ensuring that all member schools provide an appropriate educational and athletic environment. The NCAA also has the stated goal of providing a level playing field for teams. Sometimes these goals mesh. For example, recruiting restrictions limit coaches' contact with high school athletes. This makes it easier for recruits to have a relatively normal senior year while also placing all coaches under the same recruiting guidelines.

NCAA regulations primarily focus on a school's dealing with recruits and student-athletes. For example, what can a school provide a student-athlete? When is a student-athlete allowed to sign with a school? And what is the maximum number of hours that an athlete can be required to work? While the NCAA's stated goals are to provide a level playing field for all sports and to protect student-athletes, the NCAA's actions from an economic perspective are logically consistent only when interpreted from the perspective of restricting competition. In this sense, the NCAA has played a major role in shaping the level and distribution of profits in college football and basketball.

Professional sports leagues have effectively limited expansion and restricted entry into the league. This has increased competition among cities for teams. Pro leagues have enforced restrictions on a franchise's contracts with players through player drafts and limits on free agency. This has reduced competition among teams for players. And pro leagues have limited the ability of individual franchises to negotiate their own media contracts, reserving that right for the league. This has fostered competition among the networks for the broadcast rights. The NCAA also has attempted each of these strategies.

The NCAA's classification of schools into divisions, with the emphasis on Division 1, effectively restricts entry into big-time football. For example, to be in Division 1A football a school must have a minimum stadium capacity, a minimum average attendance, etc. The big-time football powers have no incentive to share their revenue with others. Thus we have seen the NCAA evolve into a number of separate divisions. You could argue that

Division IA is the major league, Division IAA is equivalent to baseball's Triple A, while Division II and III are the lower level minors. The biggest difference is that players do not move up although colleges may.

The NCAA's restrictions on recruiting and on grants-in-aid (scholarships) can be interpreted as restricting competition among colleges for players. They are the NCAA's "salary cap" and limit the amount of money that college athletes may receive for their athletic performance. The NCAA argues that these restrictions ensure that college athletes are amateurs. From an economic perspective, it does not matter whether you receive $20,000 in cash or $20,000 in tuition, room and board. Either way, a college athlete is being paid for his or her ability to catch a football or shoot a basketball or spike a volleyball.

The NCAA also has attempted to reserve negotiations of national media contracts to itself although not always successfully. In 1954 the NCAA limited the number of times a college football team could appear on national television during one season. This was the "Notre Dame Rule" since its goal was to limit TV appearances of the Fighting Irish. The NCAA then negotiated a television contract for all schools until the early 1980s when Georgia and Oklahoma successfully sued the NCAA for the right to negotiate on their own. Even then most major colleges recognized that most would be better off with a single television deal. They just did not want to share TV revenues with smaller football programs. Thus they formed the CFA which negotiated television arrangements for the football powers (except those in the Big Ten and the PAC Ten). This arrangement lasted until Notre Dame opted to make its own deal with NBC, bringing the process full circle and putting the Irish back on national television virtually every Saturday. The moral here is that while the NCAA and the CFA have not been entirely successful in restricting negotiations of television contracts, it has not been for lack of trying. They have tried to behave like a cartel. They just have not been successful.[2]

---

[2] From an economic perspective, this lack of success is no surprise. Given the number of schools in the NCAA, it is almost always in someone's best interest to go against the wishes of the cartel. In other words, cartels with many members tend to be unstable.

Interpreting the NCAA's actions first from the perspective of a cartel and only secondarily from the NCAA's preferred perspective as protector of student-athletes also puts many NCAA regulations in better perspective. Without contending that all NCAA regulations are designed to enforce cartel behavior and reduce the welfare of student-athletes, let me focus on five regulations that are most readily interpreted from that perspective.

First, the NCAA limits the number of grants-in-aid that a school can offer. The number varies by sport with football allowed 85. Over the last ten years there have been a number of attempts by college presidents to reduce the number of grants-in-aid. The explicit reason: to reduce costs. The last successful drive reduced the number of scholarships for men by ten percent across the board (for example, track used to have 14 scholarships; now they have 12.6). A reduction in scholarships to reduce costs will improve the financial status of schools. However, it is not in the best interests of student-athletes. Some student-athletes will not receive a scholarship in 1996 that would have received a scholarship in 1992.

Second, the NCAA prohibits scholarship athletes from holding an outside job during the school year. Given the number of hours athletes must spend in training, it is not clear how most could hold a part-time job. However, the logic for prohibiting part-time jobs focuses on the possibility for "abuse." A booster could provide a no-show job and effectively pay an athlete for his or her athletic performance thus subverting an athlete's amateur standing. Prohibiting part-time jobs also makes a coach's life easier since athletes do not have to juggle work commitments, school and sports. Nevertheless, irrespective of the logic underlying the prohibition, precluding athletes from the option of holding an outside job reduces their income and is not in their best interest. A common phrase in finance is "options have value." The NCAA's removal of that option costs students some value.

Third, the NCAA prohibits athletes from signing with an agent. An athlete that accepts payment from an agent sacrifices all remaining collegiate eligibility. A football player, for example, that signs with an agent but accepts no payment and subsequently renounces that agreement typically will be declared ineligible for four games. In the NCAA's eyes, only amateurs can play collegiate sports and the NCAA defines what constitutes an amateur. Is that in an athlete's best interest? Typically an agent will work on behalf of the athlete to negotiate the best deal possible with a professional team. But what would stop an agent from working for a student-athlete to negotiate the best deal possible with a college team? Only the NCAA's restriction against signing with agents precludes that - and the NCAA's restriction was voted into existence by the colleges that those agents would be dealing with. Certainly there are un-scrupulous agents that have taken advantage of athletes. However, the rule against signing with an agent deprives college athletes of an option and again "options have value." The NCAA's restrictions against signing with an agent can only be labeled self-serving.

Fourth, the NCAA allows colleges to offer only one year schol-arships. When a recruit signs with a college he or she accepts only a one year grant-in-aid. Most schools commit verbally to four years but this is not required. For example, Kentucky had a basket-ball player who would have been a senior in 1995-96 and who was not offered a scholarship for his senior year.[3] This is a case where a school has an option: to offer or not to offer a renewal of the scholarship. That option has a value for the school but at a poten-tially great cost to the student-athlete.[4]

Perhaps more fundamental, however, is the NCAA's restriction on the maximum grant-in-aid allowed. A school can provide tu-ition, room and board, plus such incidentals as money for required texts. It cannot pay for an athlete's travel from home to school nor can it allow an athlete to stay at school when school or NCAA-al-lowed training is not in session. Simply stated, the NCAA severely limits the compensation a school may provide an athlete. In con-

---

[3] There was some question about whether he would be turning pro. However, it was clear that he would not be drafted.

[4] The argument has been made that with a four year commitment, a college coach that wants to free up a grant-in-aid must "run off" the no-longer wanted athlete by making his or her life so unbearable that they quit. With only a one year commitment, these abuses are eliminated. In fact, with four year scholarships the student retains more options: quit or stay; with one year scholarships, the school retains more options. When an athlete does not perform up to expec-tations, there may be no good options. However, the one year commitment does not effectively address the issue.

trast, there are no limits on the rest of the student body. A graduate student in business might receive free tuition plus a stipend of $15,000 for performing tasks less demanding than required of a football player. Is the limit on allowable expenses in the best interests of student-athletes? If you believe that, I would like the opportunity to sell you a nice little bridge I own over in Brooklyn.

The NCAA and its apologists can argue all they want that these restrictions on compensation are in the best interests of college sports, the universities, and the overall student body. It is beside the point to debate any of those issues. My point here is that even if you concede all these arguments—which I do not—the restriction on what a college can provide a student-athlete is still not in the student-athlete's best interest. The NCAA is operating as a cartel in its dealings with athletes and is effectively reducing their pay.

Finally, consider a regulation that is very specific in its impact. After an athlete commits to a school in writing, the student-athlete loses a year of eligibility if they decide to attend school and to play somewhere else. Consider a particularly problematic example. Suppose a football coach at Illinois successfully recruits a player for Illinois. Suppose the coach then leaves Illinois and takes a job at Texas before the player ever attends Illinois or participates in a single practice. NCAA rules require that student-athlete to sit out one year if he chooses not to play for Illinois and Illinois does not release him from his obligation. A coach can move virtually whenever he likes, even if he is in the middle of a multi-year contract. In contrast, an athlete is locked in.[5] The NCAA and colleges argue that a student-athlete is attending a school primarily for the education and who is the athlete's coach should be of secondary concern. If you believe that, I can sell you the Washington Monument at a special price this week. Suppose you accept a scholarship from Harvard to study under a Nobel laureate who then takes a position at Yale. Are you under any obligation to attend Harvard and not

---

[5] Technically the coach must receive permission from the school he is leaving and the athlete also could receive permission to go elsewhere. In practice, however, schools have placed virtually no restrictions on coaches' movements and have placed substantial restrictions on athletes' movements. One other difference in this example: in the student's case it is the school that first changed the contract by changing coaches, while in the coach's case it is the coach that initiated the change.

to attempt to matriculate at Yale? This NCAA regulation, like many others, gives schools options and gives athletes nothing.

The bottom line on NCAA regulations is that they do generally provide a level playing field for teams in all sports. They also frequently protect student-athletes. However, when the economic interests of schools and athletes conflict, NCAA regulations invariably come down on the side of schools. That should come as no surprise. The schools are the ones that wrote the regulations in the first place. In a nutshell, NCAA regulations primarily protect the schools, give schools the options, and enforce a cartel among schools to reduce the costs associated with sports programs and to restrict competition among schools for athletes. Despite the NCAA's rhetoric, the only goal consistent with all the regulations is to restrict competition among colleges and to maintain or increase college profits.

WHAT ARE STUDENT-ATHLETES PAID?

Given that the NCAA has a goal of restricting competition among colleges for student-athletes, the corollary is that those athletes on average are underpaid. This conclusion begs the questions what are student-athletes paid and what should they be paid? Student-athletes "pay" is simply the value of their education. The grant-in-aid includes tuition, room and board, and some incidentals like required books. What is the appropriate dollar value? The best way to value it would be to ask how the market values it or what do other students pay for those same services? Some adjustments must be made, however.

First, state schools typically have a substantial state subsidy for in-state students. Thus, for state schools the relevant number is the out-of-state tuition. This methodology indicates that private schools like Duke, Notre Dame, and Stanford "pay" student-athletes more than public schools. However, students do pay substantially more to attend these schools than to attend Mississippi, Nebraska, and Pittsburgh. This suggests that the market values education at the former schools more than the latter. Nevertheless, in the subsequent calculations I distinguish between public and private schools.

Second, this procedure values an education at cost rather than valuing it as the potential increase in earning power. Estimates of the value of an education or the return to funds invested in education are around twenty percent or higher. Thus, one might increase the value by twenty percent over tuition costs. This adjustment is not made but would not appreciably change the following results.

Third, athletes that do not graduate have not taken advantage of their tuition. They have played not for an education but for their room and board. This assumes that they do not graduate due to factors under the school's control rather than due to factors under their own control. Given that the highest graduation rates are at schools with reputedly high academic standards—Duke, Boston College, and Notre Dame, this appears to be a reasonable assumption. If Duke can provide a climate where roughly ninety percent of its football players graduate, it would appear that Alabama or Houston could do the same. Student-athletes that graduate are viewed as receiving payment equal to their tuition, room and board and incidentals. Those that do not graduate are viewed as receiving payment equal only to their room and board.[6]

Fourth, one might argue that the compensation should include some measure of the salaries of professional athletes who have graduated from a program. For example, in 1994 North Carolina had eleven graduates playing in the NBA. Should their salaries be credited in part to UNC and should the implicit salary for UNC basketball players be increased to reflect their higher professional earnings? The answer is that their salaries generally should not be credited to UNC. If they would have received the same pro salary if they had attended Duke or Georgetown or NC State, then it is the player's talent rather than the program that is responsible for the professional salary. Does a player earn a high pro salary because he attended a particular school or because of characteristics he had when he entered that school?[7] There is no

---

[6] This procedure assumes that if they did not graduate then their tuition was wasted. While that undoubtedly is too strong an assumption, looking at the courses frequently taken by college athletes, e.g., "The Philosophy of Sport," it appears to have some solid justification.

[7] This another example of the "nature versus nurture" debate on the effects of genetics versus environment that has been discussed for years in both economics and sociology.

evidence that UNC adds anything that Duke does not. Thus no ad hoc additions are justified. A few of the top programs like UNC, Duke, and Michigan in basketball and Notre Dame, Miami, and Nebraska in football may be penalized slightly by not making this adjustment. Most programs will be unaffected.

To calculate student-athletes' pay, the last adjustment is to convert those grant-in-aid values into hourly salaries. Thus, we need an estimate of the number of hours worked. The NCAA allows coaches to require a maximum of twenty hours per week in season, and most seasons are about five months long. Football players, for example, in-season work about 420 hours. Out-of-season conditioning might require ten hours per week bringing the yearly total—from a quasi-official perspective—to 730 hours per year. However, the required hours exclude "optional" activities possibly including watching game films, additional weight training and running. The actual total is undoubtedly closer to 1000 hours per year, all quite consistent with the NCAA's mandate of a maximum of twenty hours per week. In fact, student-athletes from a variety of football programs have contended that the actual number of hours worked—including all the activities ancillary to participation in football—easily bring the total number of hours to 1200 per year.

The subsequent calculations assume 1000 hours worked per year. They also value tuition at cost rather than adjusting upward to reflect the value rather than the cost of a college degree. Making both adjustments would leave the salary numbers unchanged. If you believe only one of these adjustments is appropriate, then adjust the reported salary numbers either up or down by twenty percent. The conclusions, however, generally remain unchanged.

Table 12.1 presents graduation rates for football and men's basketball for all Division 1A football schools as well as a selection of other schools (graduation rates are for all freshman from 1985 to 1988). Also included, based on graduation rates and the methodology detailed above, are the implicit hourly compensation for athletes at these schools. The numbers indicate a wide range of compensation with some programs "paying" over $20 per hour and others pay less than $5 per hour. A few pay less than the minimum wage.

Table 12.1

Graduation Rates and Implicit Compensation

School	Graduation Rates		Hourly Compensation	
	Basketball	Football	Basketball	Football
Akron	40	37	6.93	6.68
Alabama	17	46	4.55	6.30
Arizona	20	51	5.56	8.02
Arizona State	22	38	6.35	7.62
Arkansas	31	40	4.83	5.33
Arkansas State	9	24	2.68	3.23
Auburn	43	40	6.65	6.45
Ball State	64	58	7.97	7.54
Baylor	46	56	7.45	8.22
Boston College	71	89	18.49	21.48
Bowling Green	53	47	7.56	7.06
Brigham Young	45	44	4.69*	4.66*
California	62	57	13.60	12.99
Cal St. Fullerton	0	33	3.20	6.38
Central Michigan	15	61	5.00	8.55
Cincinnati	19	44	6.20	8.53
Clemson	38	37	6.84	6.75
Colorado	62	48	11.70	9.92
Colorado State	27	55	6.37	8.84
Connecticut	43	47	10.04	10.52
Duke	69	91	16.69	20.37
East Carolina	31	49	5.63	7.08
Eastern Michigan	14	44	5.04	7.20
Florida	31	42	6.40	7.23
Florida State	45	48	7.31	7.53
Fresno State	31	33	7.22	7.41
Georgetown	86	NA	22.46	NA
Georgia	19	38	4.65	5.89
Georgia Tech	33	56	6.83	8.53
Hawaii	67	67	5.94	5.94
Houston	7	23	4.52	5.26
Illinois	13	75	5.43	10.55
Indiana	56	62	9.09	9.66
Iowa	64	65	8.64	8.73
Iowa State	29	46	6.00	7.70
Kansas	30	46	5.42	6.56
Kansas State	30	29	5.00	4.93
Kent State	47	47	6.80	6.80
Kentucky	21	61	4.30	7.02

School	Graduation Rates		Hourly Compensation	
	Basketball	Football	Basketball	Football
Long Beach	0	18	4.50	6.19
Louisville	27	37	4.97	5.53
Louisiana State	18	35	4.15	5.26
Louisiana Tech	50	62	4.23	4.73
Maryland	38	56	8.57	10.26
Massachusetts	38	66	8.61	12.09
Memphis	50	53	4.74	4.93
Miami (Florida)	50	54	14.47	15.13
Miami (Ohio)	38	62	9.39	10.75
Michigan	65	72	10.26	10.97
Michigan State	58	58	10.29	10.29
Minnesota	19	41	5.19	7.26
Mississippi	62	53	6.72	6.22
Mississippi State	27	56	4.63	6.24
Missouri	25	48	5.80	7.94
Nebraska	36	53	5.24	6.30
Nevada	20	49	5.38	7.29
Nevada Las Vegas	75	26	9.65	6.42
New Mexico	40	46	6.34	6.77
New Mexico State	36	34	5.37	5.24
North Carolina	82	66	11.33	9.88
North Carolina St.	7	50	4.04	7.95
Northern Illinois	29	47	5.64	7.25
Northwestern	69	80	16.61	18.41
Notre Dame	73	81	16.27	17.60
Ohio	46	66	7.58	9.15
Ohio State	31	57	7.22	9.68
Oklahoma	33	49	5.49	6.44
Oklahoma State	11	36	3.86	5.34
Oregon	50	67	8.49	10.17
Oregon State	44	64	7.95	10.07
Pacific	38	71	9.68	14.36
Penn State	82	80	12.76	12.55
Pittsburgh	45	48	9.37	9.71
Providence	91	NA	17.44	NA
Purdue	50	47	8.66	8.38
Rice	74	73	13.05	12.94
Rutgers	60	67	10.78	11.52
St. John's	64	NA	12.13	NA
San Diego	0	34	4.95	7.75
San Jose	8	24	5.61	6.93
Seton Hall	36	NA	10.81	NA
South Carolina	64	55	8.45	7.69

School	Graduation Rates		Hourly Compensation	
	Basketball	Football	Basketball	Football
Southern California	20	55	9.68	15.77
Southern Methodist	55	45	12.74	11.32
Southern Mississippi	27	59	3.62	5.37
Southwest Louisiana	29	30	3.50	3.55
Stanford	86	80	22.34	21.24
Syracuse	21	64	9.81	16.40
Temple	36	32	8.85	8.43
Tennessee	21	46	5.02	6.61
Texas	46	47	6.27	6.33
Texas A&M	33	42	5.90	6.46
Texas Christian	36	55	5.71	6.77
Texas - El Paso	8	32	2.27	3.51
Texas Tech	18	31	4.95	5.86
Toledo	33	58	6.16	8.25
Tulane	NA	60	NA	17.40
Tulsa	31	51	7.08	9.20
UCLA	25	58	8.37	12.28
Utah	50	55	6.00	6.37
Utah State	27	47	4.46	5.68
Vanderbilt	60	81	16.90	20.64
Villanova	83	81	19.31	19.00
Virginia	57	62	11.68	12.32
Virginia Tech	33	51	7.20	9.05
Wake Forest	53	76	11.49	14.62
Washington	27	44	6.17	7.49
Washington State	50	46	7.70	7.39
West Virginia	46	63	6.65	7.68
Western Michigan	40	56	6.86	8.03
Wisconsin	50	66	8.50	9.94
Mean	40	52	8.02	8.99
Median	38	51	6.82	7.69
Maximum	91	91	22.46	21.48
Minimum	0	18	2.27	3.23

NA - Not Applicable (No Division 1 football program).

* Brigham Young's hourly compensation is substantially understated due to subsidies from church to university.

Table 12.2 lists the top ten schools for football compensation and basketball compensation as well as the top ten public schools. The table contains few surprises. The schools with the highest compensation are uniformly private schools with high tuitions—and presumably highly valued graduates—and with relatively high graduation rates. Many of these schools also have outstanding athletic programs. For example, Stanford, Notre Dame, Syracuse, and Miami have consistently been ranked among the top football teams. Others like Duke and Vanderbilt have had minimal football success. Arguably those schools have had difficulty finding student-athletes that can survive the academic load while also playing football. The story is much the same in basketball. Villanova, Duke, and Georgetown have flourished in basketball while Northwestern and Vanderbilt have struggled.

Among public schools, many of the traditional powers show up on the list, Michigan and Penn State in football and North Carolina, UCLA, and Indiana in basketball. But some schools that do not typically crack the Top 25 polls also find a place. Looking at these rankings indicates Rutgers' football players or Penn State's basketball players do perhaps surprisingly well.

These numbers suggest that some schools may have the opportunity to substantially upgrade their football or basketball programs. For example, if student-athletes are attracted to programs that pay the most, then Duke, Vanderbilt, and possibly Rutgers may be due for football comebacks while Notre Dame and Penn State could see upturns in their basketball fortunes. However, the question in part is do high school student-athletes choose a school based primarily on academic considerations or upon sports related concerns? Based on the numbers presented in Chapter 9 on the limited number of players who make the pros, for most student-athletes academic considerations should dominate. Consider the schools that place the most players in the pros. Notre Dame leads the football rankings yet slightly less than fifty percent of Notre Dame freshman football players ever play a single down in the NFL. North Carolina leads the basketball rankings but only about thirty percent of North Carolina freshman ever play in the NBA. Despite these statistics, however, the potential for big profession paydays undoubtedly carry substantial weight.

Table 12.2

Universities with the Best Compensated Athletes[a]

| Basketball | | Rank | Football[b] | |
School	Implicit Wage		School	Implicit Wage
Georgetown	$22.46	1	Boston College	21.48
Stanford	22.34	2	Stanford	21.24
Villanova	19.31	3	Vanderbilt	20.64
Boston College	18.49	4	Duke	20.37
Providence	17.44	5	Northwestern	18.41
Vanderbilt	16.90	6	Notre Dame	17.60
Duke	16.69	7	Tulane	17.40
Northwestern	16.61	8	Syracuse	16.40
Notre Dame	16.27	9	Southern California	15.77
Miami (FL)	14.47	10	Miami (FL)	15.13

Public Universities with the Best Compensated Athletes

| Basketball | | Rank | Football[b] | |
School	Implicit Wage		School	Implicit Wage
California	13.60	1	California	21.48
Penn State	12.76	2	Penn State	21.24
Colorado	11.70	3	Virginia	20.64
Virginia	11.68	4	UCLA	20.37
North Carolina	11.33	5	Rutgers	18.41
Rutgers	10.78	6	Michigan	17.60
Michigan State	10.29	7	Miami (Ohio)	17.40
Michigan	10.26	8	Illinois	16.40
Connecticut	10.04	9	Michigan State	15.77
Nevada Las Vegas	9.65	10	Maryland	15.13

[a] While the rankings generally are not sensitive to the underlying assumptions, some rankings can change. For example, equaling room and board in basketball makes Stanford number one and Notre Dame number three.

[b] Division IA football programs only.

The bottom of the rankings may also be of interest. Table 12.3 presents the worst compensated—including all schools where the implicit wage is less than $5 per hour. Without exception they are public schools with low graduation rates. Texas-El Paso and Arkansas State are 1-2 in both lists of worst compensated because of low graduation rates and extremely low room and board. In basketball, they would still make both lists even with double the room and board based on their abysmal graduation rates. In general, schools that are the powers in the sport are not on the worst compensated lists, although ex-powers or would-be powers may be included. In football, Arkansas and LSU were perennial top 25 teams. Given their place in the bottom ten in salaries, it should come as no surprise that their football programs have fallen on hard times. Memphis spent a lot to upgrade its football program. It has had only limited success. Its lack of success also should be no surprise given its ranking of fifth worst compensated. While only one team from the SWC makes the bottom ten in football—Houston—the conference's lack of success is readily explainable given the low implicit compensation of all conference schools except Rice. Furthermore, the bottom four private schools are TCU, Baylor, SMU, and Rice—all SWC members.

The story in basketball is much the same as in football except that there are many more schools with implicit wages below $5 per hour—a result of a number of schools with graduation rates at or close to zero. Some "big-name" schools appear on this list including NC State, LSU, Kentucky, Alabama, Arkansas, and Louisville. The programs at Louisville and NC State have struggled in recent years in comparison with their past successes. These numbers suggest an explanation: some athletes do consider the value of the education offered by competing schools. Of the schools on the worst compensated list, only Kentucky and Arkansas have consistently had successful programs.

Schools like Texas-El Paso or Arkansas or Houston or LSU might argue that they are at the bottom due to a statistical accident. They do not really exploit their student-athletes but the graduation rate in a particular year was low or their students actually gain more than indicated here. Unfortunately, in virtually all cases those arguments are without merit. Schools like UTEP, Memphis, and Alabama are close to the bottom of the graduation rankings virtually every year. And the athletes at those schools face the same challenges as those at Duke or Boston College or Stanford. At some point administrators at these schools are going to have to accept their responsibility for true oversight of the athletic program, recognizing that the institution is first and foremost a university and that athletic accomplishments are only secondary.

There is one additional number not included in Table 12.1 that reveals a college's attitude toward its student athletes: what

Table 12.3

Universities with the Worst Compensated Athletes

Basketball		Football	
School	Implicit Wage	School	Implicit Wage
Texas-El Paso	2.27	Arkansas State	3.23
Arkansas State	2.68	Texas-El Paso	3.51
Cal St. Fullerton	3.20	SW Louisiana	3.55
SW Louisiana	3.50	Louisiana Tech	4.73
Southern Mississippi	3.62	Memphis	4.93
Oklahoma State	3.86	Kansas State	4.97
North Carolina State	4.04	New Mexico State	5.24
LSU	4.15	Houston	5.26
Louisiana Tech	4.23	LSU	5.26
Kentucky	4.30	Arkansas	5.33
Utah State	4.46		
Long Beach	4.50		
Houston	4.52		
Alabama	4.55		
Mississippi State	4.63		
Georgia	4.65		
Memphia	4.74		
Arkansas	4.83		
Texas Tech	4.95		
San Diego	4.95		
Louisville	4.97		

percentage of those who use their four years of eligibility also graduate? One should expect that virtually all who use four years of eligibility also would be virtually done their degree requirements. At most schools this is the case. Northwestern, Duke, North Carolina, Penn State, Ohio State, and Oregon State are among many that have graduation rates of four-year athletes over 90 percent. But there are some schools where this rate is under 70 percent. Table 12.4 lists the "Baker's Dozen" of the lowest percentages, schools with graduation rates less than 70 percent. The message sent by these schools to student-athletes is about as negative as it gets. That is, schools on this list appear to systematically exploit their athletes by employing them for four years but not taking the steps necessary to facilitate their graduation.

To give a different view of the implicit compensation in college football and basketball, the implicit compensation for all colleges in Table 12.1 were ordered from high to low for both basketball

Table 12.4

The Dirty Dozen
Colleges with the Lowest Graduation Rates
for Athletes Who Use Four-Year Eligibility

Rank	School	Graduation Rate
1	Kansas State	39
2	Long Beach	48
3	Southwest Louisiana	50
4	Houston	59
	San Jose	59
6	Nevada Las Vegas	61
7	Arkansas State	62
8	Oklahoma State	64
9	San Diego	65
	West Virginia	65
11	Mississippi State	66
12	Arkansas	69
	Wisconsin	69

and football. Charts 12.1 and 12.2 then present the compensation series graphically. The graphs suggest that athletes at the best paying schools are well compensated. The charts also suggest that student-athletes at some schools are exploited. How many are exploited depend in part on what you view as the appropriate salary. If you view the starting salary for part-time work for a high school graduate as $5 per hour, then most are well compensated and only the schools listed in Table 12.3 exploit student-athletes. If you view football in particular as difficult and sometimes dangerous work, a salary of perhaps $10 per hour might be justified. Then, there are a lot of exploited student-athletes.

Looking just at the implicit compensation paid to football and basketball players does not tell the entire story. One should ask in the absence of college football, for example, what would football players not in the NFL earn? There is no easy answer to that question but it would appear reasonable to assume that there would be more interest in minor league football. Indeed, one can easily argue that colleges have supplanted minor league football and have succeeded in marketing their product as something other than the minor leagues. While it is speculative to argue what minor league football salaries would be in the absence of collegiate football,

Chart 12.1

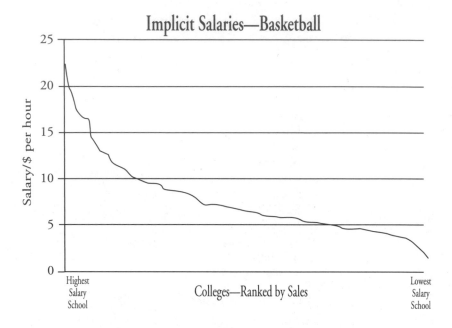

minor league baseball and hockey salaries give some indication. In hockey, the top minor leagues have a pay ceiling of $62,500 but typically pay much less. In baseball the average minor league salary is about $2,200 per month or about $13 per hour.[8] Given that football is a more physically demanding sport, a salary in excess of $15 per hour would appear appropriate. Then we again conclude that student-athletes at most schools receive less than they would if the market were allowed to determine their salaries. The exceptions to this statement, e.g. Stanford and Notre Dame in football and Duke and Georgetown in basketball, may be noteworthy but are clearly exceptions rather than the norm.

Joe Paterno was quoted at the beginning of the chapter as saying, "An athlete who does not graduate is grossly underpaid as an entertainer. One who graduates is overpaid." The numbers do not entirely corroborate this statement. One who graduates is overpaid if they went to a top university. One who graduates from an-

---

[8] This calculation assumes that baseball players work 28 days per month or have one off day every two weeks. It also assumes that they work—including practices, games, and travel—on average six hours a day.

Chart 12.2

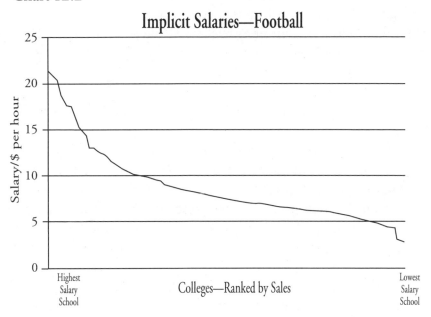

Implicit Salaries—Football

other university appears to be marginally underpaid. And one who does not graduate is grossly underpaid.

One might question whether changing some of the assumptions made at the beginning of these calculations would change the conclusions. The answer is emphatically no. Using the graduation rates for a different period may alter an individual school's standing and implicit salary. However, overall graduation rates generally do not rise—or fall—appreciably from one period to the next. Schools like Boston College, Duke, and Notre Dame consistently top the graduation rates in football while schools like Alabama, Louisville, LSU and most of the SWC consistently show up at the bottom. Do athletes work somewhat more or somewhat less than estimated here? Should public school figures be increased to reflect additional public subsidies? Making these adjustments leaves the basic conclusions unchanged.[9] In sum, college

---

[9] The conclusions here are sensitive to only one assumption: the value of a college education. If you value a college education at the NPV of the difference between a high school graduate's salary and a college graduate's salary over their working life, then you might argue that student-athletes at most schools are well compensated. However, if you use that measure, the corollary is that the average return to a college diploma is well in excess of thirty percent and the U.S. as a nation dramatically underinvests in college education.

athletes would appear to make more money if they played professional ball. Does that mean that college athletes should be paid - or at least football and men's basketball players should be paid? The answer, perhaps surprisingly, is not necessarily.

SHOULD STUDENT ATHLETES BE PAID?

The arguments that student-athletes should be paid are simple. First, they generate substantial revenue for their schools. Second, they work long hours to perform at the desired levels. NCAA rules also prohibit student-athletes from working a part-time job during the school year. Other students can work and frequently can afford things that athletes cannot—like a pizza at 11 P.M. Third, while the evidence is incomplete, it appears that at least at the upper levels of the minor leagues, professionals in hockey and baseball get paid more than their collegiate counterparts in basketball and football. And fourth and potentially most compelling, the keen competition in recruiting high school athletes suggests that colleges have something important to gain from those athletes. Otherwise, why engage is such intense competition and why so many regulations limiting that competition?

Let us consider each of the arguments in turn.

Collegiate athletes—football players at least—generate substantial revenues for their schools. Unfortunately, in general it is gross revenue and not net revenue. Only about thirty schools make money on college football. The rest struggle to break even. Michigan, Florida, and Notre Dame all make a mint. Temple and Western Michigan lose big. Even programs like Oklahoma State and Wisconsin lose money. In sum, including administrative overhead and maintenance of facilities, the only money that college football makes is the money that is given to schools in terms of donations and state funding. The total net revenues earned by collegiate football is virtually zero. Collegiate football players do generate tremendous gross revenues for their schools. But along the way those revenues are matched almost dollar for dollar with costs.

Before moving on, a word is in order about those costs. In the pros at the major league level approximately half gross revenues go to the players. At the minor league level that percentage is substantially lower since fixed costs consume a larger fraction of the revenue base. Coaches' salaries are a relatively small percentage of total costs. In collegiate football, however, coaches' salaries frequently are the largest component of costs—exceeding the value of grants-in-aid or implicit player compensation. If players were paid salaries based on competitive markets, other football-related costs would likely be reduced to bring costs back into balance with revenues. One likely source to cut: coaches' salaries.[10]

The second argument for paying football players is that they work hard. They generally do. And so do soccer players, softball players, volleyball players, etc. One can easily make an argument that swimmers or runners put in as many hours over the year as football players. If it is simply a matter of paying football players for their hard work, shouldn't soccer players, or swimmers or gymnasts be paid too? I have great sympathy for the argument that athletic effort should be rewarded. Spending twenty hours a week on football makes getting through college more difficult for a football player than for a student without that encumbrance. But the same can be said for a student who must work twenty hours a week to pay for tuition. If you allow football players to receive a stipend, what about baseball players or swimmers? Is there any line you can draw in terms of which athletes should be paid and which should not? What about scholarship athletes versus walk-ons? If you argue to pay all athletes just $1000 per year, you are talking at least $0.5 million at Division 1 schools. Few schools like Michigan, Nebraska, and Notre Dame run a surplus in their overall athletic budget.[11] If you argue for paying all athletes, something will be cut and one likely candidate is the number of athletic scholarships. To allow explicit payments to athletes would virtually guarantee that programs like wrestling and gymnastics would be widely phased out while others perhaps including volleyball, tennis, track and golf would be scaled back. If you argue that the only athletes that

---

[10] In addition, comparing collegiate coaching salaries with minor league coaching salaries in baseball or hockey suggests collegiate football and basketball coaches may be overpaid.

[11] Even relatively rich schools like Notre Dame have recently undertaken cutbacks in athletics. In Notre Dame's case the action was to eliminate wrestling.

should be paid are those that are in revenue producing sports, then you are back to the issue of net revenue rather than gross revenue, and relatively few athletes are in programs that generate positive net revenue—even in football.

Third, other minor leagues generally pay more than the implicit compensation suggested in Table 12.1 and Charts 12.1 and 12.2. What would happen if minor leagues were a way of life in football or basketball is a matter of speculation, although it would appear reasonable to infer that salaries would be higher in minor league football, for example, than they appear in college. That does not mean that football players would be better off. There are mitigating factors. Professional sports leagues are far from perfectly competitive. Minor leagues generally do not have free agency. If minor leagues in football developed along the lines of those in baseball, football players could be dramatically worse off! Typically they would sign a minor league contract right out of high school and then not be eligible for free agency and for a big salary until serving two or more years in the majors. Now they can attempt to sign for a big salary as soon as they are drafted which may be after just two years of college. That is, if a player is talented enough he can declare for the pros after only limited college experience. Furthermore, players have some ability to test the waters and judge their marketability. They now have a limited ability to go pro when it is in their best interests rather than when it is in someone else's best interests. Given the short careers of most football players, they may be better served by the current system than by a baseball-like system with minor leagues and high salaries only after a few years in the majors.

And fourth, there clearly is substantial competition for the best high school athletes. If there was a free market for those athletes, they would make dramatically more money. For example, Notre Dame's most recent two starting quarterbacks, Rick Mirer and Ron Powlus, were both rated the number one high school quarterback in their graduating year. With competitive bidding for their services, they could have received offers substantially in excess of tuition, room and board. Would collegiate salaries increase if competition was allowed even though college football does not yield any substantial net revenues? The answer is simple and has a parallel in pro sports. First, in pro sports the superstars and potential superstars are well paid in comparison with the average player. It is reasonable to believe that a similar situation would develop in the collegiate ranks. Stars would be paid substantially more while the backup nose tackle might not even receive a scholarship. And second, I repeatedly emphasized that different owners had different objectives and many were intensely interested in wins. The parallel for colleges is that something other than profits—or net revenues—may be very important to collegiate decision makers, whether that is the college president, the athletic director or alumni and boosters. The competition for the top student-athletes appears far more intense in all sports than would be justified based simply on revenue considerations. Even the competition for the top runners or softball players or gymnasts is intense although all three sports generate little revenue. This should not be a news flash. But the obvious implication is that the competition for student-athletes is largely driven by non-monetary factors. School pride—the equivalent of what I labeled "ego" in professional sports—is a prime factor underlying the competition for student-athletes. What price for school pride? Unfortunately, there is no comparable pricing procedure like comparing NPVs with actual sale prices as was done for the pros. We can state only that with a free market, school pride would push salaries of some student-athletes much higher than they are now.

THE ALTERNATIVES

(1) **Maintain the Status Quo**. The NCAA continues the sham of arguing that college athletes who receive tuition, room and board are amateur athletes, receive no compensation, and should receive no compensation. This alternative asks for trouble. The numbers here document that many college football and basketball players are underpaid. Athletes at many schools can legitimately complain that they are exploited. If the NCAA attempts to maintain the status quo, no one should be surprised when college athletes unionize. When workers are paid less than they believe they are worth, whether they are textile workers making minimum

wage or baseball players making over $1 million each per year, we should expect them to unionize. Current NCAA regulations gives many college athletes exactly that incentive.

(2) Go to a Free Market. Rather than effectively setting implicit compensation through NCAA regulations, let colleges bid for high school talent in a free market, unconstrained by the NCAA. While throughout this book I have generally argued in favor of market-oriented solutions, it does not appear to me that total reliance on the market in this case is either justified or optimal. Some college athletes would be better off, although many would not. The best high school athletes would have much improved opportunities and compensation, but the rest would scramble for the crumbs. In addition, the face of collegiate athletics would likely change dramatically. Michigan, Florida, Notre Dame, and Nebraska, for example, have substantial revenue to compete for the top talent. In the short term, those programs might grow stronger. In contrast, Wisconsin, Vanderbilt, Miami (FL), and Kansas State do not have the revenue to compete for talent. Those programs probably would grow dramatically weaker. Then who would the stronger teams play? Traditional rivalries would be lost; over time it would become clear that colleges were simply minor league teams. The implication for collegiate football could be rather stark. The sometimes-fiction that college football players are student-athletes would be irrevocably shattered and the mercenary status of those players would be apparent to all. But if college football was viewed as minor league, would there be the same interest? Would college football still be "the" Saturday fall event? I must admit my skepticism. I believe that moving to a totally free market would mean college football would be viewed as minor league football. Gross revenues would shrink and colleges and college athletes both would lose in the long-term. The big losers then could be the Michigans, Floridas, and Notre Dames as well as the alumni and boosters who flock to the fall collegiate spectacles. Not surprisingly then, there has been no enthusiasm for such a suggestion. Most willingly accept the convenient fiction that collegiate football is entertainment quite different from minor league football.

(3) Tinker with Current Rules and Regulations. Unfettered competition to pay student-athletes appears problematic. A fallback position would be tinker with current NCAA regulations and allow limited stipends. This alternative is frequently suggested by the student-athletes themselves. Two ancillary questions are important if this approach is adopted. First, who should be eligible for such a stipend? Should it be football players and men's basketball players or all student-athletes? Should it include walk-ons? And second, how would allowing these additional expenditures influence the overall athletic program or even the overall financial health of the university? The most likely result, as discussed above, is that some sports would be eliminated or severely curtailed.

From a revenue perspective, it would appear reasonable to allow more liberal NCAA regulations on the incidental expenditures a college may reimburse student-athletes. This statement might appear incongruous given zero net revenues in college football as a whole. However, when looking at the costs, the percentage directly spent on the athletes is relatively small. In addition, it would appear likely that boosters are more than willing to pay athletes just for the prospect of having increased athletic success. In other words, many associated with the college may be willing to subsidize the loss associated with a revenue-losing football program. From on equity perspective, it would appear necessary to permit the same allowance for incidental expenditures for all student athletes. After all, if the football program and the track program both lose money, why should only football players be reimbursed for some additional expenditures? In addition, boosters may be willing to subsidize the track program as well.

I am not wildly enthusiastic about tinkering with current NCAA regulations as a means for ensuring athletes are reasonably compensated. As noted earlier in this chapter, those regulations are frequently opposed to a student-athletes best interest. Tinkering with them to make them less athlete-unfriendly does not appear to be a fruitful endeavor.

From the perspective of paying student-athletes, there is a more fundamental question: are the individuals student-athletes or athlete-students? While the difference may appear semantic, I believe this distinction is crucial. If the former is the most appropriate view—and as a college educator I certainly hope that it is—

then the focus should be on the educational mission and thus on the educational pay or implicit salary of the student-athlete. If the latter is more accurate, then the individual is an athlete first and foremost and a student only secondarily. Then direct payment for services rendered is more appropriate since the pay pertains to the athletic endeavor and being a student is simply a means of maintaining eligibility and good standing given NCAA guidelines. If the former is more appropriate, it would appear incumbent to ask what can be done to increase the implicit pay of student-athletes in terms of the value of the education that they receive.

(4) **Seriously Alter the Incentives.** The last alternative would be to undertake a more fundamental revision in NCAA regulations, structuring them so that a school's best interest and the student-athlete's best interest are one and the same. One suggestion would be to improve the odds that student-athletes take advantage of the implicit educational benefit afforded them. A simple alternative: tie the number of scholarships a school receives to its graduation rate. For example, Division IA football currently allows a maximum of 85 scholarships. Pick a graduation rate, for argument's sake, say 60 percent. For every two points that the football team is over that rate over a five year period, allot the football team another scholarship. For every point under it loses a scholarship. Duke would be able to offer 100 scholarships while Alabama (pre-probation) would be down to 71, Temple down to 57 and Houston to 48. You want to see coaches internalize the goal of making sure their players graduate? That proposal would give them a real incentive and would seriously increase the implicit compensation of student-athletes.

I do not pretend that this suggestion will be greeted enthusiastically by many in the collegiate athletic community. Those who oppose it or something like it, however, perhaps do not belong in any college community. I also do not contend that this suggestion will solve all the financial woes of college athletes. They still will find themselves cash-poor during their college years. However, they do have the opportunity to graduate from college debt-free - a claim many of their classmates will not be able to make. Alternately, like their classmates they can borrow to buy a car or those 11 P.M. pizzas.

Chapter 13

Conclusion — The Financial Future of Big-Time Sports

"Greed is good! Greed is right! Greed will save the U.S.A.!"
—Oliver Stone, screenplay, *Wall Street*

"Sure it's nice to win, but there's only one thing that's important to me and that's the money that we're going to get, win or lose.... To me, baseball means money, and that's all I care about."
—Vida Blue, pitcher, Oakland A's

"You can have money piled to the ceiling, but the size of your funeral is still going to depend on the weather."
—Chuck Tanner, manager of the Pittsburgh Pirates, on high salaries

"If Gabe Paul were running a hospital, I'd invest in a mortuary."
—Bill James, baseball analyst, on baseball general manager Gabe Paul

"I can't tell you what I intend to do. But I can tell you one thing. It won't be anything rational."
—Calvin Griffith, owner, Washington Senators

The Top 25

When I initially contemplated writing this book, I was simply curious about how much a sports franchise was worth and what the return or profit for a typical franchise was. I also was curious about how collegiate sport finances compared with the pros.

313

Those questions now are easily answered. Table 13.1 presents the Top 25 most valuable franchise including all professional leagues and colleges. For professional teams, market value includes Net Present Value (NPV) based on the franchise's profits plus the league average "ego value" or how much an owner pays for the hobby of having a pro sports franchise. For some teams, like the Dallas Cowboys, the league average ego value undoubtedly understates the owner's actual ego value. For colleges, market value includes only the NPVs and does not include a corresponding value placed on "school pride." There is no easy way to place a value on school pride. Thus the college values may be understated.

The Dallas Cowboys currently are the most valuable team in sports with a market value of $428 million. The St. Louis Rams are a close second at $420 million and the Baltimore Ravens are third at $387 million. All NFL teams start with a base yearly revenue of about $40 million in television revenues and these three augment that with the most lucrative stadium arrangements in pro sports. While St. Louis currently has a slightly better stadium arrangement than Dallas, the Cowboys recent sponsorship deals with American Express, Nike, and Pepsi make them number one.

A year ago, the New York Yankees were the most valuable sports franchise. Over the past year MLB has self-destructed while some NFL franchises have signed mega-deals. Nevertheless, the Yankees are still the fourth most valuable sports franchise, worth $357 million. The Yankees' number four ranking—and the New York Met's 14th ranking—is primarily due to their media arrangements. The Yankees and Mets dwarf all other sports franchises in terms of their local media revenues. The rest of the top ten is there based primarily upon exceptional stadium arrangements.

All sports are represented in the Top 25—even hockey. Hockey franchises with good stadium arrangements—like the Boston Bruins, Detroit Red Wings, Chicago Blackhawks, and Mighty Ducks of Anaheim—are the financial equal of teams in any league. While some might argue that the NBA is a much stronger league than the NHL, the most profitable franchises in the NHL are the financial equals of the best in the NBA. Perhaps the point made most emphatically by Table 13.1 is the importance

Table 13.1

Top 25 Most Valuable Franchises[a]

Rank	School	Value
1	Dallas Cowboys (NFL)	$428
2	St. Louis Rams (NFL)	420
3	Baltimore Ravens (NFL)	387
4	New York Yankees (MLB)	357
5	Boston Bruins (NHL)	313
6	"Former Huston Oilers" (NFL)	303
7	Baltimore Orioles (MLB)	290
8	New York Knicks (NBA)	288
	Los Angeles Lakers (NBA)	288
	Chicago Bulls (NBA)	288
11	Chicago Blackhawks (NHL)	280
	Detroit Red Wings (NHL)	280
13	Mighty Ducks of Anaheim (NHL)	262
14	New York Mets (MLB)	257
	Boston Red Sox (MLB)	257
16	Oakland Raiders (NFL)	253
17	University of Michigan (NCAA)	252
18	Montreal Canadians (NHL)	246
19	Detroit Pistons (NBA)	238
	Portland Trailblazers (NBA)	238
21	University of Florida (NCAA)	223
22	Pittsburgh Steelers (NFL)	220
23	University of Notre Dame (NCAA)	213
24	Philadelphia Eagles (NFL)	212
	Chicago Bears (NFL)	212

[a] Market values for professional teams and NPVs for college teams.

of stadium arrangements. Almost any team in any league can become a financial powerhouse with the appropriate stadium arrangement.

The NFL has the most teams—seven—in the Top 25 (a year ago, MLB tied the NFL for the lead). MLB has the least—four. The Top 25 suggests that the NFL currently is the financially strongest sport—or has the most financially strong franchises. The NFL has a long-term labor agreement, a sound television contract, and a revenue sharing arrangement that gives any owner interested in profits a healthy return. Baseball has none of these. While the NFL has concerns about a developing split between richer and weaker franchises, MLB has problems with the future profitability of perhaps half its franchises. In the NFL, many old-time stable franchises make the Top 25, including the Steelers, Eagles and Bears (and a number of other franchises like the Dolphins are close behind). In MLB, beyond the Yankees and Mets only two exceptional franchises, the Orioles (lucrative stadium arrangements) and the Red Sox (media revenues and gate revenues), make the Top 25.

The NHL and NBA each place five teams in the Top 25. In many respects the leagues look very similar with teams frequently sharing arenas. Arenas are the key determinant of profitability in each league. For example, exceptional facilities shared by the Chicago Bulls and Blackhawks put them both in the Top 25. Similarly for the Detroit Red Wings and Pistons. Weaker facilities keep the New Jersey Devils and Nets off the list. While the NBA and NHL look similar based on the Top 25, below the top teams the leagues look dramatically different. Most NBA franchises make money. Many non-elite NHL franchises struggle.

Three college teams also make the Top 25. The most valuable collegiate "franchise" is the University of Michigan. The college values are understated relative to the pros since they do not include the "ego value" of a franchise. If a team like Michigan has an "ego value" of $30 million—a not unreasonable assumption given the average NFL ego value of $70 million—then the most valuable franchise in the state of Michigan is not the Lions or the Pistons or the Red Wings. It is the University of Michigan Wolverines. The other two college teams in the Top 25 are Florida and Notre Dame. The implication of college teams in the list of Top 25 Most Valuable Franchises is simple. If the University of Florida's football team played the Miami Dolphins, you should have a large supply of ambulances ready. However, the Gators—and the Wolverines and the Fighting Irish—are the financial equals of virtually any pro team.

Table 13.1 suggests one other point. Most of the teams on the list have a reputation for excellence on-the-field (or exceptional recent stadium deals). Whether you look at the Yankees or the Cowboys or the Fighting Irish, over the years these programs have won consistently. The moral? Winning pays, and paying wins. That's no surprise. But the corollary, for both colleges and pros, is that the financial rules have a considerable impact on who wins and who loses. The finances suggest that ten years from now, the Yankees, Lakers, Cowboys, and Fighting Irish are likely to still be winning. The Royals, Clippers, Bengals, and Commodores (Vanderbilt) are likely to be still losing.

While the Top 25 suggests that some sports franchises are extremely valuable, it does not indicate whether professional sports franchises have made a competitive rate of return. All the evidence presented here indicates that on average the returns have been exceptional. Given a choice between putting your money in a sports franchise or in stocks and bonds, on average over the last twenty years you would have been better off putting your money in a sports franchise in any major league. Even the NHL has had an average return in excess of the stock market average. The fortunes of individual franchises, however, have fluctuated tremendously.

The financial success of professional sports is predictable for two reasons. First, each league has a monopoly in that sport, although it faces competition in the broader entertainment market. For example, I cannot start an NFL franchise and begin play—even if I had $100 million or so to spare—because I am not a member of the club. As the American Express ad used to state: "Membership has its privileges." Monopoly profits are one of them. Anyone could attempt to form another league, and while many have tried, few have succeeded.[1] Each sports league has a monopoly in that sport and has worked hard to maintain that monopoly. Thus we should expect to find monopoly profits in each sport—which we do.[2]

---

[1] In the last 30 years one attempt, the American Football League (AFL), was tremendously successful, forcing a merger with the established league. Others have had mixed success with some teams eventually allowed into the established league, for example, the American Basketball Association and the World Hockey League.

[2] Some economists have argued that a sports franchises with higher profits should have those profits incorporated into higher NPVs, thus yielding only average returns. There are two problems with this argument. First, it ignores the riskiness of those higher than normal expected future profits. And second, it ignores the hobby or consumption value of the franchise.

Second, over time U.S. income has risen dramatically and with that rising income has come increasing expenditures on entertainment. Economists generally predict that income will continue to increase. Thus, it is reasonable to predict that entertainment expenditures also will increase and sports will continue to thrive. This implies that sports franchises' should continue to enjoy financial success.

Table 13.1 considers franchises at the top in terms of market values. What can be said of franchises at the other extreme? In October and November 1995 the press reported a number of statements by owners recounting their losses. The Pittsburgh Pirates claimed to have lost $60 million in the 1990's; the Seattle Mariners claimed to have lost $67 million in the last four years; the Houston Astros claimed to have lost $65 million in the last three years; the Cleveland Browns claimed to have lost $21 million in the last two years; the now-St. Louis Rams claimed to have lost $7 million in L.A.; the Florida Panthers claimed to be losing $1.2 million per month. The list goes on and on. Are owners with the weakest franchises losing their shirts? First, let me set the record straight with the claims. Based on public information none of these claims appear correct. The Pittsburgh Pirates lost "only" $26 million rather than $60 million; the Seattle Mariners lost $33 million rather than $65 million; the Houston Astros lost $16 million and not $65 million; the Cleveland Browns made $8 million in 1994 rather than losing money; the St. Louis Rams made $5 million in their last year in L.A. rather than losing $7 million; the Florida Panthers made $5 million rather than losing $1.2 million per month.

Some franchises have lost money. Many others have used dubious accounting to claim they have lost money. And those fictional losses have then been used in attempts to extort better stadium leases, new stadiums or league permission to relocate. Generally, financial losses have been grossly overstated. No NFL franchise has lost money.[3] Some NFL owners may have borrowed heavily against their franchise and the owner may be in financial difficulty. However, no NFL franchise itself is in difficulty. Any

---

[3] The 49ers had a loss from 1990 to 1994 but their 1995 profits will more than offset that loss.

NFL owner who claims to be losing money is guilty either of accounting gimmickry or financial incompetence. The situation in the NBA is similar. A few NBA franchises have small losses, but those losses appear either self-inflicted or due to accounting legerdemain.[4]

In contrast, the NHL has some franchises that have lost money and others that have made no money. Generally, these franchises in their current locations—Winnipeg, Hartford, and Edmonton—do not have tremendous financial prospects. Some MLB franchises also have lost substantial amounts of money. Cincinnati, Detroit, Kansas City, Milwaukee, Pittsburgh, and Seattle have all rung up losses exceeding $10 million between 1990 and 1995. In some cases the loss appears due to front-office incompetence, in others to efforts to buy a winner, and only in rare cases is it due to circumstances not of the owners own making.

Before moving on, there is one more comment related to two teams that you might have expected to find in Table 13.1: the San Francisco 49ers and Atlanta Braves. Both exclusions make a point. The San Francisco 49ers are not there despite winning their fifth Super Bowl in 1995. The point for the 49ers: not all owners attempt to maximize the franchise's profits or income. Many are in it because they want to win; the money is secondary or even irrelevant. Some are willing to spend substantial amounts to bring home a World Series title, an NBA championship or a Super Bowl victory. The 49ers' DeBartolo is a good example. He has paid for the best; he has received what he paid for; and he has not complained about not making tons of money. However, the willingness to spend freely has lowered the average return in sports. Sports returns average over 20 percent despite some owners' attempts to buy victory. If all owners were like the White Sox's Jerry Reinsdorf or the Bengals' John Sawyer and cared only about profits, sports returns could be much higher. Whether we would have exciting teams to watch is another question.

Second, the Atlanta Braves are not on the list despite being

---

[4] The Pacers loss arguably is due to the franchise not being run like a business while the Hawks loss is due to TBS's underpayment for the broadcast rights.

arguably the best team in MLB from 1991 through 1995. The point for the Braves: accounting considerations are important. Many franchises play games with the financial numbers. The Braves appear to do it better than most. If the Braves' cable TV rights were put up for auction, they might bring $10 million more than Turner's cable company is paying Turner's Braves. No one is better off or worse off, but the Braves appear poorer. The point is that the numbers employed by many teams to indicate losses are, in fact, an accounting fiction.

Summary of Economic Conclusions and Implications

At this point it is useful to go back and summarize the findings and implications.

(1) All professional leagues have average returns greater than those available from stocks and bonds. All professional leagues also have some monopoly power so this conclusion should not be surprising.

(2) All leagues have teams with great profits and a few with losses. Again, there should be no surprise. Some teams are well run and some are not. Some are run primarily to make a profit and others primarily to win. In general, however, if I were an owner of a sports franchise other than the Winnipeg Jets, I would be ashamed to say I lost money. It would be equivalent to saying that I am incompetent—or that I am greedy and want to win games and have the public subsidize my victories.

(3) A sports franchise can be run like a business or run like a hobby. As a business, you expect it to make money and on-the-field success is almost irrelevant. Try telling that to your fans! As a hobby you should expect it to cost money and on-the-field success is very important. Try telling that to your bankers! We should expect some tension between owners with different objectives. The owners and the leagues have yet to resolve this conflict. A revenue sharing proposal in Chapter 7 suggests a resolution.

(4) A game is a joint product producing both a win and a loss. That is a fairly obvious point. Owners and leagues, however, generally have yet to catch on to the corollary: since the product is shared, the revenue also should be shared. With owners frequently

adopting a "look out for Number One" attitude and ignoring what is good for the game, discussions of revenue sharing have focused on whose ox is gored and not what it is the league's best interest. Baseball has been the most egregious violator of this point, a fact probably reinforced by MLB's lack of a commissioner, but the NFL's 1995 franchise moves and Jerry Jones independent contracting suggests the NFL also will have more problems. Unfortunately, many owners appear to have flunked kindergarten—at least the lesson about sharing.

(5) College sports—at least football and men's basketball—are like professional sports. The NCAA acts like a cartel to restrict entry and divide profits among schools. The schools themselves have a range of profits running from a few like Michigan, Florida, and Notre Dame that make a lot, to another thirty that do reasonably well, to the rest that struggle. Most big-name football schools make money on football. Most others do not. The total revenue earned from football and men's basketball in Division 1A is surprisingly close to zero despite large profits at the top schools.

(6) The NCAA does not have the financial welfare of student-athletes foremost in its mind. When the welfare of schools conflicts with the welfare of student-athletes, NCAA regulations invariably are slanted toward the schools' best interest. This result is predictable given that the schools write the regulations.

(7) Strictly from an economic standpoint, some student-athletes appear underpaid and some overpaid. For many student-athletes, the value of the benefits that they receive in terms of tuition, room and board falls short of the salary they would earn in a competitive marketplace. This need not imply that student-athletes should be paid. However, there is no good method for appropriately compensating student-athletes without dramatically revising NCAA regulations.

(8) Professional athletes generally are neither underpaid nor overpaid. Historically, restrictions on player movement have resulted in underpaid athletes. Limits on free agency, salary caps, and rights-of-first-refusal are attempts to limit player salaries and would be illegal if imposed outside a collective bargaining agreement with a union. None are necessary for the survival of any

league. Revenue sharing is all that is needed to resolve the differences between rich franchises like the Detroit Red Wings and poor franchises like the Calgary Flames even in a setting of complete free agency.

(9) Players should change their negotiating approach. For example, many want to stay involved even after they retire. The easiest way to do it? Negotiate the next contract for a piece of the franchise in lieu of some salary. Owners should have no objections—although it might require changes in league bylaws. How much more motivated would a player be if he also was a part owner?

(10) Fans, take heart. Higher player salaries generally do not cause higher ticket prices. Owners charge fans the highest price they think they can get away with irrespective of player salaries. In fact, causation likely runs in the reverse direction. Higher ticket prices cause higher player salaries. The evidence, most dramatic in baseball, suggests that revenue increases are followed by increasing player salaries.

THE MAIN ECONOMIC PROBLEM IN SPORTS

We have witnessed a strike or lockout in every sport since 1993. We have seen dramatic decreases in television rights for MLB. We have seen increasing numbers of teams relocate for financial reasons. We have seen unprecedented public expenditures to build or renovate sports palaces. We have seen cities compete for teams. We have seen athletes convicted of income tax evasion and drug use. What then is the main economic problem in sports? My contention: owners do not see eye to eye. Laugh if you want, but if owners were all on the same page of the playbook many economic problems would disappear. In other words, the issues that play out in the news are merely symptoms of a more fundamental problem.

It should be obvious that all owners have differing objective (and to an increasing extent the players have differing objective). Some owners are more interested in victory and others in profits. That Steinbrenner and Selig do not share the same values or the same opinions should not be a news flash. What may be news is that these disagreements underlie much of the current turmoil in sports. In baseball, for example, some owners will take almost any settlement with the union just to get the game back on track. Other insist that a settlement must include a salary cap or a luxury tax or revenue sharing and would sacrifice a season to get one. MLB owners have not even been able to agree on a commissioner let alone agree on a rational approach to negotiating with the union. Is it any surprise that labor impasses wiped out the 1994 World Series and part of the 1995 season?

Some contend that MLB's conflict between owners and players is simply a manifestation of the traditional conflict between management and labor. The only difference is the magnitudes of the salaries and the working conditions. If that was the case, there would have been no strike in 1994. Neither the owners nor the players are stupid enough or greedy enough to risk the income involved. Unfortunately, the problem is more subtle and much more complex and lies in the conflict among owners.[5] Simply stated, owners have different views on the importance of profits and victories. Some are in sports as a business and are looking to wring the maximum possible profits and nothing else matters, won-loss records, fans, nothing. Others are in it to win. Sports owners are highly represented on the Forbes 400 list of the wealthiest people in the world. A fraction of these people would like what virtually no one can buy, a Super Bowl ring or a World Series championship. There are other reasons to want to own a sports franchise. Some owners may be in it for the ego. Steinbrenner and Turner may be the prototypes. Still others say they are in it out of a sense of civic pride, although I am too much the skeptic to take them at their word. If all you want to do is win, spending another $5 million may be inconsequential. But if someone else is in it for the profits, your spending may seriously hurt their profit. The bottom line: there is great conflict among the owners and until that conflict is resolved there can be no long-term agreement between the owners and a union because the owners have no common ground on which to base their strategy.

---

[5] The problem has been with the owners, although the NBA's turmoil in the summer of 1995 was due to an intra-union dispute rather than to an intra-ownership dispute. Further intra-union disputes are probably inevitable as different players have different financial interests.

MLB owners have said they will enact revenue sharing once players agree on a salary cap. The owners have things backwards. There will be no labor agreement—and no salary cap—until they agree on revenue sharing. The only questions are how much revenue sharing and how to implement it. I proposed a two part tax to address the underlying problem of different owner perspectives. First, tax costs in excess of the league average. Make the tax rate something other than punitive, thirty percent would be appropriate for baseball. If an owner wants to buy a championship, let him try as long as he is willing to compensate the other owners for the costs he imposes on them. Second, tax teams that consistently lose. If an owner does not field a competitive team, e.g. the Tampa Bay Buccaneers, San Diego Padres, Los Angeles Clippers, and Hartford Whalers, he also imposes costs on other owners. Place a tax that will compensate the other owners. No two taxes are going to get the owners all on the same page on the playbook. But at least they will be talking the same language in terms of the trade-off of profits and victories even if they choose alternative perspectives on how to operate.

Are Big Salaries a Big Problem?

How about a salary cap or restrictions on free agency? It certainly makes sense for owners to ask for both. They increase owners profits. It also makes sense for the players to object to both. They reduce salaries and restrict player options. More fundamentally, both represent restrictions on the operation of the free market that are without any pressing economic rationale. Salary caps and free agency restrictions both represent a movement back to the view that regulation is preferred to market incentives. There is no evidence even from the NBA that a salary cap has been effective. Restrictions such as a salary cap simply mean that accountants and lawyers search for ways around the restrictions. If you write a salary cap restriction in more than 25 words, I guarantee you that within three months I will find a way around it.

Free agency restrictions do work to lower salaries. The reserve clause, however, is as close to slavery as is currently allowed in the United States. The reserve clause was successful in eliminating any player bargaining power. While owners might enthusiastically support such a step, why it should be a matter of public policy is beyond me.

The salary cap and restrictions on free agency are bogus issues. The owners would lose in court. Why force a strike over an issue that the courts likely would throw out? The reason is that the owners disagree among themselves on bargaining strategies and then go to the players with a plan that they can agree on but that is fundamentally flawed because it does not address the underlying issues.

Salaries in sports have escalated dramatically and have become dramatically more unequal as the best performers command increasingly large sums. These trends are not confined to sports and also occur in the more general entertainment industry. Why? Because audiences are larger and more money is at stake. The best of the best are worth a lot because they generate tremendous revenues. If a Roger Clemens or Shaquille O'Neal or Wayne Gretzky will put 5,000 extra bodies in the stands, he can reasonably sit down and bargain with an owner for much of the revenue those fans will generate. Higher salaries are not endangering the games and higher salaries will not continue on their own. There is a solid economic reason for those higher salaries: higher revenues entering sports.

Without exception, when revenues entering a sport have increased—at least with limited free agency—salaries have increased thereafter, exactly as predicted by economic theory. When revenue growth has slowed, salary growth has slowed also. Owners' predictions of doom from escalating salaries are a marvelously self-serving attempt to convince the public that the players are to blame for current and recent sports stoppages. To predict that baseball or hockey or basketball or football is suddenly going to die because the players are making too much money and the owners cannot afford to remain in the game is ludicrous. Any owner that wants out can exit in a flash. At the right price, a line of people wait to buy into all four sports, alleged losses notwithstanding. When there really are losses and owners in general are in it for profits and not for wins, then and only then will owners show some self-restraint and reduce salaries. Nothing forces owners to pay high salaries except their desire to field a winning team.

Is Franchise Free Agency a Problem?

In 1995 the NHL saw the Quebec Nordiques move to Denver, the Winnipeg Jets commit to leaving Winnipeg, and the New Jersey Devils, Florida, Edmonton, and Hartford all threaten to move. In the NFL, the Rams moved from Los Angeles to St. Louis, the Raiders moved from Los Angeles to Oakland, the Browns committed to moving from Cleveland to Baltimore, and the Oilers have committed to moving from Houston to Nashville. In addition, Tampa Bay, Cincinnati, Seattle, Arizona, and Chicago also have considered franchise moves. MLB has seen no franchise shifts, but the Astros, Pirates, Mariners, and even the Yankees have threatened to move. Only the NBA appears a bastion of stability.

Is franchise free agency really a problem? It is my contention that it is a symptom of a problem rather than a problem itself. Owners that are interested in profits have an incentive to shake down anyone they can—players, TV networks, or cities. Restricting the number of franchises so that one franchise can attempt to play city against city has worked wonders for the profits of a number of owners, although it has done nothing for city finances in Los Angeles, Chicago, and New York, for example. The underlying problem is that league constraints on entry into the league together with a league's relative inability to prevent an owner from moving make it possible for an owner to cut his best deal from whatever mayor will promise the most, without respect to what is in the league's best interests or fans' best interests. Franchise free agency is simply a symptom of league rules and league financial incentives. Changes in the league rules could eliminate the problem—if owners collectively wanted to eliminate the problem!

Statistics and Whining Multimillionaires

Before concluding on financial history, there is one last point I want to belabor. Owners in all leagues have cried poverty and argued they have incurred incredible losses. However, no one has released real financial data to corroborate these contentions. Publicly held franchises, the Boston Celtics, Green Bay Packers, Toronto Maple Leafs, and Vancouver Canucks all show profits. If owners contend that they have a loss, they have a responsibility to show the numbers—all the numbers and not carefully-sanitized-accounting-justified-economically-meaningless numbers. If an owner is unwilling to open his books, he should forfeit all credibility when stating the franchise is losing money. An owner who states the franchise is losing money but does not release financial information is simple whining. Owners should put up or shut up.

In fact, I would go much further than a polite request to open the books. If owners will not open their books and yet continue to engage in economic brinkmanship in terms of labor negotiations, then I would advocate three much stronger actions. Parenthetically, I must note that I did not begin as an advocate. Economic analysis of the numbers made me an advocate.

First, owners receive extensive tax advantages. For example, sports franchises are allowed to amortize personal service contracts while other industries are not. Why should the Milwaukee Brewers have a tax advantage that General Motors does not when the Brewers are acting as much like a business as GM? If owners are going to play games with the public in terms of whether there are going to be games, then take away their tax advantages. Second, the owners in baseball have an anti-trust exemption. There is no solid economic justification for this exemption. Precipitating a baseball strike is one more reason why Congress should take it away. Third and perhaps most important, the overwhelming majority of professional sports franchises enjoy substantial *de facto* municipal subsidies. These include providing municipal stadiums, subsidizing construction of private stadiums, providing municipal services at low cost or no cost, and a range of tax breaks. When a franchise is unwilling to provide complete financial information to the public, the municipality ought to pull the plug on all subsidies. In a nutshell: no information—no tax breaks, no anti-trust exemption and no municipal subsidies.

"Statistics are like loose women. Once you get them, they let you do what you want with them."—Walt Michaels, coach, New York Jets.

"Statistics always remind me of the fellow who drowned in a river whose average depth was only three feet."—Woody Hayes, football coach, Ohio State.

When teams or leagues have released information, frequently it has been released to prove a point rather than to enlighten a discussion. What can be said about the numbers here? I have done my best throughout to get all the numbers from all sources available and then let the economic implications develop as they may. I had no axe to grind. I have no axe to grind. I have noted throughout that my numbers are based on the best information available. They are estimates and they are imperfect. However, they give a clear view on the profits in all sports, and the results and implications appear robust even to relatively large changes.

You don't like my numbers? You don't believe my numbers? Then I have a challenge. Tell me what numbers are incorrect and why and what are the corrections. Call me; write me; E-mail me! If you have information that will correct any numbers here I am more than willing to make any changes required. My address is:

Department of Finance and Business Economics
University of Notre Dame
Notre Dame, IN 46556
Email: Richard.G.Sheehan.1@nd.edu

WHAT DO THE FINANCIAL NUMBERS IMPLY FOR THE FUTURE OF SPORTS?

Turning to the future, let me briefly consider where each league appears headed based upon its current financial situation.

BASEBALL. The easiest prediction is for increasing reliance on cable and pay-per-view and additional efforts to obtain municipally subsidized new stadiums. Owners keep searching for additional revenues in an entirely futile attempt to stay one step ahead of the players. Pay-per-view represents the only obvious new revenue source on the horizon. Some clubs will push for additional revenue from a new stadium. Following Chicago, Baltimore, Cleveland and Texas, it is likely that the push for new stadiums will continue with owners from New York to Cincinnati to Seattle aggressively lobbying for municipal support. The spectacle of George Steinbrenner, netting $20 million plus per year from the Yankees, trying to shake down a financially threadbare New York City (or state) may make sense to Steinbrenner and other MLB owners. I find it revolting—not surprising, but revolting nonetheless.

It would appear that greater revenue sharing is in the cards for baseball. I say this not because I have recommended it or even because it is economically justified. It will come because the number of clubs that believe they would gain from such a plan is growing close to a majority.

I would like to say that further expansion is in the cards for baseball because a number of cities could support a well-run franchise. Expansion is economically justified. The cities at the top of the expansion list should include New York City, Washington, D.C., and Mexico City—I still like the idea of another New York team called the Brooklyn Bums. However, the owners have shown no enthusiasm for the prospect of expansion.

Ultimately, one would hope that baseball's owners and union would recognize that they are partners and may gain more by collaborating than by fighting. I am not optimistic. There has been too much bad blood. The owners have exploited the players for too long for the players to trust the owners, and the players have won for too long at the negotiating table for the owners not to seek victory regardless of the cost. At some point the owners' and players' economic self-interests will bring about a long-term settlement. Baseball politics, however, may postpone that settlement for a long time.

BASKETBALL. Basketball will see the demise of the owners' cherished salary cap. It is simply a matter of time, if not this contract, then the next. It served a purpose ten years ago; it serves none today. The NBA has been in the forefront of most economic trends in sports. Unfortunately, the union split also is a likely future trend. All owners do not have the same goals and incentives and constraints, and it would be unreasonable to think that all players do. In the past, splits among players have been masked by their desire to raise the total income of all players. At some point players will recognize that more for the stars means less for the journeymen. This will greatly complicate labor negotiations. Future labor negotiations in sports could be dramatically uglier and messier unless all parties have a dramatic change of heart. Again, the question is will there be cooperation or confrontation?

Basketball has taken the lead in terms of aggressively seeking expansion franchises and then imposing stringent restrictions on those franchises. I expect this trend to continue, ultimately with two twists. First, the expansion to Europe is inevitable. The only question is how soon. The NBA wants to continue to increase revenues, and Europe is the likely source for the next big increase. The other expansion twist will involve owners like Disney. The only surprise about Disney's entry into sports was that it did not happen in the NBA first. The cross-marketing opportunities for companies like Disney or SONY or Busch or a Baby Bell or a network, perhaps Fox, are too rich to ignore. The economic pressures will lead to these linkages. The only question is how soon. The building boom also will continue. New facilities draw more fans, even with the same old team. More importantly, however, a new arena gives a franchise the opportunity to maximize the number of luxury boxes and substantially increase revenues. The Detroit Pistons have struggled on the court recently, but owners still see the big revenues from their luxury boxes and lust for similar revenues in their home arena. A corollary is that players will get a slice of that revenue.

The last prediction for basketball: those long-term contracts are not the wave of the future. The most recent union contract begins to address this issue. Teams and players will both get burned. Teams will sign mediocre talent and be stuck with big-money payouts that will lower profits and—if the salary cap is still in place—reduce their ability to field a competitive team. Players will sign for what looks like a fortune but in a few years find that they are at the top of the talent pool but only in the middle of the salary ranking (no one should be surprised when a Glenn Robinson or a Chris Webber is a holdout in five years!).

FOOTBALL. Football has followed a very different path from the other three leagues, largely due to a more restricted schedule. One thing to change: the schedule. The NFL already has cut back the exhibition schedule and increased the length of the regular season. Ultimately it will do it again. The economics make it inevitable. The payoff from changing the last two pre-season games to regular season games is just too great to ignore. Increase the season by two games or 12 percent and each team could pick up another

$1 million in television money and perhaps another $1 million in gate revenues.

Non-gate stadium revenues will be the main growth area in the immediate future for the NFL. Franchises are going to increasingly search for income like additional luxury boxes, personal seat licenses and individual deals with major sponsors. All give the team additional revenue. Perhaps more importantly, however, all give the team additional revenue that does not have to be shared with the league. Ultimately, NFL revenue sharing will have to be expanded to include these revenue sources or current revenue sharing agreements are going to break down. No middle ground is possible.

More teams will attempt to shake down more cities for publicly subsidized stadiums and deals like St. Louis gave the Rams. Every deal that is signed puts further pressure on financially weaker franchises to cut their own deal because each deal increases next year's salary cap. Expansion into Los Angeles is a no-brainer. Overseas expansion appears premature. Football has yet to set the stage for successful international expansion. One revenue concern: if the next round of negotiations for national television broadcast rights does not match the last round, many NFL franchises would be in deep financial trouble.

The salary cap in football is an interesting experiment that will soon be history—by the owners request. It makes no more sense in the NFL than it makes in the NBA. The San Francisco 49ers first demonstrated in 1994 how meaningless it was with creatively written—and rewritten—contracts. Teams like the Cincinnati Bengals thought they would be able to increase their payroll, sign talent that other teams had to waive, and then be a contender on the field. They got one of three. They spent more but had nothing to show other than a bigger payroll and lower profits. The owners may be greedy but they are not that stupid. When they see the salary cap does not deliver as promised, it's history.

Also coming in football, more reliance on guaranteed contracts. Players are going to look at still-performing veterans like Phil Simms being cut and realize that the big contracts are meaningless unless you collect. Given a choice between a 3 year $2 million contract with no guarantee and a 3 year $1.4 million contract with a guarantee, players are going to start taking guarantees and the clubs will go along because it saves them money and makes it easier to fit under the cap. (Bonuses are a form of guarantees, generally paid in advance and used to circumvent the salary cap. Teams will attempt to move from bonuses to guarantees when the salary cap is removed because bonuses are paid up front while guarantees are paid in the future.)

HOCKEY. The primary question facing the NHL is the future of the small Canadian markets, and there is no easy call on that. If NHL owners are willing to agree on a generous revenue sharing plan, then cities like Winnipeg will retain their franchises. Without substantial revenue sharing, goodbye Winnipeg, Edmonton, and possibly Calgary and even Ottawa in the long-term (Quebec is already history). NHL owners have not been generous to anyone but themselves; thus I am not optimistic about more revenue sharing. Nevertheless, the choice is clear from an economic standpoint.

The wisdom of additional expansion is in doubt. Adding franchises in large southern cities would dilute the talent pool. It would not be profitable to the league unless the southern franchises had exceptional strength such as that brought by owners like Disney. Remember that Calgary has a franchise because the Flames could not make it in Atlanta. Nevertheless, adding franchises would make a national television contract more likely. In terms of expansion, the NHL is in a unique position with a receptive international audience in Europe. However, while a franchise in Moscow could be extremely popular it may not be profitable and would not help to secure a national television contract in the U.S.

The main economic step that the NHL must take to maintain its status as a major league sport is to package the game to make it attractive to U.S. television networks. Bringing in Disney and taking out fighting were two major steps forward. Unfortunately, the 1994 strike was a major step backward. Ultimately, though the purists will wail, the timing of the game will change to accommodate TV. From an economic perspective, hockey needs a network television contract and that contract will not come without breaks in the action for commercials and probably a shorter game.

COLLEGE FOOTBALL. The top college programs make tons of money while most of the rest lose money. Does this mean that colleges will drop or scale back their football programs? Probably not. There is too much pride at stake for many college administrators to look just at the economics of their football programs. (what state legislators might do is a different question). In the late 1960s Holy Cross commissioned a study to see whether its football program was economically justified. The answer was no, and the recommendation was made to drop football. Holy Cross still has a football program—based largely and explicitly on considerations of school pride.[6]

As in the pros, the search goes on for ways to increase revenues and decrease costs. One thing that will come: a college football playoff. Would it do away with the bowls? Perhaps, but in general who would care? With the exception of Notre Dame, the teams that gain the most from the bowls are the Vanderbilts and Northwesterns. They generally do not go, yet split the conference revenues of the teams that do. Would it further detract from the academic performance of student-athletes? The argument rings hollow. If football players need more time to study, do away with spring practice; don't leave for a Saturday away game on Thursday morning making the players miss Thursday and Friday classes; and further restrict the amount of hours that players must put in both during the season and off-season. Division IAA has a tourney and there has been no obvious impact on academic performance. Division IA could do things one better. Take the top eight teams for a three game tourney; begin with the traditional January 1 bowls and end two weeks later about January 15th. For most schools that is an academic break period anyway. The tourney will come. The potential revenues are too great to ignore.

Also on revenues, colleges will place much greater emphasis on marketing. The pros have moved far beyond colleges in terms of marketing their games (one might also argue that they have moved

---

[6] Holy Cross's football program now is Division IAA and offers no athletic grants-in-aid. However, scholarship costs are but a small part of the total cost of a football program. Thus, it is likely that Holy Cross's football program still is not justified simply from an economic perspective. It would appear that school pride is the primary factor maintaining Crusader football.

far beyond good taste). Nevertheless, a horde of marketing ideas and tie-ins—many extraordinarily tacky—will creep into collegiate sports over the next ten years simply because athletic directors will not be able to turn down the money. Potential revenue sources also include items like shoe contracts. For years they have been viewed as a perk of coaching. Get named a coach at a big-named school, win some games and sign a lucrative shoe contract. Colleges are beginning to sign those deals instead. Why should the coach get $500,000 for saying players must wear brand X shoes? Schools have winked at the practice because it was one way to pay coaches without faculty oversight committees complaining about excessive compensation. Well the cat is out of the bag and the monetary amounts are too much for colleges to ignore. A coach picking up a stray $50,000 may not pose a problem; a coach picking up $500,000 attracts university attention. A school might as well pay the coach another $100,000 and sign the shoe contract itself.

On costs, college presidents may continue reducing the maximum number of allowed grants-in-aid as a means of holding down costs. Frankly, I think those actions are largely window-dressing. Grants-in-aid are not the major factor driving the cost of college football. Coaches salaries, administrative overhead, maintenance of frequently palatial facilities and even travel and recruiting all may exceed the cost of grants-in-aid. If college presidents are sincere about cutting expenses there are other items that need their attention including athletic administrative costs, facilities costs and recruiting costs.

On compensating student-athletes, I know that something will be done relatively soon. I just do not know what. If changes are not made to increase the implicit compensation, then athletes will take it in their own hands, perhaps hiring agents to negotiate with colleges. The NCAA's only choice is to do something substantial quickly or wait for the athletes to take the initiative.

On gender equity and Title IX, it is likely that the Brown University court ruling that forty percent female student-athletes was inadequate will substantially alter the long-term picture of female sports unless Congress intervenes. Requiring colleges to go to a 50-50 ratio could dramatically change the face of collegiate athletics, either by substantially increasing the costs of athletic programs or by dramatically cutting men's programs in sports like wrestling, gymnastics, volleyball and soccer. The rationale for only forty percent female athletes was ad hoc at best, and dollar subsidies to male sports dwarfs those to female sports at many universities that do not make money on football.

COLLEGE BASKETBALL. Basketball presents a very different picture from college football. The successful schools like Indiana, North Carolina and UCLA make substantial money from their programs but not nearly as much as the top football programs. While the maximums are much smaller, the losses also are much smaller. The primary difference between basketball and football is that the lower costs have prompted many more schools to go Division I in basketball. The number of Division I basketball schools in 1994-1995 was over 300. For schools like Robert Morris, Coppin State, Murray State, or Santa Clara, an NCAA tourney bid is like winning the lottery in terms of publicity and revenue. In addition, this lottery ticket is relatively cheap. Thus we see a proliferation of Division I basketball schools although most make at best only a small profit.

Reorganization is coming to major college basketball. Nothing too dramatic and nothing that would pose a danger to the golden goose of the NCAA tourney. But the number of teams joining Division I just for a piece of the tourney pie keeps growing and the pieces are getting smaller. It is only a matter of time before basketball divides Division I into the real basketball schools and the ersatz schools. The split will come for the same reason it came in football. The North Carolinas, Kentuckys, and UCLAs simply do not need to split the tourney revenue with Brooklyn College, Florida Atlantic or Prairie View. As economic pressures grow on the former schools they will surely cut the latter out of the pie.

THE FINAL SCORE

The bottom line is that professional franchises have been very profitable endeavors, despite cries of poverty far and wide. Economic pressures have shaped the way sports has evolved and will continue to shape the way it evolves. The games themselves, however, all appear quite healthy. As a number of people have stated, "Baseball must be a great game to survive the people that run it." The same can be said for basketball, football, and hockey. Each sport seems to have a way of muddling along, perhaps not finding the best solution to its problems, but always finding the next batter in the lineup. I expect that situation to continue.

We have all heard owners cry poverty, fans decry that the games are not what they used to be, and sports analysts speculate whether a sport can survive recent economic turmoil. I have tried throughout to avoid being either Pollyanna or Chicken Little. Each sport has real economic problems. Tell me an area of life that does not! But each sport also has some major strengths and appears financially sound overall. In addition, each sport has been around a long time despite management that has sometimes been just a cut above indictable. It is reasonable to assume that all will continue to muddle along.

After examining the financial numbers, I must also admit that I am going to change who I cheer for. Some teams are run with a view principally of winning games. They are run—arguably— with the fans foremost. For example, the Green Bay Packers, San Francisco 49ers, Baltimore Orioles, and Pittsburgh Penguins have been run to win and when the owners have lost money they have not whined about it. Those are the type of teams and the type of owners that I would like to see have success. The Chicago Bears, Cincinnati Bengals, New York Mets, Chicago White Sox, Milwaukee Brewers, Boston Bruins, and Edmonton Oilers among others have been run looking first and foremost at the profit numbers. If the owners of those franchises got out of the game we might all be better off.

As I have gathered the information for this book, I have been struck by the number of people in each sport that care little for the game and are just after the money. As an economist perhaps I should not have been surprised. After all, the saying is that economists know the price of everything but the value of nothing. If that was the only criterion to be an economist, then some players, owners and a commissioner or two would make excellent economists! There are players and owners both that I am glad I do not have to associate with. But there are also players who are in the game because they love it and who would play for free and owners who place the game, the league, and the competition above their own profits. For them and for all true fans, two final thoughts from men who said it more eloquently than I and whose actions matched their words:

"When you keep the game on a high plane, the money will take care of itself."—Frank Selke, general manager, Montreal Canadians.

"I never look back. I love baseball, and you have to be patient and take the good with the bad. After all, it's only a game."—Tom Yawkey, owner, Boston Red Sox.

About the Author

Dr. Richard G. Sheehan received his Ph.D. from Boston College in the mid-70s and has kept active by writing numerous articles on topics ranging from relationships between crime rates and incarceration rates to inflation in Saudi Arabia. In addition to his own articles, he has served as co-author or editor on several articles and books, and is a reviewer for the *American Economic Review, International Economic Journal, Journal of International Money and Finance*, and *Financial Review*, to name a few. Dr. Sheehan received the Georgescu-Roegen Prize in Economics in 1990, and the Executive MBA Teacher of the Year Award in 1994. He is currently a professor in the Department of Finance and Business Economics at the University of Notre Dame. *Keeping Score* is his first solo-authored book.

/